The Man Who Was Cyrano

A Life of Edmond Rostand, Creator of *Cyrano de Bergerac*

To Neil,
with best wishes,
Sue Lloyd.
June 2004.

Previous publications:

Roget's Thesaurus of English Words and Phrases (London: Longman, 1982)
Roget's Thesaurus of English Words and Phrases, abridged edition (London: Penguin Books, 1984)
Improve Your Word Power (London: Longman, 1988)

The Man Who Was Cyrano

A Life of Edmond Rostand, Creator of *Cyrano de Bergerac*

by Sue Lloyd

Unlimited Publishing
Bloomington, Indiana

To Christopher Fry,
our own English poet dramatist

C'est avec le cire de son âme qu'il [Rostand] avait modelé
celle de Cyrano
*It was with the wax of his own soul that [Rostand] formed
that of Cyrano*

–Rosemonde Gérard

Contents

Acknowledgements

I WOULD LIKE TO THANK the many people who have encouraged me over the long gestation of this book, and in particular Geraldine Clarke and Elizabeth Bencze, who read the draft manuscript and made many helpful comments. Keiron White, of International School Moshi, gave me valuable information from the Internet before I had access to it myself. The librarians at the British Library, the Bibliothèque Nationale and various other academic libraries were always helpful. Robert Lambolle, of *Reading & Righting*, gave me useful advice and encouragement. Monsieur Henri Pac, the Luchon historian, answered my queries with courtesy and patience, while Christopher Fry earlier wrote me a witty letter about his translation of *Cyrano de Bergerac*. Finally, thanks to Geoff, my patient companion on many visits to places connected with Edmond Rostand.

Prologue

IN THE EARLY HOURS of 29th December, 1897, late strollers along the Boulevard Saint Martin, in Paris, witnessed extraordinary scenes. Knots of people were forming and reforming outside the Porte-Saint-Martin Theatre, which had only just shut its doors. They were laughing, crying, gesticulating, embracing – and none of them seemed to want to go home. Those who were present on that momentous occasion would always feel a special bond between them, as if they had been present at a miracle.

The play whose première they had just been watching had finished late because of constant interruptions for applause and encores. Even then the audience had refused to leave, demanding one curtain call after another. The young author was, however, too shy to appear. He had slipped out of the theatre and into a cab, from which he and his wife were watching with joy and amazement the exultant crowds.

Later that morning the Paris papers with one voice proclaimed a genius, who had restored to France her glorious heroic past in traditional alexandrine verse.

Who was the young poet who had won the hearts of the French people and routed the spectre of their defeat twenty-seven years earlier by the Prussians; who had revived France's confidence in herself by joyously proclaiming the Gallic virtues of wit, enthusiasm and chivalry? His name was Edmond Rostand and he was only twenty-nine years old. His play, about an obscure seventeenth-century poet and swordsman, Cyrano de Bergerac, would soon become famous, not just in France but all over the world. It continues to inspire audiences to this day.

The success of *Cyrano de Bergerac* was a turning-point in Rostand's life. His future was assured but he had to live up to the expectations of the French people. Sensitive and conscientious, Edmond Rostand did his best to satisfy them. Well aware of his own limitations, he worked unsparingly and anguished over every line. The fame he had set out to achieve from his very first book of poems turned into a crushing burden from which only death released him.

Act One: Childhood and Youth
(1868 – 1890)

Souviens-toi que ta vie eut un rose matin
Remember that your life had a rosy morning
– Eugène Rostand

Tout beau fruit, nous dis-tu, n'est qu'un ver qui se cache
Every lovely fruit, you [the devil] say, is nothing but a hidden maggot
– Edmond Rostand[1]

FEW POETS can have had such a good start in life, in spite of being born on April Fools' Day. Edmond Eugène Joseph Alexis Rostand was born at his parents' home at 14 rue Montaux (now rue Edmond Rostand) in the flourishing port of Marseilles at five o'clock in the evening on the first of April 1868.

"Remember that your life had a rosy morning", wrote Edmond Rostand's father Eugène, to his young son. Edmond was born into the affluent bourgeoisie at a time when the Second Empire seemed to be promising stability and prosperity. The house at rue Montaux, an elegant L-shaped block in white stone with elegant ironwork balconies, built just five years earlier by Edmond's maternal grandfather, was typical of the confident new buildings in this part of Marseilles.

Yet traumatic years for France followed soon after Edmond's birth: in 1870 France lost the war with Prussia, leading to the abdication of Napoleon the Third. After the brief flowering of the Commune, the Second Empire was succeeded by the Third Republic. There were riots in Marseilles. Eugène took his family for safety first to Nice and then to Luchon in the Pyrenees, returning home when stability had returned.

From now on, however, Edmond's childhood was uneventful and secure, in a warm and loving extended family. His uncle Alexis and his maternal grandparents, Jules and Françoise Gayet, also lived at 14, rue Montaux, and there were cousins living nearby. The Gayets were an old seafaring family, but Jules Gayet had abandoned the sea to become a prosperous chemical manufacturer.

Angèle-Justine Julie Rostand,[2] Edmond's mother, was vivacious and outgoing, a true Massilian, fond of telling amusing stories in her Provençal accent. Angèle was a strict Catholic and ensured Edmond was brought up in the Catholic tradition, a tradition he would value but not practise as an adult.

Edmond's father came from an old Provençal family with its roots in Orgon, in the Alpilles. The Rostands had provided Orgon with its lawyers and other notables, and intermarried with the other major family, the Estrangins. Edmond's great-grandfather Alexis-Joseph had set up the thriving Marseilles branch of the family, establishing a major new bank there after the French Revolution. Alexis-Joseph had been a prominent member of Marseilles society, and a generous philanthropist. His son Joseph had married a Spanish woman from Cadiz, Félicie de Ferrari, who had both Italian and Spanish blood in her veins, as she was descended from the Genoan aristocracy. Both Joseph and Félicie died before their grandson Edmond was born, so he never knew them, but he was proud of the Spanish element in his makeup. Unfortunately, however, Félicie was prone to nervous troubles and depression, an affliction inherited by her son Eugène and her grandson Edmond.[3]

Eugène Hubert Marans Rostand[4] had begun his working life as a barrister, and was said to have been an excellent orator, able to adapt his speeches to suit his audiences – a talent which his son inherited and put to use in a different arena. Given the chance to join the management of the family bank, however, he rose to be its president. As an economist with socialist sympathies, he became such an authority that his advice was later sought by politicians. He was awarded the Legion of Honour in 1896. And in the carriageway of the house in rue Montaux hang two matching bronze medallions, one commemorating Edmond Rostand and the other, his father Eugène.

But Eugène, though successful in his chosen profession, had really wanted to be a poet. He had already published two volumes of verse before the birth of his son, and two more would follow, along with the first translations of the Latin poet Catullus into French verse.

Similarly, Alexis,[5] Eugène's brother, was a successful financier, but he would have preferred to dedicate himself to music, for which he had shown an early aptitude. The two brothers, the poet and the musician, spent many evenings together composing oratorios and other works. When Edmond was two years old, their oratorio, *Ruth*, was a great success in Marseilles.

It was a time when people met regularly in each other's homes to hear music and poetry or discuss politics. From an early age Edmond was encouraged to recite poetry to the guests, while his talented younger sister Juliette would play the piano.

One such evening, the politician Paul de Cassagnac, famous for his duels, had left his pair of swords in the anteroom. He told Edmond that while he was duelling, the sword guards (les coquilles) continuously made a clinking sound. Edmond would remember this when he came to compose the Duel Ballad in *Cyrano de Bergerac*: "Les coquilles tintent ding-don!" (Act I, sc.iv).

So Edmond grew up surrounded by music and poetry. But there was more to the Rostands than professional success and a love of the arts. The epigraph to this chapter is taken from a poem written by Eugène for his baby son. Set in its context, it reads:

> *Mon fils...*
> My son, my dear one, when you become a man
> and read these verses where I name you, trembling,
> remember that your life had a rosy morning,
> a bright dawn, and think of those whose fate
> is painful, dark and sad right from their birth;
> who never had a dawn, and never knew but shade.
> remember that these are your brothers –
> go towards them...
> – "Eddie", *Les Sentiers Unis*

Eugène Rostand had great compassion for the poor, and put his concern into action. His books on economics focused on how to alleviate poverty. Hoping to represent the underprivileged, he stood for parliament four times between 1878 and 1893, without success. So he then concentrated his efforts on practical philanthropy. Eugène Rostand, like his forefathers, headed several charitable institutions in Marseilles, and was the first to help provide low-cost housing for working people.

The lesson of his father's poem was not lost on young Edmond, if indeed he ever needed it. He seems to have had a naturally compassionate nature and was, all his life, generous to those in need. In his youth, his generosity sometimes caused problems to his friends; in later life even his enemies acknowledged that kindness was one of Edmond's most prominent attributes.

Rostand felt drawn in particular to life's failures, whom he called "*Les Ratés*", from the verb *rater*, to fail. He would dedicate his first book of verse to *Les Ratés*; they form the subject of many of his early poems. Amazingly, given his loving and comfortable background, Rostand felt that he could so easily have been a *raté* himself. The fear of failure is the counterpart of the desire to succeed, and both are constant themes in Rostand's poetry and in his plays.

Where did this fear of failure come from? The sensitivity and tendency to depression Rostand had inherited from his Spanish grandmother may have been partly to blame. As he later progressed from one success to another, the greater the obligation he felt to his public, and the greater his fear that he would not be able to express his vision. This fear is of course shared by all original creative artists. Edmond Rostand possessed to a very high degree the conscientiousness of the artist who wishes to give only of his or her best. But there may have been a deeper cause for his lack of confidence, a kind of inferiority complex which had its roots in the circumstances of his father's birth.

Not until after Edmond's death did it become generally known that his grandparents' marriage took place over twelve years after the birth of

Eugène, the elder son. For Félicie was already married when she first met Joseph Rostand. It was not until her husband died in 1855 that Félicie was able to marry Joseph and then only in secret. The following year, when she was thought to be dying, a public ceremony took place at her bedside. She recovered, and lived to be fifty-one, dying in 1861. Eugène and Alexis were given the surnames Marans and Gasan respectively at their birth, though they were baptised under the name of Rostand. Although they were signed in as Rostands at the *Lycée de Marseilles*, Joseph's sons were not officially adopted until March 1866, when they were in their early twenties. And it was not until Eugène's marriage the following February that he was invited to join the family bank, the *Caisse d'Épargne des Bouches du Rhône*, founded by his grandfather, the patriarch Alexis-Joseph.

Although their father had looked after their interests, the effect upon the two brothers of this traumatic upbringing, and the rejection for a long period, in official eyes at least, by the family they belonged to by birth, must not be underestimated, especially as they had both inherited their mother's sensitive nature. (Ironically, Eugène in particular was said to closely resemble his grandfather Alexis-Joseph, who may not even have known of his existence.) In the eyes of the state, Eugène and Alexis were only "adopted" Rostands – they are listed under "enfants de parents inconnus" in the Marseilles register of births, and even on his marriage certificate, Eugène is still named as "Joseph Eugène Hubert Marans Rostand…fils majeur adoptif" (the 'Joseph' was added when Joseph officially recognised his son). The witnesses to Eugène's marriage were eminent members of Marseilles society with a clutch of Legion of Honour rosettes between them, but also present was a link with the past, in the shape of Dr François Roberty, the doctor who had signed Eugène's birth certificate.

We can now see a further layer of meaning in Eugène's poem. Eugène himself has experienced the fears and insecurity of those born outside the family circle. He would do his utmost to make his own son feel secure and well-loved, while seeking to inspire in him sympathy for those less fortunate than himself.

As a little boy, Eddie, as his family called him, knew nothing of his father's secret. He grew up in a warm and loving environment, with first one, then two younger sisters[6] for company, as well as his Estrangin cousins living just around the corner. Angèle Rostand later recalled her son as being a quiet, well-behaved and thoughtful child who loved to read.[7] He had a vivid imagination and excellent powers of observation. But one of his characteristics caused some difficulty to his parents: his fastidiousness. He refused to wear anything which had the slightest mark on it. This was surely the outward sign of that inner fastidiousness which Rostand was later to express through Cyrano:

> *Moi, c'est moralement que j'ai mes élégances.*
> *... je marche sans rien sur moi qui ne reluise,*
> *Empanaché d'indépendance et de franchise.*
> My elegance is of a moral kind
> ... everything about me glitters as I walk,
> independence and honesty are my plumes.
> – (Act I, sc. iv)

Such fastidiousness was part of Edmond Rostand's love of beauty, which expressed itself in every detail of his everyday life, and most obviously, unlike Cyrano, in his delight in fashion and elegant attire. In adult life, his ties were legendary. A friend, the actress Mme Simone, later wrote of him: "He loved elegance and was not afraid to show it; he always dressed not merely in good taste but with meticulous care".[8] As a child, Edmond loved the fine lace collar he wore for his portrait by Lagier so much he refused to take it off. As a young man, he would cause some amusement to his friends by the variety of coloured ribbons he wore in his boater. No wonder Rostand was later fascinated by the seventeenth century, when ribbons, plumes and clothes in many colours were fashionable apparel.

One of Edmond's favourite amusements as a child was to visit the puppet theatre set up in the square in front of the Palais de Justice, not far from his home. Besides watching Polichinelle and the little plays about Guignol which were popular at the time, he would also have first seen here the characters of the *commedia dell'arte* : Columbine, Harlequin,

Pierrot and others. They made a deep and lasting impression on him. A puppet theatre plays a major role in his last play, *La Dernière Nuit de Don Juan.* As soon as he was old enough, Edmond was also taken to see the French classics performed at the Palais de Justice, as well as the plays put on by the Marseilles *Association artistique,* of which his father and uncle were active members.

Every aspect of the theatre fascinated Edmond from childhood. When given his own puppet theatre, he spent as much time making the costumes and scenery as he did on manipulating the puppets. As a successful playwright, Rostand always took a keen interest in the production of his plays, making little sketches of the costumes and decor he wanted.

At first, Edmond's education was conventional: a local English kindergarten for three years from the age of three and a half, then a private Catholic school, *l'Institution Thédenat.* But at the age of ten his father insisted on sending Edmond not to a Catholic Secondary School, but to his own old school, the *Lycée de Marseille,* as a day boy.

The *Lycée* was a prestigious institution which could count many eminent Frenchmen amongst its ex-pupils. Here Edmond found a congenial atmosphere and began to make his mark as a student. But attendance at the *Lycée* also brought with it knowledge less welcome. Either from his parents or from schoolmates whose fathers had been at school with his own father, Edmond learned about the illegitimate origins of his father and his uncle.

When Edmond made this discovery, it must have seemed to him as if his whole world had been turned upside down. Everything he had taken for granted was now shown to have been based on shaky foundations: the comfortable bourgeois life, the respectable and honourable family line were his, not of right, but due to the condescension of the legitimate line of the Rostand family.

A less sensitive child might have taken such revelations in his stride. Illegitimacy, with later recognition and official adoption, was not uncommon in Marseilles society at that time. Edmond's family was loving and intelligent, his mother and father were respectable and respected members of the bourgeoisie. But the immediate effect of his discovery of his father's origins was apparently to turn Edmond from a cheerful, talkative little boy into one who was "shy, wild and silent" at home. This evidence, from another inhabitant of 14 rue Montaux, is quoted by Odette Lutgen in her psychological study of the Rostand family.[9] Lutgen's thesis, persuasively argued, is that the illegitimate births of Eugène and Alexis had a traumatic effect on both them and their descendants, giving them inferiority complexes from which they could only escape by making enormous efforts to succeed, all the while fearful that they would not. This would certainly fit in with Edmond's attraction to "Les Ratés" (Failures), and the constant theme of failure in his poetry and plays. Almost all Rostand's heroes fail to achieve their dreams and have to come to terms with disillusionment.

Eugène Rostand seems to have coped with his illegitimate origins by deciding to excel, like Cyrano, in everything he did. Edmond for his part would learn to have recourse to his sense of pride, a trait he also gave to his Cyrano. He would pour his own sensitivity into his idealistic heroes, who prize their dream ("Le Rêve") above mundane reality. Reality, to Edmond Rostand, meant the loss of illusions, as in the citation at the head of this chapter, taken from his last play, *La Dernière Nuit de Don Juan*. Rostand's Don Juan has no idealistic vision to sustain him when his illusions are destroyed. He is the converse of Rostand's earlier heroes, but the message is the same. Reality is not enough – human beings need a dream to survive.

The *Lycée de Marseille* is housed in a former convent. The school boarders thought it a gloomy place and were envious of Edmond: "you sensed a happy child, a beloved child, the delight and pride of his family," recalled the writer Paul Brulat.[10] Another classmate of Edmond's, Jean Payoud, remembered him as "slim, with ever-alert eyes, a rather prominent nose and a witty mouth".[11]

There were several ways for Edmond to reach the large, gloomy portals of the school, but all involved a climb at some stage, for it is set on the hill that rises up from the harbour. Many of the streets he could take were lined with gracious Empire buildings – the boulevard Louis Salvator, for example, which climbs up from the Prefecture – perhaps he accompanied his father this far on the latter's walk to the family bank, just at the end of the rue Montaux. At the top of the hill, Edmond would have crossed the *cours Julien*, now a pleasant square with Judas trees and fountains, and so come out opposite the lycée. The imposing Conservatoire adjoining it now houses the local archives, including the ledger recording Edmond's birth. Or he could have followed shopping streets such as the Place St Ferréol, lined with flower stalls on Thursdays, a memory he would treasure later when he lived in Paris.

Another route would have led him through the older and narrower streets of the town, such as the rue Moustier, at the top of which stands a pillar surmounted by a bust of Homer, in memory of the city's' Greek origins as the Phocean colony, Massilia. And after school, it would only have been a short walk down the famous street, La Canebière, to the quay and its ships, or to the ancient heart of Marseilles on the opposite hill. Even if Edmond returned straight home, he would have had constant glimpses, down the long straight streets, of the splendid church built a few years before his birth, Notre Dame de la Garde, keeping watch over the town and the harbour from its prominent hilltop site.

Once Rostand had left Marseilles, he rarely returned. It is Provence rather than his home city which seems to have left its mark on him, especially the Provence of the troubadours. But most of all he was absorbing that love of the sun which is so much a part of the Provençal makeup:

> *O Soleil! toi sans qui les choses*
> *Ne seraient que ce qu'elles sont!*
> O sun! You without whom things
> would only be what they are!
> – *Chantecler* (Act I, sc. 2)

These lines, spoken as part of his "Hymn to the Sun" by Chantecler, the cockerel who believes he makes the sun rise, are among the most revealing in all Rostand's work. Just as the sun improves on reality, the poet's imagination makes reality bearable. What would life be without a dream to aspire to, a dream that colours everything one thinks and does? This theme appears in Rostand's earliest poems and was to remain constant throughout his life. It was part of his strategy for coping with painful reality.

When Edmond was eleven, the Prince Imperial, the exiled son of the deposed Emperor, Napoleon the Third, died in an accident at the age of only twenty-three. Eugène Rostand was chosen by the Bonapartist sympathisers of Marseilles to represent them at the funeral in England. He wrote a touching series of letters home. Eugène's admiration for Napoleon Bonaparte had led him to hang a copy of Lawrence's famous portrait of Bonaparte's son, the ill-fated Duc de Reichstadt, over Edmond's bed. It is not surprising that, when looking for a patriotic subject for a play to coincide with the Great Paris Exhibition of 1900, Edmond chose to write the story of the Duc de Reichstadt, also known as "l'Aiglon", the Eaglet.

In spite of his distressing discovery about his father's illegitimacy, Edmond was doing well at the lycée. He excelled in particular at French composition and at history. Eugène took an intense interest in his progress, arranging for the whole class's French composition marks to be delivered to his house on Saturday evenings, and even getting them telegraphed to him if he was away from home. He would then read the list to his son, starting with the lowest marks, and pausing tantalisingly between each one. Even when Edmond had gained the top mark, Eugène scarcely praised him. He expected his son to do well. This kind of pressure may also have contributed to Edmond's fear of failure.

Rostand's fellow-pupils have testified to the strong impression Edmond made on his classmates. His French compositions, in particular, were usually read out to the class. As for his skill at recitation, then a school subject, Paul Brulat recalled that Edmond spoke his lines like a real actor, and Jean Payoud described Rostand as "an actor born". Rostand also loved literature and history: Sir Walter Scott was one of his favourite authors. There was, however, one subject which Rostand did not like: mathematics. In the mathematics class Edmond got bored and used to amuse himself by building Egyptian temples with his books.

In spite of his successes, Edmond was not thought of as a model pupil by his teachers. On the contrary, he seems to have exasperated them. For in class he would be lost in a dream for much of the time (preferring as he did the dream to reality). Then, when he had to hand in a composition, he would apply himself so effectively that the teacher had no option but to award him high marks. "You set a bad example", his Form Three teacher, M. Guérillot, would complain. "You daydream all the time" (Vous musardez tout le temps).[12] "Musarder"– what a lovely word for such a pleasant occupation! Edmond looked it up in the etymologies and later wrote an entertaining preface on the history and meanings of the word for his first book of poems, which he naturally called "Les Musardises".[13]

Although he enjoyed writing poems at this age, Edmond did not yet think of himself as a poet. Jean Payoud was the "class poet", and when Edmond, at fourteen, needed a poem to impress a little milliner with whom he fancied himself in love, it was to Jean that he turned. Could this incident have given him the idea of the letter-writing Cyrano undertakes for Christian? If so, it was not to be the only one.

It was at prose that Edmond excelled at school, and not only in the French composition classes. Even an essay on the Mediterranean for his geography teacher was read out in class. Not that it had won any marks, being totally devoid of geographical facts. But his evocation of the ancient turquoise sea that lapped around his home city held the class spellbound.

Edmond's forte was writing little stories in the style of Alphonse Daudet, the popular Provençal writer whom Edmond greatly admired, learning whole pages off by heart. And it was a short story of this kind that would be Edmond's first nationally-published work, some years later.

When Edmond was in Class Four, his teacher read to his pupils from Théophile Gautier's popular novel, *Le Capitaine Fracasse*. This lively novel, still read today, takes its name from the stage name of the hero, the Baron de Sigognac. Set in the early seventeenth century, this book had all the ingredients likely to appeal to the young Rostand: a brave but penniless hero; a pure and beautiful heroine wooed and eventually won; the vicissitudes of a troupe of travelling players, and all the swashbuckling excitement of that period of French history, told with a wealth of historical detail and a rich and whimsical vocabulary. This novel made such an impression on Edmond that echoes of it can be found all through *Cyrano de Bergerac*.

It was also through Théophile Gautier that Edmond made the acquaintance the following year of the historical Cyrano de Bergerac himself, when his teacher read the class the famous passage in *Les Grotesques* which gave rise to the legend of Cyrano's oversize nose.[14] As a "nasigère" ("nose-bearer" – Edmond had rather a prominent nose himself), it is not surprising that Rostand ever after felt an affinity with such a man. But Cyrano's main appeal to the young Rostand lay in his fanciful imagination, his proud independence, and, of course, his panache.

Edmond's two final years of schooling would be passed in Paris. Once he had left home, Edmond would only briefly return to Marseilles for the Easter and New Year holidays. But he would continue to spend the summer holidays with his family, as he had done throughout his childhood, in the Pyrenean spa town of Luchon.

Luchon, ville des eaux courantes,
Où mon enfance avait son toit.
Luchon, town of running water,
where my childhood had its home.
–"L'Eau", *Les Musardises* (1911 ed.) (III, iii)

Luchon, "Reine des Pyrénées", sits high in the hills of the Haute-Garonne, at the head of the valley of the River Pique. It held a very special place in Rostand's heart. Here the Rostand family used to spend the summer season, away from the dust and heat of Marseilles.

At Luchon Edmond grew from childhood to boyhood, from boyhood to manhood; he met his future wife and spent the first few summers of his married life here. During the long summer holidays it was at Luchon that Edmond grew to love nature. And here, above all, he first became fully aware of his vocation to be a poet.

Thanks to its sulphur baths, Luchon was a popular spa during the Second Empire. Its visitors had included not only politicians and aristocrats but also literary figures such as Flaubert, Taine, Dumas fils and even Victor Hugo. Every summer the cream of Empire society paraded down the Avenue or under the tulip trees of the Quinconces, a fine park in front of the Baths.

But when the Rostands built their summer villa there, Luchon was still a small place, consisting of little more than the fashionable area round the Allées d'Étigny; the medieval town with its market place, and a few holiday villas near the Baths. The railway did not arrive until 1873, the grand Casino was not built until 1880. There were simply three small private casinos; one, at the Villa Corneille (now a charming hotel), also had a ballroom and even housed the protestant church (reached by a separate staircase). The town museum was housed there too, at one time. It contained another link with Napoleon Bonaparte's son, the Eaglet: his large globe of the world.

The Villa Julia (a name inspired by Juliette, for Edmond's new baby sister, and Julie, his mother's second name), had been built well away from the fashionable Allées, beside the rushing River Pique, with a view of the rugged mountain peaks which form the border with Spain. In those days there was a little waterfall just upstream, but today the Pique runs more evenly between stone walls, past a bust of Rostand installed in 1922. The meadow beyond is now given over to a "terrain de sports". But it is possible to imagine the scene in Rostand's time, when the small villages of the valley would have been set in fields melodious with cowbells, and the River Pique would have run its sparkling course between meadows full of wild flowers, just as its tributaries do today.

In this idyllic spot Rostand spent every summer for over twenty years, developing that love of nature which is so evident in his poems and plays, especially *Chantecler*. These summers have been described by the playwright Henry de Gorsse, who became Edmond's lifelong friend from the time when their respective nurses brought them both to play under the tulip trees and catalpas of the Quinconces park.[15] Henry remembers Edmond as a child, floating flowers, rather than paper boats, down the stream, or lying on the grass absorbed in the contemplation of a gentian or a buttercup. At seven Edmond was a thin, delicate little boy, according to Henry, with deep eyes and a rather flat face framed in curls. Edmond disliked his curls, which he thought made him look too much like a girl, and envied Henry's already cropped head.

The two boys played together in the park, or in the garden of the Villa Julia, until they were about ten, when they were allowed to wander off on their own. This was also the age when they were learning to ride. What joy to explore the woods and field, looking for flowers and following the streams! Rostand would always love running water – a love he credited Luchon with inspiring. What daring adventures they had at the Castel-Viel, an ancient chateau on a knoll just above Luchon, where the Pique is joined by the Lys! Little but a ruined tower and crumbling walls was left. They would not return home until evening, called home by the bells of St Mamet just across the river, their faces, at blackberry-time, smeared with purple juice, their hearts full of high deeds and adventure.

Edmond took the lead in their adventures, for though a dreamer, he was imaginative and inventive. He also enjoyed playing practical jokes, a trait which continued into adult life. One day he discovered how to get into the attic which housed the mechanism to work the large clock on the face of the Baths and worked out how to make the hands move. For several days he amused himself and confused the visitors by putting the clock forward or back.

Usually Edmond involved Henry in his escapades. Feeling sorry for some deer that had been put on show in the Quinconces, he persuaded Henry to help him free the creatures and drive them out of their enclosure up to the hills. But their kind intentions were frustrated by the deer themselves, who insisted on following the boys back to their former prison.

Edmond's sense of justice led him into other adventures, too. In the nearby village of Montauban, the local priest had diverted a stream into his garden, creating a series of cascades which he was charging visitors 50 centimes each to view. But Edmond felt it was wrong to charge people to see something as natural as flowing water. Without telling Henry why, he asked him to help him find the source of the stream, high up on the hillside. They found the stream had been diverted by a single plank. Edmond kicked the plank aside, and the stream returned to its former course. Below, in the curé's garden, there was uproar when visitors discovered they had paid to see – nothing! The affair would have been a mystery, had the boys not made the mistake of going to see for themselves the success of their operation. Their amusement immediately revealed their guilt to the curé, who spoke to them reproachfully rather than angrily – did they not realize they had deprived the poor people of the parish of a valuable income? Edmond immediately opened up his purse, which contained some twenty-five francs, saved up by himself and Henry to give their other friends a fireworks show, and "contrit mais magnifique", handed it all over to the curé. Such a gesture was typical of Edmond – it satisfied his love of panache, as well as his generosity.

Did Rostand have this gesture in mind when he has Cyrano throw a bag of gold to the players at the Hotel de Bourgogne, after he has interrupted their performance of *La Clorise*, in Act One of *Cyrano de Bergerac*? Rostand did use events from his childhood in his plays. Another incident took place at a children's ball. Edmond challenged a young Spaniard to a fight, after the latter tried to stop a little Greek girl from dancing with him. His adversary ran to get friends to back him up, but Edmond insisted on fighting alone. The parents of both boys arrived in time to stop the fight, but Edmond never forgot the incident. Some years later, after reading Act One of *Cyrano de Bergerac* to Henry, he stopped short when he reached the point where Cyrano goes out alone to fight the hundred men waiting for him at the Pont de Nesle:

Et vous messieurs, en me voyant charger
Ne me secondez pas, quel que soit le danger!
And you, sirs, when you see me charge,
 don't come and help me, whatever the danger!
– (Act I, sc. vii)

"Do you remember the little Greek girl?" he asked de Gorsse. "We played that out ourselves when we were twelve."

As for Rostand's often impulsive generosity, examples abound throughout his life. Henry de Gorsse suffered from it on at least one other occasion. The two boys had gone on a hike to the Moraine of Garin, a pleasant picnic spot about seven kilometres from Luchon. Henry had gone on ahead for water. On his return he found that Edmond, feeling sorry for a passing gypsy woman and her children, had given them all their food.

According to Henry de Gorsse, Rostand idealised the poor almost to the point of envying them. "He always had almost a worshipping attitude towards the poor, a sort of admiring pity for needy wanderers." Rostand's compassion embraced all poor people, whoever they might be: "He loved all beggars with the same passion, whether they were sordid, inspired or violent like the ones you see in the mountains". This was the same love that inspired his fellow feeling for worldly failures, the "Ratés".

Once they had learned to ride, the boys could range further afield. By his twenties Rostand, as we can see from his poems, knew and loved the whole area known today as the Haute-Garonne. It is an area rich in history (one of Edmond's favourite subjects, of course), from the Roman ruins of St Bertrand and the Romanesque village churches to the chateaux crowning almost every hill where impoverished seventeenth-century aristocrats like Gautier's Baron de Sigognac and Dumas's d'Artagnan had lived, chateaux by then often in a picturesque state of disrepair. Edmond took great delight in the Gascon names of hills and villages and used them in *Cyrano de Bergerac* for the titles of his Cadets de Gascogne.

One of Edmond's favourite villages was St Béat on the upper Garonne River. Here, the townspeople claim, a particular heavy balcony below which a lover could stand without being seen by his beloved above, gave Rostand the idea for his balcony scene in *Cyrano de Bergerac*. However, there are many similar balconies. And round the Villa Julia itself ran a wooden balcony at first-floor level, hung with wisteria in Rostand's time.

The road to St Béat leads to the border, as does the road through the Val de Burbe to the Col du Portillon, which left almost from the Rostands' back door and was one of the boys' favourite longer excursions. Just beyond the Col, they could look down into the Val d'Aran which had, besides its own beauty, the allure of being in a foreign country – Spain! Edmond's attraction to Spain, already present because of his pride in his grandmother, grew in strength as a result of his holidays in Luchon.

From the windows of the Villa Julia, Edmond would have been able to see the mountains of the frontier, just a few kilometres away. The Pic de Sauvegarde and the Pic de la Mine are bare and craggy, contrasting with the steep but wooded hills on either side of the valley. Between them lies the Gap de Vénasque, a difficult but not impossible way across the border for pedlars, smugglers, and refugees fleeing the war then raging in Spain. Sometimes moodily brooding, sometimes breathtakingly clear, the mountains were the constant companions of Edmond's boyhood and an ever-present reminder of his closeness to Spain.

What did Spain mean to the boy Edmond? Mainly what he had read about it: the idealism of Don Quixote and El Cid; the heroism of Roland; the romantic passion and jealously guarded honour of Musset's characters in the *Contes d'Espagne et d'Italie;* the exoticism of the Moors. He felt a deep affinity with all these qualities, especially with the noble ideals and courage of his literary heroes, which he attributed to his Spanish blood, through his grandmother. What is it, he asks himself in "Les Pyrénées", that draws him back so strongly that "at twenty as at twelve, I am standing at the train window looking out for your peaks?" It must be his Spanish blood that draws him, though no mountain-lover, to the Pyrenees, still in France, but so close to Spain that "sans quitter ma France, J'entends mon Espagne chanter!" (without leaving my France, I can hear my Spain singing).[16]

When Edmond was about eight, he and Henry saw in the streets of Luchon another reminder of Spain – the tattered remnants of Don Carlos's beaten army, struggling to safety over the mountain passes after their final defeat by Alphonse XII. Weary and often wounded, these soldiers seemed like heroes to the boys, who had heard of their bravery and ingenuity, making shot from silver mined in the mountains, for instance, when they ran out of lead. With Edmond's natural sympathy for the underdog, it is not surprising that this was a very powerful experience which made a lasting impression on him. Later, Edmond found in Victor Hugo's epic verse the same kind of romantic heroism he had admired in the defeated Carlists, and vowed to write an epic about them himself. Though he never did, similar ideas recur in a late poem, "Un Soir à Hernani" and in the much earlier "Le Contrebandier", written in his early twenties, in which the poet describes himself as a modern Don Quixote, a smuggler of idealistic enthusiasm into modern life.[17]

As soon as Rostand became aware of the *fin-de-siècle* disillusion which pervaded his times, he resisted it passionately. In the Carlists he saw heroism in action, men fighting for an ideal, modern Don Quixotes. According to Henry de Gorsse it was this experience that crystallized Rostand's decision to become himself a fighter against defeatism, not only the defeatism due to the defeat of France by Prussia in 1871, but the disillusion and apathy infecting his whole generation. Passionately proud of his French nationality, Rostand vowed to re-awaken "the virility and elegant pride of [his] race".

From his holidays in Luchon, Rostand gained an abiding love of nature; an affinity with Spain and Gascony; the first stirrings of his heroic idealism and the affirmation of his patriotism, and the inspiration for his early poems. But Luchon also played its part in the awakening of Rostand's vocation for the theatre.

At first, Luchon had little to offer theatrically but a few travelling circuses, whose poverty-stricken performers had little talent but plenty of brio. The boys would re-enact the various turns the next morning for the amusement of the servants. However, in 1880 a new Casino was built in Luchon, complete with a theatre and a permanent Guignol.

The Guignol used the stock characters: Guignol, the lovable hero; his adversary, Gnafron; Madelon, the young woman, and so on. The hunchbacked figure of Polichinelle, familiar to Edmond from Marseilles, would also have figured there. The experience of watching the puppet theatre remained a vivid one for Edmond. In his last play, *La Dernière Nuit de Don Juan*, the eponymous hero evokes an image of a group of children sitting on the ground looking up at the puppet booth, just as Edmond and Henry themselves would have done.

Both Edmond and Henry (and later, Edmond's older son Maurice), traced their fascination with the theatre back to the Guignol of Luchon. Seeing their interest, Uncle Alexis gave Edmond a puppet theatre of his own. The boys spent hours learning the rather mediocre playlets which came with it, and performing them to the servants at the Villa Julia.

But their love of things theatrical received an even greater impetus when they had the chance to go on stage themselves. Through the boys' friendship with two of the leading stars of Luchon's summer season, Victor Capoul and Pedro Gailhard, they heard there was to be a special performance of Berlioz's *Carmen* at a Gala Evening to celebrate the opening of the new Casino. Edmond and Henry were not slow to volunteer to be amongst the children forming the chorus in Act One.

This experience made a tremendous impression on the boys. Both decided they would be actors when they grew up. But the immediate result of their going on stage was dissatisfaction with the playlets provided with Uncle Alexis's puppet theatre. Edmond, who was already trying to write in traditional French forms such as octosyllabic verse and alexandrines, decided to write his own play, and in verse. This was the beginning of Rostand's playwriting career.

According to Henry, this play, the first of several Edmond wrote for the puppet theatre, used the stock characters of the Guignol: Gnafron is a hairdresser, Guignol a young poet in love with Madelon, Gnafron's daughter. (All Rostand's heroes were to be poets of one kind or another.) The story was inspired by a real-life hairdresser in Luchon who kept two foxes in a cage outside his shop, advertising his "vixen milk" as a cure for baldness. In Rostand's play, Guignol tricks the reluctant father into letting him marry his daughter by threatening to expose the "vixen milk" as fraudulent. The play closes with Gnafron commenting that, for Guignol to be so crafty so young, he must have drunk vixen's milk! It seems that the little two-act play was developed with a verve worthy of the *commedia dell'arte* of which Edmond was so fond.

As Luchon expanded, more and more figures from public life came for the "Season", and many of these found their way to the Villa Julia. Among those made welcome at the Rostands' were Ernest Reyer the Wagnerian composer (a friend from Marseilles), and Francis Plante, the blind pianist. Stephen Liégeard, the writer and socialite who coined the phrase "La Côte d'Azur", also visited. He was not to know that he would be beaten by Edmond in 1903 in the election for a place in the Académie française. Joseph Galliéni, born in nearby St Béat, later became famous for his defence of Paris as Minister of War during World War One. Another future politician was the fiery young Clemenceau, who would always remain on good terms with the Rostand family. There were aristocratic visitors too, such as the Baron de Nervo, leader of Luchon fashion and a keen investor in the new railways. When Alexis Rostand moved to Paris, leading financiers also called on the Rostands during the summer. The playwright Camille Doucet, Permanent Secretary to the Académie française and an administrator at the Comédie-Française, was another distinguished visitor. Did he, one wonders, ever discuss writing for the theatre with the future dramatist?

Although Eugène and Angèle were excellent and lively hosts, they were far from being socialites. In his poem "La Maison", Edmond affectionately describes the Villa Julia as a simple house, smelling of fresh linen and baby powder (his youngest sister, Jeanne, was born in 1879), lived in by a contented family.[18] "Tous nos orgueils etaient modestes, Comme des bijoux de corail", he wrote. (All our matters of pride were modest, like necklaces of coral.) When there was no company, the family followed their own pursuits: Juliette picking out Mozart tunes on the piano, Edmond writing or reading, Eugène working on his translation of Catullus,[19] perhaps, or composing an oratorio with his brother Alexis.

The whole family believed in the value of work. It was an attitude that stayed with Rostand throughout his life. Work was a sacred duty, as he frequently stated in his plays and poetry. And work was satisfying, too: "Minutes que rendaient célestes La mélodie et le travail" (minutes made heavenly by melody and work), he writes in the same poem, relating how he worked at his Greek translation while a bee hummed in the sunshine outside the window.

In the summer of 1884, Edmond was working even harder than usual during the summer holidays, taking extra lessons with the Abbé de Montauban. For that autumn he was to start his new life at the Collège Stanislas, in Paris.

In Paris, Edmond's literary talents would be encouraged by excellent teachers; he would meet people who had a lifelong influence on his development, and he would again meet with Cyrano de Bergerac and his fellow poets of the seventeenth century. But he had to learn to live apart from his close-knit, loving family, and away from the sunshine of Provence.

Eugène and Angèle had selected the Collège Stanislas as the most suitable college for Edmond to take his *rhéto* and his *philo* (rhetoric and philosophy, the two classes taken in college before going on to university). Edmond's parents hoped their promising son would then study for a university degree before training for the Foreign Office or for a military career at Saint-Cyr.

The Collège Stanislas, just off the boulevard Raspail, in Montparnasse, was one of the major lycées in Paris. It was acceptable to both parents, being a Catholic lycée run by the Maristes, but with teachers of a high calibre from the Sorbonne. Several of Edmond's cousins had also attended this college. Here, shut off from the temptations and delights of Paris by Stanislas's high walls, Edmond would complete his schooling.

Rostand's entrance form has survived. In it Eugène declared that although his son was in generally good health, apart from being a little anaemic, he had a nervous temperament. Deeply sensitive, far more than appeared on the surface, he was inclined to be dreamy and rather melancholy. Because Edmond was absent-minded, and not very well organized, he needed, and and would respond to appreciatively, any interest and support offered, especially with material things. These characteristics, noted by his perceptive (and similarly sensitive) father, would continue into Edmond's adult life.

Eugène admitted that Edmond had no aptitude for science: "le point noir", but was otherwise intelligent beyond his years. (Ironically, Edmond would have enjoyed biology, if that had been on offer, as he was fascinated by the natural world. But it was left to his son Jean to explore this subject.) But as regards literature, Eugène had no hesitation: his son had the potential to go "as far as he was pushed".[20]

The whole family moved to Paris for three months, to make the transition as easy as possible for Edmond. He took the first part of his baccalaureate in November and then began his career at Stanislas, first as a day boy, staying in the family of a nearby priest, the abbé Danglard, but later, at the insistence of a new principal, as a boarder.

Edmond was now subjected to the spartan regime that his family had hoped to spare him. In spite of their misgivings, he soon fitted in, and apart from being teased for his Marseillais accent, was soon accepted by the other students. But Edmond did find it hard to conceal his sensitive and emotional side in such a masculine and rational environment. The chapel services, with their incense, music and candles, and the reminder of home, gave him some comfort. These outward signs of religious faith, connected by Rostand with the security of his childhood and the beliefs of his mother and sisters, remained potent symbols for him that surface again and again in his work. He employed such symbolism with powerful effect in the last scene of *Cyrano de Bergerac*, where Cyrano's death takes place in the garden of a convent, to the sound of mass being sung. Whether Rostand had any religious beliefs himself will be discussed later, in the context of *La Samaritaine* and *La Princesse lointaine*.

The teachers at the Collège Stanislas were stimulating and sympathetic. They encouraged him to read as much as he liked. It was Edmond's great good fortune to have René Doumic as his teacher in his first year at the Collège Stanislas, the year of "rhétorique". Doumic, who later became Permanent Secretary at the Académie française and editor of the influential *Revue des Deux Mondes,* was then a young man of twenty-four who enjoyed friendly relations with his pupils. He also had a passion for French literature, a passion he encouraged in "le jeune Marseillais", as he called Edmond.

It was in Doumic's class, during a course on the French poets of the early seventeenth century, that Edmond renewed his acquaintance with Cyrano de Bergerac. Doumic's remarks about this poet's integrity and independence, and his fantastic imagination, struck a chord with the young Rostand, who now devoured all the poet's works, including *Les États et Empires de la Lune,* which he would draw on later for Act Three of *Cyrano de Bergerac*.

Edmond was enthralled by this whole period of French history, the period evoked in his old favourite, Gautier's *Le Capitaine Fracasse*; the period known as "LouisTreize", which stretched, in literary terms, from the death of Ronsard in 1585 to the beginning of the reign of Louis Quatorze, the Sun King. This period was characterised in literature by a break away from the strict classical rules of the Renaissance in poetry and drama, resulting in a flowering of individualistic poetry and a tendency to free thinking as opposed to obedience to the dictates of the Church. At the same time, there was an improvement in manners, with the growing importance of the court. This was carried to extremes by the *Précieuses* ridiculed by Molière (and gently satirized in *Cyrano de Bergerac*), but the flowery formulas of the time, its elegance and fine clothes were much to Rostand's taste. He admired, too, the variety of poetic forms used by the poets, and their flouting of earlier conventions. Many poets, especially *"Les Irréguliers"*, who included Cyrano, were *"Rêveurs"* and *"Ratés"* (Dreamers and Failures) after his own heart. At the same time, Corneille was writing his heroic dramas about the conflict between love and honour.

The period "Louis Treize" was just the time in French history to engage the passionate interest of one whose family motto was *"Egerunt et cecinerunt"* (they have done deeds and sung songs), just as the reign of Queen Elizabeth the First would have thrilled Edmond if he had been born in Britain. It was a time of duels and poetry, of romantic love and the clash between love and duty, of brave deeds and flourishing speeches, of d'Artagnan and the Three Musketeers, whom he was now discovering. By introducing his pupil to this period of history, Doumic had shown Edmond a living expression of the dreams and passions of his innermost being, and given him a focus for his idealism and enthusiasm. The lifelong process of nurturing the works of art which would express them had begun.

Doumic later said that Rostand was the best pupil he had ever had at Stanislas. Certainly, Edmond's French essays were always read out to the class, and his essay on Molière's *Le Misanthrope*, "Alceste ou Philinte?" was judged worthy of inclusion in the college's *Livre d'or*. But Doumic also called Edmond a "fantaisiste" – he was still a dreamer, particularly in lessons such as mathematics, where he was often in trouble for reading poetry instead of his algebra book. Edmond once told his family he wished all the lessons could be on French literature. Perhaps not all, however – he was also making the discovery of Shakespeare and Lope de Vega, thanks to another teacher, Boris de Tannenberg. Shakespeare in particular was a revelation to one used to the strict rules adhered to in French classical drama: here there was no "Unity of Time, Action or Place", and comedy was mixed up with tragedy, poetry with prose. But what language! What theatre! Rostand would later put to good use in his own dramas what he had learned from Shakespeare.

Boris de Tannenberg and René Doumic, both only a little older than he was, became Edmond's friends. But the German teacher, Lorber, was more like a father to Edmond. Lorber would read Goethe to his pupil in the evening sometimes for a treat, and occasionally took him home with him to talk about literature. The older man's gentle manners made a great impression on Edmond, who called him in a later poem "le bon Lorber". They maintained an affectionate relationship all their lives. Edmond, as a student, dedicated a novel to his teacher (*Mon La Bruyère*, unpublished). Lorber, for his part, would never miss any of his former pupil's premières.

But though his teachers encouraged Rostand's love of literature, it was not one of them who finally awoke the desire in Rostand to be a poet himself. In his first book of poems, *Les Musardises*, Rostand pays tribute to "mon maître vrai" and "l'éveilleur de mon premier enthousiasme" (my true master...the one who awakened my early enthusiasm): it was the school *pion* or supervisor. The pion assigned to Edmond's class was a figure of fun to most of the boys. This elderly, well-educated man in a long, threadbare coat and a battered opera hat had turned to drink to console himself for his failure to succeed as a poet. The resulting red nose gave him his nickname – Pif-Luisant – "Shiny-Conk". One day the pion discovered some of Edmond's poems, hidden in his desk. From then on the two spent many hours together talking about poetry. Pif-Luisant encouraged Edmond to break the rules of regular verse according to Boileau, still taught at the lycée, and lent him books of poetry disapproved of by his teachers. This was just the stimulus Edmond needed – how could *Cyrano de Bergerac* ever have been such a success if Rostand had stuck closely to the rules of French classical verse? What was more, the old pion would also expound on the classical poets Edmond was studying – Homer, Ovid, Tibullus, Virgil, bringing them to life in a way no teacher had been able to do. Above all, he fostered the boy's idealism and love of beauty and poetry. No wonder Rostand addresses him in *Les Musardises* as "toi que j'ai tant aimé" (you whom I loved so well).

In loving the shabby, ugly old man, rather than despising him as his school-fellows did, Edmond not only revealed the compassion that his father had hoped to inspire in him, but also showed that he could see beyond appearances. It was the pion's soul that mattered to the boy. Here is the contrast Rostand would dramatise in the character of Cyrano: an ugly exterior hiding inner beauty. Was the pion's ugly red nose in Rostand's mind when he gave his famous hero such an extravagant proboscis? It seems likely. Perhaps some of the humorous remarks in the Nose Tirade were first flung by cruel schoolboys at Cyrano's predecessor, Pif-Luisant, in the courtyard of the Collège Stanislas.

Pif-Luisant is also the first of the "Ratés" (Failures) that appear in various guises throughout Rostand's work. Like Cyrano, whose dreams of love and fame come to nothing, but who dies triumphant with his idealism and integrity intact, they are failures in the eyes of the world, but within they are glorious. Pif-Luisant appears in two of the earliest poems in Rostand's first collection of poems, *Les Musardises*, and many other poems praise similar idealistic failures. In fact, the book as a whole is dedicated to the Ratés. In the "Ballade des Songe-creux" (another name for poetic dreamers who have never achieved success), Rostand realises he could quite easily become one of them himself. This fellow-feeling for the Ratés continued all his life, for even after his success with *Cyrano de Bergerac,* Rostand feared he would fail to please the public and to inspire it with his ideals.

While Rostand's love of literature was being fostered and encouraged, his enthusiasm for the stage was also being given full reign. Not only could he visit the theatres of Paris on his days off, he was able to act himself in school plays and concerts. He so excelled in the elocution lessons that a fellow pupil considered, when he acted in Molière, that Edmond was better than any actor at the Comédie-Française.

The links with home were not completely broken. Edmond's friend from Luchon, Henry de Gorsse, was also in Paris, attending the Lycée Condorcet. Many Rostand relatives lived in Paris, Jules and Albert Rostand, for instance, and from his mother's sister's side of the family, the Marquis de Barthélemy. Eugène's friends, too, such as Paul de Cassagnac, took an interest in Edmond. But in particular Eugène himself visited often and kept up an assiduous correspondence. Indeed his attentions and constant exhortations to do better became rather wearing, according to Rostand's nephew, Roland de Margerie. It was only as Edmond developed his own friendships in Paris that he was able to free himself from his father's all-pervasive influence.[21]

On Sundays and on Thursday afternoons, traditionally free time in French schools, Edmond's relations and family friends would call at the Collège Stanislas to take him out on well-meaning but often rather boring excursions. But there was one exception to the rule: Colonel Villebois-Mareuil, who was just the kind of man to inspire and entertain a young man with his head full of dreams of heroism and chivalry.

The colonel, who was married to Edmond's cousin Paule Estrangin and lived on the nearby Avenue Villars, had served with distinction in Indo-China and Tunisia and been wounded in action in the Prussian War. He was a military man who lacked the provincial inhibition to which Edmond was accustomed. He found the colonel's outspokenness refreshing and exhilarating.

On the occasion of his reception into the Académie française, Rostand would acknowledge the influence of the colonel on his development as a young man. He described how the colonel would arrive at the college to carry him off to the Bois de Boulogne and other delightful places, talking to him all day of love and war. He was "sparkling without effort, profound as if by chance", his words containing just enough tartness to be stimulating. At the end of the day, the boy returned to his college dazzled and refreshed, feeling he had effortlessly learned much about "life".

Villebois-Mareuil also took Edmond to the theatre. In his speech at the Académie française, Rostand drew a parallel between his cousin and the theatre – both were larger than life and so able to take us out of ourselves, returning us afterwards to everyday reality with renewed vigour and courage. Unsurprisingly, the colonel himself figures largely in *Cyrano de Bergerac*: many of his characteristics were given to the roistering Cadets de Gascoigne.

His year of *"rhéto"* completed, Rostand returned to spend the holidays with his family in Luchon. Because he had not devoted enough time to the classes which did not interest him he had not done particularly well in his studies, achieving only twenty-sixth place in his class of thirty-five. But he had taken first prize in French, and won another prize for a Latin translation. This entitled him to take part with other top pupils in the annual Saint-Charlemagne celebrations, eating cold veal and salad, washed down with tiny amounts of champagne. Once he was home again he spent much of his time reading the classics he had discovered at college, steeping himself in Shakespeare and the Spanish dramatists; devouring the seventeenth-century French poets, Cyrano in particular, and savouring the chivalry and action of Alexandre Dumas's *Three Musketeers*. The contemporary novels of Georges d'Esparbès, on similar themes, were also favourites of Edmond's.

Nor were his theatrical ambitions forgotten. Henry de Gorsse and Edmond were both attempting to write plays. Rostand's was a light comedy in verse about Mme. de Rambouillet's salon, set in his favourite Louis-Treize period. He was to return later to this idea. At the same time, roaming the countryside on foot or on horseback with his friend, he was absorbing the impressions of nature which he would later try to express in poetry.

Edmond often went for long walks with his father, too. At such times, the subject of Edmond's future career would naturally be broached. Eugène and Angèle had expected their brilliant son to make a career in diplomacy. But Edmond appeared to have made no plans himself, apart from vague notions of devoting himself to writing. He asked for more time to think about it, but before the holiday was over, his mind was made up. He wished to pursue a career in literature, probably as a poet.

How could Eugène Rostand fail to sympathise with such a desire? But he had had to deny his own poetic inclinations in order to support his family – would Edmond be able to make a living from writing? A compromise was reached. After leaving the Collège Stanislas, Edmond would "do his law", so that at least he would have a profession to fall back on. And as a further concession, he would be allowed to study, not in Aix–in-Provence, close to Marseilles, but in Paris, where all aspiring writers had first to succeed. In Rostand's reception speech to the Académie française, he paid tribute to his father's understanding and support, speaking of "the happiness of some sons who did not arouse doubt in their fathers, and who saw the latter, far from turning them away from the Academy, taking the trouble to show them the way themselves".

On their way back to college for their year of "philo", Edmond and Henry had the train compartment to themselves, and took it in turns to read *The Three Musketeers* all night, standing on the seat to be nearer to the dim lamp. The valour and daring of d'Artagnan particularly appealed to Edmond. "I should like to write a play about him", he enthused. And indeed, though d'Artagnan himself only has a walk-on part in Rostand's most famous play, Cyrano has all his qualities (except good looks): daring, courage, enthusiasm, idealism, verve, carelessness of consequences, the extravagant gesture – all of which can be summed up in one word – panache!

"Panache! He thought about it all the time!" wrote Henry de Gorsse of this period of Edmond's youth. The first time Henry heard Edmond use the word was one lazy summer afternoon when they were discussing clothes. They had been cycling, the latest craze, and Edmond, with his usual attention to elegance, was wearing a blue suit rather than the white trousers and black spats that were usual. He happened to mention that he would like to wear suits of many other colours, too. "Even pink?" teased Henry, but Edmond replied seriously, "No, of course not. Pink is a tender, feminine colour. For a man, it lacks panache."[22]

Panache, that extra touch of elegance, dash or wit, like the white plume ornamenting a helmet which is its literal translation, is the quality we associate especially with Cyrano. Besides being his chief characteristic, it is also the last word he speaks, and the last word of the play. Rostand himself defined panache, in his reception speech to the Académie française, as "l'esprit de la bravoure" (the spirit of gallantry and courage) – something not great in itself, but added to greatness, "quelque chose de voltigeant, d'excessif, – et d'un peu frisé" (something fluttering and rather over the top, even a little boastful [literally "twirled"]) … "c'est le courage dominant à ce point la situation – qu'il en trouve le mot" (it is courage so in control of the situation that it can make a joke about it). Panache, Rostand went on to say, came to France from Spain, but the French have given it a light touch that is in better taste – panache is a kind of heroic modesty, a refusal to take death or oneself too seriously: "un sourire par lequel on s'excuse d'être sublime" (a smile by which we apologise for having behaved nobly). A little frivolous, perhaps, a little theatrical, he concedes, but nonetheless, panache is a quality Rostand would wish for all his listeners.

Cyrano, d'Artagnan, the Three Musketeers and Rostand's Cadets de Gascogne all display panache. All were Gascons. And just at this period in his life, Edmond was a Gascon too. Did he not live for a large part of the year in Luchon, in those days part of Gascony? Did he not travel through the heartlands of Gascony as his train made its way back to Paris or Marseilles? The Gascon and the Provençal existed side by side in Edmond's heart, and always would.

On his return to Stanislas, Edmond joined Monsieur Séguier's Philosophy class. One of his new classmates was Pierre Véber, the novelist and playwright. Véber remembered him as " distant but not aloof, extremely polite, … absent-minded". This fits in well with the picture we already have of a sensitive dreamer, absorbed in a world of his own. Rostand already stood out from the crowd. Véber called him "a pupil both noticeable and noticed … [he] already seemed older [than the others] … he spoke little and hardly seemed to do any work". "Surely", he added, perhaps with a touch of hindsight, "he was dreaming of some 'distant princess'" (a reference to Rostand's play, La Princesse lointaine). Like others who met Rostand throughout his life, Véber was struck by his modesty – in particular, he did not boast of belonging to an aristocratic college by wearing his uniform (royal blue, with gilt buttons) outside school. Calling on Rostand some thirty years later to solicit his vote at the Académie française, Véber was amazed to find

Rostand again not wearing his uniform – this time the distinctive green jacket of the Academician.[23]

Edmond did well in his last year of school, apart from finding philosophy an impossibly difficult subject. Rostand always had trouble with abstract ideas – his imagination was more suited to concrete expression, which is why he felt at home in the theatre. On 27th July, Edmond passed the second part of his Baccalaureate and was able to return to his family with his father. The director's final report must have pleased Eugène: "Edmond gained attention for valuable qualities: intelligence, a subtle and discerning mind, able to appreciate literature, a pleasant personality, the manners of a refined young man".[24]

One disappointment spoiled Edmond's last few days at Stanislas. As he found it almost as easy and much more enjoyable to write in verse, he had gained permission from Doumic, still his teacher of French literature, to write his entry for the end-of-term essay competition in verse. This break with tradition was displeasing to the more conservative teachers, and Edmond was not awarded the prize, which he felt would otherwise have been his. This was a setback for one hoping to make a living from his pen – however, Doumic consoled him, saying that he, Doumic, had every confidence in his "jeune Marseillais" and would follow his career with interest.

His schooldays behind him, Edmond returned to Luchon for the summer holidays. He and Henry were now young men-about-town. As children, they had often been amused by the fashionably-dressed men and women who thronged Luchon during the summer season, and Edmond had encouraged Henry to throw burrs at them. But now Edmond was one of them himself, able to give full play to his natural love of elegance and fine attire. It was then the fashion to wear brightly coloured ribbons on one's boater, and Edmond's natural superiority was confirmed for Henry by the brilliance and variety of his ribbons. The two young men now had many other friends at Luchon, but all acknowledged Edmond as their leader.

The young people built a stage in the garden of the villa Julia, and laid on performances for their families and acquaintances. The programme was a varied one: songs, music, poetry, sketches and even dancing.

Edmond's love for the theatre found another outlet in a romantic adventure with a visiting actress. Philinte was a *divette* – a singer in the operettas and comic operas now being performed at the Casino for the entertainment of Luchon's growing summer population. Waiting for her after a performance, Edmond begged to be allowed to read her the first act of a comic opera in verse he had written. This was graciously allowed. Edmond then asked for another meeting. Philinte again agreed, and Henry accompanied Edmond on horseback one morning to the chosen spot, a secluded hillock not far from Luchon known as the Mamelon de Cier. The actress was already there. "Well, young man, what have you to say to me?" she enquired as they rode up. "Des vers!" exclaimed Rostand, and immediately began reading his poetry to her, as coolly, relates de Gorsse, as if he had been reciting in his parents' salon. At the last line, Henry tactfully galloped away. In *La Princesse lointaine*, Bertrand bursts in upon Mélissinde, the 'distant princess', with the same cry.

The comic opera Edmond read to Philinte, of which only the first act seems to have been written, was based on a novel, *La Bavolette*, written by Paul de Musset, brother of Alfred, who wrote sentimental romances set in the seventeenth century. Edmond enjoyed such novels about "la galanterie chevaleresque", and preferred gentle, sweet women – the effect, Henry de Gorsse thought, of having a loving and close relationship with his mother and his two sisters.

The summer over, Edmond returned to Paris to begin his law studies. At first he stayed with the de Gorsses in the rue Berlin. When Henry was away doing his military service, Edmond had his room across the courtyard, overlooking a pleasant garden where wood pigeons cooed. Now that his son had left college, Eugène's vigilance was more relaxed; he had asked Boris de Tannenburg, Edmond's former Spanish teacher, to keep an eye on his son instead.

Edmond did not find it easy to be once again separated from his family, toiling away at his studies and writing poetry in his spare time

in dismal Paris when he might have been with his family in sunny
Provence:

> *Si je n'avais rêvé le vieux rêve inutile*
> *A tant d'autres pareil,*
> *De me faire une place au soleil d'une ville*
> *Qui n'a pas de soleil!*
> If I, like so many others,
> had not dreamed that old useless dream,
> to make myself a place in the sun
> in a town which has no sun!
> – "La Chambre", *Les Musardises* (1911 ed.), I,ii

When Henry was home on leave, the two friends spent all their
spare time going to the theatre. There were then over fifty theatres in
and around Paris, many catering for specific audiences. In addition
there were café-concerts, revues and circuses, as well as marionette
shows. At the state theatres, the prestigious Comédie-Française and
the Odéon, the young friends could savour the French classics such as
Racine, Corneille and Molière, and translations of Shakespeare. There
were revivals of Victor Hugo's Romantic dramas, too, as well as a few
verse plays by modern poets such as Francois Coppée and Jean Richepin
who were trying to keep this tradition alive.

But most contemporary authors had to prove themselves on the
boulevard first. They were unlikely to be performed unless they
conformed to the expectations of largely bourgeois audiences, who
simply wanted to be amused while they digested their copious dinners:
the plots usually revolved around money, class or adultery, especially
the latter. Though some of these plays addressed topical social issues,
the greater part were comedies, vaudevilles or farces, relying more on
amusing, fast-moving plots than characterisation or polemic.

Because of the difficulties in getting new plays performed, revivals
abounded, especially of historical romances and melodramas, but
also of the "well-made plays" popular with an earlier generation. The
theatre, in fact, in spite of the apparent variety of plays on offer, was
stagnating. Around twenty-five mainly elderly authors, of whom

Sardou, Labiche, Meilhac and Halévy, Pailleron, Dumas fils, Ohnet and Augier, were the most popular, shared long runs on the Parisian stage between them.

But a new era was about to begin, as playgoing became more popular throughout French society with the increased security and prosperity of the now well-established Third Republic. Successful novelists began to see the potential of the stage for reaching a wider audience and acquiring instant fame and more money. But it was still difficult to break into the system, and the conservatism of audiences and critics was resistant to change. The larger theatres needed big audiences and long runs to survive, so were wary of experimenting. However, to help new writers, by the 1880s most major theatres had introduced experimental matinees for new plays or minor classics.

Many of these new plays, such as adaptations of novels by Zola or Daudet, were about real life. They challenged not only artificial situations but also production conventions and acting styles. Henry Becque's portrayals of modern victims of society were strongly resisted at first, but by 1885 his *La Parisienne* was, after a trial run at the Renaissance, accepted by the Comédie-Française. Other playwrights applauded (Rostand would later be a friend of Becque's), but audiences did not enjoy such stark realism. Becque gave up writing for the theatre in disgust, but others were inspired by his example.

Real change began when an enthusiastic amateur, Antoine, set up an independent theatre, the Théâtre Libre, specifically to give new playwrights a chance.[25] All kinds of plays were welcomed by Antoine, reflecting the various schools of literature of the time: naturalism, symbolism, idealism. He also accepted historical plays and dramas in verse, and introduced Parisians for the first time to foreign writers such as Tolstoy, Ibsen, Maeterlinck and Sudermann.

Within a few years, the theatre would become of absorbing interest to Parisians. The success of the Théâtre Libre with a minority of the play-going public would inspire other new ventures, such as Paul Fort's Théâtre d'Art in 1890 and Lugné-Poe's Théâtre de l'Oeuvre in 1893. Always an important feature of middle class life, the theatre now offered greater choice and attracted a wider audience. So popular would play-going become in just a few years that one contemporary writer would dub the Paris of that time "Cabotinville" (Actorstown). [26]

Dramatic critics would be household names, their pronouncements eagerly awaited and debated. It was already a golden age for acting with actors and actresses of the calibre of Mounet-Sully, Constant Coquelin, who would be the first Cyrano, Réjane, Jane Hading, and the queen of them all, Sarah Bernhardt. Bernhardt, whom Rostand later came to know well, was as flamboyant off the stage as on it, and she and her colleagues gave the theatre a high profile. The theatre would be seen as a kind of barometer of the French spirit: the Comédie-Française and the Odéon were a source of national pride.

While the state theatres continued to perform the French classics, and the cream of the new plays, the numerous boulevard theatres would vie with each other to attract the well-to-do bourgeois public, but with more varied fare than before. Meanwhile the new minority theatres would offer an opportunity to experimental writers, who then often progressed to the boulevard or even to the state theatres. Aspiring authors, who until now had tried to break into the literary world with poetry, began to turn to the theatre instead.

The year 1887, when Antoine founded the Théâtre Libre and Edmond Rostand turned nineteen, was a turning point for Edmond as well as for the French theatre. That May, one of his short stories appeared in print, in the popular national paper, *Le Gaulois.* " Le Costume du Petit Jacques" was a rather sentimental little piece reminiscent, like his earliest attempts at writing in school, of Daudet, especially in its concern for the poor and humble. [27] As it included both a visit to a tailor's and a children's ball, Edmond was able to revel in the description of georgeous stuffs and elegant costumes. A simple, sad anecdote about the death of the tailor's son, the piece was well-written and nicely judged, with a hint of that irony and amusement at human behaviour that were to blossom in Rostand's later work. The vivid scene-setting and natural dialogue also reveal his innate theatrical sense.

But Rostand had already taken his first steps in the literary world that year, by winning the Academy of Marseilles's "Maréchal de Villiers prize" for an essay on the subject: *Deux Romanciers de Provence: Honoré d'Urfé et Émile Zola* (Two Novelists of Provence...).

When Eugène Rostand, now the Director of the Academy, had told his son the subject of that year's essay, Edmond, his interest aroused, had returned home for three months to research and write his entry. Eugène may well have had a hand in choosing the topic, closer to his own (and his son's) interests than some earlier ones. However this should not detract from Edmond's considerable achievement. Could two French novelists present more of a contrast than Honoré d'Urfé, the seventeenth-century author of the long, flowery novel of sentiment, *L'Astrée*, bible of the *Précieuses* and their salons, and Émile Zola, Edmond's contemporary, whose naturalistic, even grim, pictures of "real life" had often shocked his readers? What could two such writers have in common apart from their rather tenuous links with Provence?

However the topic gave Rostand the chance to exercise his already considerable skills as a literary critic. His prize-winning essay, printed in the *Journal de Marseille*, and also printed privately by his proud father (but not published in Paris until 1921), is well-reasoned and well-written, with an amazing assurance and knowledge of French literature.

Many of Rostand's favourite themes and ideas are present here. We have already noted that for the poet, just as the sun transforms reality, so too the imagination makes reality bearable. Here he writes that Provence is "the land of the all-powerful imagination": just as the sun of the Midi transforms everyday things into something richer and more beautiful, so the imagination of the Provençal can make the slightest incident into a vivid, often exaggerated story. This may have been a delicate tribute to his mother's known talents in this field, but Rostand's remarks about the story-telling skills of his fellow Provençals apply equally to the dramatist he was later to become: "that facility for telling stories ... that verve...that enthusiasm in the telling which brings the story alive, and makes it colourful and lively ...marvellously chosen details which make you see what is happening."

What he saw as the transforming power of the Midi sun – the sun he yearned for in exile in Paris – always fascinated Rostand. The whole of his play *Chantecler,* and especially the well-known "Hymn to the sun" in Act One, is a paean of praise to the Provençal sun which makes the ordinary beautiful. Everyday reality was not enough for Rostand. It had to be transformed, either by the light of the sun, or by the power of the imagination, or by a vison of what might be, "Le Rêve", to bring out its true beauty.

In his essay, the young critic noted that Zola and d'Urfé represent the two extremes of the French spirit as depicted by Brunetière: the former displays "l'esprit gaulois", which tends to cynicism and coarse humour; "l'esprit précieux" is represented by d'Urfé: polite, idealistic, refined language, lapsing at times into artificiality. Neither approach fully satisfied Rostand. He wanted, "non point le réalisme, mais la nature". He abhorred coarse "gallic" humour in life and literature, but would have to guard against preciosity in his own writing.

It is clear that Rostand has already formed his own attitude to life. He was strongly attracted to d'Urfé's period of French history. This is understandable, given his love of elegance, gallantry, poetry and beautiful language. The verve and chivalry he admired in d'Artagnan and the real Cyrano de Bergerac were complementary to polite society, not opposed to it (d'Urfé himself was a soldier as well as a courtier and writer). Preciosity and swashbuckling were underpinned by the same idealism, expressed on the one hand in poetic speech and idealised love, and on the other hand, by the willingness to fight, and if necessary to die for, a woman, an ideal, or even just as a heroic, if useless, gesture.

In Rostand's eyes, this ideal – if idealised – society presented a glaring contrast with that of his own times, where, he felt, true poetry; tender and refined sentiments, and gentle social pleasures had been discarded in favour of a rather brutal realism and the demands of practicality. Materialism reigned: "Thinking is less common than reckoning" (on pense moins qu'on ne compte). What outward elegance remained was only for show, masking grossness and lack of true feeling. In matters of the heart, courtesy and chivalry were made to seem ridiculous, and women were no longer accorded special respect. Rostand believed that even the French language had deteriorated from "the beautiful, pure, rather ceremonious, language of former times".

Rostand was no prig, however. He admits to being, inevitably, a child of his time. All too easily, he writes, one becomes used to reading books that were once thought shocking. It is the decent book that one is embarrassed to be caught reading these days – and no-one reads *L'Astrée* any more!

There was more to Edmond's distate for the materialism of his times than a simple nostalgia for a lost golden age. His attitude was positive, not negative. He was inspired by his love of poetry to yearn for a life transformed by idealism, just as everyday things are transformed by the power of the Midi sun. That this would be an inspiring message for many, the success of *Cyrano de Bergerac* has shown.

Rostand closed his assessment of d'Urfé with a quotation from Zola which, he feels, applies to the earlier writer: "il planta les petites fleurs bleues de l'idéal dans la brutalité des désirs" (he planted the small blue flowers of idealism in the brutality of desire). In modern French, the expression "fleur bleue" denotes, tongue in cheek, someone who is sentimentally romantic (which proves Rostand's point about the cynicism of the modern world).[28] But Rostand came to see it as his mission in life to sow the small blue flowers of idealism amongst the materialism and cynicism of his own generation. Or, using another metaphor which we shall find in his poems, he saw himself as "le colporteur de l'idéal", a "smuggler of idealism" into the modern world. Here already is Rostand's *leitmotiv*, the idealism that runs through all his work for the theatre.

At about this time he also wrote a one-act play in verse on a theme that might have come naturally to d'Urfé's pen – he called it *Le Rêve*. A poet is in love with a woman he has never met. When the possibility arises of actually meeting her, he dies rather than risk losing his ideal picture of her. The play was destroyed, but Rostand would return to the theme of love for an unseen woman in his first serious play, *La Princesse lointaine*, based on the true story of the medieval poet Joffroy

Rudel. The idea of "the dream" being preferable to reality also reappears in his work from time to time. One could argue that for Cyrano, too, "the dream" of Roxane returning his love is too precious to risk declaring his feelings to her even after the death of Christian.

Already then, by the age of nineteen, we find Rostand has a well-thought-out attitude to life. How was he to find a life-partner who would share his love of poetry, his romantic and chivalrous attitude to women and his high ideals? Perhaps only another poet would do. This brings us to the third major event in Rostand's life in that momentous year of 1887.

That summer a young woman called Louise Rose Étiennette Gérard, known as Rosemonde, was visiting Luchon for the first time. She was twenty-one years old, and had come with her guardian, Mme Sylvie Lee, to take the waters. Eugène Rostand found himself sharing their compartment in the train that climbs up into the Pyrenees from Montréjeau. He was amused at the unselfconscious delight shown by Rosemonde at her first sight of the mountains, and began to talk to her. He soon discovered that, like the Rostands, she loved the arts and literature, and wrote poetry. As they parted at the station, Eugène invited the young woman to call. She and Mme Lee were staying just a few doors away, at the Villa Mauricia.

The next day, Edmond was reading the sixteenth-century Portuguese classic, Camoëns' *Lusiades,* when the doorbell rang. When he went to answer it, there, framed in the doorway, with the sun lighting up her blonde hair from behind like a halo, as he told a friend later, stood Rosemonde. Two years older than Edmond, Rosemonde was already well-known in the literary milieus of Paris. Her guardian Mme Lee ran an influential salon at her home in the boulevard Malesherbes, where Rosemonde recited her own poems to the guests. A contemporary journalist described his first impressions of her as: "a very young girl, very slim, very blonde, delicate and gracious … her manners were delightful, without any affectation of naivety or too much coquetterie … her poetry was ingenuous and subtle, with something airy and lingering about it".[29]

The two young people quickly became friends. Rosemonde not only wrote poetry, but was also taking elocution lessons from Maurice Féraudy, a leading actor at the Comédie-Française. The little group performing at the Villa Julia invited her to join in their concerts of songs, dances, poetry recitals and acted dialogues. The programmes for this summer, printed on silk, still survive, and show that the dialogues between Edmond and Rosemonde increased from one in August to three in September. By the end of the summer, they were deeply committed to one another.

Rosemonde had a distinguished background: her father had been Count Louis Maurice Gérard, the son of the famous Field Marshal Gérard of whom Napoleon said that, if he had listened to his advice, the French would have won Waterloo. Count Gérard was also a descendant of the eighteenth-century writer Mme de Genlis,[30] through his mother, Louise Rose de Valence, after whom Rosemonde was named.

There is a strong possibility that royal blood ran in Rosemonde's veins. Her grandmother's mother, Pulchérie, was the daughter of Mme de Genlis. But as the latter was the mistress of the Duke of Orleans, Pulchérie may have been his daughter. In that case, Rosemonde and her sons would be descended ultimately from Louis XIV himself. This possibility did not appear to concern Rosemonde; she was simply proud of her connection with Mme de Genlis. She owned the writing desk of her famous ancestor, and later she would write her biography.

Rosemonde's pedigree, however, though glittering, was not flawless. In an uncanny echo of the circumstances of Eugène Rostand's birth, Rosemonde was born illegitimately.[31] Her "guardian" Mme Lee, was really her mother. Sylvie Lee already had two sons by her English husband. Count Gérard did not recognise his daughter legally until January 1868, so Mme Lee passed herself off as Rosemonde's guardian and set up a *conseil de famille* to look after her daughter's interests. The council included the ageing Parnassian poet Leconte de Lisle and the popular dramatist Dumas the Younger, son of Alexandre Dumas the Elder, whose historical romances had so enthused Edmond. The composer Massenet was also a friend of the family. So from an early age, Rosemonde had moved in literary and musical circles. She had been writing poetry since she was twelve. At the convent where she had been educated, Rosemonde had thought herself merely Mme Lee's ward. She only discovered the truth when her father died unmarried in August 1880, leaving her the bulk of his considerable fortune.

For Rosemonde, too, 1887 was a critical year. Before her visit to Luchon, she had become engaged to someone chosen for her by the *conseil de famille*. But on her return to Paris, she broke off this loveless betrothal.

On his return to Paris that autumn, Edmond took and passed the first of three parts of his law degree. He soon moved to an attic room in the rue de Bourgogne. Here he was thoroughly miserable. However, he worked on, attending law classes in the daytime, giving private tuition to supplement his income, and writing poetry at night. Although still determined to make his living by writing, he is obsessed by the fear of failure. In a poem written while he was a student, he tells how two things help him to keep up his spirits: the red rose on his writing table, and the little mouse he can hear late at night gnawing away in the roof. The rose counsels "Pride!" the mouse "Patience!"

> *Ce sont les deux conseils dont j'ai besoin de vivre*
> *L'un gris, l'autre vermeil:*
> *Mais le second conseil est moins facile à suivre…*
> These are the two pieces of advice I need to live –
> one grey, the other red –
> but the second is more difficult to follow…
> – "La Chambre", *Les Musardises* (1911 ed.), I, ii

"More difficult to follow", because of Rostand's continuing sense of inferiority, perhaps on account of his father's illegitimate birth. It was astute of the young poet to build up his pride and so give himself the confidence he needed. Much of his later success was due to his cultivation of these two qualities: his pride, learnt in the lycée and strengthened by the example of his fellow Gascon, d'Artagnan, will not let him fail; his patient habits of work enable him to persist and eventually triumph.

One comfort was that Rosemonde was also in Paris. The two young people continued to keep in touch on their return to the capital, mainly by letter, for Rosemonde was too involved with social activities and her mother's salon to be able to meet Edmond often. Edmond's poetry took on a new urgency. He was aware of how important it was now for him to succeed in his chosen profession. Many of the poems he was to publish in his first book of verse, *Les Musardises*, reflect the debate going on inside him – should he, or should he not, devote himself to writing poetry?

Poetry had always been part of his life. His father not only wrote verse but encouraged his son to read and love poetry, a love fostered by friendship with Pif-Luisant. Edmond had recited poetry and mixed with poets in his family's salon. The dreams and fantasies he indulged in, too, were better suited to poetry than prose. Indeed, he often found it easier to write in verse – he had a natural facility for it. But could he succeed as a poet?

Along with Rostand's desire to be a poet went his love for the theatre. We have the testimony of many of his contemporaries that if he had not become a dramatic poet he would have made an equally successful actor or producer. He had an excellent grasp of all the aspects of staging a play, and could also speak verse beautifully, in a natural voice which brought out every nuance of the author's meaning. Later, at rehearsals of his plays, he would explain to the actors exactly what he wanted them to do, and sometimes, with manic energy, act out each part in turn himself.

But Rostand's affinity with the theatre went deeper than mere talent. For the theatre is based on illusion – a play is not real life, but an imaginative depiction of an alternative reality. For someone who wished to express their "dream", the theatre was the ideal environment. The theatre also fulfilled Rostand's desire for something larger than life – enthusiasm and passion that were out-of-place in everyday life could be given full rein there.

Furthermore, a theatrical performance was a group experience: the audience could thrill as one to the emotions and events being played out on stage. Rostand later came to see this unifying experience as one of the most important reasons for him to write for the theatre. His aim, as he told the audience at his reception into the Académie française, was to use the power of the theatre to give "leçons d'âme" (lessons for the soul), to inspire and unite the French people by reminding them of the idealism and panache that was part of their Gallic heritage.

It was Rostand's good fortune that the verse drama, which combined his talent for writing poetry with his love of the theatre, was a prominent part of that heritage, and one which was still very much in favour with French audiences. The state theatres, the Comédie-Française and the Odéon, regularly performed Racine, Corneille and other poetic dramatists. They were willing, too, to perform modern works in verse by writers such as François Coppée, Jean Richepin, Catulle Mendès, Henri de Bornier and Théodore de Banville. Such plays usually enjoyed a *succès d'estime* without making any money or much impact on ordinary theatre-goers. It would be Rostand's great achievement to please both lovers of poetry and the general public.

However, it took a little while for Edmond to discover his true direction. During his lonely months in Paris as a law student, he had written a number of poems, mainly inspired by his desire to be a poet. After meeting Rosemonde Gérard he began to write love poems, too. At the same time he was translating poems by modern Spanish writers such as Zorilla for his former teacher, now his family-appointed guardian, Boris de Tannenburg, who was compiling an anthology. Tannenburg was a staunch ally, both encouraging the young man and assuring him he would eventually succeed, and also doing his best to convince Edmond's parents that their son had made the right decision in choosing a literary career. At Tannenburg's suggestion, Rostand attempted a tragedy in verse, based on Lope de Vega's *Tamayo*, but Edmond only managed to compose the beginning and the end. In spite of a tendency to melancholy at times, Edmond's temperament was generally optimistic and positive. He felt ill at ease in tragedy.

Instead, he wrote a one-act play in verse, set in his beloved seventeenth century. The action took place in Mme de Rambouillet's salon, and featured her daughter, Julie d'Angoulême, and Julie's admirer Charles de Montausier. (This may have been the same play mentioned earlier.) According to Henry de Gorsse, fragments of this early attempt were later used by Rostand in *Cyrano de Bergerac* and in a later poem, "Journée d'une Précieuse".

Edmond also tried his hand at prose. In *Les Petites Manies*, a play of which only the first of a planned two acts was written, he amused himself presenting the foibles of two friends who drive each other to distraction. Some of these ideas, too, were re-used, this time in his first successful play, *Les Romanesques*. But Edmond's first venture on the French stage was in one of the forms he had not yet experimented with: vaudeville.

This rather surprising debut came about as a result of meeting Rosemonde's two half-brothers at a New Year's Day party in 1888 at Mme Lee's apartment. The Lees lived in an attractive town house at 107, boulevard Malesherbes, in the most fashionable part of Paris, close to the Parc Monceau. The elder brother, William, was intellectual and artistic, a kind of "raté génial" ("inspired failure") with whom Edmond would have felt an instinctive sympathy.[12] Henry Lee wrote for various sporting papers and was also an enthusiastic theatre-goer. He and Edmond decided to write a vaudeville together.

Vaudeville – light comedy with an improbable plot full of twists and turns – was a very popular form of entertainment in the commercial theatre at that time. The plot of Edmond and Henry's play, *Le Gant rouge*, concerned some love letters concealed in a shop sign (the red glove of the title), and the efforts of the various characters to obtain, conceal or destroy them. To the delight of the young authors, the Théâtre de Clùny accepted the piece. Rostand, thrilled, attended all the rehearsals.

The first performance of *Le Gant rouge* took place on 24th August, 1888. Rosemonde, now Edmond's fiancée, had encouraged the venture, but was, to her intense regret, away at the time, travelling from spa to spa with her mother, who was unwell. The young authors' hopes of success, however, were soon dashed. The play ran to almost empty houses for fifteen days and was then taken off. It was, of course, the height of the summer season, when audiences were thin and auditoriums stiflingly hot. But if the redoubtable Francisque Sarcey, the influential drama critic of *Le Temps*, is to be believed, the fault lay rather in the play itself, in which, he wrote, there were no witty lines at all.

There were, however, kinder reviews in the *Moniteur Universel*. "The public laughed heartily", wrote "Surtac". He praised "amusing situations, jolly cross-dressing, and very successful disguises". In more experienced hands, he thought, the play could have been a great success. "Robert Dorsal" also praised the play for its youthful verve and gaiety, while pointing out a few faults due to inexperience. This certainly sounds more the kind of play we would expect of the young man who was to write *Cyrano de Bergerac* less than ten years later. Dorsal concluded his review with the mysterious claim that he knew of better works by the same author. "This young gentleman has wit and imagination ... he is even capable of a subtlety of which I admit *Le Gant Rouge* scarcely gives an idea. You will be grateful to me in a little while for having been one of the first to bring his name to your notice", he wrote. Edmond, intrigued, wrote to thank his unknown supporter. It turned out to be none other than his old form-teacher, René Doumic.

Rostand was later embarrassed by this early effort, and actually went to court in 1903 to prevent Gaston Marot, the director of the Cluny Theatre, from staging it again after the success of *Cyrano de Bergerac*. The play apparently contained coarse expressions that were out-of-keeping with Rostand's character – he who preferred d'Urfé to Zola – and it has been suggested that Marot tampered with the script to make it more acceptable to his patrons. Certainly the copy of the play kept in the Archives de France, copied into exercise books in a rounded hand (perhaps Rosemonde's?), seems harmless enough, and even quite witty. Antoine, in his account of stage performances for 1888, lists the authors as Gaston Marot and Edmond Rostand, in that order, and elsewhere refers to Marot as Rostand's collaborator. Marot was in fact entitled to fifty per cent of the performing rights, so he had obviously played a major role in preparing the play for the stage. Henry Lee is not mentioned at all. It seems quite possible that the play started out, as Henry de Gorsse claims, as a charming comedy of bourgeois manners, such as Edmond was to write, with more success, in *Les Romanesques* just three years later.

This failure did not mean Rostand would give up his dreams of being a writer. He wrote to Rosemonde of his longing to produce something that he could be proud of, something wholly original. One day, he told her, I am sure I will write a truly beautiful play in verse.[33]

A play in verse particularly appealed to him, because it was the most difficult form in which to succeed, but he wanted to concentrate on writing something – anything – which would draw on what he felt were his main strengths: depth of feeling, and sympathetic yet gently mocking observation of human nature. Edmond was convinced he had real talent, but inspiration was slow in coming. Without inspiration, what use was talent? "Suis-je sûr de trouver ma chanson dans mon coeur?" (Can I be sure of finding my song in my heart?).[34] This refrain would echo through Rostand's life, even after the success of *Cyrano de Bergerac.*

Edmond continued to write poems in his lonely room in the rue de Bourgogne. Only three were printed: "La Ballade des Songe-Creux" (Ballad of the Dreamers) in 1888, "Les Nénuphars" (The Water-lilies) in 1889, and "La Sagesse des boeufs" (The Wisdom of the Oxen) in 1890, all in the *Nouvelle Revue.*[35] Other poems, such as one to his cousin Henri Estrangin in Marseilles, congratulating him for putting up a fountain in front of the family bank, were written for pleasure and for his friends' eyes only. Because Edmond found it easier to write verse than prose, he often wrote his letters in rhyme, doodling little pictures in the margin and on the envelope.

It was Rosemonde's poetry which first appeared in book form. *Les Pipeaux* came out in 1889, published by *the* poetry publisher of the day, Lemerre. It was warmly received by press and public, and had the honour of being "crowned" by the Académie française, at the instigation of Dumas the Younger. This was not, however, just a case of a beautiful young woman's literary acquaintances rallying to her support – her poems did have a genuine freshness and sensitivity that was widely appreciated. Several, especially the "Ritournelles", were set to music, notably by Cécile Chaminade, the popular contemporary pianist and composer.

Reading the charming poems in *Les Pipeaux* (The Reed-pipes), you realise that Rosemonde Gérard was the ideal life-partner for Edmond Rostand. The two had so much in common: a love of poetry, of course, but also an appreciation of nature, reverence for all living creatures, a taste for solitude and reverie. Both cherish their ideals – "le Rêve" (the dream) – in contrast to banal or harsh reality. Rosemonde's femininity forms the perfect counterpoint to Edmond's masculinity (a masculinity which is gallant rather than "macho"). She is receptive, tender, comforting. Both adore Nature, but Rosemonde wishes to become part of it. Edmond, on the other hand, desperately wishes to master Nature, struggling to express its beauty and its power in poetry. In love, Rosemonde again is archetypically feminine, wholehearted in her devotion and willing to lose herself in the service of her beloved. She is perceptive: knowing and accepting Edmond just as he is; she is wise, realising that the magic of first love will pass, but still romantic enough to treasure these fleeting moments of happiness.

With the success of *Les Pipeaux*, Rosemonde's success as a poet seemed assured. Meanwhile, Edmond had made the acquaintance of the composer, Emmanuel Chabrier.

Chabrier was a well-established composer. But he was now struggling to compose *Briséïs*, a tragedy in the Wagnerian style, and short of money. So he determined to write some light music for songs to be performed in the salons, and fixed on some of Edmond's poems.

This may have been at the suggestion of the Rostands' friend from Marseilles, Ernest Reyer, another Wagnerian, or the connection may have been made through Edmond's Uncle Alexis, now living in Paris in the rue du Conservatoire, and becoming well-known in musical circles as well as financial ones. Chabrier was setting to music two of

Edmond's lighthearted country poems: "La Ballade des gros dindons" and the "Pastorale des cochons rouges". They would be included in what the composer jokingly called his "Barnyard Romances".

Rosemonde too contributed to the final selection, published as *Six Mélodies* in 1890 by Enoch. The selection consisted of Edmond's two poems plus Rosemonde's "Villanelle des petits canards" and "Les Cigales", along with a further poem by Edmond, "Toutes les fleurs", and Ephraïm Mikhael's "L'Ile heureuse". Of these "petites blagues pour le chant" (little jokes for singing), as Chabrier called them in a letter to his friend, the tenor Charles von Dyck in December 1889, it is the first three songs which remain deservedly popular today. Chabrier's music beautifully brings out the humour and lightness of touch of the young people's verses.

Chabrier must have been pleased with Edmond's collaboration, for he invited him the following year to write an "Ode à la Musique", a *pièce de circonstance* commissioned by one Jules Griset to celebrate moving into his new house. This was a piece for a choir of women's voices plus solo soprano and piano accompaniment. After its first private performance in November 1890, it became part of the concert repertoire and was a great favourite of Debussy's. Even today, it is still occasionally performed – few of its listeners can associate it with the author of *Cyrano de Bergerac*.

But this is to anticipate. 1889 also saw the publication of Boris de Tannenburg's anthology, *Poésie castillane contemporaine*, which included some of Edmond's translations of Zorilla. [36]

The summer of 1889 was naturally spent in Luchon. This year, the season was more brilliant than ever, for the first "Battle of the Flowers" took place. The original idea for this event, where residents and visitors vied with each other in decorating their carriages or their horses in flowers, has been attributed to Edmond Rostand, as he was an acquaintance of Maurice Froyez, one of the first organisers. Whatever the case, the Rostand family certainly took part every year, and carried off the prizes more than once. A photograph of Edmond and Rosemonde's decorated carriage in this first "Battle" can be seen in the Luchon museum.

It may have been during this summer that Rostand had the experience that gave him the idea for the substitute wooing of Roxane, the main hinge of his plot in *Cyrano de Bergerac*. One of Edmond's friends in Luchon was very distressed because the girl he loved found him too naïve and inhibited, and threatened to leave him. Edmond took pity on him and began to give him advice as to how to court her. He even dictated his love letters. Thanks to his intervention, the courtship, like Christian's, ended in marriage.

This story is recounted by Paul Faure, and Rosemonde Gérard tells a similar one.[37] It seems likely to be true, especially as we know that Rostand did use events from his own experience in his plays. M. Henri Pac, the Luchon historian, even gives us the real names of the lovers: Jérome Faduilhe and Maria Castaing. Jérome was the son of the owners of the Villa Mauricia, where Rosemonde had stayed on her first visit to Luchon.[38]

The performances in the garden of the Villa Julia continued. Edmond wrote a lighthearted one-act play for himself and Rosemonde to perform with his friends. In rhyming couplets, *Pierrot qui pleure et Pierrot qui rit* used the familiar *commedia dell'arte* characters, and had Columbine being wooed by not one but two Pierrots. "Pierrot qui Pleure" (Weeping Pierrot) is sad and weeps at every opportunity. His rival, "Pierrot qui Rit" (Laughing Pierrot), appears to be without a care in the world and turns every setback into laughter. Here are the two contrasting sides of Edmond himself personified in drama for the first, but not the last time. It is "Pierrot qui Rit" who wins Columbine's hand, but not until she discovers he also knows how to weep. Here, too, is Cyrano, concealing his feelings behind a cheerful exterior, but a Cyrano who succeeds in winning his beloved. Rostand was pleased with the play, and revised it the following summer, without realising that it would be his Open Sesame to the world of the theatre.

On his return to Paris, Edmond continued to write poetry, much of it inspired by his holidays in Luchon. Rosemonde had persuaded him to publish his poems at his own expense with Lemerre. This was a common procedure at a time when men and women with literary ambitions were flocking to Paris. Publishing verse was at that time the most popular way to begin a literary career, until the theatre became the focus of literary ambitions.

Les Musardises was duly published in the spring of 1890, just before Edmond and Rosemonde's wedding, but of five hundred copies printed, only thirty were sold. Lacking any literary friends ("this young man will never do anything worthwhile", Leconte de Lisle had told Rosemonde), and belonging to none of the literary coteries that then abounded in the capital, Rostand's book was hardly reviewed and therefore, in the hectic literary life of the times, had little chance of being noticed.

The one enthusiastic review it did receive, however, was enough to keep the young poet's hopes alive. The respected critic Auguste Filon, writing in the *Revue Bleue*, announced that this was the most brilliant literary debut since Musset's *Contes d'Espagne et d'Italie* burst upon the world. Such exaggerated praise was perhaps partly due to the fact that Filon, formerly tutor to the Prince Imperial, was an acquaintance of Eugène Rostand's. However, as Filon wrote after the triumph of *Cyrano de Bergerac,* it came to seem something of an understatement. But whether out of friendship or perception, Filon correctly identified the attraction of this youthful book of poems:

> It's a veritable explosion of poetic talent; along with that, a new accent, this spontaneity, this boldness, something vibrant and lively … astonishingly audacious and even more astonishingly skilful.[39]

Filon also noted approvingly the young poet's attitude to life, contrasting it with the prevailing *fin-de-siècle* decadence and *ennui* :

> Beneath this exuberance, a healthy, normal mind: no neurosis or sign of decadence; a joyful, robust appetite for life laced with that melancholy where passionate souls find relaxation without anxiety.

Such praise was not undeserved, and if Rostand had been better known in literary Paris in 1890, the applause which greeted *Les Pipeaux* might have been repeated for *Les Musardises*. Again, Leconte de Lisle, the one literary figure with whom Edmond was acquainted, was unsympathetic. "If your book failed, it was only what it deserved", he remarked to Edmond. As a Parnassian poet, however, Leconte de Lisle could hardly be expected to approve of Edmond's romantic leanings and the liberties he took with the conventions of rhyme.

Filon's glowing review alone was enough to keep up the spirits of the young poet, and fill him with hope for the future. Rostand later recalled how he read this article "qui me paraissait éblouissant" (which seemed to me brilliant) as he was walking through the Parc Monceau on his way to visit his fiancée. The trees were in bloom, and Rostand began to say to himself, "Now let's see – the scene is set in a lovely garden ...". He was to recall this idea for *Les Romanesques*, his first performed success.[40]

Although *Les Musardises* did prove to be the beginning of a brilliant literary career, as Filon had prophesied, these poems could not be said to be as mould-breaking as Alfred de Musset's early verse. But they do foreshadow favourite themes and styles, and give an idea of Edmond's preoccupations at the time.

The original 1890 edition is now very rare – even the microfilm in the Bibliothèque Nationale seems to be pieced together from various sources. The book is in three parts: "Les Songe-Creux" (The Dreamers), "Poésies diverses", and "Le Livre de l'Aimée" (The Book of the Beloved). Rostand would publish a revised edition in 1911, taking the opportunity of omitting some poems and adding new ones.[41]

"Les Songe-Creux" deals with Edmond's desire to be a poet. He fears he may become one of the *Ratés* (Failures) for whom he feels so much sympathy. Both the earliest dated poems (not all poems are dated) deal with Edmond's poetic master, the old pion, Pif-Luisant, though the encounters they describe were probably imaginary.

Through Pif-Luisant, Edmond expresses his own attitudes to poetry. "Our first duty is to sing for everyone" (Notre premier devoir est de chanter pour tous), declares the old pion, "Fi on difficult art just for literary cliques! (Foin d'un art compliqué pour petite chapelle), that is, the Symbolists, the Idealists and other groups who wrote only for an elite. What does it matter if your readers understand nothing of the finer points of poetry, as long as they have a heart to be moved by it? This was and would be Rostand's own attitude – he wanted to reach people's hearts, rather than to be admired and understood only by other poets.

As he would later in the theatre, Edmond dramatizes his inner conflict, putting the arguments of his parents and other well-wishers into the mouth of the old pion, who tries to persuade him of the dangers of becoming a poet. However, Rostand does rather load the argument against the voices of reason, which proclaim:

> Ne fais jamais d'art! Ne t'ingère
> Jamais de penser du nouveau!
> Fume un gros cigare. Digère.
> Et crains les rhumes de cerveau![42]
> Don't ever do anything artistic!
> Never think about anything new!
> Just smoke a big cigar and let your meal go down well –
> and beware of colds in the head!

There is, in fact, no contest. While recognising the dangers and difficulties, Edmond is irresistibly drawn to being a poet. He would rather be a failed poet than a successful bourgeois. Besides, Edmond loves and respects the failed poets to whom his book is dedicated: "Je vous aime et veux qu'on le sache" (I love you and want people to know it). Perhaps it is sheer chance that fame and fortune passed them by, like the specks of dust in the air, of which only a few are caught up in a golden sunbeam ("Le Bal des Atomes" (The Dance of the Atoms), I, vi).

Others may have failed because they found themselves incapable, finally, of giving expression to their wonderful vision, their "rêve". Rostand's dedication is "To you who are haunted by the chimera of definitiveness and perfection, and who have finally done nothing, because you wanted to do something too well".

This could so easily have become true of Rostand himself. "The best poems are the ones you never finish", he writes in "Ballade des vers qu'on ne finit jamais..." (I, xxi) "Dans des vers terminés le rêve peut-il vivre?" ("Can the dream live on in verses that are finished?") Always dissatisfied with his work, Rostand's efforts often ended up in the wastepaper basket.

Many poems describe Rostand's struggle to capture his ideas in poetic form. He describes sitting up late in his small, cheerless room, writing in the small circle of light from his lamp. He is at least determined to win "un bonheur d'ouvrier" – the satisfaction of a job well-done. But sometimes he lies all day on his bed, dreaming and looking at the small square of blue sky framed in his window. If he stands up he will have to see the reality of the ugly walls opposite, the grim courtyard below. So he lies there, staring at the sky and dreaming, till the blue changes to indigo and the stars come out ("Le Divan", I, v).

Here again Edmond seems to prefer his dream to reality, as in the early piece already mentioned, *Le Rêve*. In this he was sympathetic to the thinking of the Symbolists, who dominated French poetry at the time. But Rostand was not content to stay in an ivory tower, writing verse only understandable to a choice few. He wanted to communicate his ideals to the general public, so he had to live in the real world as well as in his dreams. How, then, was he to keep hold of his dream? The secret, he declares in this poem and others, is to carry your dream intact inside yourself. If he does this, Edmond decides, he will be able to live in the real world without losing his courage and enthusiasm. He would follow this advice throughout his life.

There are many poems inspired by Edmond's holidays in Luchon. Lighthearted and often playful, these reveal good powers of observation and that deep love of nature which was to be a constant source of inspiration to him. Much of what he sees reveals to him something about his own nature.

In "Le Tambourineur", for example, the poet encounters a young man on his way to sing a dawn serenade to his beloved. He is playing a merry tune on his pipe (*le galoubet*), whilst beating time on his drum. (We find a similar idea in Act Three, scene six of *Cyrano de Bergerac*, where the pages Cyrano sets to keep watch are to play a light, high tune if a woman comes along, and a slow, low tune for a man.) Edmond remarks on the contrast between the light, joyous notes of the pipe, and the low, heavy note of the drum, and finds it in himself:

> *Tambourineur d'Amour, comme je te ressemble!*
> *Je vais jouant du triste et du gai ensemble:*
> *Le tambourin sonore et grave, c'est mon coeur,*
> *Bien plus lourd à porter, va, que ta caisse lourde!*
> *Mais, toujours, cependant qu'il fait sa plainte sourde,*
> *Sifflote mon esprit, ce galoubet moqueur!*
> Love's Drummer, how much I ressemble you.
> I too play sad and happy music together:
> the solemn, resonant tabor is my heart,
> much heavier to bear, you know, than your heavy drum!
> But while it carries on making its muffled moans,
> my spirit, that mocking pipe, whistles away merrily.
> – (I, xiii)

Rostand's playful, mocking spirit was the counterpart to his commitment to the ideal, and, like Cyrano's bravado, a way of keeping his melancholy side invisible to others. In the playlet he'd written at Luchon, he had personified these aspects of himself in the two Pierrot characters. But in the later plays, his heroes, like Edmond himself, combine an idealistic attitude to life with the ability to see the irony of their own predicaments. This refusal to bow down in the face of danger, and to make a joke of one's misfortunes is of course the main ingredient of that most Rostandian of qualities – panache!

Many of these early poems are infused with gentle irony, both in their choice of subject – little pigs running down the road, butterflies getting drunk on nectar – and in the stylistic liberties Rostand takes with versification. Puns and other examples of wordplay abound. He delights, too, in using old, rare, dialect or literary words, especially those which please the ear, and is not averse to making up words which he feels should exist. Why, for instance, is there no word for "singing like a nightingale"? Edmond invents one – "rossignole", and uses it for the sound made by the tambourineur's flute. The sound of the nightingale's song reappears more than once in his work, most significantly in the last play performed in his lifetime, *Chantecler*.

The Third Part of the book, consisting of poems inspired by Rosemonde, was omitted almost in its entirety from the 1911 edition. Apparently Rostand by then felt they lacked any originality. It is true that, mostly light and inconsequential – precious, even – they add little to our understanding of the poet. But the section was introduced by two poems of greater significance. "Plaidoyer", a long poem in four-line stanzas, is a recommendation of the poet to his beloved.[43] In it Edmond admits to all his failings: he is a dreamer, a scatterbrain, sometimes sad, sometimes amused by trifles: all he can offer her is his heart and his verses. Poets are easily discouraged, and need someone to love them. With her support, he is sure he can make a name for himself, and if he succeeds, it would be due to her.

Rosemonde would indeed play a large part in Rostand's success. She would cheer him when he was depressed; make fair copies from his tiny writings on scrappy bits of paper; learn his plays by heart; bring up his children and give him a peaceful and happy home in which to work.

Until he met Rosemonde, Edmond seems to have had only unhappy experiences of women. "La Première", "Ballade de la Nouvelle Année", "Le Souvenir vague", "La Chambre d'hôtel", all suggest that women are likely to break a man's heart if he trusts them. In "La Chapelle", Rostand seems to suggest the woman of his dreams cannot exist in real life:

Mon Adorée au front de Madone
Habite un pays fabuleux,
Le pays de Rêve où n'atteint personne,
Où vous fleurissez, camélias bleus!
The woman I adore has the face of the Madonna;
she lives in a mythical country,
the Land of Dreams, which no man can reach
and where blue camellias bloom!

This attitude makes the second poem that forms the Prologue to Part Three even more significant. "Vieux conte" (Rostand was always fascinated by fairy and folk tales and later had frescoes depicting them painted in his villa) refers to the story of Sleeping Beauty – it concludes: " Le Bonheur commence et les Rêves finissent" (Happiness begins and Dreams end). Perhaps, with his marriage to Rosemonde, real life would be better than the dream.

The poems in *Les Musardises* already show Rostand's originality and his mastery of the poetic medium. The expression of personal feelings, the self-awareness, he shares with Rosemonde, but his daring as a versifier, his breadth of vision and the variety of subjects and moods he chooses to write about, along with his extensive and varied vocabulary, deployed with wit and ingenuity, make Rosemonde's poems, charming as they are, seem slight by comparison.

Rosemonde herself, as Edmond's childhood playmates had done, felt Edmond's superiority. After their marriage, she put aside her own career as a poet in order to further his. Without her loving and self-effacing encouragement, it is quite possible that Rostand would never have written *Cyrano de Bergerac* or any of the other plays for which he is remembered today.

Edmond and Rosemonde were married at the fashionable church of St Augustin, in the boulevard Malesherbes, on the 8th of April 1890, just seven days after Edmond became twenty-two years old. (The civil ceremony had been held on the 5th April, Rosemonde's twenty-fourth birthday.) Edmond's parents and sisters came up from Provence, and the bride was given away by Massenet, who presented Rosemonde with a piano as a wedding present.

After the ceremony, the young couple left for Luchon, where they spent their honeymoon in the Villa Édouard, almost next door to the Villa Julia, and just across the road from the Villa Mauricia, where Rosemonde and her mother had stayed on their first visit to Luchon. And at the end of the summer, having seen Angèle and Eugène carry off the winning banner in the Battle of the Flowers, they returned to the capital to begin their married life.

Notes – Act I

1. All translations are by the author unless otherwise stated
2. Born 10th August 1844
3. Émile Ripert, *Edmond Rostand, sa vie et son oeuvre* (Paris, 1968)
4. Born 23rd June 1843
5. Jean Alexis Hubert Gasan Rostand, born 22nd December 1844
6. Juliette was born in 1872; Jeanne in 1879
7. See Paul Faure, *Vingt Ans d'intimite avec Edmond Rostand* (Paris, 1928), pp. 144-50
8. *Ce qui restait à dire* (Paris, 1967), p. 137
9. *De Père en fils (psychobiographie (1679 – 1964)* (Paris, 1965), p.46
10. "Rostand Écolier", *Annales politiques et littéraires*, 15th Dec. 1918
11. *Le Petit Marseillais*, 11 April 1930
12. Ripert, p. 16
13. Paris, 1890
14. *Les Grotesques, Book VI* (Paris, 1844)
15. "L'Enfance pyrénéenne d'Edmond Rostand", *Revue de France*, V (1921), pp. 75-102
16. "Les Pyrénées", *Les Musardises* (1911 ed.), III,ii
17. *Le Cantique de l'aile* (Paris, 1922), XXII; *Les Musardises* (1911 ed.), III,xx
18. *(Les Musardises)* (1911 ed.), III,i
19. Published in 1882
20. Quoted by Lutgen, p. 48
21. *Marseilles III*, LXX (Jan-Feb 1968), pp. 25-32
22. *Revue de France*, op.cit.
23. *Le Gaulois*, 11th May 1922
24. Margerie, Caroline de, *Edmond Rostand ou le baiser de la gloire* (Paris: Grasset, 1997), p. 40
25. André Antoine (1858-1943)
26. André Billy, *L'Époque 1900* (Paris, 1951) p. 357
27. 2nd May 1887, pp. 1-2
28. A symbol of idealism first found in the German writer Novalis
29. Gaston Deschamps, in *La Gazette de France*, 10 Jan. 1898, quoted by M. Migeo, *Les Rostands* (Paris: Stock, 1973), p. 55
30. Mme de Genlis (1746-1830). Of noble birth and many talents, she wrote, acted in and directed plays at court, and published ten volumes of memoirs.
31. On 5th April, 1866
32. According to Edmond's son Maurice Rostand, in his memoirs: *Confession d'un demi-siècle* (Paris: La Jeune Parque, 1948), p. 90
33. R. Gérard, *Edmond Rostand* (Paris: Charpentier-Fasquelle, 1935), pp. 191-4

[34] *Chantecler,* Act II sc. 3.

[35] Vol. no 55, pp. 609-610; vol. no 58, pp. 346-7, vol. no 64, pp. 582-4 respectively.

[36] Paris: Perrin & Cie

[37] Faure, pp 37-8; Gérard, pp. 10-12

[38] See *Luchon et son passé,* by M. Henri Pac (Toulouse, Privat, new ed., 1991). M.Pac has named his informant in a personal letter to the author.

[39] *Revue bleue,* 12 April 1890

[40] Ripert, p. 40

[41] All references are to the 1911 edition published by Fasquelle.

[42] "Où l'on retrouve Pif-Luisant", I, xi

[43] Cited at length in Gérard, pp. 151-4

Act Two: The Aspiring Dramatist:
Les Romanesques; *La Princesse lointaine* and *La Samaritaine* (1890-1897)

Vivre sans rêve, qu'est-ce?
What is life without a dream?
– *La Princesse lointaine* (Act I, sc. iv)

ROSTAND RETURNED TO PARIS determined to devote himself again to his writing. This time, with Rosemonde to encourage and support him, he would surely succeed.

The young couple moved in briefly with Mme Lee, then took her with them to live together in a rented house in the rue Fortuny. Number two, almost on the corner, and now marked with a commemorative plaque, was a modest house, but it was in the same newly-built and fashionable area as Rosemonde's former home in the boulevard Malesherbes.

In this house the new family – two sons would shortly arrive – would spend some of its happiest years. Here in a small room decorated with chestnut-leaved wallpaper, Edmond would write his first successful plays, culminating in the play that made his name and his fortune, *Cyrano de Bergerac*.

In spite of his desire for success, Edmond's pride would not allow him to take the usual route followed by those who wished to make their name in literary Paris. He did not wish to flatter those who had already made it to the top, or write sycophantic reviews of other writers' work. He abhorred the thought of attending literary salons. Several of the poems in *Les Musardises* express his fierce independence, but his feelings are even more strongly expressed by Cyrano himself, who declares to his friend Le Bret:

Déjeuner, chaque jour, d'un crapaud?
Avoir une ventre usé par la marche? une peau
Qui plus vite, à l'endroit des genoux, devient sale?
...
Préférer faire une visite qu'un poème,
Rédiger des placets, se faire présenter?
Non merci! non merci! non merci!
What, lunch off a toad each day?
Wear out my stomach by crawling on it?
Have a skin that gets dirty most quickly at the knees?
...
Prefer to pay a visit than write a poem?
Compose petitions, get myself introduced?
No thank you! No thank you! No thank you!

Rather, he would:

Travailler sans souci de gloire ou de fortune,
...
N'écrire jamais rien qui de soi ne sortit,
Et modeste, d'ailleurs, se dire: mon petit,
Sois satisfait des fleurs, des fruits, même des feuilles,
Si c'est dans ton jardin à toi que tu les cueilles!
[I would rather] work without worrying about fame or fortune,
...
never write anything which didn't come to me of itself,
and besides, say modestly to myself: be satisfied, little one,
with flowers, fruits, even leaves,
if it is from your own garden that you pluck them!

And Cyrano /Edmond concludes triumphantly:

Ne pas monter bien haut, peut-être, mais tout seul!
Not mounting very high, perhaps, but on my own!
– *Cyrano de Bergerac* (Act II, sc. viii)

Neither did the closed circles of the Symbolists, the Idealists or any other of the "petites écoles" attract one who had proclaimed that a poet's first duty was to sing for everyone. Like Victor Hugo, whom he much admired, Rostand wanted to reach ordinary people with his work, people who would understand his poetry with their hearts and not their intellects.

So Edmond and Rosemonde lived a quiet life together away from the spite, gossip and snobbery that characterised literary Paris. Only the old Parnassian poet Leconte de Lisle was an occasional visitor. He had refused to come to the wedding, but his affection for Rosemonde brought him eventually to see them. He was made welcome.

Rostand's father, too, often visited the young couple. He was often in Paris to advise the new socialist members of parliament on how to improve social conditions under the Third Republic.

In November 1890, the *Ode à la Musique* Rostand had written for Chabrier was performed at the house of Jules Griset, who had commissioned it. The first public performance took place at the Concert Conservatoire the following January.[1] The names of Edmond and Rosemonde were also being heard in the literary and diplomatic salons, where Maurice de Féraudy, Rosemonde's former elocution teacher, used to recite some of his own favourite poems from *Les Musardises* and *Les Pipeaux*.

It was through Féraudy, "merry, plump, pink and saucy" (gai, gras, rose et grivois), as he is described in one of Edmond's rhyming letters, that Edmond got his first big chance. Though eight years older than Edmond, Maurice had become a close friend of them both, and he and Edmond often dined together at the Brasserie Sport, near the Comédie-Française, between rehearsals. When Rosemonde had shown him Edmond's Pierrot playlet, Féraudy had been so impressed that he had suggested that Edmond should submit it to the Comédie-Française as a curtain-raiser.

Spurred on by this idea, Edmond had spent some time in Luchon that summer refining his play, for which his Uncle Alexis had written accompanying music. He renamed it *Les Deux Pierrots, ou Le Souper blanc* (*The Two Pierrots, or The White Supper*), and took it round to Féraudy as soon as he got back to Paris. Féraudy passed it on to Jules Claretie, the director of the Comédie-Française. Claretie, too, was enthusiastic, and raised Edmond's hopes by declaring that if the decision were his alone, he would accept it. However, every play accepted for performance at the national theatre had to be approved by *Le Comité*, the reading committee, composed of the *Sociétaires* (the permanent actors and actresses), and various other important people. But the play would be read to the Comité by Féraudy, which enhanced its chances of success. Féraudy's intervention also saved Rostand the usual round of visits to interest a leading actor or actress in his play, a stressful business which Rostand would have hated.

"J'étais ravi," Rostand later told Jules Huret, who interviewed him in 1901.[2] "I was thrilled! Just think! A play performed at the House of Molière! I said to my wife: When we are old, how nice it will be to tell our children that we had a play put on at the Comédie-Française." This is either rather ingenuous, as we have seen how anxious Edmond was to succeed, or suggests that at this time he was still expecting to make poetry his route to fame.

But the ways of the Comédie-Française were slow and ponderous. The Comité did not assemble to hear Rostand's little play until 13th March 1891. For Edmond, who saw the chance of his work being performed at last within his grasp, the delay was hard to bear. Meanwhile, he continued to write poetry. He also made a small contribution to a ballet-comédie, *Le Prix de beauté*, which would be performed for the first time at the Ambigu theatre on May 31st that year.[3]

When Féraudy duly read Edmond's play to the members of the Comité, they were delighted by the young playwright's skill, verve and humour. But they turned it down. The death of Théodore de Banville, responsible for the revival of the pierrot play, had just been announced. The Comédie-Française could not accept *Les Deux Pierrots* at such a time. Besides, the Comité felt that the public was beginning to tire of pierrots. Claretie came to tell Edmond the bad news in some embarrassment. "You have great talent", he told him. "It's not the writer who is being refused, it's the pierrots. Bring us another curtain-raiser. Another one-act play as good as this one is sure to get accepted." Bitterly disappointed, Edmond impulsively replied "I won't bring you one act, I'll bring you three!"

As Rostand explained in his interview with Jules Huret, he had suddenly felt a great opportunity was slipping away and he had to grasp it. Until then, he had not dreamt of offering more than a curtain-raiser to such a prestigious theatre, but suddenly he was seized by an irresible impulse to, as Cyrano might have phrased it, "faire le geste" (do the deed) and, to his own surprise, came out with the offer of a full-length play.

Edmond now set to work enthusiastically to fulfil his promise. For some time he had wanted to write a play on the Romeo and Juliet theme of divided lovers, but with a happy ending. The scene would be set in an attractive park-like garden, with pretty costumes and light-hearted, amusing verses. (This may have been the idea he was musing on that happy spring morning when he had just read Filon's glowing review of *Les Musardises*.) Rostand worked with manic energy, determined to prove he could keep his promise, and had the draft of what would become *Les Romanesques* ready in just over a month. He read it to Féraudy, who again approved. Encouraged, Rostand set himself to add the final details to his play.

Meanwhile Rosemonde's pregnancy successfully came to term, and their first son was born, at eight o'clock in the evening on 27th May 1891. Edmond's first reaction was to leap into a cab to tell Féraudy the good news, but halfway to his house, he suddenly remembered the actor would be performing that night, so he sent him a message by *pneu* instead. The child was named Maurice after his famous forebear, Field Marshal Gérard, but doubtless Féraudy was also pleased by the choice. Maurice Rostand, too, would become a poet and playwright. A nurse was engaged for him, called Adeline, a name soon shortened to Nounou. She would become a much-loved and lifelong member of the family.

Rostand had completed *Les Romanesques* by the time the summer holidays arrived. He was travelling with his family to Pougues – doubtless a choice made with Mme Lee's health in mind – and left the manuscript with Féraudy, who was to read it to the *Comité* that autumn. The villa Col, which they had rented, was peaceful after the bustle of Paris, but Rostand was restless. He had taken the manuscript of his play with him, intending to revise it still further, and post any amendments to Féraudy. "I'm practising fencing, going for walks and taking plenty of cold showers in readiness for those of the Comité", he wrote jokingly to Féraudy.

The reading of Rostand's play was to take place as soon as rehearsals for *Le Duc Job*, a revival in which Féraudy was playing the lead, were over. But on their return to Paris, Edmond and Rosemonde discovered that *Le Duc Job* had been postponed. Rostand found the suspense almost unbearable. He was unable to concentrate on any other writing. All his hopes were pinned on this play. He had put into it the best of which he was capable. If it was refused, would he have the heart to try again?

Rosemonde, realising the strain he was under, urged him to go away again. She claimed she had always wanted to visit Switzerland. Her mother had offered to look after the baby. They could spend time on their own, enjoying the mountain scenery, far from Paris and its problems. Rostand rather halfheartedly agreed. Before this, however, they were invited to spend a few days with Maurice de Féraudy and his wife at their country home at Saint Mandé, just south of Paris, where Féraudy was making the most of the postponement of rehearsals by taking a rest. Here, in congenial company, Edmond was able to relax. Féraudy, convinced of the merit of Rostand's play, had already learnt the role of Straforel, his projected part, by heart. They went boating on the lake, where "Straforel" recited his lines to Edmond and Rosemonde. Rostand later told a friend that these had been some of the happiest hours of his youth. At such times, all three were confident of Edmond's success.

However, in Switzerland, he again grew anxious and unable to enjoy the scenery to the full. They were to spend two weeks in Grindelwald, staying at the Hotel de l'Ours. One wet day when they were confined to the hotel, Edmond wrote Féraudy one of his delightful letters in rhyme, liberally decorated with little comic illustrations. Apparently written off-the-cuff, it is full of teasing rhymes, humorous allusions, unusual words and felicitous images. Verse certainly seemed to come more readily to his pen than prose – it was a more suitable vehicle for his imagination and wit. He cannot resist the temptation to poke a little fun at the English visitors:

L'orage est très frequent dans ce climat maudit.
Et les Anglais aussi le sont. Les blondes misses
Qui pour les épouseurs conservent les prémices
De leurs virginités, foisonnent. Elles ont
De tout petits chapeaux inclinés sur le front,
Des complets à carreaux et des souliers énormes.
Ce qui leur manque tout à fait, ce sont des formes!
Storms are very frequent in this cursed climate,
and so are the English. Blonde misses,
who reserve for their future husbands
the first fruits of their virginity, abound. They wear
tiny hats tilted over their brows,
checked costumes and huge shoes.
What they lack altogether is any shape![4]

Eventually word arrived from Paris that the rehearsals for *Le Duc Job* had begun. The first performance took place on the sixteenth of September 1891. Féraudy had made sure of good seats for Edmond and Rosemonde. Another long period of waiting followed. It was not until the first of April 1892, Rostand's twenty-fourth birthday, that Edmond himself read his play to the Comité. (Claretie would not let Féraudy read it, fearing the actor's professional touch would influence his listeners too much.)

But *Les Romanesques*, too, was rejected by the Comité, on the grounds this time that it was too long. The Comédie-Française had envisaged the play as forming part of a three-play evening. The time allowed to Rostand's play was just sixty minutes, and Rostand's reading had taken seventy-five minutes. The Comité's verdict was: "accepted subject to corrections". When Edmond, disgusted by this "formule ambigue et hypocrite", as he called it, asked for an explanation, he was told it meant that the play would be accepted on a second reading, on condition that it only took an hour to perform.

Cyrano's outburst in *Cyrano de Bergerac* when he is told that Cardinal Richelieu, if shown his play, might suggest some cuts in it, expresses

Rostand's own feelings at the thought of having to mutilate this child of his imagination:

> Impossible, Monsieur; mon sang coagule
> En pensant qu'on y peut changer une virgule.
> Impossible, sir, my blood clots
> at the thought of changing even a comma.
> – (Act II, sc. vii)

Rostand's play was as perfect as he could make it. The thought of cutting even one line was anathema to him. The months of anxiety, followed by such a disappointment, caused his always fragile nerves to give way altogether. For two months he could do no work at all. While appearing on the surface to be living a normal life, inwardly he was a broken man.

This was the first of the periods of depression which were to recur throughout Rostand's working life. Like his father and his Spanish grandmother, he was highly-strung. From now on, under great stress he would often break down altogether. It has been suggested that Rostand was a manic-depressive. A Dr Lyet argues this to be the case in a thesis he wrote for the Paris Faculty of Medicine.[5] He points out that the periods of depression were often associated with periods of intense elation and activity. This first depression had followed Rostand's euphoria when he was writing Les Romanesques. Then he had achieved the first draft in just over a month. Now the disappointment of having his play rejected was more than he could bear. The fact that it had not been refused altogether was no comfort. He could not face making any cuts at all.

It seems to have been Rosemonde who had the idea of simply reading the play more quickly. She persuaded Edmond to read it to her daily, noting the slowest passages, which he practised reading faster. Leaving out the stage directions also saved time. She marked with a pencil those passages which could, if absolutely necessary, be cut if he was running out of time at the official second reading.

Edmond's spirits revived as he saw the possibility of his play being accepted. A new friend, Jean Richepin the dramatic poet, whom he had met at the Comédie-Française, later told how on one of his visits to the Rostands he was treated to a performance of the whole play by its author, who took all the parts, whirling from one to another with manic energy. This pattern of elation alternating with depression would characterise Rostand's whole working life. So Lyet's diagnosis may have been correct. Later periods of depression were however often associated with, and perhaps caused by, physical illness.

On its second reading on 14th June, 1892, Edmond's play was accepted. Relieved and happy, he dedicated it to Rosemonde.

However, Rostand was just one of many playwrights whose work had been accepted by France's most prestigious national theatre. And being the newest, he was passed over many times as more established, and proven, dramatists presented their latest plays to be performed. Rehearsals for *Les Romanesques* did not finally begin until October 1893.

It is good to be able to relate that Edmond's original playlet did not disappear without trace. Féraudy read the whole of *Les Deux Pierrots* in one of the diplomatic salons, where it was greeted with enthusiasm. In 1899 a version with Uncle Alexis's music would be published as *Pierrot qui pleure et Pierrot qui rit*, under his pseudonym, Jean Hubert, by Alexis's usual publisher Heugel.[6] In Fasquelle's edition of Rostand's works, *Les Deux Pierrots* is paired with *Les Romanesques*. It has continued to be a favourite with amateurs in France and elsewhere.

Reassured as to the fate of *Les Romanesques*, Rostand was able to turn again to his poetry. Several of the poems written now would be included in the revised edition of *Les Musardises* which Fasquelle would publish in 1911. Many were inspired by the countryside around Luchon, where Edmond and Rosemonde continued to spend part of the summer holidays. Appreciations of the beauty of nature or nostalgic memories of childhood, these poems would be grouped together in the new edition under the heading: "La Maison des Pyrénées" (i.e. the Villa Julia). As with his earlier poems, the poet draws lessons from what he observes, lessons for life and lessons for being a poet.

Rostand was still unsure of his direction. How can he reconcile the two sides of his nature: the dreamy, sensitive, rather melancholy side and the mocking, ironical side which tells him he must act, not dream his life away. In "Chanson dans le soir", the Poet is moved to tears by the simple sound of a boy's song rising out of a valley in the peace of the autumn evening. "Shall I never be more than a vibrating lyre?" enquires the poet of himself in his usual tone " both sad and charming, moved but slightly mocking … Alas, there are better things to do!"

The sensitive side of Edmond's nature is easily hurt, and as before, it is his sense of pride that comes to the rescue. Not that he ever seeks to appear better than he is, and he himself is the first to denigrate himself if undeservingly praised. But he wants to be loved for what he is, with all his faults. (Is there a hint here that his parents were more demanding and critical of him than he would have wished?) In "Le Mendiant fleuri" (The Flower-decked Beggar), he admires a tramp who adorns his rags with blossoms from the hedgerows. "The sadder one is, the more one should look beautiful!" (Plus on est malheureux, plus on doit être beau!) Rostand, too, will cover his wounds with flowers – if the tramp can wear a lily on his waistcoat, he, Rostand, will hide his wounded heart with a rose. ("Roses" and "rose"(pink) abound in these early poems – Rostand was still very much in love with his wife.)

Two new poems are particulary important as they reveal Rostand's development as a poet. In "Les Deux Cavaliers" (The Two Knights), an allegorical variation on the Bluebeard theme, Edmond, horrified by the decadence and cynicism of his times, and being tortured by the monster Ennui,[7] sends his soul to the castle turrets to see whether any knights are riding to his aid. She sees only Doubt and Evil on the road. But the poem ends on a note of hope: the poet is sure that one day a dragoon and a musketeer will ride up and thrust their swords into the monster's back. When that moment arrives, the poet and his soul will find peace. Who will these knights be? Perhaps Misfortune and Love. Rostand only knows he will be saved when he hears their clashing spurs. For him, salvation from the lack of idealistic enthusiasm of his times is closely connected with chivalry and heroism. Significantly, aid is expected from without – the poet himself is immobilised by his uncertainty and lack of purpose.

But in "Le Contrebandier" (The Smuggler), prominently placed at the end of the 1911 edition of *Les Musardises*, it is Rostand himself who will take action against what he deplores in the France of his time. Perhaps remembering the heroic Carlists he saw as a boy in Luchon, he sets the scene at the frontier with Spain. An old man with a laden donkey is about to cross unhindered into France when the donkey bucks, and all kinds of ancient armour and weapons spill from the old man's sacks. His contraband discovered, the old man retreats back into Spain. The poet recognises him as Don Quixote and, fascinated, follows and talks to him.[8]

The rest of the poem has a dream-like quality. Edmond learns that Don Quixote, that archetypal Romantic visionary, knows that France needs him and his chivalrous idealism, but he is unable to cross the border himself. He is always found out and turned back. He needs an accomplice, someone who will smuggle across his arms one by one – will Rostand help? The poet, typically, hesitates, unsure of his competence. He only knows how to sing foolish songs and pick wild flowers. Don Quixote's reply is "One can pass off a lance in a bouquet of flowers, or hide a signal in a song!"

Won over, Rostand enthusiastically offers his services, and chooses, for his first attempt, Don Quixote's helmet (really just a barber's basin), because it was so ridiculed, and because, for a poet, illusion is often preferable to reality. The poem concludes triumphantly:

> *Et depuis lors, dans l'ombre où passe un vent morisque,*
> *Intéressé par l'oeuvre, égayé par le risque,*
> > *Je suis toujours sur le sentier;*
> *Je cueille des bouquets, je marche, je m'arrête,*
> *Et je chante… Et je dis que je suis un poète;*
> > *Mais je suis un contrebandier.*
> And ever since, in the shadows cooled by a breeze from Spain,
> involved in my task, amused by the risk,
> > I'm always on the path;
> I pick bunches of flowers, I walk, I stop,
> and I sing … And I say that I am a poet;
> > but really I am a smuggler.
> – *Les Musardises* (Act III, sc. xx)

Edmond's sense of mission was now clearly defined: it would be his task to restore to his beloved France something of her former heroic idealism. At last Rostand was able to resolve the differences in his own character, directing his love of beauty and his idealism into satisfying action. With the triumph of *Cyrano de Bergerac*, he would succeed in his mission beyond his wildest hopes.

The summer of 1892 was passed in Luchon, though the Rostands also spent some time in Brittany, on the banks of the Rance. Edmond wrote a characteristic poem about the little boats, tugging at their moorings ("Les Barques attachées", *Les Musardises,* II, iii). Why be so eager to travel, he tells them, better by far to imagine distant places than to see their disappointing reality.

During this period of waiting for *Les Romanesques* to be performed, Edmond and Rosemonde were able to continue their favourite relaxation – playgoing. The revolution in the Parisian theatre, which had begun in the mid-Eighties, was now at its height. Many new playwrights had forced their way into the magic circle of those writing for the prestigious state theatres. Thanks to the smaller experimental theatres, foreign dramatists such as Tolstoy, Sudermann, Hauptman, Maeterlinck, and especially Ibsen were also enthralling, intriguing and scandalising new audiences nightly. The Rostands savoured everything the theatre had to offer, from the avant-garde to the more traditional.

With Rostand's new connection with the Comédie-Française, he too, was now part of the theatre world. Besides making the acquaintance of the director, Jules Claretie, and various of the actors, he had got to know the dramatist, Jean Richepin, whose play, *La Glaive* (The Sword), was then in rehearsal. Richepin was one of the few playwrights trying to resurrect the verse drama, seen by all as one of the glories of French genius but languishing since Victor Hugo.

Rostand, who would gloriously revive verse drama, and Richepin, whose rather stilted attempts to do so gained only limited success, shared more than just their deep patriotism and their admiration for Victor Hugo and the Romantic tradition. They both detested the materialism and cynicism of their own times. Richepin forthwith took Edmond, almost twenty years younger than himself, under his wing.

Richepin and Rostand must have made a strange pair – Rostand: slim, immaculate, elegant, looked quite the opposite of stocky Richepin, whose mass of sticking-up hair used, according to Maurice Rostand, to frighten his nurse, as, no doubt did Richepin's forthright, at times blasphemous, manner of talking. Richepin had led a somewhat bohemian existence, but his pity and fellow-feeling for the poor endeared him to Rostand: in Richepin Edmond had found a "Raté" (Failure) who had finally succeeded, at least partially. He and Rosemonde were generous in their hospitality to the Richepins who, because of their chaotic lifestyle, were often short of money.

A more conventional acquaintance was the dramatist Paul Hervieu. Like the relationship with Richepin, this was to be a lifelong friendship. It would be Hervieu who later persuaded Rostand to put his name forward for election to the Académie française, and then worked hard to ensure the candidacy succeeded. In the early 1890s, after succeeding as a novelist, Hervieu was beginning to make a name for himself in the theatre with his "problem" plays. Pessimistic but full of pity for the disadvantaged, he was another writer with whom Rostand found himself in tune.

Rostand may have met Paul Hervieu through his friendship with Charles Le Bargy, whom he had met in Luchon. The two men were both about ten years older than Edmond, but whereas his attitude to Hervieu was one of admiring respect, with Charles Le Bargy he had a relationship of equals. Le Bargy was a thoroughly professional young actor who had risen rapidly through the ranks at the Comédie-Française to become one of the leading "jeunes premiers", and had already been a "sociétaire" for several years when he met Edmond. He and Rostand discovered that they had in common, besides a love of literature and the classics and a fascination with the theatre, an appreciation of beautiful things, especially old prints, which they both collected and continued to buy for each other throughout their lives. Both were also obsessively elegant and discriminating in their dress.

As Le Bargy was generally optimistic and lighthearted, he was able to cheer up Edmond sometimes when his melancholy moods came upon him.

During the summer of 1893, Le Bargy was also on holiday in Luchon. Edmond read him the whole of *Les Romanesques* and persuaded him to take the part of Percinet.

Finally Claretie summoned Rostand to Paris for rehearsals. But it was a false alarm. One of the new dramatists discovered by Antoine, François de Curel, had offered the Comédie-Française his latest play, and he had to take precedence over an unknown writer. Not for the first time, Claretie offered to return Rostand's play so that he could try to get it performed somewhere else, but Rostand was adamant. He wanted his first play (*Le Gant Rouge* did not count, for him) to be performed at the home of Molière, Racine and Corneille, however long it took.

The Rostands went away for another brief holiday, this time to Fumay, a small town on the Meuse not far from Charleville. Here they stayed with a Mme Maréschal in her "manoir féodal" as Edmond facetiously termed it, right on the quay. In the evenings, Edmond would stroll by the starlit river, inventing yet more lines for his play. He later claimed that during rehearsals for *Les Romanesques,* he not only restored lines he'd had to cut, but even added new ones. On his return to Paris he sent Mme Maréschal one of his amusing letters – decorating the envelope with a rhymed request to give the postman a glass of wine.

Once Curel's play was out of the way, rehearsals for *Les Romanesques* could finally begin. Charles Le Bargy and Mlle Reichenberg were to play the young hero and heroine, with Leloir and Laugier as their fathers. Féraudy, of course, was Straforel. Edmond could not resist attending rehearsals, though writers were not expected to interfere. He asked to be allowed at least to help put up the scenery.

Finally, in May 1894, Rostand had the satisfaction of listening to his own verses being declaimed on the stage of the Comédie-Française.

Des costumes clairs, des rimes légères, L'Amour, dans un parc, jouant du flûteau
Bright costumes, light rhymes, Cupid playing a little flute in a garden.

The lines of the final rondeau sum up the play. Many of the reviews would stress the young age of the author – he was twenty-six, and his play has all the charm and lightheartedness of youth. The two lovers, Percinet and Sylvie, are in love with romance as much as with each other. They see themselves as a modern Romeo and Juliet, for their fathers, Bergamin and Pasquinot, are enemies. Like Pyramus and Thisbe, Sylvie and Percinet meet by the wall dividing their fathers' estates. What they do not realise is that their fathers are lifelong friends who want nothing better than that their offspring should marry. Knowing their children's romantic view of love, however, the fathers' apparent enmity is simply a ploy to bring about the marriage they both desire. They employ one Straforel to carry out a pretended abduction, so that Percinet can save Sylvie, and so earn her father's gratitude and win her hand. Everything goes according to plan, and the first act ends with all parties happily reunited.

However, Rostand was not such a romantic himself as to end the story there. True love needs more than romantic notions to sustain it, and in the second act, the lovers discover how they have been taken in. Sylvie declares the marriage is off. Meanwhile Percinet, feeling he has been treated like a child, rushes off to prove himself a hero in the world outside. The act ends with Straforel realising he will have to bring the lovers together himself if he is ever to get paid for his "abduction" of Sylvie.

All ends well by the end of the third act. Straforel disguises himself as an impoverished marquis and makes love to Sylvie, offering her all the trappings of romance – he will bear her away on his horse through a thunderstorm, and they will live on dry bread under the stars, while he regales her with poetic descriptions of his passion or has furious accesses of jealousy. Sylvie realises her mistake – such romance belongs in books, not in real life. Percinet now returns, also sadder and wiser, having lived through the kind of experiences Sylvie was only threatened with. They can now see that, although their fathers' enmity was pretended, and they were deluded by false ideas about romance, their love for each other was true. Straforel arrives to claim his payment and the play ends happily.

Sylvie and Percinet have to give up their illusions. But in coming to terms with real life, they hold on to the ideals of which their illusions were a warped image. Illusion and disillusion are constant themes in Rostand's plays. This preoccupation with disillusion and ideals surely stems from Rostand's childhood, when he learned of his father's illegitimate birth. Eugène, too, had had to come to terms with the reluctance of his father to own him publicly, and with the need to become a banker rather than the poet he would have wished to be. Father and son both dealt with their disappointment by cherishing their inner ideal, "le Rêve" (the Dream). Cyrano de Bergerac, the **Aiglon**, and Chantecler all have to cope with the failure of their dream. Cyrano and Chantecler adapt to their disappointments by finding a new and noble ideal to live by; the Eaglet's death finds him reconciled to his fate. Rostand's only anti-hero, Don Juan, cannot cope with the loss of his illusions, and so loses his humanity and is turned into a puppet.[9]

The story of "The Romantics" is told humorously in Rostand's fluent verse. Much gentle fun is made of the lovers, and of the fathers too, portrayed as idiosyncratic but goodhearted. Straforel is the first of Rostand's swashbuckling individualists, and he delivers a long, amusing speech on the various modes of abduction he can supply which foreshadows the tirades of Cyrano. There are deliberate echoes of the *commedia dell'arte* and of Rostand's forerunners in this kind of play: Théodore de Banville, Musset, and Marivaux, as well as many literary and classical allusions which would have delighted the cultured audience of the Comédie-Française.

The *répétition générale* – the first semi-public performance of a new play to which friends and relations are invited, took place on 21st May

1894. Rostand's parents were in the third row, while he himself watched the performance from the wings. Two other plays preceded his own: a short play by Louis Marsolleau, *Le Bandeau de Psyché,* then a long piece in verse entitled *Le Voile* by the symbolist writer, Rodenbach. The latter play in particular was obscure and melancholy, typical of the new plays by Ibsen and other so-called "northern" writers being performed at avant-garde theatres such as Antoine's Théâtre Libre. The audience reacted gratefully to *Les Romanesques,* applauding the scenery and costumes even as the curtain rose for Act One. The music of Georges Huë must have added to their enjoyment. Rostand, waiting anxiously in the wings, almost immediately heard the audience applauding a line "of which there were crowds like it in the play". "Ca y est!" he told himself (That's it!). At the end of the first act, there were seven curtain calls, including one for the young author.

The second act was received less enthusiastically but during the interval the printed copies of the play, published by Charpentier and Fasquelle, had sold out. Catulle Mendès, the poetic dramatist, came to make Rostand's acquaintance. Mendès had striven all his life to restore the verse drama to its traditional place on the French stage, with very little success. He would later become Rostand's most devoted admirer.[10]

As the curtain finally fell to warm applause, Rostand embraced Féraudy in tears. Without his encouragement, the play might never have been written, let alone performed. And hearing the applause for his play, Rostand was convinced for the first time of his vocation.

"It was a great success" was the verdict of Sarcey, doyen of bourgeois critics, in next morning's *Le Temps.* "This first act is marvellously lively and gay ... The rhymes play unforeseen and merry fanfares; it is enchanting." Other critics were equally positive. René Doumic, writing in *Le Moniteur,* praised his former pupil almost unreservedly. He too now felt that Rostand had discovered his true vocation, after his false start in vaudeville. "He knows how to find words which get across to the audience and effects which make an impact. He has the instict of seeing things from a theatrical point of view and how they would look on stage. "This brilliant debut", he added prophetically, "is that of a writer who will be able to make a career in the theatre".

Rostand's apparent facility in writing verse has sometimes been seen as a fault. In 1894, it was seen as a virtue, a delightful contrast to the ponderous, pompous, rhetorical or obscure verses of Mendès, Richepin and other contemporaries. Sarcey noted: "the author handles verse nimbly and easily; his speech is fresh and lively", and Doumic found "this easy abundance is rather charming in itself". Doumic, knowing Rostand's personality, is more concerned about a tendency to buffoonery at times. But Rostand had distinguished precedents for deliberately combining lyricism and foolery in his work – not only Victor Hugo and the Romantics, but also Shakespeare himself had done the same.

The première proper, on 24th May, confirmed the play's success. *Les Romanesques* was awarded the Prix Toirac, worth four hundred francs, by the Académie française for the best play by a newcomer at the Comédie-Française. But in spite of this and the delight the play had given to the audience – it was even suitable for viewing 'en famille', a rare quality in those days – the Comédie-Française only rarely revived the complete play after 1894, though the first act was used almost every year as a curtain-raiser on its own. The 100th performance of *Les Romanesques* would not take place until 1911.

Edmond sent each of his actors a copy of his play inscribed with an individual sonnet of thanks. He complimented Le Bargy on his dazzling white costume. As actors at the Comédie-Française provided their own costumes, Rostand could only indicate the kind of apparel he would like – Le Bargy and the others did not disappoint him. Rostand would take great pleasure in designing the costumes for his later plays himself.

Les Romanesques proved successful outside France too. It was immediately translated into German by the poet and dramatist Ludwig Fulda. Dutch, French and English editions soon followed. George Fleming's free verse translation, *The Fantasticks*, was performed in London in 1900 and in New York in 1901.[11] The play has always been a favourite with amateur companies worldwide, and was made into an opera in 1918 by an Australian, Fritz Hart.

But perhaps Rostand's play's most famous incarnation is as the long-running American musical, *The Fantasticks*. This has been continuously performed all over the world since 1960, with touring productions in Britain during the Seventies and Eighties. Book and lyrics were by Tom Jones, music by Harvey Schmidt. On the programme was printed an acknowledgement: "suggested by Edmund [sic] Rostand's *Les Romanesques*".

After the success of *Les Romanesques*, Jules Claretie asked the young poet for more of the same. But Edmond had no wish to spend his life writing agreeable light-weight plays for the national theatre. He now had the confidence to begin to express his own innermost feelings and begin his work as a "smuggler of idealism", and he already had an idea for his next play.

In his early poems, Edmond had expressed the idea that the dream – "Le Rêve" – was preferable to reality. He had even written part of a play in which a poet, in love with a beautiful but unseen woman, dies rather than meet her, lest the reality of her presence fail to live up to his image of her. Now he would write *La Princesse lointaine,* the story of Joffroy Rudel, who also loved a "distant princess" he had never met.

Rudel, a medieval troubadour and Prince of Blaye, fell in love with the Princess of Tripoli, in Syria, after hearing her beauty praised by Crusaders and pilgrims to the Holy Land. He worshipped her from afar, in the tradition of courtly love prevalent at the time, singing her praises in poems that became so well-known that they even reached the Princess herself. According to legend, he at last sailed to Tripoli to see her, but he fell ill on the way and lived just long enough to die in her arms.

This story also inspired Robert Browning, whose poem, "Rudel to the Lady of Tripoli", is included by Viscount Wavell in his anthology of poems *Other Men's Flowers*. Wavell commented that it might be easier for a lover to be true to an unseen ideal woman, especially as the pleasures of anticipation are often greater than those of realisation.[12] The younger Rostand would have agreed with this sentiment. Now, however, the moral he would draw from this love story was rather different – that a pure and idealised love could inspire and redeem others.

Rostand may have first read Rudel's poems in François Raynouard's collection of French troubadour poetry – the first to be published in France. Raynouard was a Provençal himself, a member of the Académie de Marseille as well as of the Académie française, so his work would have been easily available to Edmond. Gaston Paris, a respected medieval scholar, had also recently retold Rudel's story through his poems in the *Revue Historique*. (Rostand knew Gaston Paris through his friends Paul Hervieu and Jean Richepin.) Paris had concluded that, even if the legend was untrue, "it contains a profound myth and symbolises man's eternal aspiration towards the ideal".[13]

Here was a perfect subject for Rostand's mission as a "smuggler of the Ideal": the story of a love so pure it inspired all who were in contact with it. And it was a story set in Rostand's own native Provence, where courtly love had its centre, and the troubadours had flourished. It is fitting that Rostand's first serious play, expressing his own ideas, should take its origin from his childhood home, and that his poet-hero's great adventure should begin, like his own, from Marseilles.

Edmond had already begun to plan a play about Rudel while *Les Romanesques* was in rehearsal. The success of his comedy made it more likely that a new play of his would be accepted at one of the boulevard theatres. But first he would have to convince a leading actor or actress of the value of his play. It was they whom audiences came to see perform, and they chose the plays they thought would make a good vehicle for their talents. It was the era of *monstres sacrés*, and the greatest of them all was Sarah Bernhardt.

Sarah, at fifty, was a legend, not only because of her golden voice and charismatic stage presence, her startling blue eyes and her tawny electric hair that rose like a halo round her tiny head, but also because of her eccentric private life. Her adventures included running the Odéon theatre as a hospital during the Commune; flying over Paris in a balloon during the Paris Exhibition of 1878; keeping cheetahs and pumas as pets, carying a pearl-embellished pistol at all times, and occasionally sleeping in her own silk-lined coffin. She was an accomplished painter and sculptor, wrote poetry, plays and her memoirs, and conducted her life in a frenzy of activity that left her entourage exhausted. In fact she lived up to her motto, marked on all her possessions, "Quand-même", which translates as "all the same, nevertheless", or, more loosely but aptly, "so what!"

Sarah's first theatrical success had been in Coppée's *Le Passant* in 1869, the year after Edmond was born. After many triumphs at the Comédie-Française, Sarah soon found being a Sociétaire too inhibiting and left the state theatre to go on tours to America and around Europe. Her classic roles had included Cordelia and Phèdre. She had played the Queen in *Ruy Blas* and Doña Sol in *Hernani* for the ageing Victor Hugo, but her most famous modern role was as "la dame aux camélias", in the play of the same name by Dumas the younger. During the eighties her partnership with the prolific Sardou had seen her playing with zest a succession of romantic historic heroines: Tosca, Théodora, Fédora, Cléopatra: lightweight but spectacular plays which travelled well on her endless tours abroad, always made special by Bernhardt's acting and presence, but understandably dismissed by George Bernard Shaw as "Sardoodledum".

Now in the 1890s, as she entered her fities, Sarah was seeking for a new direction. She gave up her lease on the Porte-Saint-Martin theatre, later to be the scene of Rostand's triumph in *Cyrano de Bergerac*, and left for a tour of Australia, which she followed up with visits to London, Scandinavia and South America. On her return in 1893, she took over the Renaissance Theatre and made it the most up-to-date and comfortable in Paris. She renounced her voluptuous style for a more thoughtful, more poetic one, typified by her new interpretation of Phèdre, agreed by all the critics to be her best ever. She chose plays by contemporary writers such as Sudermann and Lemaître and was eager to discover and encourage young poets who held the same exalted ideas of the theatre as an art form as she did.

Sarah had formerly lived at the far end of the Rostands' own rue Fortuny, where it joined the Avenue de Villiers, but had now moved to a new house at 56, boulevard Péreire, still not far from the Rostands' modest home. After Edmond's success with *Les Romanesques*, Rosemonde found the courage to write to the famous actress, asking her to meet her husband. According to Maurice Rostand, a reply was promptly received, offering Edmond an interview. This meeting was to be decisive for both the writer and the actress. For Sarah was looking out for poetical plays of just the kind Edmond wished to write, and her patronage would enable him to write them. The poet, in his turn, would give Sarah some of the best roles of her career: "l'Aiglon" (the son of Napoleon), "la Samaritaine" and "la Princesse lointaine". Sarah was Rostand's real entrée into the world of the theatre. And through her, Rostand would meet the actor who was to embody his Cyrano de Bergerac, Constant Coquelin.

Sarah had heard of the success of *Les Romanesques* but had not had time to go and see it. She was impressed by its elegant young author. In what may be an embroidered account, Sarah herself described the interview in some notes she made for a lecture tour of the United States. Edmond, overwhelmed at reading his work in the presence of the great actress, managed to read the first act fairly calmly, but broke down as he reached the last lines. Not daring to look at Sarah, he finally said through his tears "I have forgotten my handkerchief." Sarah, startled out of her attentive trance, burst out laughing. The ice was broken. A handkerchief was brought and the reading continued to the end.[14]

Sarah was enthusiastic. With this encouragement, the poet set about completing his play, his work interrupted for a while by the birth of the Rostands' second son, Jean-Cyrus, on the 30th October 1894.[15]

Two days after this, a Captain Dreyfus, a Jewish army officer, was accused of passing secrets to the German Embassy and arrested for high treason. It was this event which would set in train the Dreyfus Affair. The news was announced with delight by the ultra-nationalist paper, *Libre Parole*, which had been camapaigning against Jews being in the army since May 1892. There was in fact no evidence to connect

Dreyfus with the incriminating list of military secrets, known as "le bordereau". Suspicion fell on him simply because he was a Jew. The necessary evidence was manufactured by a Major Henry, a member of the anti-espionage section, and Dreyfus was found guilty by a secret military court, although the German Ambassador continued to insist on Dreyfus's innocence.

On 5th January 1895, Dreyfus was publicly dishonoured and stripped of his uniform at a special ceremony, and shipped off to Devil's Island. That seemed to be that. Dreyfus's family continued to maintain his innocence, but could not prove it. The army continued its investigations, as no motive could be found. A Colonel Picquart was appointed to head the anti-espionage unit and to collect more evidence. The general public assumed justice had been done and lost interest. But that was not the end of it. Eventually the Dreyfus Affair would split the nation into bitter opposing forces, pitting Semitists against Anti-Semitists; Protestants against Catholics; reformers against conservatives. Rostand would have the courage to support Dreyfus, when the time came.

At some time during 1894, Rostand was also writing a poem of 101 lines, which he called "Un Rêve" (A Dream). Found among his papers after his death, it was published posthumously in 1921.[16] "Un Rêve" is interesting for the light it sheds on Rostand's attitude of mind at this time.

The poet dreams he is wandering on a battlefield, where thousands of men lie dead, dying or wounded. He is overwhelmed by their cries and their suffering and feels despair at his inability to help them, for how could he choose which are most deserving of help, knowing he can only help a very few at the most? As he stands there indecisively, he sees a man he knows moving amongst the wounded, giving water and comfort to any that he finds still alive and likely to live, but disregarding those past hope, apparently unmoved by their piteous cries. The poet recognises the man as one he and his fellow poets have often sneered at in the past, as a man totally lacking in their own sensitivity and emotional depths. He feels superior to him – what a brute, lacking the poet's own scruples and regrets, but simply acting without any emotion.

The dreamer's attitude changes, however, as he realises that the actions of the man he scorns have kept alive three soldiers who would otherwise have died, whereas he, inhibited by his scruples, has not saved anyone. He realises that all kinds of people, practical as well as poetical, have their own worth: the world needs people who can act, as well as dreamers: "Et ce rêve depuis m'a fait beaucoup rêver" (and this dream has since given me much to dream about).

This poem can be read on several levels. It vividly recreates the suffering that follows a battle, and Rostand's humanity and sympathy illuminate the whole poem. His horror of the effects of war can be seen in several of his poems, especially those written during the First World War. In Act Five of *L'Aiglon*, the Eaglet, the Duc de Reichstadt, has a vision of the aftermath of the battle of Wagram which includes several lines from this early poem. But "Un Rêve" can also be seen as a further criticism of the more esoteric schools of poets at the end of the nineteenth century, who seemed to deny the possession of any sensitivity and poetic feeling to anyone outside their own elitist circles. We have already seen in his early poems Rostand's opinion of such circles and his own desire to communicate his idealist vision to all who have hearts to comprehend it.

On a more personal level this poem seems to be Rostand's own admonition to himself to get his ideas down on paper, and not feel so inhibited by his own inadequacy to create perfection. We know, from his wife, and from poems such as "Ballade des vers qu'on ne finit jamais" (Ballad of the poems that one never finishes),[17] that Rostand's desire for perfection often led him to destroy what he had written. In his dedication poem to "Les Ratés" (The Failures), he had suggested that many had failed to produce anything at all because their vision was too perfect to be put satisfactorily into artistic form.

"Un Rêve" may also have a symbolic interpretation, where the innumerable soldiers begging for attention represent the many ideas that thronged Rostand's brain, waiting to be given expression. How was he to choose which ones to give life to, given that a writer can only achieve so much in one lifetime? Yet if he did not choose, he might live his whole life without accomplishing anything. The moral that the poet drew from his vision was characteristically optimistic: enthusiasm leading to action, however inadequate, was better than hesitation and impotent intellectual debate.

Rostand completed *La Princesse lointaine* and was invited to read it to Sarah and her company of actors. Sarah herself was so enthusiastic about the completed play that she sent a note to her old friend and colleague, Constant Coquelin, also known as Coquelin l'Aîné (the Elder), but simply "Coq" to his friends, inviting him to attend the first reading to her company. "I can assure you, you will not count your afternoon wasted", she wrote. Indeed not, as it proved. Sarah and Coquelin had acted together at the Comédie-Française, though unlike Sarah, he had remained there until his retirement in 1893. He was now involved in a lawsuit with the state theatre, as he had had to engage himself not to act in any other theatre or risk losing his pension. However, Sarah had enticed him to the Renaissance, where she had even had the gall to advertise him acting in just the roles in which he had made his name at the Comédie-Française, currently Sosie in Moliere's *Amphitryon*. Public opinion was on the side of Coquelin, according to the chronicler of the French theatre of the day, Antoine. But the Comédie-Française was losing money because retired Sociétaires like Coquelin were no longer returning to play minor roles, as they once had done, and it took Coquelin to court. The scandal was attracting much notice, from which, of course, Sarah, no stranger to controversy, stood to benefit.

Coquelin was the most famous actor of an acting family – his brother, Ernst, known as Coq the Younger, was also at the Comédie-Française, while his son Jean belonged to Sarah's company, and would be acting in Rostand's play. At the state theatre, Coquelin had specialized in the classic comedy roles such as Molière's Mascarille and Scapin, Beaumarchais's Figaro, and Hugo's Don César in *Ruy Blas*. He had also created several new roles, including Banville's Gringoire. Gringoire, like Cyrano, hides a noble soul beneath an ugly exterior. Banville wrote of Coquelin that he was one of those rare comic actors who can also express tenderness, emotion and poetry.

Constant Coquelin was also praised by Henry James, who wrote in *The Scenic Art*: "the pathetic, the 'interesting' – including where need be, the romantic and even the heroic, these and the extravagantly droll mark the opposite terms of our performer's large gamut", and again: "his features, his cast of countenance, the remarkable play and penetration of his voice which combines the highest metallic ring with every conceivable human note, marked him out for parts of extreme comic freedom as well as for the finer shades of what is called 'character'".[18] James was also impressed by the range and tone of Coquelin's voice, "surely the most wondrous in their kind that the stage has ever known", particularly in long speeches and tirades. These qualities and skills would make Coquelin ideally suited to play Cyrano de Bergerac.

The reading of *La Princesse lointaine* to Sarah's company took place on the first of February 1895. Besides Jean and Constant Coquelin, other actors present included Lucien Guitry and Edouard de Max. All were delighted with Rostand's play, especially Constant Coquelin. He took Rostand's arm as they left and begged Rostand to write a play in verse in which he, Coquelin could star. "Write a role for me" he told the young writer, "and I'll play it when you want, where you want!" Rostand immediately thought of his longstanding desire to write a play about Cyrano de Bergerac. Here was just the right actor to portray his valiant, witty and passionate character. Coq was enthusiastic about the idea and made Edmond promise to write the play for him. The dramatist and the actor that would give *Cyrano de Bergerac* to the world had come together.

Rehearsals for *La Princesse lointaine* began at once. Sarah already knew the part of Mélissinde, the "distant princess". Edouard de Max would play Joffroy Rudel and Lucien Guitry, Sarah's leading man and reputed lover at the time, would take the role of Rudel's friend and companion on the voyage, the handsome Bertrand d'Allamanon. The part of Frère Trophime, the broadminded priest who would be the mouthpiece for Rostand's idealistic message, was taken by Jean Coquelin. All three actors would continue to be associated with Rostand's future career in the theatre.

Lucien Guitry was a popular actor in the modern plays performed at the commercial boulevard theatres. Although he had had a classical training at the Conservatoire, he was now more accustomed to speaking prose than verse. He made a splendid-looking Bertrand, but found the role so little to his liking that he was to pass it to another soon after the première. The Rostands and the Guitrys became quite well-acquainted, and Guitry's son, Sacha, later became a good friend of Edmond's son, Maurice.

The actor playing Rudel, Edouard de Max, was a year younger than Edmond. His Roumanian accent was still detectable in his guttural voice, in which he delivered tirades in a rather monotonous way. "Often handsome, always artificial" was how the pitiless pen of Georges Michel described him: a dandy "always smelling of ambergris, beringed, corseted, with a velvet waistcoat and splendid ties".[19]

At the Renaissance, Rostand could be involved in rehearsals and in every aspect of the staging of his play. Now that his play was in rehearsal, he was by turns elated and depressed, with good reason. He was thrilled that Sarah Bernhardt, the most charismatic of modern actresses, was to embody his "distant princess", Mélissinde, in just the kind of play he had wanted to write, and that his play would be performed at a boulevard theatre, where he could confront the general public with his message of idealism and enthusiasm. In addition, he had now found just the right actor, one of the greatest of his generation, to embody his idea of Cyrano de Bergerac.

But could even a Sarah Bernhardt win over a bourgeois audience to his idealistic message? Verse plays, especially patriotic ones, had been successful at the national theatres, but not yet on the boulevard. Symbolistic and idealist plays had been performed at the avant-garde art theatres, but they attracted only minority audiences. Rostand did not want to write for a small elite. Nor was he an "Idealist" or a

"Symbolist". He did not wish to replace reality by a dream, he wanted to enhance reality by means of a noble ideal. He wanted to use traditional theatrical methods to surprise, delight and excite audiences; to inspire people with an exalted ideal, and send them out of the theatre with a more noble, more spiritual attitude to life.

Sarah herself was well aware of the risk that such a poetic play might not succeed. "It's quite possible the play won't make a penny", she is supposed to have said. "I don't care a bit. I think it is wonderful and I shall perform it for my own pleasure."[20] Sarah spent a large amount of her own money on the play to ensure that at least as a spectacle *La Princesse lointaine* should not fail: scenery, decor, costumes: all would be stunning, and Gabriel Pierné would provide the incidental music. Nothing less would do for a star like herself, and such spectacular displays had played a large part in the success of her Sardou incarnations.

For Rostand, *La Princesse lointaine* would remain his best-loved play, for here he first attempted to convey on stage the power of a great ideal to inspire and uplift human beings. "Vivre sans rêve, qu'est-ce?" What is life without a dream?

In Rostand's version of the legend of Joffroy Rudel, the dying poet is accompanied on the hazardous journey to Tripoli by his troubadour friend Bertrand d'Allamanon.[21] Rudel's love for his "distant princess" is understood and approved of by the sailors, even though they are a rough, tough crew:

Son amour leur a plu, vague, mystérieux,
Parce que les petits aiment les grandes choses
Et sentent les beautés poétiques sans gloses!
His love – vague and mysterious –
has pleased them because small folk love great things
and can feel poetic beauty without needing explanations!
– (Act I, sc. ii)

Rostand always believed that ordinary people would comprehend his idealistic message without difficulty. This belief, already stated in several poems, would be pivotal in his next play, *La Samaritaine*. The success of *Cyrano de Bergerac* throughout the world and for every succeeding generation seems to justify his faith in humanity's aspiration towards the ideal.

The first act of *La Princesse lointaine* takes place on board the ship bearing the sick Rudel to Tripoli, where he hopes to gain at least a sight of Mélissinde before he dies. The ship has been battered by a storm and attacked by pirates. The sailors are hungry, thirsty, wounded and exhausted. The action opens dramatically with the hoisting overboard of a sailor dead from fever. Rostand's ideas are expounded throughout by Frère Trophime, the Prince's chaplain. "C'est pour le ciel que les grandes amours travaillent" (all great loves are working for heaven), he tells the sceptical doctor Érasme, who feels the whole adventure is misguided: the Prince should be going with his fellow nobles to the Crusades, not pursuing some amorous adventure. " In every noble aim I see a nobler one arise", continues the priest, "for when you once have a dream, you will not settle for a lesser one."

The whole action of the play is here. Bertrand and Mélissinde are physically attracted to each other, but realise they cannot fall short of the standard set by the dying Rudel. They choose to devote the rest of their lives to an ideal, rather than becoming lovers. The main characters are contrasted with people who live by purely materialistic or practical considerations: Sorismonde, Mélissinde's companion; the unscrupulous trader Squarcificio, and, until converted, Érasme, Rudel's doctor, and the pilot, who trusts in his compass rather than in prayer or faith in an ideal.

Just as Rudel, having sung one last time his ballad to his distant princess, feels he cannot hold on to life any longer, land is sighted. This gives him new hope and energy. But he is too ill to be taken ashore. Bertrand offers to take Rudel's message of love to the Princess, and swears he will return with her. The ship's master quietly tells Bertrand that if Rudel should die before he returns, he will hoist a black sail that would be visible from the palace.

The next two acts are set in Mélissinde's splendid palace. The action now is totally from Rostand's imagination. His sense of theatre is very evident as one *coup de théâtre* follows another.

Mélissinde makes her entrance in a heavy cloak covered in jewels, her hair bound up in strings of pearls, surrounded by children carrying sheafs of lilies, which also adorn the floor of the palace. She speaks kindly to the waiting pilgrims, telling them of her yearning to see Provence for herself. She gives them each a lily to remember her by – they are overwhelmed by her presence and her kindness. But when they have gone, she slips off the heavy cloak with a sigh of relief, and explains to her confidante Sorismonde that she is only "bonne par ennui" (good through boredom). But she is also kind to the pilgrims because she knows of Rudel's love for her, and wants him to hear good things about her from them on their return to Provence. It is one way of communicating with the poet who loves her from a distance. And his love has transformed her life:

> Combien, dans le médiocre où vivre nous enserre,
> Le sublime de cet amour m'est nécessaire!
> How much I need the sublimity of this love,
> stifled as I am by the mediocrity of living!
> – (Act II, sc. ii)

She adds later in the scene: "Je lui dois enfin mon âme, en quelque sorte!" (In a way, I have him to thank for my soul!). However, there is another side to Mélissinde – she admits that sometimes she resents this idealistic love that is imposed on her.

Sorismonde does not approve of her mistress's attitude: she lives too much among lilies – white, proud: pure, yes, but also mystical and troubling. Yet any young men who might come to distract Mélissinde from her ideal love are kept from the palace by the *Chevalier aux Armes Vertes*, sent by the princess's jealous fiancé, the Emperor of Constantinople, to watch over his lady.

The Chevalier himself appears at this point and forbids Mélissinde to leave the palace that day, without giving a reason. But the Genoan trader Squarcificio, who is allowed in to distract her with his wares, is quick to tell her why, hoping to gain tax concessions in return for his news. A young man, a poet, is trying to gain entrance to the palace to visit Mélissinde; he has said even a hundred men could not stop him. The women believe he must be Rudel himself. After Squarcificio has left, they hear a horn below, challenging the guards. The triumphant progress of Bertrand, which takes place offstage, is followed closely by the women. Bertrand gains entrance to the palace, and Mélissinde throws him down her sleeve as a gauge as he passes beneath their balcony. The clash of swords is heard outside as the Chevalier guards the door to the princess's apartment. Then Bertrand bursts in and throws the bloodied sleeve at her feet.

> *Mélissinde: Messire! ... Ah! ... Qu'avez-vous à me dire?*
> *Bertrand:*   *Des vers."*[22]
> Mélissinde: Oh, Sir, what do you have to say to me?
> Bertrand: Poetry!
> – (Act II, sc. vii)

Bertrand sings the first two verses of the ballad Rudel had sung on the ship, and Mélissinde completes it for him. Believing Bertrand to be Rudel, she tells him that she has not only heard of his love for her, but welcomes it. Bertrand, overwhelmed by her beauty and her gentleness to him, and already falling in love with her, is horrified to discover this is Rudel's distant princess. Fulfilling his mission, he begs Mélissinde to hasten with him to the harbour. But the contrast between this handsome young man and the dying poet who yearns to see her is too great for Mélissinde. The Act ends with her dramatic "Non!" to Bertrand's entreaties.

The Third Act hinges on whether or no Mélissinde will go to Rudel. It is now afternoon. Symbolically, roses have replaced the lilies of Act Two. Mélissinde is unwilling to admit even to herself the real reason for her refusal – she is in love with Bertrand. But after talking to him again, she does agree to go to the ship. Then, overwhelmed by her feelings, she leaves him abruptly. Squarcificio arrives hoping for great advantages from the match he imagines will take place between Bertrand and Mélissinde. When Bertrand explains he is not Rudel, and that Rudel is dying, Squarcificio reacts in character: what a wasted voyage! Bertrand's scathing reply is a sentiment that recurs throughout Rostand's work:

> *Noble aventure, élan d'une grande âme*
> *Vous auriez du servir à quelque chose!*
> So, noble adventure, impetus of a great soul,
> you should have been useful for something!
> – (Act III, sc. iv)

He berates the trader for his "ugly, narrow, mercenary brain". But the astute Squarcificio realises that Bertrand is himself in love with Mélissinde. He suggests to Bertrand that, once Rudel is dead, Bertrand, who after all shared the dangers of the voyage with him, should marry Mélissinde himself. Bertrand is so disgusted and furious that he seizes the trader violently and menaces him. At that moment Mélissinde arrives with her court. She banishes Squarcificio on the spot to please Bertrand, and the trader leaves in disgrace, swearing to get his revenge.

Bertrand goes to check arrangements for their departure. Now alone with Mélissinde, Sorismonde too becomes the voice of expediency and everyday reason. "Why not marry the other one, if you love him?" But reason has no part to play in Mélissinde's dilemma, torn as she is between pity for Rudel and her attraction to Bertrand. "Fulfil your duty to the poet first and then marry Bertrand", is Sorismonde's second suggestion. "What an unworthy trick!" exclaims Mélissinde. "I don't want happiness at the price of a low compromise." That may be the world's way, but after her dream of a sublime love she could not stoop so low. But Mélissinde, once alone, is tempted to try to win Bertrand away from his duty to Rudel for love of her. What a great victory for her femininity. Such a love, though ignoble, would have nothing mediocre about it. If she cannot reach the heights of sublime love, she will plumb its depths.

Mélissinde decides to act on this temptation. When Bertrand returns, she confesses her love for him. Then she closes the window, so that they cannot see the fateful black sail that would announce the death of Rudel. Bertrand is too weak to resist her advances, and Mélissinde pulls him down onto the cushions. But both feel too guilty to embrace. The wind blows the window open, but neither can bear to shut it. Then they hear voices mention a black sail. So Rudel must be dead.

The pair spring apart, ashamed of their betrayal. Bertrand blames Mélissinde for leading him astray "for a whim". Mélissinde is shocked. "So I was alone in dreaming my grandiose dream?" But she now realises she herself was not convinced by it. Now she is bereft – without a dream, what is left for her in life? The pair are about to separate for ever when Mélissinde catches sight through the window, of a white sail. Rudel is not dead! The black sail belonged to the ship bearing the body of the *Chevalier aux Armes Vertes* back to Constantinople. Mélissinde now returns to her nobler self and her love for the dying poet, who is now even dearer to her "because of all the evil I almost did to you!" Both now hasten to board Mélissinde's galley to go to Rudel.

Act Four takes place on the ship as the sun is sinking. Tableau: Rudel is motionless, Frère Trophime praying beside him. Squarcificio is centre stage, telling the sailors Mélissinde will not come to the dying Rudel, as she is in the arms of Bertrand. The trader wants Rudel to know of his friend's betrayal, and the fact that Bertrand will discover this will be Squarcificio's revenge. But Rudel appears to be beyond hearing anything, and the enraged sailors refuse to believe anything that would destroy their dream of the princess. They seize Squarcificio to throw him overboard. They hope he will drown, but he can swim, so someone fetches a bow and arrow. As the bow is drawn, Rudel is seen to point to the horizon. A second later, faint sounds of music are heard, and Mélissinde's galley is seen approaching.

Amidst scents and music, Mélissinde, in her heavy jewelled robe, boards the boat, treading on the ragged clothes the sailors have thrown down for her rather on the rich rugs she has brought. She is overwhelmed by their sufferings and their devotion, and by the joy she inspires. "What, me? I relieve their suffering? How my heart contracts at the thought." She braces herself to meet Rudel, now disfigured by approaching death. Rudel tells her he heard what Squarcificio was saying but paid no attention – he knew she would come. Mélissinde is inspired by such faith:

> *En croyant à des fleurs souvent on les fait naître:*
> *La dame qu'il voulut me croire, je veux l'être.*
> Believing in flowers often brings them forth:
> I wish to be the woman he wanted to believe I was.
> – (Act IV, sc. ii)

Mélissinde makes Rudel's last moments as calm and happy as possible. She gives him her ring for this is their wedding day. She tells him how his poetry and tears were not in vain: "When you wept in the evenings, tears you thought were wasted, my soul felt them streaming over my hands!" She comforts him, until he is not afraid to die.

"How many, less fortunate [than I] are worn out with a vain pursuit, and die before they see their distant princess!" sighs Rudel. Mélissinde replies "But also, how many have seen too much of her, and for too long, and only die after disillusioned days!" Better to hold on to one's dream than see it fade away and become tarnished by real life: Rudel, like Cyrano, dies at the point of realising his ideal.

The poet dies in the arms of his distant princess, surrounded by flowers, incense and music. "How beautiful our love has been", Mélissinde says to Frère Trophime, "our souls will simply have mingled wings." She is a changed woman. "At last my soul found out how to care about another soul … what are you, dream, love, red roses or pale lilies, compared to that great springtime which is forgetfulness of self?" Mélissinde gives away her jewels to the sailors and announces she is retiring to a convent. As for Bertrand, he will lead the sailors to the Crusades. All have been redeemed to a higher purpose through Joffroy Rudel's noble love. The play ends with Frère Trophime's repetition of his words in Act One: "Truly, great love does the work of heaven."

"The key poem in your work", the Vicomte de Vogüé justly said of *La Princesse lointaine* in his speech welcoming Rostand to the Académie française; "it contains the seeds of it and sums it up in advance."[23] All

Rostand's idealistic ideas are here: the holiness of pure love and its redeeming power; the need for a vision, "un rêve", to raise one above mediocrity and give one a reason for living; the dream as superior to reality, and the poet as hero.

Rostand proposed that the love of one soul for another is the best part of love: "L'amour est saint" (love is holy). Both Cyrano and Rudel appeal to the noblest side of the women they love, and both die without consummating their passions. Both have an unattractive exterior hiding a great soul. Roxane and Mélissinde are at first attracted rather by the physical beauty of Christian and Bertrand. It is only later that they come to realise that what they love is the soul of Cyrano or Rudel. This love redeems both from a life of mediocrity. Conversely, for Cyrano and Rudel, the beauty of both women is part of their lovers' search for perfection, rather than a sensual attraction. In Vogüé's words: "Supreme beauty is wedded to supreme merit in the virtue of sacrifice." The sacrifice is one of earthly happiness: Cyrano's sense of honour keeps him silent after Christian's death; Mélissinde will live chastely in a convent, as does Roxane; the Eaglet will lose his chance of reigning because of his scruples about the woman who loves him. But the heroes of Rostand's plays have chosen the better part, though they die chaste, for the dream is superior to reality. This life is flawed; the dream fades when exposed to mundane existence. Better to die without attaining it, or on the point of achieving it.

Many other contemporary poets: Decadents, Idealists, Symbolists, shared Rostand's distate for banal reality. Where Rostand differs from them is his insistence that the dream should enhance ordinary life rather than replace it. In Rudel's case, his love for his distant princess has changed his life. From being indolent, purposeless and philandering, Rudel, thanks to his pure love for Mélissinde, rediscovered his soul. "[His soul] has come alive again: it suffers, loves, desires", declares Frère Trophime. "The important thing is that a heart is beating in our body!" "La seule vertu", he says later, "c'est … l'enthousiasme" (the only real virtue is … enthousiasm!"). This is a far cry from those contemporary poets who felt that their servants could do their living for them. Rostand's enthusiastic idealism surely plays a large part in his continuing appeal to all kinds of audiences.

Rudel, like Rostand himself, is a poet. All Rostand's heroes are poets in the widest sense. The poet as hero has a deeper sensitivity, a greater insight, and above all, lives by a vision which lifts him or her above mundane reality. Even Rostand's Don Juan[24] is a poet, but a warped one, who has chosen to elevate the sensual instead of the spiritual into the ideal he lives by. The temptation to exchange spiritual aspiration for sensual reality is experienced here by Mélissinde. In Rostand's later play, *Chantecler*, it is the eponymous hero who temporarily deserts his duty and goes to live in the forest with the pheasant with whom he is in love. In *L'Aiglon*, the Eaglet, Napoleon's son, is briefly tempted to follow his mother's example rather than his father's, and devote himself to a life of flirtation and sensual pleasures. The Samaritan woman has lived a sensual life until she meets Christ and is converted to higher values.

This tension between the spiritual and the sensual, which Rostand's heroes and heroines are forced to confront, is part of the poet's own makeup. Just as, in *Les Deux Pierrots*, Edmond had personified two contrasting sides of his character as "Weeping Pierrot" and "Laughing Pierrot", so in his later plays he would make concrete in dramatic form the struggle within himself between two opposing tendencies. His heroes, either in themselves or paired with their opposites (Cyrano/Christian, Rudel/Bertrand), represent both aspects of human love: the earthly, sensual side, symbolised by a handsome appearance, and the spiritual yearning towards an ideal, which in Cyrano and Rudel is concealed by an unprepossessing exterior.

Rostand the poet believed in love as a spiritual force, an inspiring ideal which could give a man or woman a reason for living and bring them closer to God. But Rostand the human being had a strong sensual side too, the signs of which were already present in certain poems in *Les Musardises*. In "Au ciel" (I, xx), the poet arrives at the Gates of Heaven, and admits to Saint Peter, amongst other failings, a penchant for womanising. (All is forgiven as soon as he reveals he is a poet.

"Come in" cries St. Peter, "You are one of us!") In "La Chambre d'hôtel" (omitted from the 1911 edition), the poet describes an assignation in a sordid hotel room, in which the poet blames the woman for changing everything in the room except his soul.

Throughout his work, Rostand reveals a rather ambivalent attitude towards the female sex. He exalts women, especially beautiful women, as fit subjects for a man's dreams, because the love they inspire can be a spiritual force, as in *La Princesse lointaine*. Don Juan's recognition of the woman who truly loves him would save him from hell – if only he could remember who she is. Her single tear of love is so pure that it burns the devil's fingers. Sensual love, on the other hand, can corrupt. Rostand's human heroes, except Don Juan, who is more of an antihero, die chaste. Women are sometimes depicted by Rostand as sirens drawing the hero away from his duty: Mélissinde here, and the pheasant in *Chantecler* both play the roles of *femme fatale* before they are redeemed by the hero's vision: Rudel's of love, Chantecler's of duty. In *L'Aiglon*, women are more sympathetically drawn, apart from the hero's mother, the frivolous, flirtatious Marie-Louise, who has chosen the sensual above the spiritual, abandoning the memory of her heroic husband Napoleon.

In marrying Rosemonde Gérard, Edmond was able to combine human love with his idealistic aspirations. Not only was Rosemonde young and beautiful, she was a poet herself, and understood his feelings. She would encourage him in every way she could in what he saw as his sacred duty of writing inspiring plays. It was the ideal marriage for Rostand, but this would not prevent him from being unfaithful in years to come.

The first performance of *La Princesse lointaine* took place on 5th April 1895, after a short delay caused by an accident to the scenery – some of the cast saw this as a bad omen. The first-night audience, however, received the play warmly. The lyricism of Rostand's verse; the music by Gabriel Pierné; the spectacular costumes and scenery and Sarah Bernhardt's golden voice and inspired performance: all made a good effect.

But the notices next day were mixed. Although it was agreed that Rostand had shown himself to be capable of writing lyrical verse of high quality, and the costumes, scenery and music all contributed to the fairytale effect, the critics were not expecting a serious play from the author of *Les Romanesques*, and did not understand Rostand's idealistic message. "It was a wonderful opportunity", Rostand later told Jules Huret, "but nearly all the newspapers destroyed the work and made it into a semi-flop."[25]

Rostand felt that only Jacques Du Tillet, writing for the Idealist magazine, *Revue Bleue*, seemed to have fully understood all that he was trying to do in the play. Some of the bourgeois press did, however, enjoy its fairytale aspects. The critic of *Le Temps* wrote of "moments when an indescribable tenderness invaded us, or a breeze perfumed with poetry caressed our souls, tired out by life." The *Figaro*'s Henri Fouquier thought *La Princesse lointaine* interesting and successful, a work of sincere inspiration.

Francisque Sarcey, who held the fortune of a play in the hollow of his hand, according to Henry James, had not yet seen the play. His review in *Le Temps* did not appear until 8th April, but it was the deathknell for *La Princesse lointaine*. Sarcey seems to have taken against Rostand's play mainly because it was not what he had expected. He had been looking forward to a light, amusing play similar to *Les Romanesques*. Instead, he found one with an idealistic message he was unable to comprehend, with a heroine whose psychology was modern and complicated. "How tiring and painful this is!" Like Sorismonde, Sarcey failed to understand Mélissinde's soul-searching: "She is free, she hasn't promised anything, she can love whom she likes." He allowed that the music was delightful, and enjoyed the fairytale aspect of the story and the spectacle of the first and last acts. But for the rest, he was "cruelly disappointed".

The later fate of *La Princesse lointaine* suggests that Rostand's play was ahead of its time. A revised version, prepared by Rostand in 1910-11, but not performed until 1929, after the deaths of both writer and original star, was warmly received by press and public alike. However, in

1895, the lukewarm notices and Sarcey's criticisms meant that audiences became so small that Sarah was forced to close down the play after thirty of thirty-five planned performances. The last performance was on 2nd May, ironically the same night on which the Comédie-Française revived *Les Romanesques* for the fifth time since the previous May.

Sarah revived her old warhorse *La Dame aux camélias* for the remaining five days, hoping to recoup some of her losses, which amounted to 200,000 francs. However, she still believed in *La Princesse lointaine*, and took it to London that June, where William Archer was won over by it. George Bernard Shaw, however, thought Mélissinde "an unredeemed humbug from one end of the play to the other". He also felt that Sarah was relying too much on her "golden voice", though he admitted having no ear for French verse, verse which was, of course, one of the main strengths of the play.[26] Sarah gave four performances of *La Princesse lointaine* at Daly's Theatre, and an equal number of performances of Sudermann's *Magda*, Sardou's *Tosca* and *La Dame aux Camélias*, but, knowing her audience, fifteen of her most recent Sardou play, *Gismonda*.

Both Sarah Bernhardt and Rostand felt that the *La Princesse lointaine* had not received fair treatment at the hands of the Parisian press. The warmth of the play's reception on the first night had not been reflected in the critics' reviews. When some words of Sarah's to that effect, came to Sarcey's ears, he replied by offering Sarah space in his column to defend the play. Rostand took this opportunity to write a respectful letter to Sarcey, explaining where he thought the critic had been wrong. This letter was printed in full in *Le Temps*.[27] Rostand noted that Sarcey had attributed the undisputed success of the first night to a *claque* (people paid to clap and cheer). However, there was no *claque* at the Renaissance: Sarah, as one of her reforms, had abolished it. So the applause had been genuine. Nor could Rostand have packed the audience with his friends either – "I lead such a hermit's life that when I'm given author's tickets I don't know what to do with them."

Rostand also took this opportunity to clear up a misunderstanding about the "window scene", by which he meant the scene in Act Three where Mélissinde and Bertrand are unable to ignore the window, knowing it may reveal a black sail, the signal that Rudel was dead. Sarcey had not mentioned this scene in his review, and yet it was this scene which had the most effect every evening. The young author concluded his letter with polite thanks to the critic for his interest and a hope that if Sarcey found, on re-examing the play, that it was less disappointing than before, Sarcey would let him know. It is not recorded that he ever did.

However, if Sarcey remained unmoved, and other reviewers had not, on the whole, been sympathetic, at least Rostand had the satisfaction that he knew the first night had been a success. Yet his disappointment was acute. Now he entered the longest period yet of depression, which continued intermittently for almost two years – until the success of *La Samaritaine* proved to Rostand that he could get his idealistic message across successfully to the general public.

After the triumph of *Cyrano de Bergerac*, *La Princesse lointaine* became well-known across the world, both in the original and in translation. Rostand's lyrical play proved especially inspiring to musicians: the French composer, Witkowski, wrote a musical version, performed at the Paris Opera in March 1934,[28] and the Italian, Davico, won an Italian music prize for his orchestral suite in 1911. Another Italian, Montemezzo, began to set the play to music but never completed this project. *La Princesse lointaine* was also the subject of an overture by Nikolay Tcherepin.

Sarah herself always loved the play, which she revived on her tours abroad, as well as in Paris. When the theatre world gathered to celebrate her achievements at a Journée Sarah Bernhardt in 1896, the poster, by her favoured artist, Mucha, in the Art Nouveau style, depicted her as Mélissinde, her head garlanded with lilies. After her leg was amputated in 1915, Sarah hoped to perform as Rudel in *La Princesse lointaine* with Ida Rubinstein as Mélissinde .

Sarah had lost none of her faith in Rostand; she commissioned another play, *La Samaritaine*, to be performed during Holy Week the following year. Rostand also had the thought of his new play for Coquelin to cheer him.

He and his family spent part of the summer in Luchon, where they stayed with Le Bargy in the Villa Diana, not far from Eugène and Angèle's Villa Julia. While in Luchon, Rosemonde, Edmond and Le Bargy gave a performance of *Les Romanesques*: at the Casino, according to Henry de Gorsse, but perhaps only at the Villa Julia; the silk programmes, with a photo and poster, were on display at a later exhibition in the town. This performance took place on 8th August: Le Bargy played his original part of Percinet, Rosemonde played Sylvette, and Edmond, "empanaché jusqu'au ciel" (in towering plumes) was Straforel. *Les Romanesques* would not be performed again in Luchon until 1922, at a ceremony to dedicate a bust of the poet after his death. (According to Pierre de Gorsse, the Luchon journalist, the three also acted the play at Marseilles, presumably for the *Association Artistique de Marseilles*.) And in a triumphant conclusion to their close association with Luchon, Edmond and Rosemonde also carried off the banner of honour in the Battle of Flowers that year.

After 1895, Edmond and Rosemonde returned only briefly to Luchon, so it was probably on this visit that Maurice, now four, saw the lifesize Italian marionettes that he describes in his memoirs. The strong impression they made on him was one of the factors which encouraged him, too, to write for the theatre.

Rostand was now planning his play about Cyrano de Bergerac. The cast of characters was already in Rostand's mind from his earlier reading. Roxane, Christian, Le Bret, Ragueneau, the Comte de Guiche, Carbon de Castel-Jaloux, Linière: all these were real people living in the seventeenth century along with Cyrano, though not always in the relationships to him or each other that we find in the play. The character of Cyrano himself is based on historical fact – the real Cyrano de Bergerac (1616-1655) was a dueller and freethinker; a poet who delighted in breaking the rules of classical verse. But his love for Roxane and his pact with Christian were Rostand's own idea. The imagined Cyrano's failure to succeed in worldly terms, and his grotesque nose, contrasting with the beauty of his soul, recalls the pathetic figure of Pif-Luisant, the pion Edmond had known and loved at Stanislas. Rostand's boyhood hero d'Artagnan and the myth of boastful and aggressive Gascons also contributed to Cyrano's character.

But above all, Cyrano was Rostand himself: independent and proud, yet courteous and chivalrous, with the heart and soul of a poet. Cyrano would be Rostand's 'colporteur de l'idéal' (smuggler of the ideal) – a Don Quixote who would fight cynicism, materialism and doubt, and who would succeed in winning the hearts of his audience. As Rostand later told André Arnyvelde, "I wrote *Cyrano de Bergerac* in accordance with my own tastes, with love and pleasure, and also, I maintain, with the idea of struggling against the tendencies of the time, tendencies which, to be honest, upset and revolted me."[29]

Rostand's earlier experience at Luchon, when he helped his lovelorn friend to win over his beloved by telling him what to say, gave him the hinge of his plot: the pact between Christian and Cyrano to woo Roxane between them. And echoes of his boyhood reading of Dumas's *Les Trois Mousquetaires* and Gautier's *Le Capitaine Fracasse* abound throughout the play.[30]

But there were other personal memories, too. The lines in the duel ballad – "Les coquilles tintent, dingdon" – recalled the sound made by Paul de Cassagnac's duelling swords, left briefly with the Rostand family at Marseilles. Edmond had enjoyed flourishing them and hearing the clinking of the silver guards. Cassagnac had told him they made this sound all the time he was fencing with them. "Quel geste" says Cyrano as he throws his purse, containing his monthly allowance, to Jodelet (Act I sc. iv) to make up for stopping the performance of *Clorise*, and "quel geste" Edmond had remarked to Henry de Gorsse when he gave the priest at Montauban their savings as a recompense for deflecting his stream. And although the incident at the Porte de Nesle is historical – Cyrano really did take on one hundred men single-handed – we have Edmond's word for it that he was also remembering the time at Luchon when he himself was prepared to fight alone against his opponents at the children's ball.[31]

There were also characters in Rostand's earlier plays who can be seen as fore-runners of Cyrano and other characters. The witty and verbose Straforel, in *Les Romanesques*, performs two impersonations, reels off a tirade in extravagant language and relies on his own ingenuity to bring the lovers together again. Squarcificio is a less savoury character who nevertheless displays verbal facility. Rudel, disfigured by approaching death, sends the handsome Bertrand to carry his suit to Mélissinde: Cyrano's words of love for Roxane would reach her through charming young Christian. And we have already seen Rostand portraying himself in *Les Deux Pierrots* as *Laughing Pierrot*, who is witty and amusing, cheerful even while his heart is breaking, and with a delicacy which prevents him, like Cyrano, from weeping in front of others.

As for the historical background, Rostand was already completely at home in his favourite period, that of Louis Treize. Besides Gautier's portraits in *Les Grotesques* and the swashbuckling novels by Dumas the Elder and Théophile Gautier that he loved as a boy, he had read Cyrano's own works. He had also read widely for his prizewinning essay on d'Urfé. Now he read or reread the two-volume edition of Cyrano de Bergerac's works published by P-L. Jacob in Paris in 1858. This included the original biographical preface by Cyrano's friend Le Bret. Other sources were Charles Nodier's essay on Cyrano (Paris, 1841), and Professor Pierre Brun's recent thesis for Montpellier University: *Savinien Cyrano de Bergerac, sa vie et ses oeuvres* (Paris 1893), which had been made more generally available in the *Revue Critique d'Histoire et de Littérature* the following year.[32] Rostand also read or consulted the *Memoirs of the maréchal de Gramont* (the Comte de Guiche of the play), Chappuzeau's history of the theatre (republished in 1875) and Somaize's *Le Dictionnaire des Précieuses*.

But having read, he put the books aside and wrote the play "without one note", according to his wife, letting his imagination run free.

As soon as the Rostands returned to Paris that autumn, Edmond started work on his two new plays. At the rue Fortuny, his children were well aware of the need not to disturb their papa. His son Maurice's memoirs[13] give us a good idea of the life of the small family that lived together there. "Between those simple walls, in this unluxurious setting, there was nothing but joy and work." Especially work. "As far back as I can reach in my memory, it was my father's work that I always recall." Maurice and Jean were used to playing quietly so as not to disturb their father. Sometimes they would be taken to play in the nearby Parc Monceau by their nurse, Nounou. Nounou's real name was Adeline Delpech, and she stayed with the family until she died, long after both boys were grown up. Like other parents of their time and class, Edmond and Rosemonde left the care of their children mainly to Nounou. An English governess, Miss Day, later arrived. She, too, would become a longstanding member of the family.

Rosemonde's mother, Mme Lee, looked after the house and helped to care for the children. She was a rather melancholy figure, always dressed in black, and according to Maurice she seemed to be "nursing a private grief", perhaps her love for Count Gérard, Rosemonde's father, whom she had never married. Her fervent Catholic faith inspired her grandson Maurice to become a believer too. Mme Lee's pet name for her daughter was Rosette – this became transmuted to Zozette by Maurice and then Dodette by Jean, and this was the name which stuck. When Rosemonde and Edmond went out in the evening, Maurice would tie a piece of thread to Dodette's wrist, and keep the bobbin himself. Only so could he bear to be separated from her. This attachment would grow even stronger with the years.

The impression of a happy family is echoed in an article written at about this time about the two poets by Adolphe Brisson, editor of *Les Annales*.[14] "Un ménage de fauvettes" (a nest of singing birds) was his phrase to describe the Rostand household: "in spite of the elegance of their outer lives, they have stayed close to nature." Perhaps the elegance Brisson mentions referred to the splendid tapestries covered in poppies, or the two Fragonard paintings that would accompany the family everywhere. Rosemonde also treasured the small rosewood bureau that had belonged to her ancestor, Mlle de Genlis. Edmond had excellent taste, and after his marriage had money to express it. From childhood he had always enjoyed designing an interior and rearranging furniture, a valuable trait in a future writer for the theatre. Besides elegance, cleanliness was important to him, too. One major luxury which Rostand had permitted himself after the success of *Les Romanesques* was to have a bathroom installed at rue Fortuny. The writer Jules Renard, a new friend of the Rostands, noted this in his diary and added rather enviously "He has a fine study but he never works there."[35] Edmond preferred to write on a shaky table in his bedroom, a habit which he continued even after the success of *Cyrano de Bergerac*.

Rostand was telling Sarcey the truth when he claimed to have a small number of friends, but their number was growing all the time. Through Sarah Bernhardt he met more and more people connected with the theatre, some of whom became intimates of the house at rue Fortuny. Besides Féraudy, Hervieu, Richepin and Le Bargy, the actors in Sarah's company at the Renaissance were now on good terms with the Rostands. But it was Sarah herself who became their close friend – a great honour, as she herself admitted that she had very few intimates.

The actress's arrival at rue Fortuny in her cab drawn by two splendid chestnut horses was always an event. But Sarah would also invite the Rostands to her house for supper. This could be rather unnerving, for she kept a menagerie of animals as pets, and sometimes a puma or a leopard cub would pad towards the visitors. Supper at Sarah's was always an experience: guests would loll on cushions or sofas (there were no chairs), in her wonderful cluttered salon, where valuable antiques and picturesque junk from Sarah's travels all over the world jostled each other. When they went in to dinner, Sarah would sit at the head of the table ensconced in a special throne. But at heart, Sarah was "simple, bon enfant, devouée, fidèle"[36] (simple, kind, devoted, loyal). She was very good to her close friends, and to their children. Both Sacha Guitry and Maurice Rostand remember being taken to "kiss Sarah Bernhardt" in her dressing room, just as other children were taken to church. On Maurice's first visit he was given a wonderful tea with cream eclairs and even champagne, in the form of a tisane Saint-Marceaux. This was his also his first ever visit to the theatre (he was about five years old). Sarah, playing in *La Dame aux camélias*, involved the little boy, sitting in the audience, in her death scene, when she is supposed to see something through her window. Maurice, who later became a dramatist, writing plays for Sarah himself, always credited her (rather than his father), for awakening within him a love of the theatre. Sarah's generosity to the children of her friends was legendary. At Christmas, her secretaries would stagger to the Rostands' door bearing a large Christmas tree. She would also throw a huge party for her grand-daughter Lysiane, with presents for all. Sarah was good at giving presents to adults too – one she gave Maurice as an adult, he wore until his death. It was the huge sapphire ring, set by Lalique, that she had worn in the last scene of *La Princesse lointaine* .

The aristocratic Robert de Montesquiou, one of the models for Proust's Baron Charlus, who had met Edmond at Sarah's before *La Princesse lointaine* and shared a cab with him to the theatre, also once visited the Rostands at their "vilain petit hotel" (ugly little house), as he so described it. But the friendship did not flourish, though Montesquiou had to admit that Rostand was always courteous and pleasant to him, and he admired Edmond's "admirable eyes, often looking within, then suddenly flashing out like enammelled swords".

Much more amiable was the close friendship which developed between the Rostands and Jules Renard and his wife Marinette, though even here Rostand's depressed moods caused periods of estrangement. This was not altogether Edmond's fault, for, as Renard confessed in his diary, he was one who "wore out friends by the dozen". [37] Renard had come to Paris from the provinces, and was by 1895, when he first met the Rostands, a well-known figure in literary circles, having been one of the co-founders of the Symbolist-orientated *Mercure de France* in 1890. He also wrote for the irreverent review, *Gil Blas*, and the idealistic *Revue bleue.* He and Lucien Guitry were members of a closeknit group which called themselves "Les Mousquetaires". (Tristan Bernard and Alphonse Allais were the others.) Renard's novels, such as *Poil de Carotte* (still popular today) had been well-received. But as an enthusiastic theatre-goer, especially to the avant-garde theatres such as the Théâtre Libre, he was now trying his hand at writing plays.

Renard wrote to Edmond praising *La Princesse lointaine* and was invited to dinner. The two men quickly became, and remained, intimate friends.

Renard too felt compassion for the sufferings of humanity. He and Rostand also shared a love of poetry and of the theatre. But whereas Edmond was passionately idealistic, Jules was coolly realistic, cynical even, though he wrote himself that his "rosserie" (nastiness), was not to be taken seriously. It was in some ways an unequal friendship. Renard, ill-at-ease in society and living very modestly and precariously with his wife Marinette in his mother-in-law's house, envied Rostand his middle-class upbringing and manners, and the comforts of his home in the most fashionable area of Paris. He felt inferior to Rostand as a writer and as a person: he saw in Edmond a man whose character, gifts and even soul were far beyond what he himself could hope to achieve, he who could only produce what he called "oeuvres à court souffle" (sprints). But Rostand respected Renard's genuine love for the poor and his unassuming modesty, qualities which, with his humaneness, shine out of the pages of Renard's *Journal*, begun in 1887. Maurice Rostand saw Renard as a modern Alceste, but one who did not disapprove of humanity as such, but rather deplored its failure to be more human. In spite of Renard's terrifying (to a child) appearance – Maurice writes of his "his hard, craggy face" – there was in his eyes "an unforgettable tenderness".[38]

The growth of this friendship between Renard and Rostand, such outwardly dissimilar writers, but sharing many of the same ideals, can be followed in Renard's *Journal*. Renard's first impression of Edmond was: "Rostand, a bit young, a bit old, a bit bald, showing a fine talent in his *Princesse lointaine*, well-informed about *L'Écornifleur* and *Coquigrues* [his novels]".[39]

Renard soon made the acquaintance of Mme Rostand, and fell under her spell. He liked Rosemonde's modesty about her own achievements:

yes, she had written a book of verse, but she never talks about it now. She'll try to find him a copy. All Rosemonde's energies were bent on encouraging the greater talents of her husband.

Edmond's unusual self-effacement and consideration for others impressed Renard: "He's really exquisite, Rostand. He doesn't write for the reviews because he might take someone else's place. He thinks a lot about other people's suffering. He gives away a lot of money."

But in not writing for the reviews because of his scruples at depriving others of work, Rostand was also giving up opportunities to make himself better-known in literary circles, especially as he did not, as Renard did, though with some self-disgust, attend the literary salons of the time. Edmond was determined to succeed by his own efforts alone. But the drawbacks of this isolation were noted by Renard in the same entry: "As Rostand does not have day-to-day success to urge him on, he sometimes feels desperate for two or three months at a time."[40] In fact, perhaps as a delayed reaction to the semi-failure of *La Princesse lointaine*, the familiar "melancholy bird" was settling ever heavier on Edmond's shoulders.

Rostand's depression was putting great strain on his friendship with Renard. "Yesterday evening Rostand and I took a big step forward to breaking up our friendship", wrote Renard on the ninth. But when he saw him, still depressed, on 26th December, Edmond introduced him to Sarah Bernhardt. Renard was overwhelmed by the honour and charmed out of his usual apparent cynicism. He was impressed, too, by the intimacy between her and Edmond: she called him "Rostand", and "son poète", "son auteur" and put her hand up to his cheek to show how cold she is. Soon after, the Renards and the Rostands were invited to a splendid New Year's dinner at Sarah's, with several others. Sarah amused herself telling fortunes and finding ressemblances with animals for her guests: Edmond is a "rongeur" (a rodent), she suggests, and Rosemonde "un mouton" (a sheep)![41]

The next day, Sarah left on a tour of the USA from which she did not plan to return for six months. Rostand's depression, perhaps partly as a result, grew worse. The doctors could do nothing for him. This was a family ailment from which Edmond's father, grandmother and his sister Jeanne all suffered at times. In an unusually tender passage, Renard wrote in his *Journal* for 18th January 1896:

> I love R and am glad to make others love him ... he is my "distant prince", he's a little brother whose suffering face it hurts me to see. I always fear hearing he has died ... he is thoughtful and kind, he isn't malicious. He is, perhaps, very unhappy. He avoids faces he doesn't know, and he is happy to know he is loved ... his death would hurt me very very much.

Yes, concluded Renard, in spite of his comfortable home, his pretty wife and his growing fame, perhaps Rostand really is very unhappy.

But Rostand's depression was beginning to estrange him from his friends, including Renard. "He isolates himself more and more", Renard continued in the same entry: "He thinks us false, lying, malicious and rapacious ... There's only one reason left for me to go on loving R, and that's the fear that he may die soon". The same day, the friends quarrel and part.

Rostand's depression had reached crisis point. Three days later, Mme Rostand told Renard: "He's plotting to kill himself. He talks of becoming a priest. He detaches himself from everything and says it's the beginning of wisdom. He only gets out of bed to sit in his chair, and he does nothing, nothing. He just arranges his papers in a fine mess if you go to see him; on them he's written nothing, just a few scribbles of drawings, and they're not even in order... he plays with knives, weapons, bottles, glasses. He handles lethal objects...". The doctor did not know what was wrong "neurasthénie, asthénie" (nervous disorders). Rosemonde was at her wits' end. She even wished Edmond could fall in love with another woman, if that would revive him. "Is he going to die, and will I always regret never having got to the bottom of that charming but troubled soul?", Renard asks himself.

However, the crisis apparently passed, as on the first of March Renard wrote to ask whether Edmond had enjoyed reading his play, *Le Plaisir de Rompre*, dedicated to Rostand. It would be produced by an amateur group on 16th March. "Are you ill?" asks Renard. "Give me a sign of friendship."[42] The following day, the friends went to the Théâtre Libre together, sitting in Sarah's son Maurice Bernhardt's box with Henri Bauer, the journalist and dramatic critic of the *Écho de Paris*. Afterwards they all had supper together at Maire's. (Renard feels now he has really 'arrived': "Ah! Renard, he leaves his wife at home! He moves in the world. He keeps company with the rich. The Danube peasant flirts.") Rostand paid for the meal, but it was his wife who checked the bill and found they had been overcharged, as Renard maliciously told everyone and noted in his diary.

Henri Bauer, an illegitimate son of Dumas the Elder's, was a man of socialist sympathies and strong principles. He would later lose his job because of his support for Dreyfus. He was an enthusiastic supporter of Wagner, Ibsen, and the avant-garde generally, especially of the idealistic poets. He had a pleasing sense of the ridiculous, exemplified by the lifesize cardboard caricature of Sarah which he always placed beside him in his usual box at the Théâtre Libre. A tall man, his huge mane of white hair gave him a leonine appearance, and before she got to know him, Rosemonde was frightened of him and his forthright opinions, calling him the Ogre. But the Rostands soon discovered that his fierce demeanour concealed a kind heart. Bauer became a good friend of theirs and of their children.

The Rostands' circle of acquaintances was increasing rapidly. On the 15th March, for instance, Edmond's publisher, Fasquelle, had invited them to a dinner party. Also present were the Richepins, the Émile Zolas, the Octave Mirbeaus and the Goncourt brothers, who noted in their diary: "the Rostands, a poet with a pessimistic stomach and a wife with skin like a rose in milk."

Other new acquaintances at this time included Renard's friends Alphonse Allais, the humorist, and Tristan Bernard, who would later become well-known for his light comedies. Renard's diary for 12 March 1896 describes a dinner party at the Bernards' which they all attended, along with Lucien Mühlfeld, who became a close friend of Edmond's, even though they moved in very different circles. Lucien had married into a Jewish banking family; his wife Jeanne Meyer, had high social ambitions for them both, and Lucien too was intent on making a name for himself as a man of letters. Their salon later attracted a wide swathe of those who mattered in Paris at the time. Edmond admired Mühlfeld's literary talent, not only in his much-admired articles for the *Revue Blanche*, one of the new symbolist reviews, but also in his now long-forgotten novels.

At the Bernards' dinner party that evening Rostand was again suffering from depression, and made no attempt to hide his boredom. This occasional rudeness, in marked contrast to his habitual courtesy, was probably an inevitable accompaniment to his depressed moods. At such times, he preferred to be on his own and could not find the energy to be sociable.

But another reason for his impatience with social occasions at this time was that he was eager to get on with *Cyrano de Bergerac*, which was beginning to take shape in his mind. He had recently been to see Coquelin backstage during the play in which he was currently starring, Sardou's *Thermidor*. During the interval, Edmond had expounded his ideas for the play to an enthusiastic Coq and both had become so engrossed the interval had become rather protracted, to the impatience of the audience.

It was a great relief to Edmond when the family were able to leave Paris and its social obligations for a quiet country villa at Boissy-St-Léger, just outside Paris.

Here they settled down for the summer. Edmond went fishing or took a gun to look for rabbits. But he brought back neither fish nor rabbits, for his mind was on his new play for Coquelin. But first he had to write the play Sarah wanted for Holy Week the following year. Religious and mystical plays were enjoying a revival in fin-de-siècle Paris, and this would be another opportunity to convey his message of love, idealism and enthusiasm.

The idea of writing a play about the Samaritan woman who is converted by Jesus at the well had come to Rostand even before *La Princesse lointaine* had been given its first performance. He had been reading Renan's *Vie de Jesus*,[43] a favourite of his wife's. His play, *La*

Samaritaine, closely follows the Gospel of St John (John 4, vv 1 – 42), but in order to make Photine, "la Samaritaine", the central character, Rostand had to invent the second act (as he had in *La Princesse lointaine*). The whole of this act is based on one sentence in the gospel account, telling how Photine goes back to the town to convince her neighbours that she has met the Messiah, and returns triumphantly with them to Jesus. This is also the only act which contains any kind of dramatic tension, though there are many *coups de théâtre* in the rest of the play. Perhaps for this reason, and because the play was to be a visual as well as an aural experience, Rostand called *La Samaritaine* an "Évangile en trois tableaux".

Rostand's choice of subject was obviously influenced by the need to provide a star part for Sarah: there were already several plays about Mary Magdalen, a possible alternative. The character of the repentant courtesan, too, was one of Sarah's specialities. But it is tempting to speculate that Edmond's holidays in Luchon also played its part in his choice. Luchon being a spa, there were wells and fountains in plenty – Edmond wrote poems about them. There were also portrayals of the Samaritan Woman in the parish church: a tapestry by Camenade and a fresco in the choir by Romain Caze, as well as a mural at the thermal baths. The image of a woman with a waterpot may also owe something to a large stained-glass window on the stair of the Villa Corneille, once the town museum. A youth and a maiden pose in medieval-style dress beside a gushing spring; the woman is resting a double-handled amphora on her hip, an amphora similar to the one in Rostand's play.

The theme of *La Samaritaine* is similar to that of *La Princesse lointaine*: sensual love can be sublimated into spiritual love and so lead to the love of God. Rostand's Jesus, like Frère Trophime, teaches that love has the power to redeem and inspire all kinds of people. In this play, Rostand was again exploring the tension between the sensual and the spiritual which fascinated him so much because he experienced it in his own character. "Isn't this the most extraordinary of moral dramas?" Rostand said later. "Imagine Liane de Pougy [a well-known courtesan] going to the Bois de Boulogne, meeting Christ, and rushing back to

Paris with only one crazy desire, to evangelise her compatriots."[44] This was, of course, Rostand's own crazy desire, too: to win the French public back to a more idealistic and spiritual way of life.

On his return to Paris at the end of the summer, Rostand continued to write, but was still plagued from time to time by depression. Fortunately he was well enough to take part in the splendid "Journée Sarah Bernhardt" on 9th December. This was an act of homage to Sarah, arranged by her friends, notably Henri Bauer. Rostand was one of six poets chosen to honour her with a sonnet.

The Day was in two parts. First came a banquet. Five hundred guests assembled in the Salle Zodiaque of the Grand Hotel, the men in black tie and tails, the women in evening dress. Suddenly, Sarah appeared at the top of the spiral staircase, her slight figure draped in a wonderful white dress in her usual spiral line, tighter at the knees than the ankles, and edged with chinchilla, which trailed back behind her. With her accustomed grace, she descended so smoothly that, as Renard put it in his *Journal*, she seemed to stand still while the staircase turned around her. Once Sarah had taken her place between Bauer and Sardou at the head of the table, the banquet began. The menus, designed by Sarah's artist friends Abbéma, Chéret and Mucha, displayed an ingenious and delectable choice of delicacies, including Poularde de Mans à la Sardou, Gâteaux Sarah and BombeTosca.

After a speech by Sarah, describing how she had served her country by making the glories of French literature familiar to foreigners everywhere, she was presented with a gold medal designed by Lalique and telegrams of congratulation from all over the world. Sardou, whose collaboration with Sarah had made him a fortune, naturally gave the toast; Sarah replied simply "my heart, my whole heart is yours". The guests then drove in a procession of one hundred carriages to Sarah's theatre, the Renaissance, where a huge crowd waited to acclaim their heroine.

Sarah had chosen two contrasting pieces in which to perform, both of which had been amongst her most successful roles. First came the second act of Racine's tragedy *Phèdre*, followed, after an entr'acte, by

Act Four of Parodi's *Rome Vaincue*, a minor classical tragedy. But the apotheosis of the day was still to come. After a further interlude, the curtain rose on a splendid tableau: Sarah, in the flowing Greek robe she had worn for Phèdre, was seated on a flower-decked throne before a backdrop of red and white camellias and flanked by palms threaded with orchids. Garlanded young women sat at her feet, while the poets who were to pay homage to her sat on her right.

One by one they rose to celebrate Sarah in sonnets specially written for the occasion: François Coppée, Catulle Mendès, Edmond Haraucourt, Theuriet, then Eugène Morand speaking the absent Jose-Maria de Hérédia's verses. Last of all came Edmond Rostand. In a clear vibrant voice, he read from the heart:

> *En ce temps sans beauté, seule encore tu nous restes*
> *Sachant descendre, pale, un grand escalier clair,*
> *Ceindre un bandeau, porter un lys, brandir un fer,*
> *Reine de l'attitude et Princesse des gestes!*
>
> *En ce temps sans folie, ardente, tu protestes!*
> *Tu dis des vers. Tu meurs d'amour. Ton vol se perd.*
> *Tu tends des bras de rêve, et puis des bras de chair.*
> *Et, quand Phèdre parait, nous sommes tous incestes.*
>
> *Avide de souffrir, tu t'ajoutas des coeurs;*
> *Nous avons vu couler – car ils coulent, tes pleurs! -*
> *Toutes les larmes de nos âmes sur tes joues…*
>
> *Mais aussi, tu sais bien, Sarah, que quelquefois*
> *Tu sens furtivement se poser, quand tu joues,*
> *Les lèvres de Shakespeare aux bagues de tes doigts.*[45]

In these times without beauty, you alone still remain to us,
knowing how to palely descend a fine, well-lit staircase,
how to fasten a headband, carry a lily, brandish a sword:
Queen of attitudes and Princess of gestures!

In these times without madness, you protest vehemently!
You declaim poetry. You die of love. Your ecstasy fades away.
You hold out arms of dreams, and then arms of flesh.
And when Phèdre appears, we all feel incestuous.

Eager to suffer, you won hearts;
we have seen flow down your cheeks – for they do flow, your tears –
all the tears of our own souls…

But also, you know very well, Sarah, that sometimes
when you are acting, you are aware that Shakespeare himself
is furtively putting his lips to the rings on your fingers.

When Edmond had finished, the applause, noted Jules Renard in his *Journal,* was as much for Rostand as for Sarah.[46] "Success as great as if his sonnet had been in five acts." Renard was convinced Rostand was in love with Sarah: "she is like the sun", he wrote elsewhere,[47] "and he is hanging from one of the rays. She is necessary to his life …."".

It is easy to understand Rostand's admiration for Sarah, which comes across clearly in his sonnet: she embodies the ideals he believes in himself: she lives passionately, loves passionately, suffers passionately. In the mediocre materialism of the times, she shines like a blazing torch. Sarah also shared his love for the theatre and had faith, like him, in its power to move souls. Like his boyhood hero, Colonel Villebois-Mareuil, she was larger than life, as theatrical off the stage as on it. Was Edmond in love with her? Quite possibly. It would have been surprising if the young poet had not responded with admiration touching on idolatry for the most glamorous actress of the time, who had deigned to take such an interest in a young poet.

The admiration was mutual. Sarah, in her book *L'Art du Théâtre,* would later place Rostand (and her former lover Richepin), on a level with Racine, Lamartine, Musset and Victor Hugo, as the greatest of French poets. She also had a great affection for Edmond and his family, sending generous gifts and visiting them often. All her life, Sarah would consider the Rostands as amongst her most intimate friends.

This homage to the great actress concluded the celebrations for the *Journée Sarah Bernhardt,* but many of the participants went on to spend the evening at a theatrical performance of a very different kind: the première of Alfred Jarry's *Ubu Roi* at Lugné-Poe's Théâtre de l'Oeuvre. The contrast could hardly have been greater – "en ce temps sans beauté", many of the audience who had been at the former celebration must have reflected as they watched Jarry's scurrilous, foul-mouthed antihero, Père Ubu, perform his antics. As the play's opening line: "Merde!" (Shit!) rang out across the theatre, there was pandemonium. Some of the audience could not contain their outrage, others were highly amused. Rostand was seen to smile indulgently, but he may have been warned of what was to come by Henri Bauer, who had encouraged Lugné-Poe to stage the play. Whatever the reaction of individuals, there could be no doubt, as Catulle Mendès pointed out in his review, that the play and its public performance actually were facts, and facts with which the theatre in France, and abroad, would eventually have to come to terms. The twentieth century had begun.

At the beginning of 1897 Rostand's depression was worse again. "Il me fait peur", Rosemonde had told Marcel Boulenger, who, reporting this to their mutual acquaintance Jules Renard, had added that Rostand depressed him with his dejected air and empty gaze. "I'd give my little finger to say something that really interests him", said Boulanger, to which Renard replied: "Only talking about the theatre animated him."[48] This was probably true. Renard and Bauer were invited to the Rostands on 4th January and talked of literature; on the 6th, the Rostands, with Renard and Le Bargy, went to applaud Sarah in her new *travesti* role as *Lorenzaccio*, in the first public perfomance of Musset's play. Renard also accompanied the Rostands to see Hervieu's new play, *La Loi de l'homme*, at the Comédie-Française. But apart from visits to the theatre and seeing a few close friends, Rostand kept to himself, nursing his depression.

When his depression did lift for a while, and he was able to work on *La Samaritaine* or on *Cyrano de Bergerac*, Rostand was even less inclined to be sociable, and could be rude to his friends, sending them away if they interrupted him, as he did when Renard hurried round to see him on 18th February after the first reading of his own one-act play (dedicated to Edmond), *Le Plaisir de Rompre*.

On March 7th, Rostand took the now-completed version of *La Samaritaine* to Sarah's Renaissance theatre to read it to the cast.

Renard, who was invited to be present, was gratified to find that his own high opinion of Rostand's talent was fully justified. "Delightful verses, delightful as hearts", he wrote in his diary. "I have no trouble in telling Rostand he is a great poet, like Musset, Gautier, Banville, that he's stronger than all contemporary poets, and that he is in poetry what I would like to be in prose." Rostand was pleased with Renard's praise for *La Samaritaine*, but told him: "J'aime bien mieux *Cyrano de Bergerac* que je suis en train d'écrire" (I much prefer *Cyrano de Bergerac*, which I'm writing at the moment).

A few days later another public appearance was necessary. Rostand had, at Sarah Bernhardt's request, agreed to take part in a matinee arranged at the Renaissance in aid of refugees from the Greco-Turkish war. He recited a long poem he had specially composed for the occasion: "Pour la Grèce".[49] In it he called on youth to support Greece, not for political reasons but because Greece was the cradle of classical and hence Western civilization, the home of beauty and the ideal. To Rostand, born in the former Greek colony of Massilia, this was a crusade comparable to that led by the Romantics in 1830, the spirit of which he called on the young to revive. "Nous reprendrons la Foi, l'Enthousiasme, l'Ode". As with his boyish admiration for the supporters of Don Carlos, Rostand's sympathies were based on emotion rather than rational politics. This is not one of Rostand's best poems, but it is further proof of his desire to inspire the public, and youth in particular, with his own high ideals.

The success of Renard's first play, *Le Plaisir de Rompre*, on 16th March established Renard as a recognised playwright. The published version would bear the following dedication: "to the young master of dramatic poetry, Edmond Rostand, the homage of a writer and the remembrance of a friend".

Rehearsals for *La Samaritaine* were soon under way. Sarah again spent her own money lavishly to make the play a sumptuous visual as well as aural experience. The hundred and fifty costumes were based on Tissot's classic illustrated life of Christ. She herself designed the stage sets and lighting, and directed the crowd scenes and tableaux, winning much applause from the critics for her efforts. Gabriel Pierné once more provided the incidental music which was to play an important role in creating the right atmosphere. The art-nouveau poster by Mucha, of Sarah leaning pensively against an amphora, has become one of the images by which she is remembered.

For the sensitive role of Christ, Rostand had chosen Louis Brémont, the first actor to portray Christ on the Parisian stage some six years earlier, in Edmond Haraucourt's *La Passion*. Even so, some critics were not satisfied, feeling that such a role was beyond any actor, and especially one who, as Sarcey grumbled, had been kissing the actress Jeanne Granier on another boulevard stage the previous night.

La Samaritaine was performed for the first time on 14th April 1897, the Wednesday of Holy Week. This time there was no doubt – Rostand's play was a success with both public and critics. Jules Lemaître called it one of the most brilliant successes it had ever been his fortune to attend. Émile Faguet described the play as "a triumph of tenderness, and of emotion full of and sweet with religious sensitivity". Even Sarcey, the third and most powerful of the triumvirate, admired and enjoyed Rostand's play this time, in spite of feeling uncomfortable at seeing Jesus portrayed on the stage at all. As for the blasé Parisian audience, "for three hours [the audience] found again the delicious source of tears", noted Jean Lorrain.

Rostand now at last felt confident that he could succeed in getting his idealistic message across to the crowd. In his dedication to the published version of *La Samaritaine*, Rostand not only thanked his interpreters, especially Sarah Bernhardt, "who was a flame and a prayer", but also his audience, "the public of Paris, whose attentiveness, emotion and intelligent thrilling even to the most concealed intentions, once more came to reassure poets".

The main action of *La Samaritaine* follows St John's gospel closely, but Rostand first sets the scene with a dramatic Prologue. The stage is in semi-darkness. Three phantoms talk by Jacob's well: they are the ghosts of Abraham, Isaac and Jacob himself, drawn by a mysterious force to celebrate the imminent arrival of the Messiah at this very place. The stage fills with other shades also drawn to the well, then all fade away as dawn breaks, leaving the scene to the living: Samaritans from Sichem, the nearby town, who have come to discuss their grievances against the Jews and the Romans. Some believe the Messiah will come to free them from oppression, others do not. But no one recognises Jesus when he arrives with his weary disciples. The Samaritans leave, refusing to talk to Jews, and are cursed by the disciples. But Jesus teaches them to love all people, Jews or pagan, and tells them the story of the Good Samaritan.

The disciples go off to get food and drink from the town, leaving Jesus alone by the well. Photine appears in the distance, carrying her waterpot on her head. Jesus describes her before she is visible to the audience. While understanding her character ("she has sinned much"), he admires her beauty and grace:

> *Elles vont, avec un sourire taciturne,*
> *Et leur forme s'ajoute à la forme de l'urne,*
> *Et tout leur corps n'est plus qu'un vase svelte, auquel*
> *Le bras levé dessine une anse sur le ciel!*
> [Jacob's daughters] move along, smiling silently,
> and their shape is joined to the shape of the vessel,
> so that their whole body is one smooth vase,
> with their upraised arms making a handle against the sky![50]
> – (Act I, sc. iv)

Photine is dreaming of Azriel, her latest lover, and singing to herself a love song which echoes the Song of Solomon. She fills her pot without even glancing at Jesus, and is about to leave when Jesus takes pity on her and asks for some of her water to drink. She refuses, as he is a Jew, but when he begins to tell her about the living water he can give her, her attention is caught. When he further tells her he knows about her lovers, she believes he is a prophet, and asks him whether it is on the Jews' holy mountain or on the Samaritans' that God should be worshipped?

Jesus replies, as in St John's Gospel, that God is to be worshipped in spirit and in truth, rather than in any particular place. He reveals himself to Photine as the Messiah whom she and others believe will come to teach them about God and free them from persecution.

Photine reacts in the only way she knows – she worships Jesus in the words of the love song she has just been singing. When she realizes what she is doing she is ashamed, but Jesus reassures her, saying: "I am always present a little in all words of love. But until they are addressed to me, people are only trying out expressions of affection". Human love is a preparation for love of God, Jesus tells Photine, "For everything comes back to me".

Photine has now found the true love for which she had been searching in her human love affairs, the love of God. She seats herself at Jesus's feet and listens raptly as he tells her how he will instruct her about the Kingdom of God, the lost sheep, and God the Father. As Photine repeats reverently "J'écoute" (I am listening), the Tableau ends on a peaceful, almost mystical note.

The second Tableau opens in contrast on the bustling, worldly day-to-day life of Sichem, where the disciples are trying in vain to obtain food from the hostile Samaritans. They leave almost empty-handed in a hail of insults. Azrael arrives, concerned that Photine has not yet returned. According to gossip, she is about to be hounded out of the town in disgrace. But then Photine herself arrives, out of breath and dishevelled. Having reassured Azrael that there is nothing wrong, she sets about convincing the townspeople to come with her to the young man who may be the Messiah. At first she is disregarded, then her ecstasy gives her such lyricism that a crowd gathers to listen:

Près du Puits de Jacob un jeune homme est assis!
Ses cheveux ont la couleur blonde;
On croit voir l'arc-en-ciel qui rassure le monde
Dans chacun de ses beaux sourcils....
On le reconnaîtrait entre mille à son calme
Et c'est Celui que j'attendais!

By the well of Jacob sits a young man!
His hair is fair;
you'd think you saw the rainbow which reassures the world
in each of his lovely eyebrows....
You would recognise him out of thousands by his air of calm
and He is the One I have been waiting for!
– (Act II, sc. iii)

The priest arrives and is amazed when Photine argues with him in
the words of the Old Testament. When the priest claims the Messiah
would never speak to a woman like her, Photine kneels in front of
them all, confessing her sins and asking them to forgive her. Jesus, she
tells them, has already forgiven her – "The indulgent saviour who has
come to us today loves precisely those whom no one loves". The debate
between Photine and the priest continues, he positing the old order,
"la loi" (law), she the new : "la foi" (faith). A few people are prepared
to leave for the well, but Photine now says she will not go unless
half the town accompanies her. Meanwhile the subversive nature of
Jesus's teaching is becoming apparent, and the priest secretly sends
someone to fetch the Romans. Photine wins over yet more people, but
now says she will not go without the whole town. In a long, lyrical
speech, she tells the crowd that Jesus's teaching can be expressed in
one word – love.

Photine is so eloquent that the crowd falls to its knees, crying out
"Le Roi, fils de David! – Le Christ! – Le roi des cieux!" They rise to
follow her to Jesus, but at this moment, a Roman centurion arrives
with his soldiers, blocking the exit to the town. Hearing seditious cries
about a king, they arrest Photine, who defends herself, saying she was
only telling them about love and pity. "And the Messiah" shouts the
priest to the disgust of the crowd. This is a serious charge and Photine
is about to be marched off to Pilate when the priest mentions that the
so-called Messiah is from Nazareth. This changes everything – the
Centurion has seen Jesus throwing the money-changers out of the
temple at Jerusalem. "He's just a poor Jew crazed with melancholy...
you're allowed this Christ, he's not dangerous. That one will never

disturb the world." Photine is released and with her at their head the crowd moves off enthusiastically, singing psalms.

For the third Tableau we return to Jacob's well. The sun is about to set. The disciples have finished their meagre meal and are grumbling to each other about Jesus, who is still sitting by the well. Driven by thirst, they eventually taste the water left in Photine's waterpot, and find it delicious. Jesus tells them this is because she has left her sins behind in it. He tells them the fields are ready to harvest, and as he speaks, they see the distant fields apparently moving, even though the grain will not be ripe for months, and hear distant voices. The townspeople are approaching. They finally appear, singing psalms, led by Photine, exultant, decorated with flowers, her eyes blazing. The children, waving olive branches, rush past her towards Jesus and the crowd follows. Photine presents the people to him. She is ecstatic, almost delirious. The crowd then listens quietly as Jesus tells them he is their good shepherd. He heals the sick and they beg him to stay with them. He promises he will stay for two days. The scene ends with Photine kneeling before Jesus, repeating the prayer he has taught her: "Père que nous avons dans les cieux, que l'on fête/Ton nom ....". (Our Father, who art in heaven ...), and on the crowd's reverent "Ainsi-soit-il" (Amen), the curtain falls.

Apparently even the cast found this last Tableau so moving that it brought tears to their eyes at every performance. Rostand's lyrical verse; Sarah's presence and thrilling voice, enhanced by the music; the attractive costumes and decor, and the impressive tableaux must have combined to make the play an almost mystical experience, as many testified. Some, like the musician Reynaldo Hahn, a friend of Sarah's, did not miss a single performance.

Rostand was following Renan in portraying Christ as a gentle, softly-spoken young man, attractive in character and looks. But he was also looking even further back, to his admired Victor Hugo, whose portrayal of Jesus as "the beloved of souls" in *La Fin de Satan* is similar. Some critics found Jesus's good looks hard to accept. But

Jesus is beautiful and eloquent because God's love shines through him. It is Jesus's message of the love of God for all people that is stressed in *La Samaritaine*. And Rostand again suggests, as he had in *La Princesse lointaine,* that ideal love can transform ordinary human love into an aspiration towards God.

Rostand shared Renan's view of religion as a religion of the heart, which had no need of temples or priests. Both give prominence to Jesus's teaching according to St John: "true worshippers worship the Father in spirit and in truth". But Rostand had already made the same point in *La Princesse lointaine,* with his "prêtre pas gênant" (unembarrassing priest), Frère Trophime, who had also preached that the way to God was through the human heart.

It is fundamental to Rostand's spiritual attitude that ordinary people, especially the poor, the slighted and the humble, find it easiest to accept and understand the simple message of redemption through love. In his poem "La Brouette", for example, Jesus, on returning to earth, finds an old woman who believes she can collect the winter sunshine in her barrow, to take to comfort her dying grandson. Her faith is rewarded, much to the astonishment of St Peter, who has accompanied Jesus. Jesus remarks: "People do not know how much the love of simple people can accomplish!"[51] Photine seems to the disciples an unlikely person to convert the townspeople, but she succeeds.

Rostand himself, unlike his wife and mother-in-law, never went to church, and teased his wife for "trying to believe".[52] His childhood, however, was imbued with the Catholicism of his mother, and he had attended Catholic institutions in his earliest years and again for his pre-university studies. He was well-acquainted with the background to Christian belief, and sometimes seems to regret his loss of the simple faith which was his as a child. In "Le Carillon de Saint-Mamet",[53] the church bells remind him of his former innocence, and of the simple faith of the family servant. "God! could one then, if one wished, have it back again, that holy simplicity?". But even the memory of this faith is comforting – the poem concludes: "Oh, bells of Saint Mamet, ring on this ringing that brings more calm to our soul!".

In *La Samaritaine*, Rostand was expressing his own sincere, if unorthodox, religious feeling, which, portrayed in the most artistic way and in the most reverently lyrical verse of which he was capable, struck a corresponding chord in his audience. He was able to succeed because his whole attitude to life was a spiritual one. His compassion for the poor and the failures of this world was given practical expression in his generosity and kindness. In his writing he exalted love and urged idealism. For Rostand, the theatre was a place where divine enthusiasm could be aroused in people's hearts. In the reception given to *La Samaritaine* he had succeeded.

La Samaritaine played to full houses for ten performances over eight days. Rostand was formally introduced to the President of the Republic, Félix Faure, during one of these performances. Sarah then had to leave with her company for an engagement in Brussels. But on her return, she gave another eight performances. Altogether the play had brought in 100,000 francs – a very satisfactory return.

The Samaritan woman remained one of Sarah's favourite roles. She revived the play the following May, and during a further revival in March 1899, the play reached its fiftieth performance. Sarah continued to perform in *La Samaritaine* at home and abroad, especially at Easter. When she was later invited to make one of the new gramophone recordings, she chose to include some of Photine's speeches.

Another sign of the success of *La Samaritaine* was a request for some of Rostand's poems by the *Revue de Paris*. Fernand Gregh, the poet, remembered him, "courteous and nervy", meticulously correcting proofs alongside Barrès and Loti.[54] Rostand chose five poems he had written since *Les Musardises* was published. They would be printed on July 1st 1897.[55]

For many of his contemporary idealistic poets, *La Samaritaine* would remain Rostand's best work, even after *Cyrano de Bergerac*. For modern poets, too, and not only in France, it has a special attraction. An English version, *The Woman of Samaria* was broadcast by the BBC in July 1945.[56] *La Samaritaine* has been translated into many other languages, including German, Italian, Hungarian and Polish. A musical version of Rostand's play was prepared by Max d'Ollone for the Paris Opera House in 1937.

NOTES – ACT II

[1] Enoch, 1890
[2] *Le Figaro*, 10 June 1901
[3] There were seven performances and Rostand had only one percent of the rights.
[4] Quoted in P. Apesteguy, *La Vie Profonde d'Edmond Rostand* (Paris: Fasquelle, 1929), p. 79
[5] "Le Style et le psychose maniaco-dépressive, Edmond Rostand", unpublished thesis, 1949
[6] This version was for singers with piano accompaniment, but in 1913 an orchestrated version appeared. An English translation by Amy Lowell was published simultaneously in Boston.
[7] Ennui – literally translates as Boredom, but is also a state of mind connected with the world-weariness of some of the Romantics and with the fin-de-siècle decadence of Rostand's own time.
[8] Cervantes was understandably one of Rostand's favourite authors. There are references to Don Quixote in *Cyrano de Bergerac*, and in Rostand's garden he would place a bust of Cervantes in an honoured position, alongside Shakespeare and Victor Hugo.
[9] *La Dernière Nuit de Don Juan* (Fasquelle, 1921)
[10] The admiration was mutual. Rostand's "Ode à Catulle Mendès" would be published in *Le Journal* on 23rd Feb. 1895.
[11] George Fleming was the pen name of Julia Constance Fletcher, novelist and dramatist (1858-1938)
[12] London: Jonathan Cape, 1944, p. 137
[13] Nov-Dec. 1893
[14] Quoted by Margerie, pp. 70-71; p. 256 ftnt.4, who found this account in Sarah's own writing in a sale of documents in 1997. The loss of the handkerchief and the emotion felt by Rostand in Sarah's presence have the ring of truth: as a child, Edmond was always forgetting his handkerchief. According to Margerie, the introduction was made by Suzanne Reichenberg, who had played the part of Sylvie in *Les Romanesques*. Others have suggested it was Jean Richepin, a former lover of Sarah's and still her friend, who had brought Sarah and Edmond together.
[15] Jean-Cyrus, later known simply as Jean, would become a renowned biologist.

[16] *Les Oeuvres Libres,* vol.1 (Paris: Fayard et Cie., 1921). Note the choice of a Rostand work for this first issue of unpublished work by famous authors.

[17] *Les Musardises* (1911 ed.), I, xxi

[18] (London, 1949), pp. 202-07

[19] *Gens de Théâtre que j'ai connus 1900-1940* (New York, n.d.), p. 31

[20] Maurice Rostand, *Sarah Bernhardt* (Paris, 1950), p. 46

[21] A fictitious character with the name of a real person

[22] "des vers" – an echo of Rostand's reply to the singer, Philinte, at Luchon, in his youth, but also his perpetual declaration of intent to his audiences.

[23] *Sous les Lauriers* (Paris, 1911), p. 212

[24] In *La Dernière Nuit de Don Juan*

[25] *Le Figaro,* 10 June 1901

[26] *Dramatic Essays and Opinions* (London, 1907), vol I, pp. 142-152

[27] Reprinted in Sarcey, *Quarante Ans de Théâtre*, VII, pp. 213-5

[28] Paris:Heugel, 1934

[29] *Les Annales,* 9 March 1913

[30] The first of three volumes of d'Artagnan's memoirs would be republished in 1896 in Paris; it was reading the earlier edition in the Academy of Marseilles's library which gave Dumas the original idea for his novel.

[31] See Act One

[32] 1894, nos. 27, 28

[33] *Confession d'un demi-siècle* (Paris, 1952), p. 18

[34] *Portraits Intimes* (Paris, 1896), vol II., pp. 39-47

[35] *Journal* (Paris, 1925-7), 7 Feb. 1896

[36] Robert de Montesquiou, another of her friends, writing of Sarah in *Les Pas Effacés* (Paris, 1923)

[37] *Journal,* 9 Dec 1895

[38] M. Rostand, p. 43

[39] *Journal,* 30 May 1895

[40] *Journal,* 13 Nov. 1895

[41] Journal, 2 Jan 96

[42] *Lettres inédites,* p.138

[43] Paris, 1863

[44] Ripert, p. 65

[45] *Le Cantique de L'Aile* (Paris, 1922), XIII

[46] 10 Dec.1896

[47] *Journal,* 18 Feb 1897

[48] *Journal,* 19 Jan 1897; 18 Feb 1897

[49] *Le Cantique de L'Aile,* VIII

[50] This passage aroused much controversy. Many admired its lyricism, but others considered it was wrong to portray Jesus as an admirer of female beauty. Even more offensive to some was the way Jesus

went on to say he reveres this gesture as his mother must have used it herself, when still a young woman. In fact it is Renan who draws attention to the beauty of the Syrian women and their graceful gesture, which the Virgin Mary must also have made. However, the image of a vase is Rostand's own.

[51] *Les Musardises* (1911 ed.), III,xii

[52] Renard's *Journal,* 13 Nov. 1895

[53] *Les Musardises* (1911 ed.) III, vii. Saint Mamet was the church near the family villa in Luchon.

[54] Gregh, in *L'Age d'or,* quoted Billy, p.310

[55] "Ombres et Fumées", "La Branche", Nos Rires", "L'Heure charmante", and "A une petite lumière". All except the last poem would be published in the new edition of *Les Musardises* (Paris, 1911)

[56] freely adapted by Wilfred Grantham and May Agate, with music by Maurice Jacobson

Act Three: *Cyrano de Bergerac* and *L'Aiglon* (1897 – 1900)

C'est avec le cire de son âme qu'il [Rostand] avait modelé celle de Cyrano
It was with the wax of his own soul that [Rostand] formed that of Cyrano
– Rosemonde Gérard

REASSURED AS TO THE SUCCESS of *La Samaritaine*, Rostand was able to concentrate at last on writing *Cyrano de Bergerac*. The atmosphere in rue Fortuny was hushed and anxious, as Rostand always found composition a slow and often painful process. He would write feverishly, then, when inspiration flagged, sit twirling his moustache and gaze unseeingly at the wallpaper, covered with large chestnut leaves. Many of the pages covered in his tiny writing ended up in the wastepaper basket.

Edmond could think of nothing but his play, and found the usual distractions of polite society hard to bear when inspiration was flowing. He would suddenly say, "I'm tired, I'm going home", and rush off. But when he got home, instead of collapsing into a chair, he would go straight to his work-table, pick up his pen and start working again on his play. It was as if, to him, work was all the relaxation he needed.[1]

Edmond's son Maurice, too, though only six at the time, re-membered how devoted Rostand was to his future masterpiece:

> As soon as the première of the play [*La Samaritaine*] was over, my father went back to work. He worked ceaselessly … his whole life was given over to his work, and that work never stopped! Even during those times when he seemed to leave it suddenly and become for the duration of a merry meal, a father like other fathers, even when he walked in one of those gardens where we spent the summer, it was clear that his apparently interrupted work was continuing in the depths of his distant gaze![2]

For the summer of 1897, the Rostand family rented a villa in the Forest of Compiègne, where the poet could continue to work undisturbed. While Edmond concentrated on his play, Rosemonde amused the children by painting the shells of snails red, gold, or silver, and hiding them in the garden for them to find. (This game would inspire Maurice to write his first play, *L'Escargot rouge*.)

All the main characters are introduced in Act One: the beautiful Précieuse, Roxane; the handsome, lovelorn, but tongue-tied Christian, Baron de Neuvillette; the haughty and powerful Comte de Guiche, also in love with Roxane, with his companion, the Vicomte de Valvert, whom de Guiche planned to marry to Roxane as a husband complaisant enough to overlook his own overtures to her. Cyrano's friends, the faithful Le Bret and the poet-pastrycook Ragueneau, prepare the way for the dramatic entrance of Cyrano de Bergerac himself: "The most exquisite of beings beneath the moon!" "Rhymer!" "Swashbuckler!" "Physicist!" "Musician!"; "Bizarre, extreme, eccentric, wan-faced"; "Prouder than any Artaban … he bears … a nose!"[3] Surely it's a joke, he will take it off. But he never does, and woe betide anyone who draws attention to it.

The setting for Act One, the theatre known as the Hôtel de Bourgogne, gave Rostand the chance to set his play clearly in seventeenth-century Paris. Here are the arrogant marquises, in all their finery; the Précieuses, with their elegant manners and over-refined language; the musketeers, including d'Artagnan himself; the naughty pages, and the invisible but powerful presence of Cardinal Richelieu. The actor Montfleury waddles onto the stage and begins to recite the mannered verses of *La Clorise*, but Cyrano sends him packing for reasons of his own. Accosted by Valvert, eager to show off in front of Roxane, Cyrano replies to his banal insults by the Nose Tirade, an outpouring of witty remarks about his nose, which he would not allow anyone else to make. Beaten in the contest of words, Valvert is drawn to resort to his sword. But Cyrano improvises a ballad as he fences, thrusting home on the last line.

When the crowds have left, Cyrano admits to Le Bret that he is in love with Roxane, but dare not tell her so. How could she love someone as grotesque as he? But Roxane's duenna arrives with a message from Roxane herself, asking for a rendez-vous. Could it be that she loves him after all? He is filled with frenetic energy at the thought. "I need giants to fight!" he tells Le Bret. Opportunely, his friend Lignière, the drunken poet, arrives. He is too frightened to go home because he has been told that one hundred men are waiting to attack him at the Porte-de-Nesle. "I'll take you safely home tonight! No one is to help me" Cyrano tells Lignière. He strides off into the moonlit Paris night, followed by a colourful crowd of friends and actresses eager to see the fight.

Cyrano, we learn in Act Two, was successful in routing the assassins. But disillusion waits in store for him at Ragueneau's café, where he meets Roxane. She confesses to him that she loves Christian, even though she has never spoken to him, and she is sure her love is returned. But he is to join Cyrano's regiment, the Cadets and she fears, with reason, that as he is not a Gascon he will be victimized. Cyrano, who has spoken no word of his own love for Roxane, now has the bitter experience of having to promise to protect his own rival. When she has gone and his fellow Cadets arrive, eager to hear the tale of his exploits of the night before, Cyrano is at first in no mood to recount them. When he eventually does so, he is interrupted constantly by Christian, who persists in making puns on noses to show he is not afraid of Cyrano or the other Cadets.

Finally Cyrano thrusts everyone else out of the room and to Christian's surprise, embraces him. He tells Christian that Roxane loves him and expects a letter. When Christian confesses his inability to express his feelings in appropriate language, a wild idea occurs to Cyrano. He, with his facility with words, will write poetic letters to charm Roxane; he will tell Christian what to say when they meet face to face. Together the ugly poet and the handsome cadet will make the perfect suitor to woo Roxane, and Cyrano's pain will be assuaged by being able to express his love to his beloved, even though under another's name.

In the course of the third act, "Le Baiser de Roxane", Roxane is wooed and won, thanks to the poetry spoken from Cyrano's heart, as he hides in the gloom below her balcony, pretending to be Christian. The latter climbs up to receive the kiss obtained for him by his friend. As Cyrano is left below alone, a naïve monk arrives with a letter sent to Roxane by de Guiche, declaring his intention of arriving that very evening to woo her. She pretends the letter is telling her she must accept her fate and marry a man she does not love: Christian. The monk is persuaded and Roxane and Christian go inside with him for the marriage ceremony.

Cyrano is again left alone outside, to intercept and delay de Guiche. This he does by falling on him from a tree and pretending he has come from the moon. His account of several methods by which he could have done this is so intriguing that de Guiche, in spite of himself, is forced to stop and listen. (These ingenious methods are taken from the historical Cyrano's book, *États et Empires de la lune*.) Because of this ruse, de Guiche is too late to stop the marriage, but he takes his revenge by separating the new couple immediately: he had promised Roxane that the Cadets would remain in Paris, but now, as commanding officer of their regiment, he orders them to march with the rest of the army, that very night, to the town of Arras, which is being besieged by the Spanish.

Love was the subject of the third act, but war would be the theme of the fourth. The Cadets are besieging Arras, but in their turn are being besieged by the Spanish. No supplies have been able to get through and the Cadets are starving. Cyrano, however, without telling Christian, is slipping through the Spanish lines twice a day at the risk of his life to send letters to Roxane. De Guiche arrives and tells the Cadets they have been selected to hold off a Spanish attack which he has arranged through a double agent as a diversion while he makes a sortie for supplies. It is likely that they will all be killed.

Cyrano, forseeing this, has already written a farewell letter to Roxane which he gives to his friend. But when Christian sees a tear on it, he begins to suspect the truth. At this point, a carriage arrives: to everyone's amazement, it contains Roxane and Ragueneau, and it is packed with food. As the starving soldiers begin to eat and drink, Cyrano confesses to Christian how often he has been writing to Roxane. Now Christian understands everything: Cyrano is in love with Roxane himself. When Roxane tells Christian that it was the power of his letters that brought her to the battlefield, and that she no longer loves him for his beauty alone but even more for his soul, Christian insists that Cyrano should tell Roxane the truth and ask her to choose between them.

Cyrano's hopes revive as Roxane assures him she would love the writer of the letters even if he were ugly, but as he is on the point of confessing the imposture and his own love, Christian is killed with the first shot of the attack. Cyrano cannot now destroy Roxane's illusions. As she is led to safety by de Guiche, Cyrano rallies his men to defend their standard, Roxane's lace handkerchief. He now has two deaths to avenge: Christian's and his own happiness.

The serenity of the Fifth Act is in contrast to the battle scene of the previous act. The autumn leaves are falling as Roxane works at her tapestry in the grounds of the convent where she has lived since the death of Christian. She is waiting for the weekly visit of Cyrano, who is late for the first time in fourteen years. He finally arrives, his head swathed in bandages beneath his hat. He has been hit on the head by a falling beam, and knows this visit will kill him. Only now will he let Roxane guess the truth, as he reads aloud, in spite of the fading light, the letter Roxane keeps in her bosom, the letter she found on Christian's dead body, but which was written by Cyrano.

Having revealed his love, Cyrano is ready to meet death, as he has met lies, injustice and compromise all his life, with a drawn sword. He may have failed as a lover and had his best scenes stolen from him as a playwright, but he has never lost his integrity, symbolised by his "panache" – the pure white plume he wears in his hat, and which, he tells Roxane with his final words, he will flourish with justifiable pride as he bows low on the threshold of heaven.

Cyrano would be Rostand's most successful hero yet: a poet, of course, idealistic, courageous, a man of deep feelings, his bravado an attempt to foil pity for his appearance, his wit a cover for his suffering heart. He follows in the line of "Laughing Pierrot", though with the panache of Straforel, in *Les Romanesques*. Cyrano's exaggerated nose, and the contrast between his ugly exterior and noble soul may have been inspired by Pif-Luisant,[4] but into the character of Cyrano, Rostand had poured all his own romantic ardour and passion for the Ideal. Cyrano's characteristics, too, are his own: integrity, independence, courage, enthusiasm, refusing to compromise with the ways of the world, hiding his sensitive poet's nature behind a joking exterior. And although Rostand did not have Cyrano's grotesque exterior to discourage him, his character's fear of failure was his own – a fear due, as we have seen, to an inner sensibility connected with his family origins. Truly Rostand modelled Cyrano from the wax of his own soul, as his wife claimed.[5]

Although, as a "heroic comedy", *Cyrano de Bergerac* is written in a different style from the preceding "idealistic plays", *La Princesse lointaine* and *La Samaritaine*, its themes are similar. The pursuit of the ideal is more important than its achievement; disillusion must be overcome by courage and the determination to hold on to one's vision. The supremacy of spiritual love over sensual love is reaffirmed. The handsome Christian duly receives Roxane's kiss. But if Roxane falls in love with Christian because of his physical beauty, she later learns to love him for the beauty of his soul, that is, Cyrano's soul. Cyrano himself keeps his love for Roxane secret and unfulfilled at first, because he fears rejection. But even after Christian's death he remains silent, partly out of loyalty to his friend, partly because his sense of honour will not let him destroy Roxane's illusions, but also because, perhaps subconsciously, he prefers the ideal to reality.

Rostand did not have to make many changes to the historical Cyrano de Bergerac[6] to create his hero. Cyrano de Bergerac really was a poet, a wit, a free-thinking philosopher, a duellist and a soldier, adept with his sword, especially in the service of his friends. He was not, as Rostand knew very well, born in Gascony, but in Paris: the patronym, Bergerac, comes from the family chateau nearby. But at heart and in his behaviour, he was a Gascon. He joined the Cadets de Gascogne, under Castel-Jaloux, at the suggestion of his dear friend, Le Bret. A bold spirit, he railed against stupidity and injustice, but also wrote poetry, love letters, plays and the first science fiction. He did quarrel with Montfleury and successfully routed a hundred men at the Porte de Nesle. He was badly wounded at Arras, but his death at thirty-five years old from a beam falling on him may have been an accident. Cyrano is buried in Gascony, at the convent of *Les Filles de la Croix* in Toulouse, where he went to live after this accident.

Ragueneau, Lignière and many other minor characters are also historical figures, as is the Comte de Guiche, nephew to the Cardinal. Madeleine Robineau (not Robin) really was the historical Cyrano's cousin; she married the baron Christophe (not Christian) de Neuvillette, and entered a convent after his death at Arras. She was not a Précieuse, but Rostand also drew on a Marie Robineau who was a Précieuse, and who was known as "Roxane". The intrigue which knits the main characters together, however, was of Rostand's own imagining.

Cyrano's nose, too, was exaggerated by Rostand for the purposes of the play, but in this he was following the legend created by Théophile Gautier in *Les Grotesques*, the book Edmond had read at college. In real life, Cyrano did have a rather large, hooked nose, but it was not so grotesque as to make him ugly. But Gautier noticed that in Cyrano's own work, *Les États et Empires de la lune*, he writes that, on the moon, a large nose is the sign of wit, passion, courage, a great soul. So highly do the moon people praise large noses, Cyrano continues, that they castrate any child born with a snub nose. Gautier suggested that this praise of large noses arose from Cyrano's sensitivity about his own, and the legend was born.

The Rostands' summer villa was close enough to Paris for favoured friends to be able to call in. Constant Coquelin was a frequent and welcome visitor. He would arrive for lunch, sometimes with his son Jean or with Sarah Bernhardt, and take away the latest batch of lines. Coq was becoming a close friend of the family. Though he had not the glamour of a Bernhardt, Coq impressed the young Maurice by his upright character and honest bearing. Maurice later said Coquelin was the only actor he had seen who really **was** Cyrano, because he was like him in real life. He showed "that independence, that disdain, that physical courage and moral courage, it's because he was able to stand up to a minister, compromise himself for a friend, refuse an honour so that it would be given to another, to sacrifice even a love affair for affection".[7]

Rostand had found not only the right model for his hero, but just the right actor to embody him. In writing the part, he took into account Coquelin's virtuosity, which coincided marvellously with the kind of verse that came naturally to Rostand: vivacious, brilliant, flowing, amusing, – and Coq excelled in tirades. Even Coq's weaknesses were not a disadvantage – he did not like playing love scenes and so the proxy wooing, where it is Christian who climbs up to receive Roxane's kiss, was ideal for him. Coq had been reduced to playing in revivals on the boulevards, after his quarrel with the Comédie-Française, and was thrilled at the chance of creating a completely new role in his own style. He demanded from Rostand yet more theatricality, more verve, more text even, often taking over other actor's speeches until they grumbled there was little left for them to say.

Rostand's play was to be performed at the Porte-Saint-Martin theatre, where Coquelin was acting at present. Rostand could have waited in the queue at the state theatre for his work to be considered, and probably accepted, now that he had made his name. But he wanted Coq to be Cyrano, and now that his play was almost finished, he wanted to get it performed quickly. The Porte-Saint-Martin was an apt venue for *Cyrano de Bergerac*. It had been connected with some of the great successes of the Romantic period, and was still known for historical dramas and pageants; it had also been the scene of Sarah's successes in Sardou's historical spectaculars. Paul Meurice's *Fanfan la Tulipe*, an amusing play also set in the seventeenth century, had earned a modest success at the Porte-Saint-Martin two years before.

Now that Rostand was able to devote himself to his writing, the verses flowed fast from his pen. He later told his friend Guillaume de Saix: "I wasn't at all rich that year, and yet I was very happy".[8] At times,

Rostand seemed possessed of an almost manic energy. According to Jean Coquelin, the poet one day described his plans for the "moon scene" (Act III, viii) over lunch. Coq asked when he could have his lines. Rostand sent the rest of the party off to Paris for the afternoon and reappeared for dinner that evening brandishing the completed scene of two hundred and fifty lines! As with previous depressions, however, the manic phase alternated with low periods when Rostand felt everything he wrote was worthless. During August a more serious bout of depression lost Rostand much writing time. He did not feel fit to return to Paris until after rehearsals had begun. By the end of November things were going well enough for a date to be fixed for the first performance: 28th December.

But doubts recurred now that Rostand's play, into which he had put so much of himself, was actually going to be performed. A five-act play in verse, to be performed on the boulevard? Such plays were put on, if at all, at the Comédie-Française, where a cultured audience might give them a "succès d'estime". And a play with an unknown hero. Who would be interested in this Cyrano, this obscure seventeenth-century poet? But Paul Meurice, the author of *Fanfan la Tulipe* and like Rostand an admirer of Victor Hugo, told the theatre journalist Jules Huret "M. Rostand is on his way: his *Cyrano de Bergerac* will, I predict, be one of the great successes of this winter".[9]

Coq, too, was enthusiastic. He had had to take part shares with the brothers Fleury in the Porte-Saint-Martin theatre in order to stage *Cyrano de Bergerac*, as his fellow-directors did not share his confidence in the new work (they even hesitated whether to announce on the billboards that the play was in verse). The budget was 60,000 francs, but the cast was huge and six separate sets were needed. Edmond and Rosemonde paid for most of the decor and some of the wages themselves. Even so, the scenery was secondhand, the furnishings were painted rather than real, and the Cadets de Gascoigne were dressed in cut-down old costumes from an earlier play. But the programme, selling at twenty-five cents, was innovative in having photographs of the actors instead of the usual engravings.

Unfortunately Coq's enthusiasm was not shared by the other actors, apart from his son Jean, the Frère Trophime of *La Princesse lointaine*, who was to play Ragueneau, the pastrycook. The female lead, a rising young actress called Maria Legault, would only sign up for a week, which was how long she expected the play to last. As for the rest of the company, in her biography of Edmond, Rosemonde paints a depressing picture of petty jealousies, a failure to understand Rostand's intentions, and lack of loyalty. The actor playing Le Bret was said to have responded to a journalist enquiring about the play's prospects: "noir", leaving the word "four" (flop) to be understood. A friend of Rosemonde's urged Edmond to withdraw the "Nose Tirade ", as it would make the whole play collapse into ridicule.

In such an atmosphere, and given his own modesty and lack of confidence in himself, it is hardly surprising that Rostand suffered some black moments. One of the worst was on 20th December, when he arrived to see the first rehearsal with the staging in place. He was horrified to discover that the gallery of the theatre of the Hôtel de Bourgogne in the first act had been erected back-to-front, with the result that the public would not be able to see Cyrano's first dramatic appearance. Edmond lost his temper. "Are you making fun of me?" he shouted. To replace the gallery the right way round would take several hours, so Rostand cancelled the rehearsal without even consulting Coqelin, who was resting in his dressingroom. The next day he was overcome with confusion and shame, and begged Coq's forgiveness.

Although it was Rostand's right, as the author, to cancel a rehearsal, he would never have done so normally. He felt too much respect for the great actor, who was like a spiritual father to him as well as a friend. It was one of Edmond's greatest anxieties that if his play failed to succeed, he would have betrayed the cast, and in particular Coquelin, who was putting on the play at his own risk. The night before the final dress rehearsal, he was found weeping in Coquelin's dressingroom. As Coq entered, Rostand threw himself into the actor's arms. "Forgive me, friend, for having dragged you into this disastrous adventure" he cried. "There is nothing to forgive", was the reply. "You have given me a masterpiece".[10]

Even Coquelin, however, occasionally became infected with the general pessimism and Rostand's own lack of confidence in his play. One night he was apparently seen with his head in his hands, moaning "What am I going to play in ten days time?"[11] But there was one person who never lost faith in Edmond and his play: his wife Rosemonde. Without her reassurances, perhaps Edmond really would have withdrawn it, as he threatened to do at least once, and the world might never have known *Cyrano de Bergerac*. In countless ways Rosemonde continued to encourage Edmond, keeping a small flame of optimism alive amidst the general despair.[12] On the night of the première she bought some real loaves and legs of ham to make Ragueneau's café look more genuine.

It was Rosemonde, too, who saved the final dress rehearsal from having to be cancelled. While the audience was already arriving, Maria Legault, who had a sore throat, was declared unfit to perform, without the risk of losing her voice for the *générale* the following day and the première the day after. Rosemonde, who knew the whole play by heart, played Roxane instead, with great success.

The *répétition générale* on 27th December was warmly received by the traditional *générale* audience of friends and relations. But the real test would come with the première on 28th December.

It was traditional to wear full evening dress at these occasions. Rostand exchanged his sober costume for the finery of a seventeenth-century marquis and joined the extras on stage in Act One. He had not been happy with their movements at the dress rehearsal. Since they had been recruited from a local wine shop at twenty sous each, this was hardly surprising. Rostand determined to direct them from within. This would be preferable to waiting anxiously in the wings for the audience's reaction. The audience was at first rather confused by all the activity on stage in Act One, where Rostand is setting the scene. After the dramatic entrance of Cyrano, however, interest began to quicken and by the duel scene, where Cyrano improvises a ballad at the same time as he fences with le Vicomte de Valvert, the audience was completely enthralled. Rostand slipped away to Coquelin's dressingroom. As he changed back into evening dress to receive his friends' congratulations, he kept repeating to himself in disbelief "C'est un triomphe! C'est un triomphe!" Later Rostand told a journalist he preferred not to attend premières of his later plays and only did so at his wife's insistence. Nothing could ever equal that evening of 28th December. "Never again shall I experience another moment like that".[13]

The first night of *Cyrano de Bergerac* was one of the great historic moments of the French theatre. As one marvellous scene followed another, the audience's excitement increased, rising to a crescendo at the end of Act Three, the balcony scene, when Coquelin led the young author on stage to receive the applause. Ladies threw their gloves and fans on stage and gentlemen, their opera hats. Friends invaded the wings to congratulate Edmond and Coquelin.

But this was nothing to the uproar when the curtain finally fell at the end of Act Five. After Coquelin had taken forty curtain calls, the curtain was simply left up. The audience just could not bear to leave. Edmond's play had reawoken, just as he had hoped to do, the traditional Gallic spirit of heroism and chivary: a tremendous feeling of national pride had swept through those present. At one point the audience even spontaneously sang the Marseillaise! Families divided by the Dreyfus Affair were reunited there and then: their reawakened sense of being French overriding their differences of opinion. Two writers who were due to fight a duel the next day embraced publicly and called the duel off. Meanwhile Edmond, too modest to appear again and rather overcome, had slipped out with Rosemonde to watch the ecstatic scenes on the pavement outside the theatre.

An exhausted Coq finally reached his dressingroom, which was thronged with wellwishers. "It's a pleasure to kill yourself for a work like that" (On se tue avec plaisir pour une oeuvre comme ça), he sighed. Sarah Bernhardt, still in her stage makeup from acting in Mirbeau's *Les Mauvais Bergers* at the Renaissance next door, hurried in to congratulate him. Her son Maurice had kept her informed on how each act was going. She had "hurried up her death scene", and so had got to the Porte-Saint-Martin in time to see the last act. In her enthusiasm, Sarah almost devoured Coquelin, as Renard relates it, and when Rostand finally entered, "she seized him for herself, by the head again [as with Coquelin], but this time, like a glass of champagne; better: like a glass of the Ideal".[14] Catulle Mendès, an admirer of Rostand since *Les Romanesques*, and still without a success himself for his own verse dramas, addressed Edmond as "mon maître", though he was nearly thirty years his senior, in a conscious imitation of Rotrou's homage to Corneille at the première of *Le Cid*.

The cast were ecstatic, their doubts forgotten. Coq sent Rostand a telegram next morning which read in part:

> My dear Rostand. I won't inflict a speech on you. You and I are both too tired. So I'll just say a couple of very brief and very simple words. You have given us a masterpiece. The day you read us *Cyrano*, those of us who were to be its humble interpreters proclaimed and acclaimed it instinctively by the indescribable emotion we felt. The public, perhaps with more authority, has ratified this judgement by an explosion of enthusiasm and amazement so great that even the most experienced theatregoers say they have never known anything like it.[15]

Jules Renard, whose friendship with Rostand was more than tinged with envy, was fulsome in his praise and wrote in his diary that night:

> Flowers, nothing but flowers, simply all the flowers for our great dramatic poet! ... So now there is one more masterpiece in the world. Let's rejoice. Let's relax, go for a stroll. Let's go from theatre to theatre to hear the latest nonsense. We are reassured. When we want to, we can return to the masterpiece. We can rely on it, shelter under it, get away from others and from ourselves with it... How happy I am! How well I feel! Rostand's friendship consoles me for having been born too late and not lived in the company of Victor Hugo ... I feel decidedly inferior to that fine genius, Edmond Rostand.[16]

The second night was equally successful. Between the fourth and fifth acts a small ceremony took place in Coq's dressingroom, where

M. Cochery, the Minister for Finance, pinned the red ribbon of the *Chevalier de la Légion d'Honneur* on Rostand's breast, in the presence of his parents and sisters, along with Rosemonde and her mother. How full must Eugène's heart have been, and how glad his son, to prove finally to his father he could succeed as a poet. Coquelin and Edmond had been told the night before by two ministers present at the première, M.Méline and M.Rambaud, that the poet would be given this recognition. The President of the Republic himself, M. Félix Faure, was to attend on January 6th to complete the compliment. It was Coquelin, convinced of the merits of Rostand's play, who had ensured the ministers' presence at the première.

Quel bonheur! Quel bonheur! … Voilà le joyeux soleil de la vieille Gaule qui, après une longue nuit, remonte à l'horizon
What happiness! What happiness!….here is the joyous sun of old Gaul reappearing again on the horizon after a long night
– Francisque Sarcey

The critics vied with each other in enthusiasm – *Cyrano de Bergerac* was not only a triumph, but the most unanimous triumph in the history of the French theatre. Above all, there was widespread relief that a poet had at last been found worthy of the great French tradition of popular dramatic verse. "Can it be true? It is not over? There will still be in France a great poetic literature worthy of 1550, worthy of 1630, worthy of 1830! It is there! It has appeared! I have lived long enough to see it! … My God, Monsieur Rostand, how grateful I am to you for existing", enthused Émile Faguet in his front-page column for the *Journal des Débats*.[17]

"Quelle bonheur! Quelle bonheur!" exclaimed the redoubtable Sarcey in *Le Temps* on the 3rd January; "What happiness! What happiness! Here is the joyous sun of old Gaul reappearing again on the horizon after a long night!" Henri Bauer's piece for the *Écho de Paris* was one long dithyramb of praise for Rostand: "Yesterday, on the stage of the Porte-Saint-Martin, in front of a public transported by enthusiasm, a great heroic-comic poet took his place in contemporary dramatic literature

… this time, Edmond Rostand has surpassed anything that could be foreseen, he has soared aloft and hovers above our admiration. What a triumph in one night!" And Rostand will have read with especial pleasure the article by Henry Fouquier of *Le Figaro*, for he commented on "the happiness of seeing a poet make the most delicate sentiments, the most subtle refinements of the heart, understood and acclaimed by the general public."[18]

So "le contrebandier de l'idéal", the smuggler of the Ideal, had succeeded in his dream, beyond his wildest hopes. After his early disappointments, he was now soaring above all his fellow dramatists. He had given expression to the emotions of his own soul, and found them accepted with enthusiasm and joy by the French public. He had sown the "little blue flowers of the Ideal" and they had not been trodden underfoot, but lifted tenderly and pressed to the bosom of the public. Rostand, modest and aware of his faults, always striving for perfection, was exhilarated but also overwhelmed. And one of Faguet's delirious paragraphs may have caused him a passing chill in the midst of the plaudits being thrown at him from all sides:

> Here is great hope of noble, brilliant and moving dramatic productions. Let Monsieur Rostand, without haste, make use of his marvellous gifts. May he give us, with slightly more discipline in matters of taste, those vigorous, exquisite things which such a work promises. Above all, let him give us one of those pure and exalted glories of the dramatic art which from time to time assert, and have asserted for three centuries, the superiority of France. *There is no doubt that now all this depends on him.* [My italics.]

Vous qui connaissez les plus grandes joies, êtes-vous heureux?
[Now] you know the greatest of joys, are you happy?
– Jules Renard, letter to Edmond Rostand, 3rd February 1898 [19]

The days that followed were full of excitement and further congratulations. Sarah, who could claim some of the credit for having brought Coquelin and "her" poet together, sent Coq a telegram reprinted in *Le Figaro*. "I can't tell you what joy I feel after your triumph yesterday and this evening. What happiness, my friend, what happiness! It is art and beauty that triumph. It's your immense talent! It's the genius of our poet! Oh I'm so, so happy! I embrace you with my heart beating with the purest of joys and the most sincere friendship. Sarah."

Both Coquelin and Sarah were overjoyed that they had found a poet-playwright who was also a real man of the theatre. Coq told an interviewer: "I've never seen anything like it. It's the most marvellous collection of theatrical qualities you could possibly dream of. This young man has everything and knows everything. He is as good a director as he is a playwright. He sees everything, he looks after everything, he is incapable of neglecting the smallest detail and nobody would play Cyrano better than he himself".[20] High praise indeed from the actor whom all contemporaries agreed **was** Cyrano.

Rostand was equally delighted with Coquelin. When *Cyrano de Bergerac* was published by Fasquelle, in the first of the editions of Rostand's plays with pale-green covers, the dedication read:

> *C'est à l'âme de Cyrano que je voulais dédier ce poème. Mais puisqu'elle a passé en vous, Coquelin, c'est à vous que je le dédie.*
> It is to the soul of Cyrano that I wanted to dedicate this poem. But since it has passed into you, Coquelin, it is to you that I dedicate it.

By the first of February, the published edition had already been reprinted five times. *Cyrano de Bergerac* continued to play to full houses for five hundred performances without a break – a theatrical record for any Paris theatre. It was impossible to get a ticket, and some critics who had missed the première thinking the play would be a flop did not get to see it until weeks or even months later. At later performances, many in the audience already knew passages by heart. One Sunday, Coquelin, tired from playing the role three times in twenty-four hours, missed four lines from the "Non merci" tirade. A stentorian voice from the audience was heard: "Le texte, monsieur, le texte!" Coq apologised and repeated the whole speech with such panache that when he finished, he had to wait several minutes for the applause to die down.

Cyrano fever reigned in Paris. Songs about the big-nosed hero were sung in Montmartre cafés. Parodies were swiftly composed for the music halls and café-concerts, with titles such as *Cyraunez de Blairgerac*, performed at the Eldorado in February, or *Cyraloeil de Tarascon* ("five quarter acts in almost verse").[21] Edmond's photograph appeared in shop windows, surrounded by a host of knicknacks on the Cyrano theme. Manufacturers were not slow to see the selling points of Rostand's hero: there also appeared *vins Cyrano, fromages Cyrano, savons Cyrano* and even *bonbons Cyrano*, which Coquelin used to buy for Jean and Maurice on his way to the theatre. The famous nose appeared on plates, glasses, ashtrays, pipes and even hats. Cyrano was everywhere. And when, a few years later, *Le Journal* did a questionnaire to see who was the favourite literary hero of the French people, Cyrano de Bergerac headed the lists of both male and female respondents, well ahead of his nearest rivals, Victor Hugo's Jean Valjean and Dumas's d'Artagnon. This inspired a double sonnet from Rostand, daringly linked by "Mais" at the end of the first sonnet:

> *On m'aime, moi? ... Mordious! ...*
> *...*
> *J'ajoute à ma gazette: 'Aujourd'hui, vingt-six mai,*
> *Monsieur de Bergerac, à soi-meme infidèle,*
> *Trouve très bon de plaire et très bon d'être aimé.*[22]
> They like me ... me? *Mordious!*
> ...
> I add to my gazette: "today, the twenty-sixth of May,
> Mr Bergerac, disloyal to himself,
> finds it is very nice to please and to be liked.

Edmond, too, found it "très bon de plaire", receiving importunate journalists and well-wishers with his habitual courtesy. Rosemonde was perhaps even more delighted by her husband's success, as it confirmed her high opinion of his talent and fulfilled her dreams for him of becoming famous. Edmond's photograph appeared in the newspapers, often with Rosemonde beside him. They were such a charming family: the elegant writer, only twenty-nine years old, his beautiful young wife, their two small sons! The author of *Cyrano* was soon known and loved throughout France. Every day the post brought letters of admiration and congratulation. Friends called with flowers and yet more congratulations. It was a time of euphoria for the young couple.

The Rostand family had moved to 29, rue Alphonse-de-Neuville, in a fashionable area of elegant new town houses.[23] It was only a few minutes' walk to Sarah Bernhardt's house in the boulevard Péreire. The decision to move away from the small house in rue Fortuny, which was only rented, was deplored by the young Maurice, who was no longer taken by his nurse to play in the parc Monceau. Not that the new house was extravagantly large: Simone, the actress, who often visited the Rostands after she married Le Bargy in 1899, called it "un petit hôtel". Here Rostand was able to indulge himself and show his good taste in choosing the decor and arranging the furniture, which gave him intense pleasure, the same pleasure that he got from designing stage sets and costumes, or in choosing his wife's dresses. For Rosemonde was always sumptuously turned out to please her husband, whom she loved, wrote Simone, "with the most perfect love". Simone had the impression that Rosemonde would have happily worn rags and lived in an attic, as long as she was with those she loved.[24] As for Edmond's clothes, his expensive tastes shocked his father, who claimed that his son spent in one season what others might spend over five years.

The move seems to have taken place before the success of *Cyrano,* which suggests the Rostand household was not short of money. Rosemonde had of course inherited a considerable fortune from her father. In his diary, Jules Renard wryly contrasted his own life with that of Rostand:

> Rostand, who gets to the top all on his own, without making his way in the little magazines but in the big ones, who doesn't go into editorial offices but out into the world, who doesn't drink beer in the brasseries with bohemians, but would rather dine with the rich, who prefers to the theatre critics the directors of theatres themselves, and Sarah Bernhardt to Lugné-Poë.[25]

Renard could not aspire to the Rostands' way of life: a combination of simple living and luxury: "He dines in a red silk shirt, no tie, rather badly shod in skimpy slippers. There are five of us [with Mme Lee] at the dinner table and there are two servants standing behind us".[26] On another occasion, the Rostands had taken great pains to make their home seem less of a contrast to Renard's, only to find that they had forgotten to hide the visiting cards from the rich and famous that littered the hall table.

It was certainly true that the Rostands were getting to know many of the most important people in Paris society. Edmond had already met the President informally at his daughter's house (she had asked him for a poem for charity). The government elected in May 1898 contained many socialists who knew Eugène Rostand, and with whom Edmond too would become acquainted, including Jean Jaurès himself. The radical politician Georges Clemenceau, who had known Edmond's parents in Luchon, had also remained a friend of the family. It does seem ironic that, although Rostand's own fear of failure gave him so much sympathy for *les Ratés* (Life's Failures), Renard seemed to be living a life closer to them than he. But Rostand's sympathy was for idealistic, impractical dreamers, not for poets whom success eluded because they chose to write for an elite. Besides, his natural preference was for a life of elegance, comfortable surroundings and good taste, all of which required money. The social circles in which he moved were those in which he was accustomed to move from birth, in contrast with Renard's background of provincial poverty and restriction.

While Coquelin continued to play to packed houses in Paris, *Cyrano de Bergerac* was taken on tour to the provinces, visiting Marseilles in March. One hundred and fifty thousand copies of the play were sold in 1898 alone. *Cyrano*'s fame quickly spread abroad: reviews appeared in foreign newspapers; there were performances in French in many European capitals and very soon translations were made into English, Italian, German, Dutch and eventually into almost every tongue.[27]

René Doumic was in the States when the first copies of the play in French arrived: the bookshops could not keep up with the demand; people were learning the play by heart. France was "the country where Cyrano de Bergerac was written". And when Édouard Rod visited a year later, it was just the same, people always asked him to tell them about *Cyrano*.[28]

The famous American actor Richard Mansfield closed his New York theatre early in order to come and see Coquelin perform. He bought the US rights and played Cyrano in an English translation by Howard Thayer Kingsbury for the following two seasons. Altogether he would play the part three hundred and eighty times. But *Cyrano de Bergerac* would not be performed in French in the United States until 1900, when Mansfield would welcome Coquelin to his own Garden Theatre. There were three other unauthorised performances of the play in 1898 in the United States, including a version by Rostand's German translator, Fulda. The enthusiasm for Rostand's play also inspired many parodies, such as *Sir Andy de Bootjack*, by Carle and Aarons, and *Cyranose de bric-à-brac*, by HB. and Edgar Smith. In September 1899, *Cyrano de Bergerac* was "freely adapted" by Stuart Reed for a musical comedy, with music by Victor Herbert.

The British playwright George Bernard Shaw may have been instrumental in getting *Cyrano de Bergerac* translated for Mansfield; he mentions in a letter that he put the actor's brother Felix in touch with a literary friend of his. Shaw's letters reveal how much interest there was in Britain in the phenomenon of Rostand's play. "Ellen [Terry] says she gets dozens of *Cyrano*s by every post. She says Gilbert [of Gilbert and Sullivan] ought to translate it!"[29] *Cyrano de Bergerac* would not be performed in English in London until 19th April 1900, when the star actor Charles Wyndham performed in an unpublished translation by Louis Napoleon Parker and Stuart Ogilvie. Later the same year, Coquelin would perform the play in French. But many people had already crossed the Channel by then to see the play in Paris. When Shaw's future wife is late back from a trip to France, he assumes she has stopped off to see *Cyrano de Bergerac* ... again.

While the success of *Cyrano de Bergerac* in Paris continued, not everyone in the world of the theatre was enthusiastic about it. Antoine, who had done so much to introduce modern plays and staging with his Théâtre Libre, appreciated the play's worth, but was apprehensive lest this success should mean a return to old-fashioned dramatic values. Thanks to Antoine and his disciples, the Parisian stage had changed dramatically since the late Eighties. The theatre now played a far more important role in Parisian life – this had contributed to the amazingly widespread effect of *Cyrano's* success – and offered a much greater variety of experiences to the general public. Audiences could now see, not only "northern" plays (gloomy, serious plays by authors such as Ibsen, Tolstoy, and Maeterlinck), but also vague and dreamlike symbolist dramas, and conversely, realistic portrayals of the seamy side of modern life, or "Problem Plays" dealing with moral or psychological dilemmas.

Many critics had suggested that at least one factor in the public's overwhelming delight in *Cyrano de Bergerac* was precisely that it offered a welcome respite from such plays. Would Rostand's success with *Cyrano de Bergerac* now lead to a rejection of the "new theatre" in favour of a return to the high Romantic drama in verse?

Other critics felt however that Rostand's play was rather a new flowering of one aspect of French literature. "[*Cyrano de Bergerac*] prolongs, unites and blends together in itself, with no effort, and certainly sparklingly, and even with originality, three centuries of comic fantasy and moral grace, a grace and a fantasy, moreover, which are very French",[10] opined Jules Lemaître. *Cyrano* would not lead to anything new.

This proved to be the case. While Rostand's own later verse plays were successful, there was no widespread resurrection of the Romantic drama. A handful of dramatists tried to profit from the triumph of *Cyrano de Bergerac*, but without Rostand's lyricism and grasp of the theatre, and especially without his heart and soul which, as Lemaître had written, "are the most ingenious and vibrant of our day", they achieved little or no success.[31]

Significantly, the only unfavourable press review of Rostand's play appeared in the elitist symbolist revue, the *Mercure de France*, above the byline A.-F. Hérold.[32] Hérold was voicing the discontent felt by many idealist and symbolist poets who had felt that Rostand, in *La Samaritaine* and *La Princesse lointaine*, was a poet in sympathy with their ideals, even though he had never frequented their circle. They now felt Rostand had abandoned them in order to write a populist comedy. They did not understand that in writing *Cyrano de Bergerac*, Rostand's intention was to carry his idealism to a wider public; since *Les Musardises* it had always been his clear intention to write "for the people" and not for a small poetic elite. The elitist poets would also have noted the stage Cyrano's aversion for the "petites écoles" of his own time, and his disparaging reference to the "Mercure français" in Act Two. So Hérold's reaction to *Cyrano*'s success was a bitter one. He called *Cyrano* "a masterpiece of vulgarity"; the author's only talent was "the art of writing badly".

But even some of Rostand's friends felt that *Cyrano de Bergerac* was being overpraised. As early as 3rd January 1898, Jules Renard noted in his journal after a visit to the Mühlfelds' salon, that Rostand was being praised there as the **only** poet! Renard had to protest: this would have placed Rostand higher than Victor Hugo. In Renard's opinion, *Cyrano* was simply a magnificent anachronism and no more. It was plays like *La Samaritaine* that would impress other poets.

Other dramatists, who had been trying unsuccessfully to re-establish the French tradition of verse drama themselves, such as Catulle Mendès, could not help but be a little envious. But the strongest feelings, as we have seen from Hérold's review, were those of the idealists and symbolists, who felt Rostand had betrayed them. Léon Blum told Jules Renard, with whom he worked on the *Revue Blanche*, that he felt Rostand had lost his way as a poet.[33]

Renard and his friends at the *Revue Blanche* were very much involved in the Dreyfus Affair, which was beginning to arouse strong feelings and divide friends and families. They and many others were now convinced that Captain Dreyfus, the Jewish officer found guilty of treason in 1894, had been wrongly condemned. In 1896 Colonel Picquart, the investigating officer, had discovered evidence incriminating, not Dreyfus, but another officer called Esterhazy. When he told his superiors that he would not keep quiet about his findings, he was posted to Tunisia. The War Office did not want the case reopened, as they had no real evidence against Dreyfus. But by July 1897, Picquart had managed to get word to a friend in Paris, Leblois, that Dreyfus was innocent. Leblois had persuaded the much-respected Vice-President of the Senate, Scheurer-Kestner, to request a retrial.

The government refused to change its position, restating that Dreyfus was guilty, but Clemenceau, the radical politician and a friend of the Rostands, was convinced by Scheurer-Kestner and began questioning the official line in October in a new paper, *L'Aurore*. The novelist Émile Zola also wrote in support of Dreyfus in *L'Aurore*, while the popular national daily, *Le Figaro*, was also sympathetic for a while. This sparked off a violent anti-Dreyfus and anti-Semitist campaign in the nationalist press. The battle would continue to rage, sometimes literally, for the next two years.

As the evidence against Esterhazy grew, there were renewed demands by Dreyfus's supporters, known as Dreyfusards, to reopen the case. But thanks to the lies told in the nationalist press, and new evidence fabricated by Major Henry, who had been instrumental in making the case against Dreyfus, public opinion was mainly on the side of the government, which refused to consider a retrial. At this stage, most writers and intellectuals felt detached from the Affair. On January 11th 1898, the War Office took just three minutes to try and to acquit Esterhazy, and Picquart was moved to a military prison. It looked as if no more would be heard of Dreyfus.

But on January 13th 1898, just two days after Esterhazy was acquitted, Zola's passionate denunciation of the government's handling of the case and his declaration of Dreyfus's innocence, "J'accuse", appeared in *L'Aurore* and re-opened the whole Affair. This time the whole intellectual and artistic community was moved to get involved. On the following day, *L'Aurore* published a petition, the "Manifeste des Intellectuels", demanding that the Dreyfus case be reopened so that justice could be done.

Zola deliberately provoked arrest to raise public awareness. His trial took place in February, to the accompaniment of riots and demonstrations. Sentenced to a large fine and a year's imprisonment, he fled to England, but he had achieved his purpose: the question of Dreyfus' innocence could not be ignored any longer.

Now the whole world looked on as France split into two camps violently opposed to each other: the Dreyfusards and the Anti-Dreyfusards. On the whole, the establishment – the right-wing, the nationalists, Catholics, the military and anti-Semitists – was either convinced of Dreyfus's guilt or felt one man's fate should not threaten the honour of the army and political stability. Dreyfus's supporters, mainly the left-wing, Jews and Protestants, the young and the avant-garde, believed that the Affair raised questions of human rights as well as of justice.

The bulk of public opinion was against the "Dreyfusards", who were thought to be threatening the survival of the Republic itself. The rightwing and nationalist press were far more powerful than the handful of independent papers supporting Dreyfus; the anti-Dreyfusard salons exercised more influence. It took courage to be a Dreyfusard: Rostand was one of only a few dramatists who committed themselves either way. His friends, too, were mainly Dreyfus supporters: Sarah had encouraged Zola. Jules Renard, Tristan Bernard, Paul Hervieu and Jules Claretie were also Dreyfusards. Most theatre people, however, either came out against Dreyfus or felt it was not seemly to get involved in the Affair.

With Rostand's sense of justice for the individual, he was bound to support Dreyfus. But in doing so, he ran the risk of alienating his audiences and upsetting his relations. (His former mentor, for instance, Colonel Villebois-Mareuil, was one of the founders of the anti-Dreyfus *Action française*.) Even within his own household, there may have been a division, for Rosemonde and her mother were Catholics and her grandfather, after all, had been a field marshal. Maurice Rostand hints as much when he tells us: "From the first moment, my father was a Dreyfusard; he supported Dreyfus with passion, with courage, with an energy which show that if he had wanted to, he would have been a brilliant politician. But not everyone in the family shared his opinion!".[34]

At the beginning of March, Rostand had the gratifying experience of being invited back to his old college, Stanislas, for a gala performance of *Cyrano de Bergerac* for past and present pupils, staff and parents. He was accompanied by Rosemonde and his parents and sisters, who were staying with them in Paris. This occasion was the idea of "le bon Lorber", Edmond's former German teacher, who had given Edmond so much encouragement as he took his first steps as a dramatist. Coquelin rose splendidly to the occasion, and between the Third and Fourth Acts, a Stanislas pupil spoke a set of verses in Rostand's honour. Rostand replied in verse, though he spoke the lines so naturally that the audience did not realise this at first. The critic Sarcey, who was present, was very impressed. Not only did Rostand recite his poem with consummate acting skill, but he did so with the easy grace of a man of the world.

The first part of the poem was an almost emotional recollection of his own time as a student at Stanislas. But Rostand did not intend to miss this chance of influencing the younger generation. By the eleventh verse, he had turned to exhortation:

> *Monsieur de Bergerac est mort; je le regrette.*
> *Ceux qui l'imiteraient seraient origineaux.*
> *C'est la grâce, aujourd'hui, qu'à tous je vous souhaite.*
> *Voila mon conseil de poète:*
> *Soyez des petits Cyranos.*

> *S'il fait nuit, battez-vous à tâtons contre l'ombre,*
> *Criez éperdument, lorsque c'est mal: C'est mal!*
> *Soyez pour la beauté, soyez contre le nombre!*
> *Rappelez vers la plage sombre*
> *Le flot chantant de l'Idéal!*

> M. de Bergerac is dead, I am sorry to say;
> anyone who imitated him would be original.
> It is the style I wish for all of you today.
> Here is my advice as a poet:
> be little Cyranos.

> If it is night-time, fight feeling your way through the dark;
> when something is wrong, don't be afraid to yell out "It's wrong!"
> Stand up for beauty, stand out against the crowd!
> Call back to the gloomy shore
> the singing wave of idealism!

This recalls Rostand's poem about becoming a modern Don Quichotte, but now it is Cyrano's white plume – his "panache" – that symbolises the revolt against modern ennui and materialism. Yes, you may be laughed at for your high ideals, says Rostand – but although panache is no longer visible as a white plume, it is still there in the hearts of the brave.

"And that's why I ask you for panache!" Rostand continued. "Put your shoulders back! Stick out your chest! March. Keep time … And twirl your moustache, even if you haven't one! Never be afraid of appearing ridiculous; you can make even modern peaceful pavements ring with the heels of your ancestors, and it is spurs which are invisible which jingle best!"[35]

Those old Stanislavians who fought in the First World War took Rostand's message to heart. Many wrote to him that they carried *Cyrano de Bergerac* or *Chantecler* in their rucksacks to give them courage and inspiration.

Meanwhile the incredible success of *Cyrano de Bergerac* continued. The hundredth performance was celebrated on 25th March. Trays of cakes were carried round the audience by Ragueneau's cooks during the interval, and all the ladies were presented with flowers. By then, the play had taken almost a million francs – the total received for 1898 alone would be 2,286,000 francs. The 150th performance would take place in May, the 300th in December. Coquelin continued to play the demanding role of Cyrano without missing a single performance until the theatre closed for the summer break in June. Rostand sent Coq a letter: "Here is the hundredth performance; here is my gratitude five times over; you have been Cyrano a hundred times, without ever being him less. I'd like to add some more scenes."[36]

Honours of varying importance continued to be given to Rostand. L'Académie des Jeux Floraux at Luchon awarded him its "Lettres de Maîtrise", an honour given earlier to Victor Hugo and Chateaubriand. His father Eugène was welcomed, in what was surely an indirect tribute, though well-earned by the recipient, as a member of the Académie des

Sciences Politiques in Paris. And letters and telegrams continued to flood in.

Rostand's knowledge of seventeenth-century France was being challenged by a young historian, Émile Magne, who wrote a series of articles in the *Revue de Paris* that summer under the title: "Les Erreurs de documentation de *Cyrano de Bergerac*"[37] Rostand replied in the same magazine that he was well aware of the anachronisms in his play, which was a work of art, not a historical document. "Local colour is not at all a result of a narrow exactitude, as you well know. A poet never does anything by chance and is only inexact on purpose."

Rostand est Cyrano de Bergerac: la plus belle âme du monde
Rostand is Cyrano de Bergerac: the most beautiful soul in the world
– *Simone.*[38]

What was the effect on Rostand of so much celebrity? The German poet Fulda, who had translated *Les Romanesques*, and who stayed for a while with the Rostands to discuss translating *Cyrano de Bergerac*, described Edmond in a Dutch paper as "l'ami le plus exquis, denué de toute pose, et d'une modestie sans pareille."[39] (The most exquisite friend, devoid of any posing, and of unequalled modesty.) There is also the testimony of Doctor L. Moreau, who told how in his youth he and his friends played a trick on a fellow student, who was, like them all, a passionate admirer of Rostand and had sent him some of his poems. They sent him a letter purporting to come from the great man himself, inviting him to dinner on Sunday. The boy duly called on the Rostands. As a practical joker himself, Edmond was simply amused. Instead of sending the student away, he chatted to him about poetry and his plans for the future. In the end he enjoyed his caller's company so much he really did invite him to stay to dinner.[40]

Fame offered many such joys to Edmond. His fear of failure was allayed for the time being. It was so good to be appreciated and feted, to meet on equal terms with other celebrities, to see his face in the papers and be recognised when he went out, to be able to thrill a young student such as he himself once was. But there were duties too.

Rostand's postbag continued to grow. But now there were more requests than congratulations. Poets sent him their verses. Lovers of literature begged to become his secretary. Edmond's innate conscientiousness would not let him ignore them. With Rosemonde's help, he courteously answered them all.

The glow cast by success and fame over Edmond's handsome figure and elegant outfits also attracted young and beautiful women. For now, perhaps, he could resist their temptations. But on outings with his friend Le Bargy he enjoyed their company.

Rostand seemed to Renard unchanged by his fame. He told amusing stories about wearing his *Légion d'Honneur* rosette in public. He felt it would have been better deserved after *La Samaritaine*; Renard agreed. In spite of the enormous triumph of the *Cyrano de Bergerac*, neither Rostand nor Renard felt the role of a comic-heroic versifier suited Edmond; it was too restrictive. Rostand still thought of himself chiefly as a poet writing for the theatre, rather than a dramatist writing in verse. Poetry was better suited to his idealistic message. Yet it was precisely Rostand's theatrical gifts which made him successful, and so able to get his ideas across to the general public. And it was the theatre which he loved and wished to work for. "He loves everything about the theatre", noted Renard "even down to its smell of urinals".[41]

The Dreyfus Affair continued to inflame the nation. Jules Renard felt Rostand was not as committed as he was. But Rostand did not want to spend his precious energy and time on political campaigning. He had a wider agenda: his desire was to move hearts by means of the theatre. He had refused to sign the "Manifeste des Intellectuels", telling Clemenceau he only put his name to poems. Later, he changed his mind, signing the "Hommage à Picquart" later in the year, and also the petition against Zola's suspension from the Legion of Honour.

Edmond preferred to support Dreyfus in his own way. He had befriended Colonel Picquart, whose Cyrano-like courage in standing up for the truth at all costs he admired. Picquart had now been released from military prison and dismissed from the army on a charge of indiscipline. Rostand had accompanied the colonel to a meeting at

Zola's house the previous December, and been booed by the crowd outside. This may have been the same occasion as when Sarah Bernhard appeared on Zola's balcony and shamed the mob into silence.[42]

On 8th May, Rostand took the even bolder step of inviting Colonel Picquart to join Rosemonde and himself in their box at the Théâtre de l'Oeuvre for the première of Romain Rolland's controversial new play about the Dreyfus Affair, *Les Loups*. As a result, the Collège Stanislas cancelled a reception for Madame Rostand. There was also a move by right-wing papers to urge people to boycott *Cyrano de Bergerac*, but it came to nothing. The 150th performance of *Cyrano de Bergerac* was sold out, just as all the earlier performances had been, and Rostand's play continued on its triumphant way.

One of the drawbacks of fame was the request for "poèmes de circonstance". "*La Fête au manège*"[43] was written for the War Horse Society to raise money for the *Société de secours aux blessés militaires*. One senses that Rostand's heart was not really in these verses. He acknowledges the glory and splendour of the panoply of war. But, typically, he reminds his listeners that war horses are trained for battle, and battles mean death and injury. In these verses, Rostand harks back to his own early poem, "Un Rêve", and anticipates the battlefield scene in his next play, *L'Aiglon*.

Far more to Rostand's own tastes was "La Journée d'une Précieuse".[44] This long poem follows one day in the life of "Doralise", a Précieuse. Rostand pokes gentle fun at Doralise from his late-nineteenth-century standpoint, and revels in the details of the clothes, food and literature of his beloved seventeenth century.

"What would you do next if you were me?" Rostand had asked Renard one day in March. Edmond said he had at least fifty ideas for plays as good as *Cyrano de Bergerac*.[45] For the moment he was working on a verse tragedy, provisionally entitled *La Chambre des amants*, intended for the Comédie-Française. By March 1899 the play had a new title but was still hanging-fire, and it seems only two of five acts were written.

As the year progressed, the Dreyfus Affair reached a critical point. A new investigator had realised that the evidence against Dreyfus was forged.

Colonel (formerly Major) Henry, the man responsible, was arrested in August and committed suicide in prison. Esterhazy, his guilt now evident, fled the country. However, to declare Dreyfus innocent was not politically possible: it would mean admitting that the War Office had deliberately tried to obstruct the course of justice. There were calls for retrials yet again. Public opinion was swinging behind Dreyfus at last.

That summer Rosemonde and her mother visited Vichy for the sake of Mme Lee's health. Meanwhile Rostand was on a rare visit to Marseilles for the wedding of his younger sister Jeanne to Pierre de Margerie.[46] He spent the rest of the summer with Rosemonde, Madame Lee and the boys in a quiet country villa near Paris. At "Soupizeau", in the forest of Compiègne, Rostand began to work on a new play for Sarah Bernhardt: *L'Aiglon*.

L'Aiglon

Et ceci n'est pas autre chose Que l'histoire d'un pauvre enfant
And this is just the story of a poor child
– frontispiece to *L'Aiglon*

After *Cyrano de Bergerac*, *L'Aiglon* is perhaps the best-known of Rostand's plays in Britain and America. It tells the sad story of Napoleon's son, François Bonaparte. After Napoleon's downfall and exile to St. Helena, his young son was taken by his mother, Marie-Thérèse, back to the Imperial court in her native Austria. François became Franz and was raised as an Austrian prince, his birth-title of Roi de Rome reduced to that of Duc de Reichstadt, though he was known as l'Aiglon (the Eaglet) in France. Bonapartists continued to hope the Eaglet would return to France as Napoleon II, but he was far too important a hostage for Metternich, the Austrian chancellor, to give up. He lived the rest of his short life in exile. Always in fragile health, the duke died of lung disease in 1832. He was only twenty-one years old.

During his lifetime, there was much interest in and sympathy for the young prince, who seemed a truly Romantic figure. Rostand, too, evokes sympathy for the Eaglet, who is unable to fulfil what he sees as his destiny. Rostand's Franz considers himself French rather than Austrian; he yearns to return to France to take up his rightful place as the son of Napoleon Bonaparte.

Rostand had been familiar with the story of the Eaglet since his childhood. Eugène had hung a copy of the portrait by Lawrence in his son's bedroom. "The young man in the portrait became a kind of friend", Rostand later related. "I saw him from my bed every morning when I opened my eyes … he presided over my studies when I sat alone at my little table. He was there for my first reading, my first dreams, my first emotions. So you see, it's thanks to him that I wrote *L'Aiglon*. I was being haunted by a ghost from my little bedroom in the rue Montaux at Marseilles".[47]

There were other links, too. The duke's globe of the world was on view in the town museum in Luchon. More significantly, Rosemonde's grandfather Gérard had been one of Napoleon's field marshals: she and Edmond had called their elder son Maurice in his memory. And Edmond will not have forgotten those poignant letters his father wrote home from England in 1879 while attending the funeral of another young Bonaparte who died young: the Prince Imperial, son of Napoleon the Third.

But Rostand's "kind of friendship" with the Eaglet went deeper. He felt a close affinity with the duke. Like him, he had a vision of what he wanted to achieve, but feared, in spite of the success of *Cyrano de Bergerac*, he might still be unequal both to the task he had set himself and to the high expectations of others. Like the Eaglet, too, he was the son of a famous father, both biologically and even more so in the literary sense, for Rostand was aware that some were seeing him as a new Victor Hugo. Rostand never aspired to such heights. His own gifts, as he well knew, were suited to a smaller, lighter canvas.

The patriotic, idealistic Eaglet is a typical Rostandian hero. Like Cyrano, Franz sacrifices his one chance of success because of his sense of honour – he refuses to abandon the woman who is in danger for his sake. His dream, too, comes to nothing, but he comes to terms with his disappointment and accepts his fate nobly.

The story of the Eaglet was an apt choice in other ways, too, for Rostand at this time. Sarah Bernhardt was expecting from him a suitably patriotic subject for performance during the *Exposition Universelle,* to be held in Paris to usher in the twentieth century. With the story of the Eaglet, Rostand hoped to offer a play with a patriotic theme that could unite his compatriots, riven as they were still by the Dreyfus case, with a shared enthusiasm for their history.

A wave of bonapartism was currently sweeping France as a result of increased national confidence, encouraged by the militant patriotism aroused by the Dreyfus Affair. Between 1890 and 1900, Napoleon Bonaparte had appeared in over thirty plays or revues in Paris, and figured in works by Barrès, Paul Bourget, and Georges d'Esparbès. The Eaglet appeared less often, but Coppée's poem, "Le Fils de l'Empereur" was popular in the salons, while Desnoyer and Beauvallet's play, *Le Roi de Rome,* written in 1850, had recently been revived. Émile Pouvillon had just offered a new play about the Eaglet, also called *Le Roi de Rome,* to Sarah, but she had refused it because it was in prose. But she must have seen the possibilities for a star role, and so may have suggested the subject to Rostand herself.

However, this epic and tragic subject was on a grander scale than the poet had yet attempted. And though a patriotic subject was essential, it was also dangerous. For the most vocal patriots were the anti-Jewish, anti-Dreyfus right-wingers, who might see the play as supporting their extremist views. Rostand decided to deal with this by making it clear that his play had no political agenda. It was simply the personal story of the Eaglet. He stressed this by giving subtitles to the different acts: "Les ailes qui poussent, qui battent, qui s'ouvrent, les ailes meurtries, les ailes brisées, les ailes fermées" (The wings which grow, which beat, which open, the wounded wings, the broken wings, the folded wings).

Rostand threw himself into the task of researching his subject with enthusiasm. He and Rosemonde combed the bouquinistes and the printshops for contemporary engravings and writing about the Eaglet. According to Rosemonde, Edmond read none of the recent literature inspired by Napoleon's son, lest another's imagination should colour his own. His main historical source was Henri Welschinger's biography, *Le Roi de Rome*, published in 1897 and given to Rostand by the author, who was a friend of the family. Welschinger portrayed the duke as conscious of his own identity as a Frenchman and the son of the former Emperor of France. This was the attitude which became the pivot of Rostand's play. But there was then no historical evidence to support this view. The historian Frédéric Masson, who was writing a historical study of the Eaglet at this time, came to the opposite conclusion. It was not until the discovery of the duke's letters to his mother in 1957 that Rostand and Welschinger were proved right and Masson wrong.[48]

The memoirs of Prokesh, the duke's closest friend, were another important source.[49] Rostand also read *Le Fils de l'Homme*, the account by the Marseillais writer Barthélemy of his frustrated attempt to meet the duke, to whom he wished to present his epic poem about Napoleon in Egypt. Rostand incorporated several ideas from this account into his play, including the key phrase used by the duke's tutor Dietrichstein to Barthélemy: "Le duc n'est pas prisonnier, mais... il se trouve dans une position toute particulière." (The duke is not a prisoner, but is in a very special position.) (Act II, sc.ii)

Throughout that summer of 1898 Rostand worked on his play, in a room whose walls were covered in engravings and portraits of Napoleon's son, including David's portrait and one by Daffinger showing the duke as "dressed to the nines with hair well-curled", as well as various deathbed scenes. Books about the Eaglet were piled up everywhere. The name of their summer villa amused Rostand, who doodled on a page of his manuscript: "Soupizeau! Qui commence en soupir et finit en oiseau" (Soupizeau! Which begins as a sigh and ends asu a bird). Even Rostand's doodles were in verse.

The Rostands returned to Paris in the autumn. *Cyrano de Bergerac* had resumed on 15th September after the summer break and was well on its way to its three-hundredth performance, on 21st December. Coquelin had not missed a single performance. Neither had Rostand's fame diminished. 1899 would, if anything, see an increase in it, as his earlier plays were revived for an admiring public. The Comédie-

Française performed *Les Romanesques* again, while *La Samaritaine* reached its fiftieth performance at Easter. The play became part of Sarah's Easter repertory – she would perform it almost every year until the war. *Les Deux Pierrots* was published, under its original title, with Alexis Rostand's original music.[50]

Meanwhile *L'Aiglon* was gradually taking shape, but not quickly enough to please Sarah. In a reply to a query from her about the play's progress, Rostand begged her to be patient. The work of creation was slow and exhausting. He was trying hard, he wrote, but hard work was not enough. "There is a mystery in producing poetry", and the inspiration he needed was not always there.[51]

As with *Cyrano de Bergerac*, this would be the pattern for Rostand's creative life: feverish activity when he felt inspired to create, alternating with periods of exhaustion and nervous debility during which the poet was unable to produce any satisfactory work at all. Even as a child, Jean Rostand was aware of the seriousness of his father's work, and the way in which it depended on this mysterious thing called "inspiration" which could not be relied upon or called up at will. He came to see his father as both hero and victim of an unceasing struggle to work, work which was both his torture and his reason for living.[52]

The difficulties of creation were familiar to Rostand. But his new status as a public figure was putting him under increasing strain. Renard noted in his diary in March: "Rostand – always tired, always suffering from a migraine, always burdened by his fame".[53] There seemed to be no end to the requests for prefaces, poems, contributions to revues, appearances, and so on and so on. Some requests, from mere acquaintances, he refused, causing offence and even enmity. But he would not refuse to help his friends. He was writing a preface for Jules Huret's book on Sarah Bernhardt, and agreed to appear at one of Sarah's "Samedis Populaires" for the general public – an initiative after his own heart.

Rostand, a private man only really at ease with his family and close friends, had evolved a way of coping with his fame when in public, as the sharp-eyed Renard noticed: "Rostand arrives. He's certainly a great man. He only offers the hand which is holding his cane. He hardly replies". But this aloofness did not extend to his friends, Renard was relieved and even flattered to discover: "I'm quite happy with that, because he makes an exception for me".[54] This public reserve, essential for the poet's own peace of mind, gave people who did not know him well an erroneous impression of superiority and pride.

Rostand's apparent reserve was a defence erected by his modesty. With people he knew, it was not necessary. Gérard Bauer, the son of the Rostands' friend, the critic Henri Bauer, found Edmond perfectly accessible when he met him as a child. "Truly this man had the charms of a troubadour; he ressembled his poetry and his writing, also decorated with narrow-waisted capitals replete with flourishes. Such as he was, and anxious to please, surrounded by the glow of an incomparable fame, he succeeded in leaving an adolescent boy with an ineffaceable impression".[55]

To his friends, Rostand was generous with his time and with himself. He went, for instance, with his wife and Lucien Mühlfeld, to visit his fellow playwright Henry Becque, who was dying. Becque's realistic plays were more appreciated by the public after his death than during his lifetime, and he was dying in poverty and squalor. To Rostand he said: "Your fame is already great, but I see it growing even greater. It will fill the whole century". Mühlfeld whispered maliciously to Edmond "he's becoming delirious."[56]

So even some of Rostand's friends could not help being envious of his success. But in Jules Renard, such envy struggled with the real admiration he felt for Rostand: "in his presence, you envy him. You feel the total waste of effort it would be to try to catch up with him; so you take your revenge in finding him frail, thin, bald, but with a few rather ridiculous long strands on his neck".[57]

Cyrano de Bergerac finally closed at the Porte-Saint-Martin theatre on 4th April 1899, after five hundred performances to full houses. Since September, there had been only six days when it was not performed. The swashbuckling hero then went on tour to the provinces, but without

Coquelin, who remained in Paris to play the part of Napoleon in Émile Bergerat's *Plus que reine*. In May, after a great success playing Hamlet *en travesti*, Sarah Bernhardt took her company on tour, too, travelling with them for six months around Europe. Feeling cramped at the Renaissance, she had taken over the municipal theatre on the place du Châtelet, formerly the Théâtre des Nations, and planned to make it the most beautiful theatre in Paris, a fitting setting for Rostand's new play. The alterations would be done in her absence.

Perhaps partly because Sarah was away, Rostand was restless again. Most of *L'Aiglon* had now been written, and he was no doubt anxious to get on with the casting. Talking to Renard on 29th May, he said he was fed up, and wanted a theatre where he would be master. He also felt he had few true friends – a result of fame. That summer, he was going to tell everyone he was going to Pougues, and then, perhaps, he would get some peace. Edmond had at least one official engagement, however: on 24th July he was formally admitted to the Legion of Honour. He had nominated two "grand old men" of literature as his sponsors: the poet Sully Prudhomme, who considered Rostand had taken his place as the French national poet, and Ludovic Halévy the dramatist, a tireless encourager of young talent.

Rostand spent part of the summer of 1899 in Vienna, where Sarah's company were on tour. Although he disliked travelling, he wanted to see for himself the chateau of Schönbrunn, where the Eaglet had lived out his brief life. Having obtained special permission, Edmond and Sarah were able to visit the duke's apartments as well as the rest of Schönbrunn and its grounds. In the print and antiquity shops of Vienna, they also sought out contemporary engravings and other authentic period items for the production, which was to be as historically accurate as possible.

Sarah's company were performing in the evenings at nearby Brunnen. They travelled by special train, Rostand with them. One of the stations they passed on their route was Wagram. Wagram had been the scene of a decisive battle won by Napoleon against the Austrians: there had been great slaughter on both sides, with over 50,000 men killed. Here

Rostand's Eaglet would have his terrible vision of war in Act Five of *L'Aiglon*. Sarah decided they should make a kind of pilgrimage to the battlefield and impulsively told her Austrian impresario to organise torches and transport from the station. On Rostand's last night before leaving for home, an amazing spectacle met their eyes at Wagram: a band was playing, carriages waiting, horses neighing, all in the light of flaring torches. The impresario had taken Sarah at her word. The actress, delighted, was about to leave the train when the station clock caught her eye. "Can it really be two o'clock?" she exclaimed. It was: the performance in Brunnen had ended later than usual. "On, on!" cried Sarah, and the train swept on, leaving behind a bemused impresario and his companions. Rostand later recounted this episode, typical of Sarah's enthusiasm and extravagance, with great amusement. It appealed to his boyish sense of humour.[58]

On Edmond's return, he told Rosemonde, who had stayed with the children, that Schönbrunn had been exactly as he had imagined it. Rostand was fascinated by the elaborate furnishings and décor and had taken many photographs which were used to recreate these on stage. But the main result of his visit was that he was able to imagine l'Aiglon himself more vividly, his heart wrung with pity for his character. This pity comes through clearly, particularly in the last act, which would depict the duke's death. Rostand had thought of adding a seventh act, in which the visitors to the Eaglet's tomb would speak only German, but instead he wrote the two sonnets which conclude the text in the published version.

L'Aiglon opens in 1830. In France, Romanticism was all the rage amongst the young, the "Jeunes Frances". 1830 was the year of Victor Hugo's *Hernani* and the accession of Louis-Philippe to the throne of France. Franz, Duc de Reichstadt, is spending the summer with his mother, Marie-Louise, widow of Napoleon, in the villa of the Austrian chancellor Metternich at Baden, outside Vienna. The room and its furnishings are lovingly decribed in the stage directions. Later in the Act, Rostand was also able to indulge his delight in clothes and fabrics, when a tailor arrives from France with the latest fashions to show Marie-Louise. The frivolity of the court, and especially of Franz's mother, is contrasted with the political manoeuvrings of the chancellor.

There is a revival of Bonapartism in France, but this must be kept from the Eaglet, in case he tries to escape and lead a rebellion to take his father's place. Franz, however, seems to have no ambitions of that kind. He is a charming blond young officer who dresses elegantly but appears to have no energy or interest in anything. His main leisure pursuits are riding out on his own or choosing his clothes. However, it soon becomes apparent that he is proud of his French ancestry, and yearns to emulate his famous father and rule over "his" France as Napoléon Deux. He is secretly learning about his father's achievements from a dancer, Fanny Essler, who pretends to be his lover. His cousin, the countess Camerata, whose mother was Napoleon Bonaparte's sister, arrives in disguise as the French tailor's assistant; she is an ardent Bonapartist, and urges him to escape – the plans are all ready and he would be welcomed by the French people as his father's son. Here is the duke's chance to gain the throne of France, but he rejects the offer because he does not yet feel ready to rule.

Act Two takes place the following year in the Salon des Laques in the palace of Schönbrunn, at Vienna. Here, too, the décor is copied from the original. (Rostand liked it so much he later had a similar room built for himself.) The duke's cough, already noticeable in Act One, has got worse and he has had to return unexpectedly from parade. He catches the Chief of Police examining his wastepaper basket. The duke knows he is surrounded by spies; his best and only friend, Prokesch, has been sent away: he is bitter and lonely. However, his sympathetic aunt the Archduchess manages to bring back Prokesch. To him, the duke pours out all his troubles: he is surrounded by people he does not like. His mail is always opened: he receives many love letters but will not let love distract him from his duty, even though he is attracted to Thérèse, his mother's young companion. Yet he feels he will never be fit to rule France.

Prokesch consoles and reassures him. He is teaching the duke tactics. They get out the box of soldiers they use for the lesson and find someone – who? – has painted them all in the correct uniforms of Napoleon's army. This someone turns out to be Séraphin Flambeau, the person appointed to stand guard outside the Duke's door at night. He is a former grenadier guard, one of those who followed Napoleon with unvarying loyalty; a survivor of the *Grande Armée*. The duke is thrilled to meet, at last, a true *grognard*, as such soldiers were affectionately known. Flambeau shows Franz all kinds of objects with the duke's name on, brought from Paris, to persuade him how much he is loved in France. (All were genuine relics of the time, lent to, or bought for, the play.) Flambeau is one of the conspirators working with the duke's cousin Camerata: new plans have been made and only await the duke's consent. If Franz can be in Paris in three weeks' time, the people will acclaim him Emperor. This time the duke agrees to the plan, but he must first keep a promise he made to the Archduchess, to ask his grandfather, the Emperor Franz of Austria, for his permission to leave for France. If this fails, he will try to escape: he will leave an obvious signal for Flambeau, who will then alert the conspirators. The Act concludes on a high note of hope.

The character of Flambeau was written with Coquelin in mind. His enthusiasm, his tirades, his fighting spirit, his integrity, his courage and above all his panache, all recall Cyrano. Flambeau calls his version of panache "du luxe":

> ... *mon défaut*
> *C'est d'en faire toujours un peu plus qu'il ne faut!*
> ...
> *J'aime me battre avec, à l'oreille, une rose!*
> *Je fais du luxe!*
> It is my failing
> always to do a little more than necessary!
> ...
> When I fight, I like to wear a rose tucked behind my ear!
> It's my luxury!
> – (Act II, sc. ix)

The name Flambeau (flaming torch) is symbolic. In this play, the grenadier represents the idealistic, enthusiastic side of himself that Rostand had portrayed in the character of Cyrano, while the Eaglet embodies his pessimism and fear of failure. Here again Rostand is dramatising two contrasting aspects of his own personality. Flambeau and the duke make up yet another of Rostand's "pairs", complementing each other in a similar way to Bertrand and Rudel: the idealistic, physically weak dreamer and the energetic man of action.

Act Three takes place the same evening. The Emperor is receiving his subjects, among them Franz, in disguise. Once recognised, Franz charms his grandfather into admitting that the French people would support him if he returned to France. He even cajoles the old man into giving him permission to leave for France. This tender scene of reconciliation and hope is interrupted by Metternich. By astutely demanding certain conditions from the duke if he returns to France as Napoléon Deux, the Chancellor turns the Emperor against his grandson. The Emperor is a conservative, an autocrat, while the duke is a liberal and believes that an emperor can rule over a republic.[59] They part as enemies.

Franz, now determined to escape, gets out his most treasured possession, Napoleon's own hat, and puts it on the table as a sign to Flambeau before he retires for the night. Flambeau understands and makes the signal to the conspirators to go ahead. Then, as he usually does, it seems, he sheds his Austrian lackey's uniform and becomes a Napoleonic grenadier. Proudly he takes up his post for the night outside the duke's bedroom. Metternich arrives to speak to the duke. He sees Napoleon's hat in the moonlight and vents his hatred of its wearer. When Flambeau, in his grenadier's uniform, steps out of the darkness and challenges him, Metternich thinks he is hallucinating. But the tables are turned when the duke himself opens his door; Flambeau escapes through the window, and Metternich destroys all of Franz's newfound confidence by showing him himself in a mirror, where he persuades Franz he has not inherited his father's character, but that of his mother, weak and frivolous, like her Hapsberg ancestors, who were also susceptible to madness.

The fourth act opens by contrast in an atmosphere of frivolity: it is the night of Metternich's ball. Cloaked and masked figures wander through the picturesque imitation ruins in the gardens of Schönbrunn. But the duke is still depressed from the previous night; Metternich has broken his spirit. Convinced he is unfit to rule, he'll seek amorous intrigues instead:

> *C'est logique, Don Juan fils de Napoléon!*
> *C'est la même âme, au fond, toujours insatisfaite!*
> *C'est le même désir incessant de conquête!*
> …
> *Soit! Je serai le reflet blond du héros brun,*
> …
> *Mes soleils d'Austerlitz seront des clairs de lune!*
>
> It's logical, the son of Napoleon as Don Juan!
> At bottom, it's the same unsatisfied soul!
> The same unceasing desire to conquer!
> …
> All right! I'll be the fair reflection of that dark hero
> …
> my suns of Austerlitz will be moonlight nights!
> – (Act IV, sc. iv)

Yet again Rostand depicts this struggle between the ideal and the sensual sides of himself. For the duke, this brief yielding to temptation will be the cause of the failure of his plan to escape. Franz persuades the gentle and chaste Thérèse to agree to a rendez-vous later that night in his secluded hunting pavilion. But seeing his mother flirting with her latest admirer brings him brusquely back to himself and restores his sense of purpose. Fanny brings him details of the plot and Flambeau makes a surprising appearance from his hiding place, still in his grenadier's uniform, which is not at all out of place at a fancy-dress ball. The duke changes places with his cousin Camerata, according to plan, and slips away with Flambeau, not knowing that Thérèse's brother, an Austrian by adoption, has found out about his sister's rendez-vous and intends to surprise the duke there.

Wagram, a vast plain where Napoleon defeated the Austrians, is the atmospheric setting for the fifth act. The conspirators assemble. The duke is transported by joy, expressed in a lyrical poem which surely expresses Edmond's own aspirations too:

> *Régner! Qu'on va pouvoir servir de grandes causes … faire de belles choses!…*
> *Je ferai … je ferai … je veux faire … je rêve …*
> To reign! What great causes I will be able to serve, what beautiful
>   things I will do!…
> I will do … I will do … I want to do … I dream …

The conspirators are about to leave for France when the duke discovers that his rendez-vous with Thérèse is known to the Austrians. When they find Camerata there disguised as the Duke, they will realise the real Franz has escaped. The conspirators must leave immediately, or the chance will be lost. But the duke urges them to return – he cannot bear to leave the countess to her fate. Camerata herself arrives and is furious to find the duke still here. She urges them to leave, but it is now too late. The police have arrived and the conspirators are surrounded. The police turn a blind eye as they flee, but Flambeau is recognised as a wanted man. He kills himself rather than be taken. Even in dying, "il fait du luxe", making a play on words as he drives his knife home: "Séraphin, c'est la fin! Flambé, Flambeau! Bonsoir!" (It's the end, Séraphin! You're flambéd, Flambeau. Good night!)

The duke is left alone with the dying Flambeau, his hopes in ruins. He comforts the old soldier by evoking the battle of Wagram, until he expires in the duke's arms. Alone, Franz begins to hear the voices of the dead; he has a vision of the plain after the battle, covered in dead and dying French soldiers.[60] Is this the counterpart to the glory of his father's campaigns, then, all this suffering? But first one voice then another is raised, calling "Vive l'Empereur! " The Eaglet sees that his destiny is to be quite other than his father's: he is to be an offering, an expiation for the suffering of so many sons of France. He offers himself as a sacrifice, and is accepted by the dead. Now the glory of the battle can return. Still absorbed by his vision, he sees an Austrian regiment riding towards him and rushes to the attack. But it is his own regiment, assembling as ordered for manoeuvres. The act ends with Franz back in his role as an Austrian officer.

The sixth and final act, *Les Ailes fermées*, takes place later the same year. The duke is dying. The scent of Parma violets fills the air.[61] According to Austrian tradition, all the members of the royal family must be present when Franz takes his last communion, but to avoid the duke's realisation that his last hour has come, they are hidden behind a curtain. Thérèse's involuntary sob reveals the deception. The duke accepts his fate and thanks the women who have loved him: Thérèse, his cousin Camerata, the Archduchess. He also forgives his mother, who finally calls him François. He asks to be put on his father's camp bed to die. The cradle he lay in as the Roi de Rome is put beside him, and an account of his splendid christening in Paris is read aloud as he quietly gives up the ghost. "Maman" and "Napoléon" are his last words. The poignancy of this death scene is increased by the closing lines: Metternich orders the duke to be dressed for burial in his white uniform, the uniform of an officer in the Austrian army.

L'Aiglon was to be performed at Sarah's new theatre, now renamed the Théâtre Sarah Bernhardt. The revenues from a revival of Sardou's *Tosca* had enabled her to completely refurnish the theatre in honour of *L'Aiglon*. In a departure from the traditional red, the entire auditorium, twice as large as that of the Renaissance, was carpeted and draped in buttercup-yellow, set off by white walls. The one thousand six hundred seats were also upholstered in yellow. The polished marquetry stage was horizontal, rather than sloping, as was customary, and without the usual prompter's box. Sarah reserved for herself a luxurious suite of three rooms in the Empire style on the second floor, while on the ground floor was a dining room for twelve, with its own kitchen. The great actress was always surrounded by her little court of admirers, and she liked to dine at the theatre between rehearsals or after the performance. Her intimate friends were often invited here to lunch on Sundays. The foyer was decorated with ten life-size murals by Mucha in his Art Nouveau style, of Sarah in her most famous roles, including the Samaritan woman.

Sarah, at the age of fifty-seven or so (she would never divulge her correct age), was now queen of the Parisian theatre, feted and adored by all her subjects. As the actress Simone described her at this time, "Mme Sarah Bernhardt dominated the French stage from her buttercup-yellow Olympus", thanks to:

> Her genius, her splendour, her talent, her courage, her mistakes, her triumphs, her choices, her noble preferences, her voyages round the globe, her scorn for obstacles, her defiance of nature, the fame of her name which reached even to straw huts, her court of friends, of parasites, of servants ready to undertake any task, and the tributes falling over each other to reach her from the five parts of the world.[62]

To this woman at the peak of her powers, Rostand offered the part of the young Duc de Reichstadt, and she made it her own.

Sarah and her company returned to Paris in the autumn of 1899 and rehearsals for *L'Aiglon* began in November, even though Rostand was still writing the last act. Not all the roles were cast yet. In particular, the important role of Flambeau, the old soldier, which was written with Coquelin in mind, was still unfilled. Coquelin was not happy about appearing in only four of six acts, and found various excuses to put off making a decision. Sarah also wanted Edouard de Max to play the Emperor of Austria, but he had just played the Eaglet himself in Pouvillon's play. Nor would Le Bargy, a frequent visitor with his wife Simone,[63] agree to play Metternich, though he claimed to be interested for a while. But the main women's roles were settled: Maria Legault, who had created the role of Roxane, would play the duke's mother, Marie-Louise; Blanche Dufrêne, a later Aiglon herself, would create the duke's enthusiastic cousin, Camerata.

With his usual attention to detail, Rostand, with Sarah, minutely supervised the decor and the action. He even chose the accompanying music himself: works by the duke's contemporaries in Vienna: Schubert, Strauss and Lanner. The fashionable interior designer Jansen was in charge of creating the scenery and furnishings, closely copied from the originals. The military painter Édouard Détaille, was consulted to ensure the accuracy of the model soldiers' uniforms in Act Two. Sarah had borrowed the actual cradle of the Roi de Rome from Vienna and had it remade, complete in every detail. She had let it be known that she wanted to borrow or buy relics of the period, and hats, pipes, rifles and other items arrived at the theatre from old Bonapartists. In return, they and any survivors of Napoleon's exile on Saint Helena were offered free seats for the performance. An old senator had lent her the very cockade once worn by Napoleon, to place in the Emperor's hat. No expense was spared. Sarah even had new uniforms made in Paris when the ones ordered from Austria did not reach her exacting standards. Her own famous white uniform was Paul Poiret's first success as a fashion designer.

Rehearsals were lively affairs. Sarah, although a hard driver of herself and others, was always ready to make everyone laugh with her quick wit and apposite remarks. Theatre friends called in, eager to see how the play was progressing: Armand Silvestre, Catulle Mendès, Sardou, eating little cakes and chatting to each other during the breaks while Sarah's artist friend Georges Clairin, known as Jojotte, made sketches of them and of Rostand, wrapped up in various coats, including a very expensive sable of Sarah's. Theatres were chilly places, and he was susceptible to draughts. His insistence on attending rehearsals in spite of this was to have almost fatal results.

But Rostand was in his natural element: the theatre. Working with Sarah, he was able to play a full part in the production of his play. Rosemonde has described how Edmond, in between advising on staging, lighting, exits and entrances, sometimes playing all the roles himself, was also writing the sixth and last act, often sitting on the stairs leading up to the stage from the auditorium.

Rewriting, too, would sometimes be called for, and Rostand was engaged in just this when Jules Huret dropped in one day to see how Rostand's preface to his biography of Sarah was progressing. Edmond was working on the corner of a table already laid for a meal in Sarah's palatial dressingroom. He seems to have been able to write anywhere, but his best ideas, he once told Renard, came when he was travelling in a cab or a train, almost as if the jolting movement activated his brain, he joked.[64] Sarah was called to the stage, and Rostand watched her go with admiration. He said to Huret, "Never has she has never been more beautiful; she brings to this role a liveliness, a youth, a charm, a brilliance really amazing."[65]

It was true that Sarah seemed made for this role, which became one of her most famous. She was no stranger to acting *en travesti*, especially in the guise of a young man, and these roles had included some of her finest performances from the start of her career. Sarah's small body elegantly fitted into the white uniform worn by the duke as an Austrian officer, while she strode around like a man, having worn the uniform for weeks to get this just right. Unable to find a suitable wig, she had cropped her hair for the role and made up for the stage her youthful presence belied her years. One young woman who saw the play actually fell in love with her. (Sarah made her come to her dressing-room to see her without her make-up.) When the first night finally arrived, it would be as much a triumph for Sarah as for the author. L'Aiglon became one of her most famous roles and she would continue to play the part well into her sixties. Even after her leg was amputated in 1914, she would continue to perform the death scene of Act Six.

But Rostand himself did not have Sarah's self-confidence and stamina. Again he was having doubts about himself and about his play. Depression began to dog him again. He was unable to sleep and began, like his hero, to cough. Still he insisted on attending rehearsals, until the doctors ordered him to stay at home. The fourth act was rehearsed at rue Alphonse de Neuville. On December 16th, Sarah's company began their first season in the newly decorated Théâtre Sarah Bernhardt with a revival of *Hamlet*. The following day, Rostand, though unwell, read the whole of his play to the cast on stage. He was then diagnosed as having a lung infection, probably brought on by anxiety and overwork, and confined to bed for most of the month.

Meanwhile the problem of who was to play Flambeau had been resolved. Lucien Guitry, the handsome and elegant actor, the adored stage lover of the boulevards, who had created the part of Bertrand d'Allamanon in *La Princesse lointaine*, had agreed to take the part, mainly to please Rostand, who was afraid his two great friends, Coq and Sarah, would become estranged from each other if Coq continued to put off making a decision.

Sacha Guitry, Lucien's son, has described their interview in his memoirs. Rostand apparently read the first act very quickly to Guitry, having warned him that he did not appear in it. Guitry was enthusiastic; the second act also delighted him. The fourteen-year-old Sacha, listening and watching from the next room, recounted that Rostand did not so much read his play as act it. He acted it rather like Sarah Bernhardt, and he acted it admirably. He knew it by heart, often forgetting to turn the pages. His youthful fame, his delicate face, his attractive voice, all combined to make him in Sacha's eyes the most charming of men. The third act was read to similar effect. "Admirable!" cried Guitry,"I can't see what would prevent me from acting in this excellent play."

But both men were well aware of the difficulties for Guitry in accepting: not only does Flambeau take no part in the First Act, but he dies in the penultimate act. As Rostand came to the fourth act, he hesitated, said he was sorry, but he felt quite faint and needed to eat something. Off they all went to lunch at Prunier's and before the end of the meal it was decided that Guitry would create the role of Flambeau. Both men realised that a little play-acting had taken place, but were not going to allow that to spoil their pleasure.[66]

At Christmas, Sarah's secretary arrived at the Rostands' door as usual with a huge Christmas tree. She had also sent, amongst other treats, a special present for Maurice, the would-be playwright. It was a model theatre, a replica of her own, with "Théâtre Sarah Bernhardt" written across the façade. Two tiny posters were displayed outside, advertising "*L'Escargot rouge*: pièce en cinq actes en vers de M. Maurice Rostand".[67]

By January, Rostand had recovered from the lung infection, though he continued to be unwell and suffering from his nerves. "Poor Rostand", noted Jules Renard. "He is unhappy. He thinks *L'Aiglon* is boring. He can no longer live. He can't get to sleep before six o'clock in the morning; every evening his doctor gives him an injection of goodness knows what".[68]

Lucien Guitry did not share Rostand's doubts. Excited at the thought of playing Flambeau, he told Renard "[*L'Aiglon*] is wonderful!" "Rostand, he's a genius", agreed Renard. "Yes, to write something as good as *L'Aiglon* you have to be ill" was Guitry's reply.

Even though he was unwell, Rostand was making great efforts to obtain the cross of the Legion of Honour for his friend Renard. He had written a letter to the minister concerned which brought tears to Renard's normally dry eyes. He had even sent Rosemonde to the Renards with a little diamond cross. But in spite of encouraging reports in the press, Renard was passed over at the last minute.[69] Rostand was furious. Rosemonde came herself, in her kindly way, to tell the Renards the bad news in person. But later the same year, Rostand would be successful, and in August 1900, Renard would be awarded his Legion of Honour cross.

1900. A new year; a new century. France could welcome the twentieth century with some confidence. Material prosperity had been restored after the humiliating defeat of France by the Prussians. The Third Republic had now survived for thirty years and a new stability seemed assured by the centre-left government of Waldeck-Rousseau. The Dreyfus Affair was effectively over, thanks to a face-saving official pardon, though attempts continued to clear Dreyfus's name. The riots, anarchist attacks and nationalist uprisings of the previous year were mostly left behind, along with the embarrassing Fashoda incident, where France's ambitions to own colonies right across central Africa had been foiled by Britain, whose own Empire was flourishing. Anti-British feeling was intensified by French sympathy for President Kruger and the Boers in South Africa; France now looked to Russia as an ally rather than Britain.

To celebrate the new century and give expression to their national pride, the French government had invited the world to an *Exposition universelle* in Paris. A new era, it was felt, was dawning: the wonders of electricity were replacing the old reliance on gas; the metropolitan railway was being constructed; automobiles had appeared on the roads –

France had over two million of them, and they could reach a speed of more than thirty miles an hour. The wireless and the phonograph were in their infancy but the use of the telephone was growing. Moving pictures were now being made with phonograph soundtracks: the early "talkies". Rostand's play was to be one of the highlights of this exhibition, a demonstration of France's cultural supremacy and a reminder of her glorious history.

At the Théâtre Sarah Bernhardt, *Hamlet* continued to be performed in the evenings, while during the day rehearsals for *L'Aiglon* were taking place. The actors assembled at one-thirty every afternoon. Lucien Guitry would arrive at two-thirty, Rostand at about three o'clock. Sarah would not arrive until about ten minutes to four. The sixty or so people present would assemble to kiss her hand and she would disappear to get dressed. The rehearsal would then begin, but it would stop again at five o'clock for "Madame Sarah's cup of tea". It is not surprising that rehearsals took several months.

One minor role still had to be filled, that of Captain Foresti, who is the officer leading the duke's regiment to manoeuvres at Wagram in Act Five. Sarah, as the duke, throws herself at this officer, believing, in her hallucinatory state, that he is the enemy. She always did this with such energy that no one so far had been able to stay upright. René Fauchois, who eventually got the part, described how he first had to recite Racine to Sarah and to Rostand, also present, "very elegant, dressed in black, a monocle in his eye and papers in his hand". Rostand complimented him on his voice, and Fauchois was given his one line to learn. They then rehearsed the scene. Fauchois resisted Sarah's lunge so well that this time it was she who nearly fell over. "That was fine", said Sarah, "You can have the part, but next time, remember to say your lines". In the effort of withstanding Sarah, Fauchois had completely forgotten to speak his part.[70]

As rehearsals progressed, the interest in the play became intense, taking first place in the newspapers even over more serious matters such as the Boer War. What would this young playwright produce next? Could he match, or even surpass, *Cyrano de Bergerac*? The nationalist press acclaimed the patriotic theme, which made the left-wing, Dreyfusard papers uneasy. *L'Aurore* grumbled that "the brilliance of [Rostand's] talent is aiding the abominable legend [of Napoleon]". [71]

But Rostand was well aware he would have to tread a careful path. A patriotic subject had had to be chosen, but his treatment of it would not be bonapartist or chauvinistic. Nor would he glorify war. To make clear his intentions, he put a quotation from Heinrich Heine on the title page of the printed edition: "you cannot imagine the effect produced ... by the death of the young Napoleon ... I even saw young republicans weeping." And at the suggestion of Jean Jaurès, Rostand put the following verse on the dedication page:

> *Grand Dieu! ce n'est pas une cause*
> *Que j'attaque ou que je défends*
> *Et ceci n'est pas autre chose*
> *Que l'histoire d'un pauvre enfant.*
> Good God! I am not attacking
> or defending a cause here,
> this is simply
> the story of a poor child.

Rostand's disclaimer was stating the truth. Without playing down his hero's love of France, Rostand had succeeded in writing a patriotic rather than a chauvinistic play, a play not about a conqueror of lands but about a victim of politics. Rostand's vision of the Eaglet as a kind of expiation for his father's victories, won at so great a cost in human lives, was his own. Nor did he make any attempt to evolve a solemn style; his verse is generally less exuberant than in *Cyrano de Bergerac*, but still typically Rostandian: natural, lively, flowing, witty. Although l'Aiglon's story is a tragic one, there is much humour in the play, including puns. For this Rostand would be criticised, but as he explained, he wrote to the best of his ability in the way that came naturally to him.

Eventually a date was set for the première: 17th March 1900, just a month before the opening of the Universal Exhibition. The *répétition générale*, for family and friends, would take place on 15th March.

Rostand insisted on this going ahead as planned, even though he was too unwell to be present. (A new device, the "theatrephone", enabled him to listen to the performance from his bed.)[72] The moment awaited by the theatrical world had finally arrived. "The play unfurled its splendours before an audience where every man in tails, with a flower in his buttonhole, every woman covered in her diamonds or her pearls, all genuine in those days, was fully aware of the glorious privilege of being present at the entry into the world of a work not just watched out for, but passionately awaited", wrote Simone.[73] The audience was not disappointed. Applause was soon ringing out, especially for Flambeau's patriotic speeches. Renard thought Guitry even better than Sarah. Rostand was reassured – his play was a success.

But the real test would be the première, two days later. The audience at the *répétition générale* were invited guests. But the public at the première had had to pay fantastic sums for their tickets. This had not prevented the Tout Paris from being present. Never was such a glittering audience gathered together of the rich and famous in every walk of life: fellow playwrights such as Sardou, Hervieu, Brieux and Mendès, some hoping to find fault; writers such as Anatole France, Robert de Montesquiou, and the bilious Jean Lorrain, beringed and corseted; Rosemonde's family friend Massenet and other musicians; politicians such as Casimir-Périer, a future president, and Louis Barthou. The aristocracy were there in all their finery: the Duke and Duchess de Rohan, Prince Murat, the Duchess d'Uzès and the Countess de Greffulhe, model for Proust's Duchesse de Guermantes, who was dressed all in gold. Count Primoli had paid, it was said, thirty louis for a mere tip-up seat. Professor Pozzi, the favourite doctor of society, was there too, and so, of course, were all the critics, except Sarcey, who had died the previous year.

In the gallery were several old men wearing Legion of Honour decorations. They were the survivors of St. Helena, invited by Sarah. People had even come from England. The American playwright Louis N. Parker was present, too: he had been asked to translate *L'Aiglon* for the impresario Charles Frohman. "The first night of *L'Aiglon* was a thrill from beginning to end", he wrote in his memoirs. "Here was the real, genuine, Tout Paris…come to set its seal on [Rostand's] immortality."[74] Also present was eight-year-old Maurice Rostand. He sat in a box with his mother, gazing in wonder at the famous faces surrounding him. It was his first ever première, and even more special because *L'Aiglon* was dedicated to him and to his famous great-grandfather Count Gérard, Field Marshal of France under Napoleon Bonaparte himself.[75]

The curtain rose at 8 pm and did not finally fall until 2 a.m. the next morning. There were twenty curtain calls. Rostand finally appeared, after repeated demands from the audience. This, to Louis N. Parker, was the finest moment: when Sarah announced the name of the author, "she became the Angel of Glory, proclaiming the Poet's apotheosis; and the final words Edmond Rostand, even with the preliminary bourgeois Monsieur, seemed written across the quivering heavens in characters of flame." When she led Rostand forward, the audience's delirium became a frenzy. Parker usually found the author's appearance an anti-climax. But Rostand! "Beau Brummel would have taken his hat off to him; and even Sarah seemed insignificant beside him."

There was no doubt about the public reaction to *L'Aiglon*: it was a triumph. Sarah's acting and Rostand's verse swept the audience along and made them want to cry "Vive l'Empereur!" The Eaglet's death scene had the audience in tears. Indeed, Rosemonde remembered that at certain passages in the play, the action seemed almost to stop because of the emotion of the audience. Rostand's aim had been to move hearts at the plight of Napoleon's son, and to unite the French people as he had with *Cyrano de Bergerac* – he had succeeded. There had been no confrontation between nationalists and Dreyfusards, no unwelcome demonstration of support by the bonapartists, who had been instructed by their leaders to merely show their enthusiasm by their applause. "Tomorrow, if he wants, he could be King of France", noted Jules Renard after the *répétition générale*.[76] Paul Morand, too, evoking the mood of the première, has someone exclaim: "if Rostand wanted to, he could march this evening on the Elysée [palace]".[77]

The critics were harder to please. Though united in their praise for Sarah, they were less enthusiastic about Rostand's verses. In part, this was an inevitable reaction against their excessive praise for *Cyrano de Bergerac*. Most agreed that Rostand had carried off a tour de force, even sustaining at times comparison with Victor Hugo. He was praised for his brilliant verse and ingenious scenes. But this very brilliance and ingeniosity, it was felt, were carried to excess. They were not always appropriate to such a serious theme: there had been lapses of taste. The brilliant tirades and monologues were almost overwhelming in their virtuosity and the play was overlong, it was felt, with too many diversions from the main plot. Jules Renard had felt the same: in his diary on returning from the *répétition générale* he had written: "A prodigy, rather long, of virtuosity. Its beauty, and, a little, its boredom, are crushing. You admire without being moved. Extraordinary and banal. A play where the spectators yawn with admiration. It's like being in front of a wonderful waterfall: after a while you want to go away".

One of the most thoughtful reviews was by René Doumic, Edmond's former teacher, writing for the *Revue des Deux Mondes*. " [The critics] are now making our subtle poet pay for [their] disproportionate enthusiasm", he noted. Rostand remains what he always was, a marvellously gifted writer. His talent – pleasant, light, relaxed, lyrical, tends to fantasy and gently mocking, even cheeky, irony. Even his faults are traditional French ones: preciosity, sentimentality, and buffoonery, and they too had played a part in his earlier successes. But they are less suitable for a serious subject such as *L'Aiglon*. Rostand should be congratulated for trying something new to him, but it is now time for him to write something with "with more soul, more thought, more interior life, and on a more personal note".[78] This is just the kind of play Rostand would in fact write next in *Chantecler*.

While most critics' reviews combined praise and criticism of Rostand (even Hérold, who had so damned *Cyrano de Bergerac*, granted the author of *L'Aiglon* some good scenes), Émile Faguet, who had heaped exaggerated praise on the earlier play, was virulent in his condemnation this time. Not only did he find *L'Aiglon* overlong; he felt personally threatened by the brilliance and inexorability of the verse.[79]

The public, however, loved *L'Aiglon*. The play became one of the essential experiences for visitors to the *Exposition universelle*, which opened a few weeks later. Sarah continued to perform in *L'Aiglon* right through to the end of October, only taking a break during August. The triumphant fiftieth performance was celebrated on the 30th April, the 200th on the 25th September. The theatre was still fully booked in October, but Sarah had long ago arranged a tour of the United States for November. She promised to revive the play on her return.

What should have been a triumphant and joyful year for the Rostand family was, however, one fraught with anxiety. The chill that had kept Edmond away from the *répétition générale*, aggravated by his already weak condition because of tiredness and overwork, had deteriorated into pleurisy. This threatened to become pneumonia, which, the doctors warned, could easily be fatal. Maurice remembered how pale his father had been at the première. Simone, too, had noted he was unwell, shaking with fever, but not wanting anyone to pay attention to it. On the 19th March, according to Rosemonde, he had gone to visit Faguet, in hospital for an emergency operation on his leg. "But he was the only one to write a bad review!" she had cried on his return. "Perhaps he was the only one to be right", Rostand had replied. The following day, he had had to take to his bed, and by 21st March, the newspapers were reporting that he was seriously ill. Bulletins continued to appear daily in the national and even international newspapers, such was Rostand's importance. The Crédit Lyonnais posted up news of Rostand's health in all its branches. France feared to lose its brilliant young poet. Renard, reading of his friend's illness in the papers, was ashamed of joking after the *répétition générale*: "only Rostand could do better". He had also defended Rostand rather halfheartedly recently at the Théâtre Antoine. Now this man "tout de même unique" (unique, after all) might be at the point of death.[80]

Sarah's doctor, Dr Pozzi, was called in: he diagnosed pneumonia and extreme weakness, amongst other things. Pozzi recommended a lung specialist, Dr Grancher, who called on Edmond daily. Rosemonde nursed her husband anxiously, remembering that after Edmond's illness last December, she had been told another lung problem could be fatal. Rostand's mother and his sister Jeanne, in Paris for *L'Aiglon*, stayed on to help her. Pozzi wanted to operate, but Dr Grancher, who had suffered from a similar complaint himself, managed to prevent the operation and in doing so probably saved Edmond's life.

Telegrams came from all over the world, while in Paris a constant stream of callers came to the rue Alphonse de Neuville to register their concern. The most illustrious names in Paris signed the visitors' book, but Maurice thought his father was most moved by hearing that ordinary people had also come to hear the latest news of 'their' poet. Gradually Rostand's condition improved, but he was still very weak. Against the advice of his doctors, he stayed in Paris correcting the proofs of his play. He was anxious to restore cuts that had been made for the performance, and to add the detailed stage directions which would conjure up the ornate rooms of the palace of Schönbrunn. After a month in bed at the rue Alphonse de Neuville, he finally agreed to leave Paris to convalesce. For the rest of the summer, the Rostand family stayed at the former home of the duc de Dino, at Montmorency, just outside Paris. This ugly red building with over-ornate gates had a large and pleasant garden where Rostand could rest in the shade of the trees.

Visitors came from Paris to cheer Rostand up. The most eagerly awaited was Sarah herself: Montmorency was close enough to Paris for her to be driven over in her cab every day. Dressed in summer muslins under her fabulous chinchilla wrap, announced from afar by the jingling bells of her two chestnut horses, she seemed like a character from a fairy tale. She never failed to bring a bunch of violets from the previous night's death scene – Edmond joked that, just by sniffing it, he could tell how successful the performance had been. Maurice and Jean enjoyed the actress's visits as much as their parents, especially if Sarah had brought her grandchildren, Lysiane and Simone. Besides, Sarah was such good fun! She shared their father's delight in practical jokes and unconventional behaviour. One day she poured a bottle of champagne over her hair, to prove to the boys that it was naturally curly.

Sarah was already thinking of her next project: an "opéra parlé", perhaps based on the Orpheus myth, for which Reynaldo Hahn would write the music and, she hoped, Rostand would write the words. Hahn – witty, charming, a dazzling pianist and amusing mimic, a favourite of the salons, was a friend of Marcel Proust's as well as Sarah's. Sarah also talked of reviving *La Princesse lointaine*, with decors by Fortuny.[81]

Coquelin, too, came to see Edmond, also hoping for another play. Coq had a project for which he needed to earn some money: a rest home for retired actors, which he would build in the grounds of his own property in the country. A generous thought, which later became a reality. He had been performing Cyrano again since the fifteenth of May this year, and would continue in the role after the summer break, right up to the end of October.

Edmond's great friend Le Bargy came to dinner often with his wife Simone. Almost by chance, taking up a challenge from her husband, Simone had decided to become an actress. She studied the art with the serious discipline she had earlier given to her studies of psychology. Taken before Sarah to demonstrate her new skills, she had gained the approbation of the older actress. "Here is the person who should play the Eaglet in my place, if I am ever ill", Sarah told Le Bargy. Prophetic words, for Simone would indeed later play the part, which became associated with her almost as closely as with Sarah.[82]

Many other friends found their way to Montmorency. As Edmond was at first too tired even to read, he asked Maurice and Jean, with typical consideration, to cut the pages of books sent to him, so that their authors' feelings would not be hurt when they called.

Meanwhile in Paris, *L'Aiglon* continued its triumphant course. For many of the fifty-one million visitors to the Exposition Universelle a visit to the Théâtre Sarah Bernhardt to see Rostand's latest masterpiece was a must. The exhibition covered over forty acres alongside the Seine, where countries from all over the world could display their attractions. But the main star was *La Fée Électricité* (the Fairy Electricity), who had her own Palace, with illuminated fountains. The wonders of electricity were everywhere. Moving pavements and an elevated railway took visitors from one attraction to another. There was also a monster Ferris Wheel. Then were the moving pictures, shown on a huge screen. Both Sarah and Coq figured in these new films: Sarah as Hamlet, and Coq as Cyrano. The duel scene from *Cyrano de Bergerac* was part of the Pathé *Masks and Faces* film. The sound had been recorded at a performance in 1897 and was played on a phonograph to synchronise with the pictures. Jules Renard visited the Exhibition with Lucien Guitry and was flattered to be taken sometimes for Edmond Rostand, as Guitry was known to be Edmond's friend.[83]

It was not only at Sarah's theatre that visitors could enjoy Rostand's plays. Coquelin was reviving *Cyrano de Bergerac* at the Porte-Saint-Martin. (The falling leaves for Act Five that year would be provided by Rostand's sons, who gathered them by basketfuls at Montmorency.) The Comédie-Française performed *Les Romanesques*. *L'Aiglon* was also touring France and Belgium; at the end of April the company were playing in Rostand's native Marseilles. In cafés and revues, Rostand's name was again everywhere: the parodists had been prepared this time, and takeoffs of *L'Aiglon* proliferated: *Aiglons-nous les uns les autres*; *L'Aigle-Dindon*; *Napoleglon*; *Le Petit Moucheron*, along with various Aiglon guignols, were being performed in Paris and the provinces. Even Rostand's Uncle Alexis may have joined in the fun: *L'Aiglon pour rire*, a one-act parody performed in Versailles in December, is listed in the British Library's catalogue as being by Jean Hubert, his musical pseudonym. And just as with the success of *Cyrano de Bergerac*, there was a proliferation of knicknacks and other objects on the same theme, especially fashion items such as the Aiglon belt, and the Aiglon cape for women, but also Aiglon writing paper and Aiglon lampshades. Gouche, the pâtissier, was selling Aiglon cakes. A new bonapartist magazine that was started in April was also naturally entitled *L'Aiglon*.

Sarah would take *L'Aiglon* on her next visits to New York and London, but already in London Rostand's name was constantly before the public. Charles Wyndham was playing Cyrano in a translation by Louis N. Parker and Stuart Ogilvie at his own Wyndham theatre. *Les Romanesques*, translated into English with the title *The Fantasticks* by George Fleming (Julia Constance Fletcher) was being successfully performed by Mrs Pat Campbell that June. And *Captain Satan*, a novel by Louis Gallet romanticising the real Cyrano's life, published in 1898 in Paris, had been published in translation to favourable reviews.

It was only to be expected that Rostand would now be made an Officer of the Legion of Honour: the message came on the 13th August.[84] In the same letter, Edmond was told that Jules Renard would also at last get his cross, the cross of a chevalier, in the Exhibition Honours list. The government would have liked to decorate Sarah, too, but the Legion of Honour could not be given to an actress! (Some people suggested her Jewish ancestry and her kindness to Dreyfus's wife counted against her, too.) To get round this problem, honorary posts had been offered to her, but she refused to accept them. It would be many years before Sarah became a member of that august company.

In the autumn of 1900, Edmond finally managed to tear himself away from Paris. The doctors had told Rosemonde some months earlier that her husband could not survive another winter there. Dr Grancher suggested the Rostands go to Egypt, or, better, to the Pyrenees. There was a little town called Cambo-les-bains in the Atlantic Pyrenees which had an excellent mild climate – he himself had convalesced there, and had liked it so much, he now lived there for much of the time. Cambo was decided on. Rosemonde had already visited it in preparation in July; she now rented a house for the winter. The house, at the far end of the town, on the road to Bayonne, was almost new: its red-painted balconies and beams gave it the name (in Basque dialect) of "Etchegorria": "The Red House".

Notes – Act III

1. Gérard, pp. 35-6
2. M.Rostand, p.30
3. Artaban: hero of a *précieux* novel by La Calprenède – one of many such contemporary allusions.
4. See Act One
5. Gérard, p. 37
6. Savinien Cyrano de Bergerac (1619 – 1655)
7. M.Rostand, p. 30
8. *Comoedia*, 2 Dec. 1926
9. *Loges et coulisses* (Paris, 1901)
10. Apesteguy, pp. 154-5
11. Renard, *Journal*, 15 Feb.1905
12. Edmond's poem of gratitude to his wife, "A une Petite Lumière", had appeared in the *Revue de Paris*, 1st July 1897. Cited in full in Gérard, pp. 24-26
13. *Lectures pour Tous*, January 1906
14. *Journal*, 30 Dec.1897
15. Maurice Pons, "L'Année Cyrano", *La Revue de Paris*, March 1956
16. *Journal*, 28 Dec. 1897
17. Faguet, 3 Jan 1898. The dates he quotes mark milestones in the history of the French theatre: 1550, Jodelle's *Cléopatre*, the first classical tragedy in French verse; 1630: Mairet's *Sylvanire,* which reintroduced the rules of classical drama; 1660: Corneille's *Discours,* prefacing the collected edition of his plays.
18. 29 Dec. 1897
19. *Archives Arnaga*. Quoted Margerie, p 259
20. Interview quoted by Ripert, p. 95
21. Similar skits and parodies continued to be written for many years.
22. Quoted in full in Gérard, pp. 18-19
23. The house is no longer there
24. *Sous de Nouveaux Soleils* (Paris, 1957), p. 63
25. *Journal*, 3 Jan. 1898
26. *Journal*, 7 May 1898
27. Best-known of the English translations would be Gertrude Hall's (Boston & New York, 1898) and Gladys Thomas & M.F.Guillemard's (London & New York, 1898)
28. *Le Théâtre Nouveau* (Paris, 1908), pp 323-4.
29. *Collected Letters 1898-1910* (London, 1972), pp. 19-20, 23.
30. *Revue des Deux Mondes*, 1 Feb 1898

[31] The best-known of these were Miguël Zamaçois, François Porché, Louis Gendreau, who died young, and of course, Catulle Mendès.

[32] Feb. 1898

[33] *Journal*, 30 Dec. 1897

[34] M. Rostand, p.48

[35] "Aux Élèves de Stanislas", *Le Cantique de l'Aile,* XVIII

[36] Margerie, p. 124

[37] June, July and August 1898. Also published as a book with the same title (Paris, 1898), with an autograph letter from Rostand.

[38] Quoted by André Maurois, *Nouvelles Littéraires,* 1964

[39] M.J.Premsela, *Edmond Rostand* (Amsterdam: J.M.Meulenhoff, 1933), p. 97

[40] *Hommage à Edmond Rostand* (Avignon, 1931)

[41] Journal, 31 Mar 1898

[42] W.Emboden, *Sarah Bernhardt* (London, 1974), p. 104

[43] "The Riding School Fete", *Le Cantique de l'aile,* XVII

[44] *Lectures pour tous* , January 1900; *Le Cantique de l'aile,* XXI

[45] *Journal,* 31 March 1898

[46] Juliette, Edmond's other sister, was already married, to the Marseilles ship-owner, Louis Mante.

[47] Ripert, p. 115

[48] See André Castelot: *L'Aiglon: Napoléon Deux* (Paris, 1959)

[49] *Mes Relations avec le duc de Reichstadt,* A. de Prokesch-Osten (Paris, 1878)

[50] *Pierrot qui pleure et Pierrot qui rit* (Paris:Heugel)

[51] Letter quoted in Claudette Joannis, *Sarah Bernhardt* (Paris, 2000), p. 147

[52] Talking to Albert Delauney, *Nouvelles littéraires,* 2119 (1968), 1,2

[53] *Journal,* 5 March 1899

[54] *Journal,* 1 May 1899

[55] Gérard Bauer, "Le Panache de Cyrano", *Les Annales Conferencia,* 15 Dec. 1948

[56] M. Rostand, p.49

[57] Journal, 29 May 1899

[58] Faure, pp 29-33

[59] This attitude, unthreatening to the Third Republic, was Rostand's own interpretation of the duke's ideas.

[60] Rostand used some lines from his early poem, "Un Rêve" in this act.

[61] Marie-Louise was Duchess of Parma.

[62] Simone, *Sous de nouveaux soleils,* pp. 25-27

[63] Le Bargy had married Simone in March 1899, with Rostand and Hervieu as witnesses.

[64] *Journal,* 31 March 1898

[65] Huret, quoted Ripert, pp. 121-2

[66] Sacha Guitry, *If I remember right* (London, 1935), pp. 76-8

[67] A reference to Maurice's first play, written the previous summer. Sarah was the first to encourage the boy's dreams of becoming a playwright, and he adored her ever after, writing several plays for her as well as an admiring biography.

[68] *Journal*, 1 Jan. 1900

[69] *Journal*, 12 Jan. 1900

[70] Ripert, p. 123

[71] 13 March 1900

[72] A photograph of the Rostand family listening to the first theatrephone was used to advertise this device.

[73] Simone: *Sous de Nouveaux Soleils*, p. 38

[74] *Several of my Lives*, (New York, 1928), p. 192. Louis N. Parker (the "N" stood for Napoleon: he was born in France) would also translate *Cyrano de Bergerac*, *La Princesse lointaine* and Rostand's next play, *Chantecler*.

[75] In 1928, Maurice would write a play on a similar theme, *Napoléon IV*.

[76] *Journal*, 15 March 1900

[77] *1900* (Paris, 1941), p.139

[78] 1 April 1900

[79] *Journal des Débats*, 19 March 1900

[80] *Journal*, 19 March 1900; 21 March 1900.

[81] R.Hahn, *La Grande Sarah: Souvenirs* (Paris, 1930), pp. 110, 121, 130, 158

[82] *Sous de Nouveaux Soleils*, p. 36

[83] *Journal*, 4 July 1900

[84] Rostand would have the honour of accepting the decoration from the hands of his Uncle Alexis in October.

Act Four: Cambo : Arnaga and *Chantecler* (1900 – 1910)

Une âme Se forme donc loin de la vie et sa drame?
Can a soul develop then, far from life and its drama?
– *Chantecler* (Act I, sc. vi)

CAMBO-LES-BAINS, a small Basque town set on a forested hillside in the Atlantic Pyrenees, was quite different from Luchon in the High Pyrenees, where Rostand had spent his childhood holidays. It was a quiet, sleepy place, where on Sundays the priest rolled up his sleeves to play pelote. The climate was mild and wet; the views over the round, wooded hills and the not-so-distant blue mountains of Spain, superb. There was no need for haste, no cause for stress. Life here had continued at the same pace for centuries.

Rostand's doctor, Dr Grancher, had built himself a villa, Rosaenia. Here, on Sundays, he held open house for his friends and acquaintances, as well as for any visitors in Cambo for their health. That autumn of 1900, the talk at Rosaenia was the same as the talk all over town: Edmond Rostand, who had been Dr Grancher's patient, was coming to Cambo! For the fame of *Cyrano de Bergerac* had spread even to this remote part of France, and the youth of its author, and his sudden rise to glory, had inspired all imaginations.

The Rostands arrived in early November in the dead of night, having come from Paris by the Sud Express. They had travelled from the station in Bayonne in a horse-driven carriage. Maurice, then aged nine, remembers that it was raining, and continued to rain for several days. When he and Jean could finally go out into the garden, they found, in contrast to the bare trees of Paris, camellias and laburnum in bloom.

The people of Cambo gave Rostand a warm welcome: flowers, fruit, berried holly, were brought to the house; Basque songs were sung to him, a poet from a neighbouring village came to salute him in a long and incomprehensible speech. He was shown the views, the sunsets, the blue hydrangeas that bloom everywhere in Cambo. Instead of the trams and carriages of Paris, the traffic consisted of the occasional mule or oxen-drawn cart. But the greatest contrast with the Paris Edmond had left behind was the peaceful atmosphere, the tranquillity broken only by church bells or cartwheels.

One of Rostand's new neighbours was Paul Faure. Faure was an elegant young man, never without a flower in his buttonhole, and passionately interested in literature. A friend later described him as "silent, secret, withdrawn, elusive, a lover of mystery, of the unexpressed, dreaming ceaselessly of the impossible, never satisfied"[1] – very like the poet of *Les Musardises*, in fact.

Faure was to become Edmond's intimate friend at Cambo; his book, *Vingt Ans d'intimité avec Edmond Rostand*, gives us a vivid picture of this period of Rostand's life.[2]

Faure went to Etchegorria the day after the Rostands arrived, curious to see the writer he admired, and hopeful of telling him of his admiration. Edmond came out of the house just then. His face was fuller, his figure more upright, than Faure remembered, having seen him once before, at Luchon. He was wearing a fur wrap, white gloves, and carried a cane. His monocle and his elegance gave him a rather haughty appearance. Faure did not dare to speak to him. But the following Sunday, he met Rostand at Dr Grancher's. He found him courteous but reserved, not at all as he expected the famous author of an exuberant play like *Cyrano de Bergerac* to behave. Rostand was naturally the centre of attention, but he scarcely took part in the conversation, having the air of being "dans la lune" (in the moon). This was his way of protecting himself from the effects of his fame.

Rostand was not as unapproachable as he seemed. On hearing that a fellow writer, Paul Faure's good friend Louis de Robert, was also convalescing at Cambo, Rostand immediately decided to visit him. He and Rosemonde arrived in a carriage drawn by two horses, with a coachman and postilion in grey liveries. Both Louis and Paul were charmed by Edmond's easy manners and natural kindness. He invited them to join him on his daily walks in Cambo, and to visit him whenever they liked. He and Rosemonde also came more than once to visit the sick man. "Rostand is simplicity itself" wrote Faure of these second impressions. "His kindness comes from the depths of his nature, it is not put on. Not the slightest hint of a pose. He seems to find the deferential way people talk to him intimidating. You can see in his manners a visible effort, a charming desire, to make you forget his fame."[3]

Louis de Robert agreed: "It is true that this dreamer, this solitary man, this absent-minded person, was somewhat distant and reserved, but all in all he bore his crushing fame with much simplicity ... everything about him displayed genuine modesty".[4]

Rostand's physical appearance at this time was quite striking. He had now lost almost all his hair, so that his broad, pale brow was even more obvious. His eyes were always direct, but their expression varied: they could be penetrating, witty, ironic, magnetically intense in argument, or softened with compassion. Faure describes Rostand's normal voice as gentleness itself, but when he read poetry or plays it could become a powerful and infinitely varied instrument. However, for long periods Rostand would never speak at all, remaining lost in his thoughts. Then he would suddenly come alive again, taking up a conversation where it had been left off the previous evening or speaking volubly on any subject that took his fancy. Or he might suddenly withdraw into himself in the middle of a conversation. It was as if, thought Faure, he was a jack-in-the-box, leaping suddenly out of his box, then going back inside it, pulling the lid down after him.[5]

To Louis de Robert, Rostand had something youthful and gracious about him; he was something of a musketeer. He wore a different suit every day (which annoyed Robert but impressed Faure) and sported a variety of hats. He was always taking off the monocle he wore for his short sight, and when making a point he jabbed the air with his cane, a cane which was "light, impertinent, sparkling in the air and noble as a sword". When he smiled, a little hollow formed each side of his moustache, and at the same time, his short-sighted eyes took on a mocking, witty look.[6]

Edmond was at first bored in Cambo, missing the activity of the capital. But he gradually became used to the town and its inhabitants. Besides, the setting was incomparable: from his windows, he could see the whole valley of the Nive, stretching towards Bayonne, Saint-Jean-de-Luz and eventually the sea at Biarritz. In the evening, when the slopes became clear, he could sometimes see the distant villages of Hendaye and Fontarabie.

Rostand gradually regained his strength. He went for a walk every morning up and down the quiet, tree-lined Allée of Cambo, which ran right through the town, from the villa Etchegorria to the terrace overlooking the Nive valley. Sometimes he enjoyed the company of Paul Faure or Louis de Robert, but he was frequently alone. Often as he left the house his valet would run out after him with his monocle, his wallet or his watch – Edmond's forgetfulness had not improved with adulthood. He was also oblivious of the time and made Rosemonde anxious more than once when he was late for lunch. Rostand and his companions met few people on their walks, and always the same ones: the postman, the almoner of the local convent, the customs officers, various visitors also here to regain their health. All greeted Rostand with deference as they passed. Once, to the poet's embarrassment, an elderly peasant brought his son to Edmond for his blessing.

The villa Etchegorria was bright and cheerful and shaded by mimosas. The windows were thrown open to let in the sunshine, and the servants were helpful and friendly. There was an atmosphere of peace and harmony. Paul Faure soon became an intimate of the Rostand household. He has left us a vivid picture of the two sons of the house, who could not have been more different from each other. Maurice, the aspiring playwright, was confident and chatty, while Jean, the future biologist, then aged six, ignored the visitor totally. Oblivious of his elegant velvet costume, he was lying in the garden at full length on the ground, totally absorbed in scratching at the soil for insects. The English governess, Miss Day, was treated as one of the family.

Rostand was reluctant to talk about himself. But Rosemonde was eager to explain, in his absence, how hard he worked, and how he was always so dissatisfied with what he wrote that, without her encouragement, much of his work might have been thrown away.

Rosemonde was very protective of Edmond, trying to ensure the privacy and peace he needed to work. She ran the household and saw to the children's education. Until Rostand obtained a secretary, she also managed their finances. Freed from practical considerations, Edmond's mind was almost always on his work: he carried around with him small notebooks in which he noted ideas and lines of poetry in his tiny, almost illegible, writing, surrounded by sketches or doodles. But whether at work or relaxing, absorbed in his thoughts, Edmond would easily become oblivious to his surroundings and the passage of time.

Paul Faure and Louis de Robert, so different in character, but both literary men, were welcome at Etchegorria. But other local visitors were not encouraged, and Rosemonde also kept away visitors from Paris as far as possible, so that her husband could recuperate in peace. One permitted exception was Coquelin, who wanted to go over with Edmond the role of Flambeau. Sarah had persuaded him to take it on for their joint tour of the USA, in return for *Cyrano de Bergerac* being chosen as one of the six plays to be performed. She had been very disappointed that Coq had refused the role Rostand had written especially for him, and this was a manoeuvre to ensure he would continue to play Flambeau on their return to Paris. She herself would take the part of Roxane – a role she was never to play professionally in France.

Sarah and Coquelin left for their tour of the United States in mid-November. They would be away for six months. It was Sarah's fifth visit – she had been visiting the USA since 1882 – and Coquelin's third. He was taking five trunks and his faithful valet, Gillett. Sarah took a company of over fifty, plus innumerable trunks and cases.

The première of *L'Aiglon* in the USA, with Coq's first appearance as Flambeau, took place at Richard Mansfield's Garden Theatre on

26th November 1900, and continued there for a fortnight to packed houses and critical acclaim. The New York public also had the chance to see *L'Aiglon* in English, as Maude Adams was simultaneously playing the duke at the Knickerbocker theatre in Louis N. Parker's translation. *Cyrano de Bergerac*'s first French performance in the United States took place on 10th December, and ran for a week before the company moved on. Many Americans already knew the play in English translation, thanks to Richard Mansfield, to whom Coquelin was favourably compared by the critics. Sarah was thought by the *New York Dramatic Mirror* a little too melodramatic for the part of Roxane!

Edmond was not allowed by his doctors to work on any more plays until his health improved. But the visit of President Kruger of South Africa to Paris in November inspired him to write and publish a poem supporting the Boers. Many Frenchmen had gone as individuals to the Transvaal to fight alongside them, including Rostand's cousin, Colonel Villebois-Mareuil, who had so inspired Edmond with heroic stories when he was a boy. The colonel's heroism in South Africa earned him the soubriquet "Le Lafayette de l'Afrique du Sud", but he had also met his death there. So Rostand had a personal reason as well as his own sense of justice for writing his poem in support of Kruger. As in "Pour la Grèce", the poet here is concerned not with politics but with questions of idealism and integrity.[7]

In December, *L'Aiglon* was finally published. Jules Renard, reading the play for the first time, was be completely won over. "Rostand is certainly the only person for whom I would acknowledge a dazzling supremacy. He has wings while we can only crawl ... Five or six times I felt strangled by emotion: I would have liked to have been him."[8]

The peaceful days at Cambo had done much to restore Edmond's health and happiness. His step took on a new confidence, he twirled his cane with the relaxed indifference of a happy man. After the first few weeks, Edmond did not miss Paris at all. This was hard to understand for his friends and acquaintances in the capital. Asked by Pierre Mortier, the editor of *Gil Blas*, how he passed his time, he replied in verse:

> *Ce que je fais, monsieur? Des courses dans les bois,*
> *...*
> *...Je fais quelquefois une lieue*
> *Pour aller voir plus loin si la Nive est plus bleue;*
> *...*
> *Je rêve, ou je travaille.*
>   Edmond Rostand
>   Cambo."*

What do I do, sir? I go for walks in the woods, through brambles which pull at my sleeves; I walk round my garden under the arching branches; I walk round my house on a wooden balcony. When the hot peppers have made me thirsty, I drink cool water straight from the jug. When time wipes out the white road, I listen to the evening, filled with angelus bells, cowbells and barking. What do I do? Sometimes I walk a league to see whether the [River] Nive is a deeper blue further on; I come back along the bank ... and that's all, if it's fine! If it rains, I drum on the window, or read, scribbling things in the margin; I dream, or I work.
       Edmond Rostand,
           Cambo.[9]

Although Edmond was not allowed by his doctors to do any sustained work, his mind as he went on his walks was full of ideas for plays he wanted to write. Both Sarah and Coq were hoping for a new play from "their" poet. Sarah's idea for an *Orpheus* never seems to have been taken seriously by Rostand. He was more interested in revising *La Princesse lointaine*.

It was in any case Coquelin's turn for a new play, especially as it was less easy for the actor to find a role that suited him in the contemporary theatre. *Cyrano de Bergerac* had been ideal, enabling him to express both his comic and his heroic sides. Coquelin was relying on Rostand to give him another play suited to his talents. Rostand was well aware of this, and was thinking of writing a play about his hero, Don Quichotte, for his old friend. But he was also meditating a trilogy, in which Faust, Don Juan and Polichinelle (Punch) would represent aspects of the spirit of doubt, which destroys human hearts and turns them from creativeness to destruction.

Rostand also thought of writing a *Jeanne d'Arc* for Sarah, to be called *Les Cloches*, or *Le Coeur*. According to legend, Joan's heart did not burn. In Rostand's version, a young foundry-worker would rescue the heart from the pyre and throw it into the molten metal used for making bells, so that Joan of Arc's patriotism would ring out in the bells of France. Inspired by a visit to Roncevaux, where Roland and Olivier perished, with his historian friend Gaston Paris, Rostand had also had the idea of rewriting the medieval "Chanson de Roland" as a modern patriotic epic.

Edmond's dreams of bringing his ideas for plays to fulfilment undisturbed at Cambo were rudely broken into very soon. In the spring of 1901, the verse dramatist Henri de Bornier died, and his seat at the Académie française became vacant. Into several minds sprang the same thought – who better to replace him than Edmond Rostand? Jules Claretie, Émile Faguet, Gaston Paris, Ludovic Halévy and especially Edmond's friend Paul Hervieu, himself elected to the Académie only the previous year, all urged the poet to stand for election. Rosemonde was delighted at this further sign of recognition, but Edmond was shocked and amazed. He wanted to be left in peace to get on with what he saw as his true work of writing plays. Like his hero Cyrano, he had a horror of making visits and begging for votes, all the time-wasting duties that would have to be undertaken.

Finally Rostand gave in. He would stand for election only if there was competition, and he refused to compromise on his Dreyfusard sympathies. Two other candidates were found: the historian of l'Aiglon and Napoleon, Frédéric Masson, and the literary socialite Stephen Liégeard, who had been a visitor to Edmond's parents' salon in Luchon. Paul Hervieu now proved himself to be a true friend. As Edmond had still not regained his full strength and was unfit for a long stay in Paris, he, Hervieu, would do all that was necessary to get his friend elected.

The election was to take place on 30th May 1901. The Rostands closed up the villa Etchegorria and returned to their Paris home on the first of

May. Rostand refused all visitors except his closest friends, relying on others, particularly Hervieu, to obtain votes for him. "He has a world of admirers" noted Renard admiringly "and he sees no one."

Two friends Edmond was delighted to see again were Sarah and Coq, just back from their six months in the United States. *L'Aiglon* had been a triumph, performed more than eighty-three times, a third of all performances. There had been fewer representations of *Cyrano de Bergerac,* as that had been played in English many times over the past four years, notably by Richard Mansfield, but Rostand's two plays had been the most performed in the repertory. Sarah asked after Rostand as soon as she came off the boat. She had brought back the skin of a crocodile she had shot, and planned to make of it a wallet for "her poet". On hearing of his candidature for the Académie française, she was disapproving: in his state of health, he should not be making vote-seeking visits. "He is such a child", she said, smiling indulgently.[10]

There was a certain resistance in the Académie to electing Rostand, not only because of his known support for Dreyfus, but also because *L'Aiglon* had made him many new enemies. It was felt that Rostand's depiction of Metternich was a caricature of that eminent statesman. Edmond's youth, too, was against him: never before had there been a literary candidate so young; he was only thirty-three years old.

The vote was very close: Masson had much support. However after six counts Rostand was declared the winner, by three votes. His immense popularity in the country had carried the day.

Now followed an exhausting few days while Edmond's jubilant friends and supporters, along with many literary hangers-on, called at the rue Alphonse-de-Neuville to congratulate him. (Dr Grancher would not allow him to go out.) Jules Huret was granted an interview and asked the poet, lying on a couch in his study, surrounded by souvenirs of *L'Aiglon*, whether he was an ambitious man? Rostand replied, in his "voice of brass wrapped in cotton wool", that like everyone else, he liked to succeed. As for his recent success at the Académie française, "It's true", said Rostand, smiling slightly, his eye sparkling with malice behind his monocle "that my enemies have so arranged matters that my success should be even more pleasant." "So could one say you are now a happy man?" A shadow of bitterness passed across the poet's smile. "You mustn't think that. One is never happy. I am an anxious man. My unhappiness comes from my anxiety. At rest, I doubt everything. I am suspicious of fate and of things and of people. And this spoils my joys." [11]

Rostand went on to tell Huret how frustrated he felt not to be able to give theatrical form to the many ideas that passed through his head, because of his poor health and lack of stamina. "I would like to have done an infinity of things … I envy those who have vigorous and abundant natures; I wish I had that enormous faculty of work which would allow me to give life to all the characters which tempt me, of whom many are bound to die with me, because I do not have that physical strength which allows excess, the great and intoxicating excess of work!"

With Rostand's unstable temperament and far from robust health, an excess of effort led to attacks of nervous depression, and sometimes buzzing in the ears or bells ringing in his head which could go on for months. As he told Louis de Robert, Rostand paid with his health for the masterpieces he created. He could not work without being in a state of exaltation, "a giving of his whole being, an exhilaration, a transportation, in a word, a sort of mental fever … when he tensed all his strings, he vibrated and sang from his head to his feet; and then he liberated that amazing eloquence". But then he became exhausted and was forced to stop working and rest.[12]

The Rostands rented for the summer a small chateau at Saint-Prix, outside Paris, a delightful retreat, with a terrace overlooking a lake with swans. Here came only their closest friends, including Coquelin and Sarah, who was sculpting a head of the poet. Sarah and Coq had not stayed long in Paris after their return from the States. They had taken *L'Aiglon* and *Cyrano de Bergerac* to Lyons, Geneva and Brussels, always to rapturous audiences. By June they were in London. Here, at

Her Majesty's Theatre, English audiences had had a treat the Parisians would never enjoy: Sarah had played Roxane alongside Coquelin's Cyrano, as she had in the States. The company was back in France in time for 14th July, Bastille Day, when they gave a charity performance of *L'Aiglon*, the 241st representation, with Coq as Flambeau for the first time in France. Sarah and Coq dined with the Rostands that evening. Sarah had brought along Reynaldo Hahn, who sang for them.

Especially welcome at Saint-Prix after all the help he had given Edmond were Paul Hervieu and his close friend the Baroness Pierrebourg, who wrote poetry under the pseudonym of Claude Derval. The young painter Eugène Pascau, whom the Rostands had got to know in Cambo, came to stay too, to paint their portraits in pastels. He also painted their friends, and provided Rosemonde with an instant "ancestors' gallery" by copying old portraits of her distinguished forebears, Mme de Genlis and Field Marshal Gérard.

Rosemonde was also having her portrait painted by Hébert, much in vogue that season, at the chateau de Saint-Gratien nearby. This was the home of Princess Mathilde, the niece of Napoleon Bonaparte and so one of the Aiglon's cousins.

Rostand's standing in France was now such that the government had asked him to write a poem of welcome for the Empress Alexandra of Russia, who was visiting France with the Emperor Nicholas. With relations between England and France at a low point (though Edward, Prince of Wales would soon succeed in improving them), the French government was trying to build an alliance with that other great non-German power, Russia. François Coppée and José-Maria de Hérédia, the Parnassian poet, had already officially welcomed the imperial couple in solemn verses at the Académie française. Rostand's poem, "A Sa Majesté l'Impératrice de Russie",[13] was to be in lighter mood. It would be delivered by Julia Bartet on 20th September at the small theatre in the chateau of Compiègne, where the distinguished visitors were to stay.

Rostand's poem, which opened the evening's entertainment, was in light, skipping octosyllabic verse. Mlle Bartet, her dress decorated with leaves and with heather in her hair, represented the Nymph of Compiègne, who is amazed to see the old chateau come to life for the visit of the Empress. The poem's tone is relaxed, almost frivolous; the images fanciful; objects such as carpets and mirrors personified, the whole typically Rostand in his lightest mood. The poet even allowed himself several allusions to his own plays, such as [the Empress is] "Notre Impératrice Lointaine".

The concluding lines, however, were serious, and make Rostand's main point: here, where the great Emperor of War [Napoleon] once walked, the nymph is moved to see the great Emperor of Peace. This message was generally overlooked by the press, to whom Rostand's poem seemed over-precious and even facetious. The more satirical papers and those who hated Edmond because of his support for Dreyfus, were delighted to have a chance to mock the poet and his poem, claiming to see it as an insult to the illustrious visitors.

Jean Lorrain, poet, playwright, critic, moralist, man-about-town, had long hated Rostand and resented his fame. At the première of *L'Aiglon* even the young Maurice had noted his hostility. Lorrain now gleefully announced "le grand krach de la maison littéraire et commerciale Edmond Rostand et Cie" (the great crash of the literary and business house Edmond Rostand and Co.)[14]

"What's all this about a poem that might make you end up in court?" wrote Jules Renard on the 27th September from his home in the Nièvre. "I suppose it was some clever way of shouting 'Vive la République' to these Russians! Do send me your poem." Renard's verdict on the poem is a just one: "his lines are delicious, but made of such fragile stuff that clumsy hands could easily destroy them". The critics are being unfair and ungrateful. Let them go away hungry for once – they'll come back. Give us another *Aiglon*, Renard tells his friend, and the shoulders which tried to rise will bow again with depression and respectful resignation.[15]

Rostand himself had foreseen the press's reaction. "To tell the truth", he wrote to his friend Guillaume de Saix in October, "when writing these lines I knew what prejudices I was wounding, and what ignorance. In fact nothing is less easy to understand than banter and preciosity, and yet nothing is more traditionally French!".[16]

Meanwhile in Paris Sarah had put on once more the white uniform of the duc de Reichstadt, this time with Coquelin playing Flambeau, as she had intended. The revival continued at the Théâtre Sarah Bernhardt until early 1902, when Coquelin left to return to the Porte-Saint-Martin Theatre.

Other famous Eaglets at the Théâtre Sarah Bernhardt would include Edouard de Max in October 1902; later, Blanche Dufrêne, Andrée Pascal, Simone, Véra Sergine and Mary Marquet would take the role. But Sarah herself was most associated with l'Aiglon. She would also record excerpts from the play on gramophone records. *L'Aiglon,* like *Cyrano de Bergerac,* soon became famous all over the world, both in its original French and in translation.

In 1914, Sarah wanted to make a film of Rostand's play.[17] There was some misunderstanding between herself and Rostand about the rights, but it was all settled amicably. A film was made that year, by the French cinema pioneer Émile Chautard, starring J. Guilhène. In 1931, another film was made by the Russian director Tourjansky, in a simultaneous German and French version. A few years later, Henri Cain wrote the libretto for a musical version, with music by Ibert and Honegger. This was performed at Monte Carlo in 1937 and later in Paris at the Opéra, but Mussolini cancelled a performance planned for Naples. Other musicians inspired by *L'Aiglon* were Glinski and Aubert. In January 1939, Edmond's son Maurice would take the part of the duke for a French radio version.

Perhaps the most poignant performance of *L'Aiglon* was on 17th December 1941, at Vichy. An authoritative-sounding German civilian suggested to the Comédie-Française that Rostand's play should be revived to commemorate the return of the ashes of the duc de Reichstadt to the Hotel des Invalides. The German authorities disclaimed any knowledge of the mysterious civilian, but they did permit a dress rehearsal to take place, in the presence of assembled French and German dignitaries.[18]

At the end of the summer of 1901, Rostand and his family returned to Cambo. Like Doctor Grancher, they had grown to prefer this beautiful, secluded spot to the capital. Rostand had rediscovered that love of nature which had awoken in Luchon; he was also relieved to be away from the pressures of fame. Delighting in his rural surroundings, however, he found it hard to concentrate on his Discours de Réception for the Académie, and did little work. In the evenings, he and Rosemonde often went for a drive in their victoria, drawn by two horses with bells and pompoms. Later they would read or chat to friends such as Paul Faure, who often called in after dinner, sometimes with his wife.

It was on one such evening that Rostand revealed unsuspected (by Faure) artistic skills. A box of beautiful new fabric samples had arrived from the fashionable couturier, Doucet. As if possessed by a sudden inspiration, Edmond moulded some figures out of the cardboard box containing the samples, and swiftly clothed them in garments snipped out of the material. There was no mistaking what they were meant to be: Cyrano, Roxane and other characters from his famous play. Edmond amused himself in similar fashion the following night, this time modelling the characters of L'Anglais tel qu'on le parle, the popular play by his friend Tristan Bernard.[19] After a visit by the sculptor Auguste Maillard, Rostand tried his hand at clay modelling, too, with some success.

Although a few uninvited visitors did call, in spite of Rosemonde's efforts to keep them away, only a few close friends were invited to stay, such as Paul Hervieu. Maurice remembered him as "élégant et distant". Coquelin, too, came to stay, hoping to hear news of a new play. Although they were his friends, Edmond almost dreaded visits by

Coq and Sarah, visits which were demanding for the whole household. He knew they would be pestering him for new roles.[20]

Sarah herself generally spent the summers every year on her estate in Jersey, Belle-Isle, and kept in touch by means of long telegrams, but she did call at Etchegorria at least once, as there is a photograph of a reception given for her there. However, a member of her little court, the painter Georges Clairin, "Jojotte", did come to stay, and left a tangible memento of his visit: a huge picture of the four members of the family. The result pleased only the painter himself. As a joke, Rostand hung the painting over the mantelpiece in the dining room, where it caused visitors who were not familiar with his sense of humour great difficulties as they tried not to laugh.

That November, *Les Romanesques* was revived at the Comédie-Française at the same time as the first production of Hervieu's *L'Énigme*. Because his play consisted of three acts rather than just the two of *L'Énigme*, Rostand received more in fees. This offended the poet's sense of justice. In a typically generous gesture, he gave one hundred francs to the *Société des gens de lettres* to create a prize, the Rostand-Hervieu prize.[21]

But by the end of the year Rostand was suffering from depression again. This may have been a result of his visit to Paris and the stresses caused by his election to the Academy, or caused by the thought of having to write his reception speech. His physical health was still not completely restored. Perhaps to try to distract him, Rosemonde and Edmond spent a few days in Paris at the beginning of January 1902. Rosemonde paid a New Year visit to Marinette and Jules Renard. "The joy of being alive, rich and famous", noted Jules in his diary. But then she told them of Edmond's illness. He wouldn't see anyone except her; she never left his side for more than a few moments. She thought he was probably upset at not being able to work, when his mind was full of ideas for plays. He had such an amazing imagination. If only he had Renard's health![22]

While they were in Paris the Rostands surely managed to see Le Bargy's wife Simone's debut in the theatre. She was starring in a modern comedy, Henri Bernstein's *Le Détour*. Its success confirmed Simone, rather to her own surprise, as a true actress. Her subsequent brilliant career would include creating a major role in Rostand's next play.

Home again in Cambo, Rostand's health was fast returning to normal. He resumed his usual walks, taking great pleasure in the local countryside. But his peace was disturbed in February when he received a letter from Ange Galdemar, editor of *Le Gaulois*, announcing a visit. "Galdemar is a nice chap, but he's bound to ask me to write something for his paper. If journalists are going to come bothering me here in Cambo, I shall wish I had chosen to go to Cairo," grumbled Rostand to Paul Faure.[23] He had been hoping to throw himself into writing – he could not pick up work and then drop it for a few days. He needed time to immerse himself in his work and to achieve the state of mind in which inspiration would flow.

Galdemar had had an idea which he hoped would appeal to Rostand. The centenary of Victor Hugo's birth would fall on the 26th February 1902. The village of Hernani, whose name Hugo had chosen for his most famous hero, was not far from Cambo, just across the Spanish border. Galdemar suggested that, after a visit to Hernani, Edmond should write a poem in honour of the predecessor he so much admired, and with whom his name had so often been linked.

At first Rostand was reluctant. He did not enjoy travelling, and had only visited Spain twice since his arrival in Cambo, and then only to please friends. But the idea of commemorating Hugo's anniversary was an attractive one, especially as Rostand did not intend to visit Paris for the celebrations. The next day Edmond, Rosemonde and Galdemar set off at dawn, returning the same evening. They had an amusing story to recount: a self-declared guide had led them to an old house where, expecting no doubt a large tip from these visitors so interested in Hugo, he showed them a study which he claimed was the very study in which the writer had composed his famous play. He perhaps did not know, as his visitors did, that Victor Hugo had done no more than glimpse the Spanish village on passing through it as a child of ten – its name had made an impression on him but he had never returned.

Rostand found the visit to Hernani moving and inspiring. Within a few days he had composed a long, evocative poem, "Un Soir à Hernani". Unlike his earlier "pièce de circonstance", "A L'Impératrice", this more personal poem, full of his admiration for Hugo, won immediate acclaim. It was written mainly in alexandrines, but with "poems within the poem" – a virtuoso performance, with allusions to Hugo's own works throughout. As usual, Rostand makes concrete his ideas, setting them in the context of his own visit to Hernani. He evokes the impression made by the town, the first Spanish town he had seen, on the young Hugo, "a marvellous child whose soul is full of stars". Rostand's own youthful enthusiasm for romanesque Spain infuses the poem, which ends on a prayer to his great predecessor:

> *Souris, Père d'un siècle, aux humbles fils d'une heure!*
> *Que quelque chose, en nous, de ce grand jour demeure!*
> *Donne-nous le courage et donne-nous la foi*
> *Qu'il nous faut pour oser travailler après toi...*
> Smile, Father of a century, on the humble sons of one hour!
> May something of this great day remain in us!
> Give us the courage and give us the faith
> that we need to dare to work after you.

Rostand's sincerity and lyricism give the poem a depth and an emotion which won the hearts of its readers. It was published in *Le Gaulois* on the 4th March 1902.[24] Congratulatory letters and telegrams were not slow to arrive. Sarah, who had known Hugo in his old age and had acted Doña Sol for him, wrote: "Friend, your genius has magnificently celebrated the genius of Victor Hugo"; Catulle Mendès was full of joy: "How beautiful it is, how charming, how powerful, tender, exquisite, and sublime ... I am very proud of my love for you". Léon Daudet, son of Alphonse, who had much admired Rostand, was moved to write not one but two articles for *Le Soleil*, as well as sending Edmond a telegram: "I shall always be on the side of those who reawaken in us the sense of heroism and the taste for beauty and harmony".[25]

At Cambo, the Rostands' life had settled again into its usual gentle rhythm. Both Edmond and Rosemonde were happy there; he, because he loved the countryside and climate of Cambo, and because he was free there from the demands of society and his fame; she, because she no longer had to share her husband with the charming Parisian ladies who so admired him. And in the country, she did not have to wear the latest fashions to please her elegant husband, but could dress as simply as she wished.[26] The way of life at Etchegorria was free and easy. One visitor even found the maid doing the ironing in the salon![27]

But fame continued to impinge on life at Cambo in the form of the huge amount of post Rostand continued to receive. He could not bear to let people down, when they had written to him for help or to share their thoughts with him, and he took immense pains with his replies. But the sheer volume of letters and requests for autographs threatened to overwhelm him, and was keeping him from his real work of writing plays and poetry. Eventually he decided to appoint a secretary, and was lucky enough to find Louis Labat, a journalist and writer from Bayonne. Intelligent, good-humoured, full of energy, Labat was well-known in local literary circles. He quickly became far more than a secretary, he became a close friend, and would be chosen by Rostand as one of his executors.

In addition to his other duties, Labat immediately began learning Latin in order to teach it to Rostand's sons. Maurice and Jean were being educated at home. The governess Miss Day taught them English, while other teachers were recruited from Bayonne, including, to the great excitement of the boys, a fencing teacher. As duels were still being fought in Paris, self-defence could be thought of as a necessary skill. But their father's admiration for the Three Musketeers is just as likely to have played a part in the decision to teach Maurice and Jean how to use foils, swords and even sabres! Maurice notes wryly that these skills were never needed.[28]

Now that Rostand's health was fully restored, he bought a white Arab mare, Zobéïde, and began to explore the countryside around Cambo. Rosemonde, ever protective of her husband, insisted he always be accompanied by a groom: while Edmond's mind was on his work, he might let his horse wander anywhere and get lost.

Edmond's walks during his convalescence had never taken him much beyond the park at Cambo. Now he was able to roam further afield, seeing and hearing with a poet's eyes and ears the delights of the lush, rain-drenched countryside of the Basses Pyrénées. On his return, he would often recount his travels to Paul Faure, who was impressed by his sensibility and powers of observation. "Nothing escaped him about this countryside whose charm is not revealed immediately, which only lets itself be understood little by little. ... All the poetry of nature had suddenly entered him. He was delighted ... as if he had acquired another treasure for his poetic soul."[29]

On his wanderings through the countryside, Edmond's mind was on his work. He had put aside, for the moment, his plan to write about Don Quichotte, and was instead concentrating on *Polichinelle*. But as he passed a farmyard near his home one day, he stopped to look at the animals. As he watched the hens strutting about, the sleeping cat, the dog roaming round, and all the usual inhabitants going about their business just as humans would, he suddenly saw the cockerel enter "fier, dominateur, avec du dédain dans son regard ..." (He enters, imperious, proud, with disdain in his look and in the rhythmic movement of his head, and something heroic and irresistible in his walk. He advances like a swordsman, you'd have thought him a man looking for amorous or deadly adventures, or a king amongst his subjects ... There was general excitement! ... Really, there were arguments about this cockerel.)[30]

Suddenly it seemed to Edmond that here was the subject of a play. He had a vision of how it would look on stage, the birds and animals behaving just as he saw them in the farmyard, but they would be expressing human ideas and emotions. He went back several times to the farm, called Miremont, and the action of the play took shape rapidly in his mind. The cockerel would be his hero, a typically Rostandian hero: a poet, of course: idealistic, proud, protector of the weak and champion of the light and the sun. An ideal – and apposite – role for Coquelin, "le Grand Coq"!

On his wanderings, Rostand was now alert for images for his play. But he was also looking for a suitable plot of land on which to build a house. He and Rosemonde had agreed that they did not wish to live again in Paris. The frenetic atmosphere, the enviousness of other less successful writers, the constant pressure, was exhausting and prevented Edmond from doing what he most wanted to do: write plays. They both liked the Basque countryside, the mild and sunny climate, the quiet life. They would sell their house in the rue Alphonse-de-Neuville and maybe buy just a small pied-a-terre for their visits to the capital. But their real home would be here, in the Basque country. They would find a lovely setting and create for themselves a house and garden of their own where their sons could grow up and Edmond could concentrate undisturbed on his writing.

One day Rostand called unexpectedly on Paul Faure. He was jubilant. "I've found just the place", he cried, "Come and see!" The two men drove in Edmond's carriage along the road to Bayonne and stopped near a farm called "Les Trois Croix". Here they got out and struggled up the hillside through the brambles and bracken. At last they stood on the flat top of a spur between two river valleys. All around lay the rolling Basque countryside, with its green fields, tranquil flocks of sheep and white farmhouses. To one side of the spur lay the valley of the Nive, with its villages: Halsou, Jaxtrou, Ustaritz, Larresore. To the other rose line after line of wooded hills and beyond, the blue wavering line of the Spanish Pyrenee. It was the perfect spot for Rostand's house. Unfortunately, however, the land belonged to three different people. Rostand asked Dr Juanchuto, a well-known local figure, to negotiate on his behalf.

Meanwhile the reception speech for the Académie française was still unfinished. In fact by early spring Rostand had only, as he joked to Paul Faure, written one word of it: "Messieurs". His absorption in his land and his new play made him further postpone the writing of the speech, and his reception was put off for another year.

In Paris, Coq was again playing Cyrano during April and May. But in the United States, a farcical situation had arisen that would keep *Cyrano de Bergerac* off the stage there for almost twenty years. In 1899 an American playwright, Samuel Eberly Gross, claimed that Rostand had borrowed ideas for *Cyrano de Bergerac*, notably the balcony scene in Act Three, from Gross's own unsuccessful play *The Merchant Prince of Cornville*. Gross claimed Rostand must have read the English script he had left at the Porte-Saint-Martin theatre in 1889 and at the Comédie-Française in early 1897.

Rostand thought the claim so risible (he wrote a witty letter to *Le Temps* in which he admitted having borrowed the whole of the seventeenth century from M. Eberly Gross of Chicago) that he did not take it very seriously. Neither did Richard Mansfield, the actor who held the American rights and had been performing as Cyrano in the English version. Gross filed a lawsuit for breach of copyright against Mansfield in Chicago, but, fearing the case would go to New York, where he thought he would lose, he offered to reduce the damages he was claiming from $50,00 to $1 plus costs if Mansfield would not defend the case. In view of the high costs inevitable whether he won or lost, Mansfield agreed. After a preliminary hearing in June 1899, the Supreme Court of Illinois had no option, the case being undefended, but to give judgement three years later in Gross's favour.[31] The press of Paris, New York and London were scathing in their comments. "Gross has ruthlessly torn off the laurels from M. Rostand's brow and clapped them on his own" wrote the Chicago Tribune.[32] "The charm of *Cyrano de Bergerac* is the soul breathed into it by the poet", proclaimed the Mayor of Chicago in the same paper four days later. But this could not change the verdict of the courts. Gross was awarded an injunction preventing *Cyrano de Bergerac* from ever being performed again on the American stage! This would not be overturned until 1920. Coquelin could no longer tour the United States as Cyrano and would take the play to South America instead.

At the beginning of June, Maurice, now aged eleven, was to take his first communion. Rosemonde made extravagant preparations for what became a major local event. There is a sign here of the attachment between Rosemonde and Maurice, which would become stronger with the years. Jean, ressembling Edmond in his fierce but silent passions, was more devoted to his father, and as a small boy, turned for maternal affection to his nurse, Adeline Delpech, whom he kept with him, even after his marriage, until her death in 1939.

On 15th July 1902 the deeds of sale for the plot where Rostand wanted to build were finally signed. He immediately started to get the site cleared of scrub and brambles. Rostand had already decided to call his new home after the stream running round the base of the hill, the Arraga. But as this sounded rather too harsh, Rostand softened its name to "Arnaga". His new home and his new play were to absorb all Rostand's creative energy for the next seven years.

On Coquelin's next visit, Rostand told him of his idea. Coq, who had been expecting either a *Don Quichotte* or a *Polichinelle*, was rather surprised he would play neither of these eponymous heroes, but a bird! But he was delighted that his poet was writing a new play for him. Rostand made Coquelin promise to mention the play to no one, as he knew the papers would seize on the idea and probably ridicule it before it was even written.

Edmond was able to greet the New Year of 1903 with satisfaction: he had at last finished his "Discours de Réception" for the Académie française, and a date had been set for the ceremony: Thursday 4th June. Now he could concentrate on his new play and his new house. Hervieu, who had done so much to get Rostand elected to the Academy, wrote to him that January "I wish this poet and sage's house was finished so that you only had to meditate on plans of works that are winged, considerable and destined for the universe."[33]

But for Edmond, Arnaga too was to be a work of art, a creation into which he would put as much of himself as into his plays. He wanted to make it as beautiful as possible, a fitting home for the family of a poet. He spent every evening after dinner drawing up plans, but soon realised he would need an architect. His father recommended Albert Tournaire, who had worked on the family bank and won a prize at the 1900 Exhibition.

Tournaire came to visit the Rostands and was shown the sketches Rostand had made so far. Rostand envisaged a Basque-style house that would fit naturally into the landscape. But his house also had to be large enough for entertaining his guests in style, a splendid house worthy of a poet. Tournaire spent several days touring the countryside round Cambo, and finally offered to design for the Rostands a much larger than usual Basque farmhouse, with typical vernacular features. He then returned to Paris to draw up the detailed design. If he expected Rostand to leave the rest to him, he was mistaken. The plans he sent Rostand returned with annotations and sketches. The two continued to exchange plans and ideas almost every day. Arnaga was to be Rostand's own artistic creation and he wanted it to embody his own ideas, down to the smallest details.

Jean Rostand remembered many happy evenings spent at Etchegorria after dinner, with his father poring over his plans and sketches, spread out on the table. As the work of designing the house progressed, Rostand made exquisite little models out of cardboard. Silk paper was used for the windows, matches for the beams and window-mullions, while the doors were made out of cigar box lids.

In March 1903, the first stone was laid to form the wall of the garden terrace. The garden would be built first, as it would take time for building materials for the house to arrive. Edmond was now going almost every day to the site, where a team of workmen was already engaged in clearing the plateau of scrub and levelling it ready for the garden. His house, at the far end of the plateau, would overlook the confluence of the Nive with the Arraga, and have its back to the prevailing westerly winds. Its windows would face east, across a formal

French garden, with ornamental ponds and flowerbeds, to the blue Pyrenees beyond.

Meanwhile in Paris excitement was growing over the poet's reception to the Academy. There was some criticism of Rostand for not returning immediately to the capital. But Rostand was busy correcting a new edition of the proofs of *La Samaritaine*, which was about to be published. (At the same time, Sarah was recording excerpts from the play for the HMV Gramophone Company.) And Coquelin had asked Edmond for a poem for a gala charity performance to raise funds for the retirement home for actors he planned to set up at his country retreat just outside Paris. Rostand responded with "Le Verger".[34]

The departure for Paris was further delayed when in March Mme Lee was taken ill with pleurisy. So it was not until 3rd of May that the Rostand family and their entourage finally left for Paris by train. It was so hot in the compartment that Rostand seriously thought of abandoning the trip until the weather changed. On their arrival at sunset at the Gare d'Orsay they found crowds of journalists awaiting them. The ultra-modern Hôtel d'Orsay, chosen by Rosemonde for its closeness to the station and the Académie française, was gained with difficulty.

A hectic three weeks followed. Labat, who had arrived the day before, greeted the poet with a huge heap of letters to answer. The telephone never stopped ringing. Friends and relations called, selected photographers and journalists were admitted, while others less fortunate lay in wait in the corridors or by the hotel entrance. Edmond submitted to the demands of his fame. He was amused by reports that he had asked a fashionable tailor to display his uniform in the window, but annoyed when it was reported that he had smiled disdainfully at the mention of Henri de Bornier, whose seat he was to take in the Academy, and that he had spoken badly of Porto-Riche, a successful contemporary dramatist whom in fact he admired. Such invented stories against Rostand were to become more and more frequent.

A certain excitement was caused at the end of May by the appearance in *La Nouvelle Revue* of lines purporting to be Rostand's first attempts to write his Discours de Reception, in verse. The poem spoke of "le rythme immortel de la mer" which brought "l'arôme des lauriers et des myrtes d'Athènes" to Edmond when a child in Marseilles (the eternal rhythm of the sea [bringing] the scent of the laurels and the myrtles of Athens). Reproduced in nearly all the papers, the poem delighted Rostand's admirers; Jules Claretie wrote a whole article in *Le Figaro*[35] praising it in detail. What was his embarrassment the following morning to discover that the poem was a pastiche by Willy.[36]

Meanwhile preparations for the Reception were going ahead. The secretary of the Academy had been overwhelmed by the demand for seats. There were over five thousand requests for places, and only one thousand five hundred people were eventually admitted, far too many for comfort, even so. The day before the reception, unallocated tickets went on sale at midday. By 3.00 pm these were changing hands for more than twenty francs, and were soon unobtainable at any price.

At dawn on the morning of the Reception, the courtyard of the Academy was already full of people who had been queuing since the previous evening. Those who could afford it had sent their servants to keep their places; soldiers were keeping order. Meanwhile, at the Hotel d'Orsay, the Rostands' apartment was so full of flowers that they were being stacked wherever there was room, even on the floor. Maurice and Jean, over-excited, ran shouting from room to room. Suddenly amidst the hubbub, the voices of hucksters were heard in the street outside. They were selling copies of Rostand's speech for two sous, even before he had spoken it! Luckily the boys were making so much noise that Rostand did not discover this till later. As it was, he had "le trac" (stage fright). After all, when he had written his plays, he had then handed his work over to others to speak his lines for him. Now any success depended on himself alone.

June 4th was a fine day, the sunshine lighting up the sombre interior of the Académie française. The doors opened at one o'clock and those fortunate enough to have tickets poured in. The cream of Parisian society was there, including the queen of the aristocracy, the Countess de Greffulhe, "slender as a dragonfly" in black; *mondaines* and even *demi-mondaines*; actresses, too, not normally seen in such numbers in these austere surroundings. Literature and politics were also well-represented. Edmond's friend Paul Faure took his seat in plenty of time and hardly dared move for fear of losing the few inches of bench he had managed to secure. Jules Renard and Le Bargy were high up in the amphitheatre.

When Rosemonde made her entrance with her two sons, both rather over-awed in their smart velvet suits, the assembled company gave her an ovation. In her summery silk dress, white with hand-painted roses, and fresh-faced from living in the country, Rosemonde looked, thought Jules Renard, like a young English girl. Next to her sat Sarah, whose large hat with green feathers was not appreciated by those behind. Coquelin, too, was there, having returned on purpose from abroad, happy to see his young friend receiving such an honour. Pascau was making sketches of the family and the audience.

A stir went through the chamber as the academicians themselves entered. Edmond's father Eugène, was among them, as a member of the Académie des Sciences morales et politiques. He was seated next to Hervieu, in a place of honour. His son would pay him a moving tribute in the speech to come.

Finally Edmond himself came onto the stage, flanked by his two sponsors, Paul Hervieu and Jules Claretie (taking the place of Ludovic Halévy). Elegant in his tightly belted academician's green uniform, his ceremonial sword (a present from Hervieu) by his side, he was greeted by warm applause. This seemed to put him at his ease, and with his right hand resting on the lectern, he began to deliver his speech with all the aplomb and skill that he had shown at the reception at the Collège de Stanislas. "He captured his audience from his first words", noted Renard in his diary. Rosemonde, who knew the speech by heart, followed the words with her lips; Sarah applauded continually, her hat nodding in time to "her" poet's cadences.

By tradition, the new academician must give a speech extolling his predecessor. In Rostand's case, this was Henri de Bornier, whose patriotic verse drama, *La Fille de Roland*, had given France new hope after the defeat by the Prussians in 1871. In masterly fashion, Rostand wove into his praise of Bornier all his own passion and hopes for the theatre. He was not going to waste this wonderful opportunity to influence "le tout Paris". As he had at Stanislas, he used his speech to attack the cynical attitudes of his day, and to exalt idealism and enthusiasm. He deplored the fact that in modern times the theatre had degenerated into a mere "jeu de société"; actors often gave the lie to the sublime verses they were declaiming by winking at the audience, and audiences themselves were more interested in the actors than in the characters they were representing. Spectators had forgotten that the theatre had sacred origins, and was still a place where the power of imagination could lift them above the everyday.

For even in modern Paris, the theatre still had a sacred dimension: "there is hardly anywhere else except at the theatre where souls, side by side, can feel they have wings". (Ce n'est plus guère qu'au théâtre que les âmes, côte à côte, peuvent se sentir des ailes.) The theatre had the power to unite the spectators and arouse in them noble, heroic and patriotic enthusiasm: "There are words which, spoken before people gathered together, have the quality of a prayer; there are thrills experienced together which are equal to a victory, and this is why the wind that comes from the luminous blue depths of the stage … can cause flags to flutter).[37]

Passion and enthusiasm had been devalued in modern times, continued Rostand, to be replaced by banter and cynicism, the knowing smile, an ironic remark. Rostand exhorted his hearers: "Il faut réhabiliter la passion. Et meme l'émotion, qui n'est pas ridicule…" (We must rehabilitate passion, and even emotion, which is not ridiculous; it is time to remind these timid French people that a resolute eye can express modern sensibility perfectly well.)

Edmond was leading up to his main point: "And that is why we need a theatre where, inspiring us with beauty, consoling us with grace, poets, without doing it on purpose, give us lessons for the soul ("leçons d'âme"). That is why we need a theatre which is not only poetic, but heroic!" For only a hero – here Rostand digressed to tell his audience about his own boyhood hero, the larger-than-life Colonel Villebois-Mareuil – only a hero can take us out of everyday life, only to return us there refreshed and exhilarated.

Just as in the theatre an experienced dramatist, having brought the audience to a pitch of enthusiasm, closes with a quieter scene, Rostand now gently brought his hearers back to themselves with a few remarks about the close of Henri de Bornier's life. Then he sat down, to tremendous applause. He had been speaking for almost an hour.

When the applause finally died away, the Vicomte de Vogüé rose to pronounce the speech of welcome on behalf of the Academicians.[18] The president of the Academy then formally declared the ceremony at an end. The Rostand family emerged into the sunlight of the courtyard of the Académie to the cheers of a huge crowd, and were driven away with Claretie and Hervieu in an open carriage to the fashionable pâtissier Boissier for a celebratory tea. Some time later, when Paul Faure returned to the hotel apartment, he found the new academician alone, still in his official uniform, and amusing himself by trying to balance, point down on his index finger, his ceremonial sword.

The next few weeks were crowded with interviews, photographers, and hopeful advertisers eager to capitalise on Rostand's popularity. Rostand's image, in his academician's uniform, stared out at passers-by from the covers of magazines and from postcards. He was invited to the presidential palace; officially inspected the new Victor Hugo museum in the place des Vosges, and attended, with Rosemonde, parties given by Adolphe Brisson, now drama critic for *Le Temps*. On the 26th, he lunched with his publisher Fasquelle. There was plenty to celebrate. Three thousand copies of Rostand's speech had been published. Rostand's "Discours de Réception" was one of the very few such speeches ever to interest the general public. As for *Cyrano de Bergerac*, it was in its two-hundred and fifty thousandth printing, while *L'Aiglon* was in its hundred and ninety-fifth thousand. Nor would these be the last printings.

Amidst all the adulation of the poet, there was one sour note. The poet Jehan Rictus published a malicious brochure, in which he accused the poet of neglecting his duty to the poor and disadvantaged by not writing about their hard lives. Oblivious of Edmond's idealistic mission, Rictus claimed that Edmond's only reason for writing was to make money. Unaware of Rostand's personal generosity and his sympathy for socialist ideals, Rictus threatened him with the revenge of the proletariat.[39]

This publication was too exaggerated to be taken seriously by the poet. But it was symptomatic of the maliciousness of some of his contemporaries. Writers who were envious of Rostand's success were all too ready to believe, or pretend to believe, the worst of him. Émile Bergerat, for instance, whose own uninspired poetic dramas continued to flop, was to remark to Renard later that year, "Oh! Dame, je n'ai pas, comme Rostand, 30,000 francs à donner pour qu'on reprenne *Les Romanesques* à la Comédie-Française" (my goodness! I haven't got 30,000 francs like Rostand has, to get the Comédie-Française to revive *Les Romanesques*).[40]

The Rostands were not sorry to leave behind the gossip and other pressures of Paris. Rosemonde was also eager to get back to her mother, whose health had again deteriorated. On 27th June, after seeing Coquelin once again perform as Cyrano de Bergerac, the Rostand family returned to Cambo.

Je pense à la lumière et non pas à la gloire!
I am thinking about the light, not about fame!
– (*Chantecler*, Act II, sc. iii)

If the Rostands had slipped quietly into Etchegorria on their first arrival, this time it was not possible. The whole of Cambo had turned out to welcome the poet. As Rostand and his family drove from the station in their open landau under triumphal arches, bands played and the crowds cheered. It was indeed a heartfelt welcome from the local inhabitants to the poet who was making his home among them.

From now until 1910, Rostand's attention would be divided between two major projects, equally dear to his heart. He had always preferred to work on two plays simultaneously, relaxing from work on one by turning to the other. But now, only one of his projects was a play: the other was his new house and garden at Arnaga.

Rostand now settled into a routine "for the first time in his life", according to his friend Paul Faure. (This "routine" probably did not last long. When Rostand was absorbed in writing a new play, he would work all day and often into the night.) In the morning, he would go for a walk, either on his own or with Faure, in the Allée of Cambo, often stopping to exchange a few friendly words with the local people, who were now used to him, unlike the tourists from Biarritz who stared and even took his photograph without asking permission. There would also be time to read the main Paris papers and the latest books. After lunch with the family, Rostand would retire to his room to write. Then, sometimes in the company of Paul Faure, he would ride out to Arnaga to see how his house was progressing.

In the evenings after dinner, his favourite form of relaxation was to draw and colour little sketches of stage settings or the actors' costumes for his play. Or, if Arnaga was uppermost in his mind, he might design some new feature of his house. If inspiration caught Rostand's imagination before the end of the meal, he had been known to draw on the tablecloth, in ink, to the amusement of his family and the horror of the servants. Besides adorning his notes, letters and manuscripts with little illustrations, Rostand also had a talent for portraiture. This first became evident when he made a quick pencil sketch of Tournaire, who was visiting Etchegorria. From then on, Rostand often amused himself, when his work had gone well, by sketching his family and friends.[41]

But there were times when work did not go well, and after a sleepless night, Edmond would shut himself in his room and refuse to see anyone. He would not even open his post. At such times, woe betide any visitor who hoped to see him, however important. On one such day, a government minister who was staying at nearby Biarritz called on Rostand. Rosemonde, knowing the poet was in one of his black moods, grabbed a glass of water and some pills from somewhere as she came to greet the minister. "I'm afraid Edmond has a terrible migraine, but I'll tell him you're here", she said. But upstairs, Rostand's voice could be heard loudly exclaiming "Je m'en fous!" (I don't give a damn!). The minister was understanding. "Genius is excused everything", he said, and departed.[42]

On Tournaire's frequent visits from Paris, Edmond would spend all day with him, either at the site or at home, poring over plans. The clearing of the plateau and layout of the formal garden were proceeding well. Edmond had been able to buy locally some fourteen-year-old lime trees. Plane trees, cypresses and yews would soon join them.

When Edmond's parents arrived for a brief visit in the summer, they were amazed at the scale of Rostand's project. But such was Rostand's prestige that the project would be finished in an unusually short time for such a huge enterprise, thanks to the goodwill of those working on it.

Simultaneously, Rostand was working on his new play. Edmond had now decided on its title: *Chantecler*, after the cockerel in the medieval French classic, *Le Roman de Renart*. The plot was a simple one: Chantecler, the cockerel, is famous throughout the countryside for the brilliance of his crowing, due, it is said, to a secret. Chantecler, like Rostand's other heroes, is also a poet: the hymn he sings to the sun has become one of those poems known to all French school-children. One day a golden pheasant rushes into his farmyard to escape from a hunter. It turns out to be a female who has exchanged domesticity and her usual drab colours for the male pheasant's glorious plumage and independence. Chantecler falls in love with her and, hoping to win her heart, tells her his secret: it is his cry that causes the sun to rise every morning over their valley!

But a conspiracy is forming against the cock by the animals who hate the light and prefer the darkness, which conceals their misdeeds. They arrange a contest between Chantecler and a fighting cockerel who will surely kill him. The contest is to take place at the guinea-fowl's salon, her "Five o'clock". *Chantecler* survives the fight. Disillusioned by the way even the animals in his own farmyard turned against him, out of envy, he still intends to do his duty living amongst them. But finding he can no longer crow properly in their presence,[43] he agrees to go and live with the pheasant in the forest. Here he learns to see through the flattery of the toads and to appreciate the song of the nightingale. Enchanted, he listens to her song as the night begins to end. The pheasant, jealous because Chantecler puts the sun and his duty before his love for her, does not alert him to the coming dawn. He fails to crow in time and the sun rises without him.

The pheasant thinks she will now be able to keep him in the forest with her for ever. But Chantecler, disillusioned but not cynical, says she will never be able to come before his duty; he must continue to sing in praise of the light. He leaves to return to the farmyard. A shot is heard. The pheasant realises that she loves Chantecler. In trying to distract the hunter from him, she is caught in a net. She resigns herself to living in captivity with him in the farmyard, and to taking second place behind his duty to the sun.

Chantecler was already in Rostand's mind when he was writing his *Discours de Réception*. Like the poet's earlier plays, *Chantecler* is a "leçon d'âme", a lesson for the soul. The light of the sun, symbol of the Ideal, and the sacredness of duty, are the two main themes of the play, and they are linked by the figure of Chantecler himself. Chantecler believes it is his duty to crow every morning to make the sun rise, so that light will banish the darkness, which hides wrongdoing; the sun reveals the beauty of nature, and enables daily life to continue. Chantecler is totally committed to his vocation and adores the light-giving sun. His idealism is contrasted with the worldly attitudes of those around him.

In his cockerel hero, Rostand was again portraying himself. Both are poets, with poets' hearts and imaginations. But most of all, Chantecler's devotion to his work and his duty of bringing light to banish the darkness of materialism and cynicism, is what Rostand felt to be his own duty. And Rostand, too, had experienced the malice of his enemies and the envy of those who formerly praised him. Both Chantecler and

Edmond experience disillusion with regard to their former success. The temptation is then to give up one's God-given task: the task of singing at sunrise or trying to give "leçons d'âme" in the theatre. But both resist this and return, wiser from their experiences, to their work.

Chantecler is the most personal of all Rostand's plays. His cockerel's lyrical speeches convey his own idealistic attitude to life:

> *Je pense à la lumière et non pas à la gloire!*
> *Chanter c'est ma façon de me battre et de croire.*
> I am thinking about the light, not about fame!
> Singing is my way of fighting and having faith.
> – (Act II, sc. iii)

Contrary to what their enemies claim, Rostand and his cockerel do not sing for their own aggrandisement, they sing because that is their vocation. And they sing in the only way they know how: "I dare to give my song as a rosebush gives its roses", says Chantecler when questioned as to his "schéma dynamique". ("As an apple tree gives apples", Rostand had said of himself.[41]) He does not know how he sings, only why. Nor can poets change their song, even though they may think another's song is superior, as Chantecler feels when he hears the nightingale. "Nul … N'a tout à fait le chant qu'il rêverait d'avoir!" the nightingale comforts him. "No one has exactly the song they dream of having. You must go on singing, singing even when you know that there are other songs you prefer to your own." Rostand writes poetry in the only way he knows how, and is not claiming to be better than other writers, whom he may even think superior. .

Likewise Chantecler's despair, once he has, as he thinks, caused the sun to rise, is Rostand's own. Rostand, like Chantecler, is modest, though both present a proud front to the world.

> *Je me trouve indigne de ma gloire.*
> *Pourquoi m'a-t-on choisi pour chasser la nuit noire?*
> …
> *Comment! Moi, si petit, j'ai fait l'aurore immense?*
> *Et, l'ayant faite, il faut que je recommence?*
> *Mais je ne pourrai jamais! Je suis au désespoir!*

I am unworthy of my fame.
Why was I chosen to chase away the dark night?
…
What, I, so small, I brought about the vast dawn?
And having brought it about, I have to do it again?
But I'll never be able to! I am in despair!
– (Act II, sc. iii)

This desperate cry expresses Rostand's anguish before the public's and the critics' high expectations of him after the success of *Cyrano de Bergerac.* He cannot be sure of the inspiration he needs in order to create, and he also lacks the energy for sustained creation. For inspiration alone is not enough. To do one's work well, it must come from the heart. "Moi, je chante en m'ouvrant le coeur", Chantecler tells the cynical blackbird. "I sing by opening my heart. Do you know what it costs me?"

Work demands great effort, but it alone makes life worth living. And work is a sacred duty:

L'effort! Qui rend sacré le plus infime!
Effort! Which makes the tiniest [creature] sacred!
– (Act II, sc. v)

The sacred nature of work was a constant theme of Rostand's from his earliest poems. Commitment to one's work can dignify the humblest calling. This is why, to the surprise of the Pheasant, Chantecler is content to live in the farmyard and fulfil his duty to its animals and to the inhabitants of his own small valley, for whom he causes the sun to rise. "I can tell you have a soul", she sighs "but can a soul be formed, then, far from life and its drama?" (On sent que vous avez une âme, mais une âme Se forme donc loin de la vie et son drame…?). One can almost hear the accents of Rostand's friends here – how can he prefer to live in the country, far from Paris? Chantecler's reply is the same as Rostand's :

Quand on sait regarder et souffrir, on sait tout.
Dans une mort d'insecte on voit tous les désastres.
Un rond d'azur suffit pour voir passer les astres.

When you know how to look and how to suffer, you know everything.
You can see all disasters in the death of an insect.
A circle of sky is enough to see the stars pass by.
– (Act I, sc. vi)

Chantecler and Rostand find their surroundings full of beauty and interest, because of the sunlight, which continually alters the appearance of even the most ordinary things. "As for me, I never get over the luxury of these things ... nothing is ever the same beneath the sun, because of the sun. For It changes everything!" An ordinary life lived by the light of a great ideal, such as Rostand and his hero aim to lead, is made glorious just as the earth is transformed by the light of the sun.

Rostand was a true southerner. Born in Marseilles, he needed and adored the sun. Perhaps this is why he found it such a potent symbol. The theme of light and sunshine inspired some of Rostand's most poetic and moving verse. The Hymn to the Sun ("Je t'adore, Soleil! ... toi sans qui les choses Ne seraient que ce qu'elles sont!" (I adore you, O Sun... you without whom things would only be what they are) (Act I, sc. 2), is well-known, but there are other equally lyrical passages, especially in the scene where Chantecler believes he is making the sun rise. Here he is explaining to the Pheasant that when he crows to make the sun rise, he feels he himself becomes the means by which the yearning of the earth for the sun expresses itself:

Et ce cri qui monte de la Terre,
Ce cri, c'est un tel cri d'amour pour la lumière,
...
Enfin, c'est tellement le cri vers la clarté
De toute la Beauté, de toute la Santé,
...
Mon chant jailli si net, si fier, si péremptoire,
Que l'horizon, saisi d'un rose tremblement,
M'obéit!

And this cry which rises from the Earth,
this cry is such a cry of love for the light,
it's such a furious roar of love for that golden thing,
the Day, which all things desire to have again:
the paths bumpy with twisted roots under their moss;
the oats with their delicate heads, and the smallest pebbles,
right down to their smallest grains of mica
…
In fact, it's such a cry towards the light
from everything beautiful and healthy,
…
when I feel this vast call to the daylight rising within me,
I enlarge my soul so that,
being more spacious, it becomes more sonorous,
and so that this huge cry can get even bigger there,
…
then my song leaps out so clear, so proud, so peremptory,
that the horizon, seized with a pink trembling,
obeys me!
– (Act II, sc. iii)

Chantecler could not have been written if Rostand had stayed in
Paris. Cambo and its countryside had revived his love of nature. Like
Chantecler, he is again full of wonder at the beauty of the world. He
delights in even the smallest creatures: the fly – "la petite musique où
bourdonne un coeur" (the small song of a humming heart); the frail
pink snail – "trying all on its own to cover a twig with silver". He had
become what the French call "un poète du Terroir". Rostand now felt
that the Basque countryside was his home. This corner of France was
now as dear to him as France itself. Throughout the play, not only the
speeches, but also especially the Prologue and the stage directions (in
sonnet form), describe in detail the sights and sounds of a landscape
familiar to the poet. And the forest where Chantecler goes to live in
peace with the Pheasant in Act Four, "the green refuge sought by all
disappointed hearts" (l'asile vert cherché par tous les coeurs deçus), is
Rostand's home at Cambo.

In *Chantecler*, the humble, ordinary, country life of daily duties and
simple pleasures is contrasted favourably with the "modern spirit" which
Rostand detested and strove against in all his plays, but particularly

here. Nowhere else, except in his *Discours de réception*, does he criticise quite so directly what he saw as the snobbish and increasingly cynical attitudes, mocking all idealism, which he had experienced again recently in Paris.

The minor characters personify contemporary Parisian types: at the guinea fowl's "Five O'clock", the peacock, "the arbiter of fashion", shows off, using unusual or obsolete words which make the salon guests swoon with admiration. For the brainless guinea fowl, the desire to have a splendid salon is her main reason for living: the more exotic and foreign the guests the better. As for the pedantic turkey, he is so obsessed with his own importance that he hates Chantecler simply because he is now adult and cannot be bossed around.

The blackbird (*le merle*), is a more complex character. Chantecler tolerates him more than the others, as he is at least intelligent, and claims to be his friend. But the blackbird misuses his quick mind, making continual facetious remarks that infuriate Patou the farm dog: honest, loyal, idealistic and Chantecler's only true friend. The blackbird models himself on his own idea of a Parisian sparrow and calls himself "le titi du poulailler" (the gamin of the farmyard). His speech is full of slang words, because it is chic to be loutish. But Patou can see the danger to public morals that the blackbird and the peacock represent:

> Their mission is to extinguish love and work; they have brought to us here in the golden light those two scourges which are the saddest in the world: the remark which always has to be a witty remark, and the fashion which always has to be the latest fashion. – (Act I, sc. iv)

And their bad example is already having an effect, says Patou. "Every day I hear hearts and vocabulary becoming more debased."

In the forest of Act Four, in contrast to the artificial conversation and frenzied attempts to be sophisticated in the farmyard, life is lived naturally and each day begins and ends with a prayer. Yet even here, there are enemies of beauty and truth: the toads, who praise Chantecler extravagantly, telling him his song is superior to the nightingale's. Chantecler is at first flattered, but when he hears the nightingale for

himself, he realises they are only praising him because they are envious
of her beautiful song.

The nightingale sings in the night but is a creature of light. She
is the heart of the evening, the voice of love, "la Chanson Éternelle"
(the title of one of Rosemonde's best-known poems). Chantecler has
a high ideal of love. He stops the Coq Cochinchinois from telling
scandalous stories in the guinea-fowl's salon because they "revolt his
love of Love". His love for the pheasant is made stronger and nobler by
his love for the light and his duty to the Dawn. "Il n'est de grand amour
qu'à l'ombre d'un grand rêve" he tells her, in an echo of *La Princesse
lointaine* (there is no great love except in the shadow of a great dream).
But the pheasant wants to be Chantecler's only love, and is jealous of
Chantecler's devotion to the sun.

Chantecler comes to see the pheasant a threat to his work. "You
still remain a female for whom ideas are always the great adversary!"
Rostand would explore the same theme in "Les Douze Travaux", a
poem based on the story of Hercules and Omphale, which he would
write in 1909. The idea that woman, with her need for an emotional
relationship, is a distraction for a man from his own ideals and heroic
enterprises, was in the air at the time.[45]

But the strong sensual side of Rostand's own personality affected
his attitude to his female characters. Rostand the man was very much
attracted by feminine charms. He therefore depicted woman as a
temptress, distracting a man, if he was not careful, from his work. In
La Princesse lointaine and *La Samaritaine*, the heroines are both, at the
beginning of the play, sensual women whose beauty is capable of either
inspiring a man to higher ideals or tempting him away from his duty. By
the end of the play both Mélissinde and Photine have learnt to prefer a
nobler attitude to love, taught by the example of the hero (Rudel, Jesus).
In *Chantecler*, too, the heroine would finally be "redeemed" by her love
for Chantecler. The pheasant represents "the New Woman" who was
appearing in Britain and France: independent, proud, and treating
men as equals (like his friend Simone, who would eventually portray
her). But she is finally willing to give up her independence and live in

the farmyard in order to be with Chantecler. As Chantecler insists on doing his duty, she will do hers.

Although Rostand portrays this struggle between the higher (i.e. spiritual) and lower (i.e. sensual) natures of human beings as a struggle between the sexes, one should not read too much into this. Rostand was no woman-hater; he enjoyed the company of spirited modern women such as Simone. But his talent was for making ideas concrete, and to embody higher feelings in his heroes rather than his heroines perhaps came more naturally to him, being himself a man, and very much aware of feminine powers to tempt a man away from what he saw as his duty.

In writing *Chantecler*, Rostand was taking the risk of alienating his public. This would be a completely different kind of play from his earlier successes. The story was totally imagined, not based on history or legend. He was also expressing his own feelings in a much more direct way, and criticising the manners of his own times quite explicitly. In addition, the problems he was setting himself in making his characters non-human were almost insurmountable: his characters had to think and talk like people, but he wanted their behaviour and appearance to be as realistically animal-like as possible. In the days before cartoon films, this was a novel idea.

Rostand re-read Aristophanes, who had successfully overcome these problems in *The Birds*. The animals of La Fontaine's *Fables*, too, had portrayed human foibles. *Le Roman de Renart*, which had given him a name for his cockerel hero, also inspired him.

No historical research was needed this time. But Rostand, perfectionist that he was, took great pains to be as accurate as possible in his depiction of his animal characters. He acquired a shelf-full of scientific tomes, which included Toussenel's *Le Monde des Oiseaux*, Brehm's *La Vie des Animaux*, *Le Traité de Zootechnie* by Charles Cornevin, Menegaux's *Ornithologie* and the *Animaux domestiques* of Gos de Voogt, with its coloured illustrations. As a child, his son Jean looked respectfully at these books, ranged on a special shelf, but did not dare touch them.

Edmond also obtained, from Deyrolle, a collection of stuffed birds, including pheasants like his heroine the golden pheasant, along with many exotic birds, even ibises and toucans. But he wanted to study from life the birds who would be his characters. So he set up a poultry-yard, with a cockerel, naturally, along with hens, ducks, geese, guinea fowl, pigeons and a blackbird in a cage. Later, at Arnaga, a black swan would swim alongside the white ones on the pond in the formal garden, and for some months the usual inhabitants of the poultry-yard were joined by the exotic cockerels of Act Three.[46] The only bird missing was a golden pheasant – Edmond thought it wrong to keep such a glorious, independent bird imprisoned. The cockerels were packed into baskets every evening and taken off to another villa, named by the family "la villa des coqs", so that they would not wake the poet too early.

Jean Rostand remembered how his father would stand watching the birds' behaviour for long periods, twirling his moustache with a distracted air. The fruits of these musings, and of Edmond's research, are evident in *Chantecler*. At nine years old, Jean was already showing signs of the great biologist he would become. In 1903, he had read an extract from Fabre's *Souvenirs Entomologiques*, and was so enthralled by it that he asked his parents for the full work. Fabre, who lived like a hermit in Provence and had only recently become famous, had devoted his long life to the study of insects. Jean wrote to Fabre and the latter replied, sending Jean some insects to study.

Rostand, too, became fascinated by Fabre, whom he saw as a hero, living only for his work. He later wrote a series of sonnets about him.[47] Although Jean, at this age, was still intimidated by his father, a rather remote presence, he knew that Rostand was glad he was interested in living creatures. It might be going too far to suggest that Jean's love of nature created a bond between two such private individuals, but Edmond did acknowledge their shared interest in a concrete way: *Chantecler* would be dedicated "to my son Jean".

Excited by his ideas, Edmond shut himself in his room and worked on his play, in tandem with his plans for Arnaga. When inspiration was flowing, he would eat lunch in his room. If the work had gone well, he would descend to dinner in good humour, sharing his latest lines with his family. According to Rosemonde, all the speeches concerning the sun and the daylight were written now, and each one was written in one single burst of enthusiasm, the handwriting becoming smaller, the words more abbreviated as the poet desperately tried to get down his thoughts.[18]

Rostand had been sending Coquelin fragments of the play as he composed them, still insisting that he tell no one about it. That autumn he invited the actor, just back from another tour abroad, to Etchegorria, and read him what he had written so far. Coq was enthusiastic and departed for Paris sure that he would soon be performing in the new play. More than six years, however, were to pass before *Chantecler* even went into rehearsal.

That November an event took place which was to shake the household to its foundations – Rosemonde's mother Mme Lee died, after two years of failing health. Rosemonde's grief was overwhelming. Her sunny, resilient personality, which usually kept the whole household in good spirits, was quenched, and it was now Edmond who had to comfort her, rather than the other way round. The two boys felt the change, especially the sensitive Maurice, who wrote later that the fairytale atmosphere of his childhood suddenly vanished. Work on *Chantecler* was temporarily interrupted.

By December, however, when Coquelin returned to Cambo with his son Jean and Hertz, the director of the Porte-Saint-Martin theatre, they found enough material for the first two acts, spread over the floor on loose sheets of paper. Perhaps spurred on by the actors' presence, Rostand worked "like a demon", staying up all night to work on Act Four, the final act. He left Act Three, "Le Jour de la Pintade" ("The Guinea-fowl's Salon) for later. Early in 1904, Henri Bauer, who had called on the Rostands on his way back to Paris from Bayonne, was able to tell Coquelin that *Chantecler* was almost finished.

Rostand, however, had been prostrated by his manic efforts: he underwent three nervous crises in January alone and his doctor ordered absolute rest for at least six months. Rosemonde did not want this to be generally known and told enquirers that her husband had had a reoccurrence of his lung trouble. She told Coquelin that Rostand was anxious about his major revival of *Cyrano de Bergerac*, with new staging, at the Gaîté theatre. This may well have been true: with his customary self-doubt, Rostand perhaps feared that the public would not see in the play the merit it seemed to have in 1897. Naturally, his fears were unfounded. Coquelin played to full houses until March, then took the play up again in June, from when it ran until the end of the season. Sarah was again playing *L'Aiglon* during her now traditional tour to London that summer. She had revived *La Samaritaine* in February.

At Cambo, serious writing was abandoned while the poet recovered his strength and nervous energies. Instead, Edmond wrote various "Lettre-préfaces". Rostand disapproved of fulsome prefaces, believing a work should stand on its own, without the patronage of a famous name. But since he hated to refuse a request, he instead would agree to send a friendly letter, which could be used instead. One was for his old friend Henry de Gorsse, who with J. Jacquin had written an imaginative reconstruction for children of *La Jeunesse de Cyrano de Bergerac*, set in their old haunts as boys in Luchon.

Edmond concentrated the rest of his energy on Arnaga. He spared no expense in obtaining the finest materials and workmanship. Building had now begun on the house. The windows would be large so as not to impede the view which was the main reason for choosing the site. The wood-panelled walls would be adorned by frescoes by fashionable decorators such as Gaston La Touche, Henri Martin, Georges Delaw and Hélène Dufau. Edmond visited the site every day, talking to the workmen and keeping a close eye on the formal garden, which was now taking shape.

One of Rostand's favourite amusements as a child had been rearranging the furniture. Later, when moving into a house of his own at rue Alphonse de Neuville, he had taken great pleasure in exercising his taste in choosing the furnishings. But he had never had the chance to design a garden before. Now creating the gardens of Arnaga was giving him immense pleasure. He obtained catalogues of roses and other plants, ordered trees and shrubs. He pored over seventeenth and eighteenth-century books of garden design so that the formal garden, looking towards the Pyrenees, would be right in every way, with geometrical flowerbeds and *pièces d'eau* with fountains. On the western side of the house, the garden was to be smaller and informal. There would be a pergola, and a terrace from which to enjoy the view.

By the summer of 1904, Rostand felt sufficiently recovered to do a little work on his play, mainly corrections. In August, when Le Bargy and Simone, holidaying in Biarritz, called on him, Edmond was able to read them what he had written so far.

But he had still not completed *Chantecler*, nor was he in any hurry to do so. He wanted to be sure it was perfect before handing it over to Coquelin, who was again this summer a frequent visitor at Cambo, asking for more lines to learn. Coq did not realise that his visits simply made it more difficult for the poet to work. Frequently Rostand would refuse to see him. But on his return to Paris in the autumn, for another revival of *Cyrano de Bergerac*, Coquelin was so sure the play would soon be in rehearsal that he broke his promise of secrecy and told a journalist that Rostand had written a new play for him, without giving its title. The press seized on the news. Soon the title *Chantecler* was also known. This was just what Edmond and Rosemonde had hoped to avoid until the play was finished. Rosemonde knew how hard it was for her husband to work under pressure and Edmond was still lacking energy and inspiration.

The pressures on Rostand finally became more than he could bear. That November, he wrote to both Jean and Constant Coquelin that he had decided not to finish *Chantecler*. To Jean he wrote: "It would be monstrous to get performed purely for money reasons a poem written unwillingly and of which I only like two or three passages. As soon as I set foot in this impasse, I realised it was an impasse: why wasn't I listened to! Why did I lend an ear to admiring exhortations, when I myself was not admiring."

To Coq he explained that he desperately wanted to rest and spend more time with his beloved wife and family:

> I no longer have anything but a huge desire to rest. My horror of all company, the need to feel myself forgotten, the desire to live simply in the countryside and in the love of my family, all these have violently contributed to the denouement of this crisis [i.e. the recurrence of his nervous problems], so long foreseen, which I have just been through.
>
> I'm not to be pitied because of the creature I keep beside me, and to whom I shall be able to consecrate myself more in future from now on. Rosemonde is worth more than Fame, and my children are worth more than my author's rights.[49]

It was certainly true that Rostand had long neglected his family for his work. His son Jean remembers how his father always seemed rather a remote figure. "In the mists obscuring my childhood, I can hardly discern the profile of my father", he later told Albert Delaunay. At the rue Alphonse de Neuville, there were no "little games" such as fathers usually play with their children. At Cambo, while he was writing *Chantecler*, Rostand frequently stayed in his room working, rather than join the family for lunch or dinner. In spite of their shared interest in nature, Jean continued, "I didn't dare disturb my father, I didn't dare talk to him or ask him the least question".[50] This did not stop Jean loving his father. When work had gone well, and Rostand joined his family at table, reading them what he had just written, Jean "melted with tenderness", partly because he was aware, even then, of his father's lack of confidence in himself, of his fear of failing.

For this was the main reason for Edmond's decision to stop writing *Chantecler*. He was all too aware of the demands of fame and the expectations of the public. His desire for perfection made him feel that his work was not good enough, perhaps could never be good enough.

Besides, Rostand was becoming more and more convinced that his play was not suited to the stage. It was not merely the difficulty of dressing up actors to look like birds; Edmond had already taken great delight in sketching possible costumes and scenery. It was more that, in spite of some theatrical moments, the action was mainly psychological. *Chantecler* was more of a poem than a play. It was also to be his most directly personal play so far. Into the character of Cyrano, before fame had overtaken him, Rostand had put his own youthful enthusiasm and panache, as well as his pride, his sense of chivalry, and his idealism. But Chantecler, renowned far and wide for his song, but unsure of himself; feeling unworthy of his fame; humbly doing his job with all his heart, and experiencing the exaltation and despair of creation, Chantecler **was** Rostand as he was now in his most secret heart. Even Rostand's family were shocked to realise the depths of the poet's depression when he read them extracts from his play.[51] Did he really want to share this revelation with the public? Even more, did he want to reveal himself at his most vulnerable to his enemies, who were determined to believe the worst of him?

In complete contrast to the picture painted of him by his enemies, Rostand was above all a private man and a modest one. He never claimed to be a great poet, and was embarrassed by admirers such as Catulle Mendès who linked his name with that of Victor Hugo. He intensely disliked flattery. "Everything about him testified to a genuine modesty", wrote Louis de Robert, who once asked Rostand whether his fame gave him any pleasure. "I cannot say I enjoy it…(but) if I did not have it, I would miss it", he had replied.[52] As a young man he had been eager to succeed, in order to convince himself and those he loved of his own worth, and above all, because he wanted to counter the cynicism of his times and preach a message of idealism and heroism to the general public.

Now Edmond found his fame a burden, a burden which weighed on him so much that it made him ill and prevented him from doing what he saw as his duty, the duty to give of his best even when his work and motives were misunderstood. *Chantecler* was another clarion call to people's higher natures; Chantecler's championship of the light and of the duty of work was the faith Rostand himself lived by. But he was well aware of the possibilities for ridicule he was offering his critics: not only because of the sight of actors strutting about dressed

up as birds, but also because of his idealistic sentiments, so out of tune
with his times.

> *La Faisane: .....Comment reprend-on du courage Quand on doute de
> l'oeuvre?*
> *Chantecler:*   *On se met à l'ouvrage.*
> The Pheasant: How do you regain your courage when you lose faith in
>   your work?
> Chantecler: You set to work.
> – (Act IV, sc. vii)

Having written virtually nothing new during 1904, Rostand's energy
and inspiration began to return in the spring of 1905. He now wrote the
whole of the only act so far unwritten, Act Three, in which Chantecler
attends the guinea-fowl's "Five O'clock". This gave Rostand the
opportunity to satirize salon behaviour. In this act, the conspiracy
to kill Chantecler almost succeeds. But while Rostand's hero is being
viciously attacked by his chief enemy, the exotic cockerel Le Pile-blanche,
he gives himself courage by actually inviting the hatred and derision of
the crowd. (Cyrano, too, used this ploy, claiming to prefer hatred to
admiration when he discovered Roxane did not love him.) The cynicism
of his times and the malicious inventions of some journalists and critics
made Rostand all the more determined to continue to praise idealism,
nature and the inspiring power of love. "You have to be able to show
yourself in your true colours!" declares Patou the farmdog, finding the
courage to shout "étoiles!" (stars!) openly in the farmyard, even though
he knew he would be mocked for doing so.

Meanwhile the news that Rostand had written a new play, in which
the main characters would be birds, had travelled round the world.
Journalists pressed continually for the latest news of his creation and
were told, as the poet had told Adolphe Brisson in January: it is almost
finished.[53]

Although Arnaga and *Chantecler* were his main concerns at this
time, Rostand permitted himself a short diversion in the form of a
long poem, "Les Mots", inspired by the current work of the Académie

française. As in England, there was a movement to "reform", that is, simplify, spelling. Edmond abhorred the thought of imposed changes; he felt that words had a character of their own, and should only alter if they changed naturally themselves, over time. Putting his ideas into concrete form, as usual, Edmond imagined the words themselves lamenting their proposed fate. "Les Mots", dedicated to Jules Renard, was published in *Le Figaro* on 9 April 1905.[54]

Rostand also felt constrained to make a short visit to Paris that June to support Maurice Barrès's candidature at the Académie française. Barrès, a passionate nationalist who had now given up politics to concentrate on his writing, had been on the opposite side to Rostand during the Dreyfus Affair, but the two writers respected each other's integrity. Rostand had written to Barrès on 8th April: "no consideration, political or otherwise, could have lost you my vote". It was the only time he felt strongly about an election, he told Barrès, and he hoped with all his heart he would succeed. Unfortunately Barrès did not succeed this time. [55] The day after the vote the Rostands gave a reception for Barrès at the Hotel d'Orsay, where they were once more staying. One of the guests was the poet Anna de Noailles. Rostand and Paul Faure had enthused together over her novel, *La Nouvelle Espérance*. At this first meeting, the two poets had little time to get to know one another, but later they would become close friends.

During his brief stay in Paris, Rostand enjoyed strolling along the quays looking for interesting volumes for his library at Arnaga. He wanted to cover its walls with books, especially old books. He also planned rather unusual doors for his library, faced with false books purporting to be the works never actually written by the writers who had imagined them. If someone were planning such a feature today, Rostand's unwritten but dreamt-of works would furnish a whole shelf.

On his return to Cambo, Rostand was able to give Coquelin, just off on a tour of South America, a neat copy of the cockerel's lines so far, so that he could learn them while he was away. Coq naturally assumed yet again that the play was almost finished, and that he would soon be performing it in Paris. But on his return in the autumn, he would find that *Chantecler* was still not completed. He would be reduced to reviving *Cyrano de Bergerac* at the Gaîté yet again.

The summer of 1905 passed quietly. Without any of the razzmatazz that had accompanied Maurice's first communion, Jean received his in the village church along with the boys from the village. It may have been this summer that Edmond sent for puppets from Bayonne and repainted them as the characters from *L'Anglais tel qu'on le parle*.

In August, Edmond invited Le Bargy's wife Simone to Etchegorria and offered her the part of the golden pheasant, la Faisane. Simone was now a star, noted particularly for her portrayals of spirited, modern young women. Rostand's play had seemed to Simone almost complete: Acts One to Three had been written, along with the major speeches of the fourth and last act. But hearing nothing more from him, she accepted a part in Bernstein's *La Rafale*. In Paris that autumn a *Don Quichotte* in verse by Rostand's old friend Richepin gained only a "succès d'estime" at the Comédie-Française.

Rostand was still returning the same reply to enquiring journalists: "[*Chantecler*] is almost finished". In fact, Arnaga was absorbing Rostand almost to the exclusion of everything else. The artist in him was taking great delight in seeing his vision take shape. Jean Veber's fairy-tale paintings already adorned Rosemonde's maplewood boudoir; in the great hall, Henri Martin's vision of a basque Angelus was in place above the fireplace. A decorator from Bayonne, Henri Perret, was overseeing the installation of the panelling, light fittings, and other details. Finally, at the beginning of 1906, with decorators and painters still busy, the Rostands began to move into their new home.

From the outside, Arnaga looks a simple, if large, basque farmhouse.[56] But inside, it was a palace where the poet had let his fancy and his love of beauty run free, celebrating all the finest styles of French history in sumptuous fashion. Every detail had been imagined and planned by him, and if executed badly, he would demand that it be done again. Nothing less than perfection was good enough for him and his family. But Arnaga was also a response to the ugliness and materialism of his own age.

The large, arched windows of the colonnaded hall face east towards the formal garden and the Pyrenees. In Rostand's time, glass cases, illuminated at night, stood before them, displaying precious pieces of jade, brought back from the Far East by Edmond's diplomat brother-in-law, Pierre de Margerie. Gaston La Touche's delicate frescoes inspired by "La Fête chez Thérèse", one of Rostand's favourite Victor Hugo poems, adorned the upper walls. A wrought-iron gate led to the Art-Nouveau library, with Hélène Dufau's large nudes depicting the seasons. Next to the library was "le salon Genlis", named in honour of Rosemonde's famous ancestor. The Louis-Sixteenth diningroom, with its marble floor and *trompe-l'oeil* columns and medallions, was at the other end of the hall, and off it, a small study in Empire style, panelled in lemonwood, with gilded bronze decorations and a marble fireplace. Edmond never worked there, but sometimes entertained visitors there in the evenings.

From the spacious entry lobby, an elegant curving stone staircase with a wrought-iron balustrade led to the upper rooms. Facing it across the lobby was a "studio" originally planned as a place for Maurice and Jean to work and relax. Decorated by Georges Delaw's frescoes of the old songs of France, a favourite theme of the time, it is an intimate and comfortable room: it was here the family would relax and take their meals when they were on their own or with close friends.

Upstairs Rosemonde, Jean and Maurice all had spacious bedrooms facing east towards the Pyrenees across the formal garden. At the back, overlooking the river valley, was Rosemonde's boudoir, along with a small salon in Empire style, and another large room intended for Rostand himself, but which became an office for his secretary, Louis Labat. After trying out almost all the upstairs rooms, Paul Faure tells us, Rostand settled in the two small rooms over the porch, with windows facing both east and west. Here he worked in bed, often from eleven o'clock in the morning until six o'clock at night, when inspiration was flowing. From his window he could see the countryside he describes in *Chantecler*.

Once installed at Arnaga, Edmond settled down to concentrate on his play. However, he still found it hard to complete the last act, even though all that remained to be written were the scene where Chantecler is flattered by the toads, and the links between the main speeches.

From now until 1909, work on *Chantecler* would proceed sporadically. Sometimes Rostand would find the energy to write a major speech for Act Four, such as the nightingale's song or the toad scene. But at other times he shut the door of his room and sat vainly waiting for inspiration.[57] Sometimes the sheer difficulties of staging his play seemed to overwhelm him – he would renounce it, and turn to other work. Always he was haunted by his fear of not living up to the public's expectations. He was determined to give only of his best – but perhaps even his best was not good enough.

> *Ah! Le cygne est certain, lorsque son cou s'allonge,*
> *De trouver, sous les eaux, des herbes; …*
> …
> *Mais moi, dont le métier me demeure un mystère*
> *Et qui du lendemain connais toujours la peur,*
> *Suis-je sûr de trouver ma chanson dans mon coeur?*
> Ah! The swan, when it stretches out its neck,
> is sure of finding plants beneath the water
> …
> but I, to whom my work remains a mystery,
> and who am always afraid of tomorrow,
> am I sure of finding my song in my heart?
> – (Act II, sc.iii)

Meanwhile Coquelin, and his son Jean, now co-director with Hertz at the Porte-Saint-Martin, were becoming more and more impatient. Since 1904 they had been told that the play was "almost ready". Coquelin, who knew Rostand well, understood his apprehensions, but he desperately needed a new play, and the public were expecting it to be by Rostand. He called frequently, uninvited, at Arnaga, as he had at Etchegorria, but the poet would often refuse to see him at all. On one of these occasions, as Rosemonde recalls, Coq dressed up as a servant bringing his lunch to the poet's room. When Rostand recognised his friend, he apparently was so amused by the trick played on him that he shook off his depression and consented to work again with Coq on his play. But after such accesses of energy, the poet would invariably relapse into despair, and refuse to let *Chantecler* be performed until he felt he had perfected it.

Hertz, too, made the same journey to Cambo several times a year, with even less success, as Rostand knew that Hertz was only interested in his play for the income it would bring. At least Coq appreciated his work as a fellow artist. But as the years passed, Coq himself began to feel *Chantecler* was a burden, forcing him to revive *Cyrano de Bergerac* every season, and between seasons, to travel to South America on tour. These tours were great triumphs for Coquelin, and as he could not resist the opportunity to share his friend's wonderful poetry everywhere he went, including the long boat journeys there and back, some of the major speeches of *Chantecler* became well-known long before the play was performed. But Coq was not young any more. The constant travelling, needed to earn money, and the long, demanding role of Cyrano, constantly revived, was taking its toll on him. Besides, "this role of Chantecler is crushing, I dread it" he would tell Paul Faure in 1908.[58]

In July 1907, the staging of *Chantecler*, at last planned to go ahead that autumn, received a further setback. But this time it was fate, not Rostand's qualms, which held up the performance. Taken ill with peritonitis, Rostand was too ill to be operated on until October 2nd. After a long and difficult convalescence, Rostand again succumbed to depression and would not give Coquelin *Chantecler*. Coq had to revive *Cyrano de Bergerac* again, this time at the Porte-Saint-Martin theatre, scene of Cyrano's original triumph; the theatre had been refurbished completely over the summer, in anticipation of *Chantecler*. Simone, also waiting for her chance to play the Pheasant, had instead to accept a part in *Samson* at the Renaissance.

A new tutor, Raymond Lerouge, had arrived at Arnaga that July. Lerouge later described life at Arnaga in his memoirs.[59] From the time when he arrived, Edmond's new play was never mentioned in the Rostand household until one evening in January 1908. When Lerouge showed an interest, Rosemonde encouraged her husband to read him the play. But after reading the first act, Edmond seemed to get tired. Afterwards, he was sufficiently interested to make a few corrections. But then he put the manuscript away in the drawer again.

However, a few weeks later, Rostand's depression lifted and with his renewed energy he turned again to *Chantecler*. Coquelin, Hertz and the designer Edel were called to Arnaga. They discussed details of the production and allotted roles: Jean Coquelin would play Patou the dog and Galipaux, the blackbird. Marthe Mellot would be the nightingale. When the visitors had left, Rostand settled down to designing the stage sets and sketching out how he wanted each scene to work on stage. Lucien Jusseaume was to create the scenery for Acts Three and Four, set in the kitchen garden and the forest. Rostand and Jusseaume sent each other designs and suggestions through the post. The poet also got to grips with the costumes, which he wanted to look as realistic as possible. He used scraps of material to clothe tiny models of his characters, as he had done for amusement on other occasions. With such an ambitious project, totally unlike anything else that he had previously attempted, and unique on the French stage of his time, he wanted to leave nothing to chance.

Comoedia announced on 2nd February 1908 that *Chantecler* was definitely going to be staged during the 1908-9 season. Renard noted in his *Journal* the same month: " Rostand's genius has returned with his health. They'll be in Paris on first September and we'll see *Chantecler*. We're all hoping for a flop", he continued maliciously, "but it's not possible. Only, a triumph would give him hardly any pleasure, and a failure will kill him".[60] Renard knew that everyone who had heard parts of *Chantecler* ("and that's almost everybody"), said it was marvellous. But perhaps they were just saying that to be "with it". It could be a prodigious success just out of curiosity – everyone would want to see just how bad it is.

Such sentiments hardly seem those of a friend of Rostand's. But Renard frequented the *Revue blanche* and the *Mercure*, magazines that hated Rostand for his popular success. In their view, poetry should be mysterious, veiled, and reserved for an elite of noble souls. In such circles, it was not done even to admit that Rostand's plays had any virtues at all.

In April 1908, a visit to Paris was necessary to check on whether Rostand's wound was healing properly. It was, but the Rostands stayed on a few more weeks. While Edmond rested at the hotel, their tutor Raymond Lerouge took the boys to his former place of employment, Boris de Tannenberg's school. Jules Renard did not call– perhaps Edmond was not receiving visitors, or it may have been Renard's envy that kept him away, as it would in October, when he visited Bayonne.

On his return to Arnaga, Rostand again suffered doubts about *Chantecler* and refused to give Hertz or Coq the play. He put it away again and turned his attention to other work: Le Bargy had asked him for a rhymed pantomime to recite to accompany a mimed action on film.

Rostand's long poem for Le Bargy, *Le Bois Sacré* (The Sacred Wood), is an amusing fantasy where the immortal gods of ancient Greece are confronted with the twentieth century in the form of a young couple with a car. Here, in contrast to *Chantecler*, there is no satire of modern life, no obvious "leçons d'âme" (lessons for the soul). It is almost as if Rostand was taking a holiday from serious writing and giving his imagination and sense of fun free reign. Having recently discovered the joys of driving himself (Edmond's was the first car in Cambo), he takes great delight in describing what is very likely his own forty-horsepower Delaunay-Belleville, as amongst the baggage are discovered a young author's verses (Maurice's), a diabolo (perhaps belonging to Jean), and the various toiletries and accessories essential to contemporary elegance from "the exquisite rue de la Paix".

The gods are relaxing in a sacred wood on Mount Olympus when a car breaks down on the road nearby. The beautiful young couple who emerge take off their bulky coats and dance the boston before sitting down for a cigarette. The god Vulcan is excited by the car and wants to examine it, so Morpheus sends the couple to sleep. Mercury (patron of thieves, amongst his other titles) opens the suitcases and the gods curiously explore their contents. Meanwhile Vulcan has been inspecting the motor, and found out how it works. He repairs the fault. Aeolus (god of winds) is called on to fill the tyres with air, Psyche lights the headlights, as it is now dusk, and the more adventurous gods go off for a drive, with Vulcan in the driving seat. When they return, it is quite dark.

The gods put everything back as it was and disappear. When the young couple wake up, they discover to their amazement that the car is mended, the tyres are hard and the lamps are already lit. Bemused but relieved, they put on all their furs and set off home. But unbeknown to them, Cupid has stowed away in the back. As the car speeds along, he stretches out luxuriously on the cushions with a stolen cigarette, regarding the oblivious pair in front with mischievous intent.

This scenario would be performed on stage in 1910, accompanied by Reynaldo Hahn's music. Another project of Rostand's this year, but an unfinished one, was a prose play, *La Chambre sans miroir*, about Helen of Troy. But Rostand wrote only the first act. He much preferred to write in verse, which, in times of inspiration, flowed readily from his pen. The poet also began a verse translation of Goethe's *Faust*, which had long fascinated him.

Somehow news of *Faust* leaked out, and although Rostand had only written a hundred lines or so, it was rumoured in Paris that Sarah would perform it before *Chantecler* reached the stage, because the poet had fallen out with Coquelin. Rostand had to telegraph his journalist friend Pierre Mortier to scotch this rumour; he reiterated that *Chantecler* would be performed at the beginning of the 1908-9 season. *Faust* was intended for the Comédie-Française, he said, not the boulevards, and would be performed later.[61]

When Coquelin had first announced that *Chantecler* would be performed in the 1904-5 season, a frisson of expectation had run through the capital. But as time went on and there was still no sign of a play, the mood changed to one of gentle teasing. In the cafés, every chansonnier in Paris, it seemed, was making fun of Rostand and his non-appearing play. It was the question on everyone's lips: "When will Rostand finish his play?" But as season followed season, and *Chantecler* still did not appear, Parisians became less tolerant. Some of the fault must lie with Coquelin, who was so eager to perform *Chantecler* that he announced it every year for the coming season. Rostand had had no intention of letting even the existence of his play become known before he had finished it to his own satisfaction.

Coquelin's presumption greatly damaged Rostand's reputation. The poet's delay in getting his play performed was incomprehensible even to his friends; it was presented by his enemies as a deliberate ploy to increase public interest in *Chantecler*. Salon gossip took pleasure in denigrating the absent poet. It was even said that he was out of his mind, but his visit to Paris that spring had shown this to be untrue. Parisians, already affronted by Rostand's self-chosen exile from the capital, now dubbed him "Edmond à bout" ("Edmond at the end", a reference to the deceased popular novelist, Edmond About), while scurrilous postcards pictured him as a cockerel surrounded by lascivious fowls, "eager to experience the vigour of his song". (Edmond's attractiveness to society women had not gone unnoticed.) Ridiculous rumours were circulating about *Chantecler*: there would be live reptiles on stage; a butterfly would flirt with an ox; the cast of characters would include a dog and its fleas. [62]

Rosemonde, ever protective of her poet, had managed to prevent Edmond from hearing about most of these malicious rumours. But he finally became aware that autumn that his enemies were destroying his reputation. This awoke his fighting spirit. He was determined to affront his critics and put on his play come what may.

So, in December 1908, Jean Coquelin at last read the whole play to the assembled actors, and rehearsals, originally scheduled for September, finally began. Rostand intended to come immediately to Paris. But fate again intervened with an attack of influenza that kept him in bed. Finally in January 1909, he and his family set off, not by train, but in his car, hoping by this means to slip unseen into the capital. Vain hope: his departure from Arnaga was quickly discovered and details of every stage of the journey relayed back to eager journalists in Paris. On 24th January, after spending the night at Tours, the Rostands arrived to the welcome of a large crowd and settled into the select and discreet Hotel Meurice. Now *Chantecler* would surely be performed this season!

Coquelin had been unwell and had missed some days of rehearsals. The weekend the Rostands arrived in Paris, he was resting in the country at the retirement home he had set up at Pont-aux-Dames. He sent a message to Edmond, inviting him to lunch on the Wednesday, along with Jean, Hertz and Edel, the costume designer. Edel arranged for the costume of *Chantecler* to be ready then, to give Coq a surprise. The actor had asked Simone to come to Pont-aux-Dames to go over with him the climactic scene in Act Two, where the cockerel hero believes he makes the sun rise. She found him in bed, but cheerful. He said he would be well enough to come to rehearsals after another couple of days. But on the morning of the 27th, Coquelin was struck down by a heart attack. He died immediately.

In fact, unbeknown to Rostand, Coquelin had been unwell for some time. Simone had already mentioned her fears for his health to Rosemonde and Maurice. But they did not take this information seriously, thinking it was just another of the rumours that had bedevilled the play.

Rostand delivered a moving speech at the funeral of his friend and interpreter. He was in despair. Not only had he lost a dear and respected friend, but it was as if his play, which had caused him so much anguish, had died with its interpreter. Who but Coquelin could play Chantecler? Which other actor so sympathised with his idealistic intentions? Now he regretted criticising Coq for reciting his verses all over the world, and wished he had instead thanked and encouraged him. As for his play, he said as he stood by the grave of his friend, he would have liked to throw the manuscript into it. Instead, he declared in his funeral speech that "these pages of the poem I had given you, moved to see you give them a value that I could not comprehend, these pages that you were handling again on the morning of your death, which you gave me the painful honour of making your last joys, these pages are for you, that is, now, for your son Jean. When, weeping, he finds them amongst your papers, he alone will decide their fate!"

While Rostand mourned his friend, and Jean Coquelin his father, the Paris papers were not slow to try to guess who would replace Coquelin in *Chantecler*. The interest in Rostand's play was still intense. Jean Coquelin had no doubts that his father would have wanted the play to be performed. Hertz, too, did not intend to let the chance of such a money-spinner slip away. Edmond reluctantly began to consider who might play Chantecler in place of Coquelin.

There was of course, no one who could fully replace Coquelin, but the actor who came closest to him in the art of declaiming verse with panache was Edmond's friend, Le Bargy. Le Bargy, however, was tied to the Comédie-Française with chains of iron. If he took the part, he would be liable to expensive lawsuits and might lose the chance of creating many interesting roles already promised to him by other dramatists. Le Bargy asked for leave of absence after thirty years service – the other *sociétaires* refused. In what seemed to Rostand a most dishonourable suggestion, Claretie even offered Jean Coquelin a place at the Comédie-Française, provided he brought *Chantecler* with him! Eventually it became clear to Edmond and to Jean that Le Bargy was not prepared to break with the Comédie-Française, as Sarah and Coquelin himself had done, and that they must look elsewhere for an interpreter.

There were not many actors of the stature and experience needed by this demanding role. Pierre Brunot, who was similar to Coq in his acting style, was still too young and he, too, was a member of the Comédie-Française. Edouard de Max, who had already played Rudel and l'Aiglon, was suggested: he was a wonderful speaker of verse, but could this eminently patriotic role (for Chantecler is "le coq gaulois"), be taken seriously if played by a swarthy Romanian? Even Sarah's name was mentioned – she would have played the part splendidly, but this was definitely a case where cross-dressing was not suitable. The only name left was that of Lucien Guitry.

Guitry was by then director of the Renaissance theatre. He was in his prime, a much-admired actor in modern prose plays. His acting was natural, according to life; he spoke, rather than declaimed, and never raised his voice. Audiences, especially women, admired his masterful manner, the impression he gave of great power under control. But was he the right man for Chantecler? He had already acted in two of Edmond's plays: as Bertrand d'Allamanon, in *La Princesse lointaine*, where he felt so uncomfortable in the role, he had handed it over to someone else within days, and as Flambeau, in *L'Aiglon*. In this latter role, written for Coquelin, he had acquitted himself well, by most accounts, though without the panache it demanded.

Rostand was horrifed at the thought that Guitry might take on the role he had written for Coquelin, and which expressed his own innermost thoughts and fears. It was not just that Guitry's acting style was so different from Coquelin's, and that his participation in the earlier plays had not been an altogether happy experience. Although Guitry and he had been friends when they first met in 1894, Guitry was now part of a circle which included Tristan Bernard, Capus and Donnay: modernists all, hostile to Rostand and sarcastic about his success. Maurice Rostand and Simone shared Edmond's apprehensions. In Maurice's opinion, Guitry was more like the mocking and cynical blackbird than the idealistic cockerel.

However Hertz and Jean Coquelin were determined the play should be performed, and so was Rosemonde. She went to see Jules Renard on 25th February and told him she thought Guitry was the only actor to play Chantecler, but Edmond would not make the first move, nor would Guitry. According to Renard, he then wrote to Guitry, his close friend, telling him the role was his for the asking.

What part this letter had in resolving the issue, we do not know. But on 9th March 1909, a contract with Guitry was signed. It was a generous one: Hertz had tripled his first offer and additionally offered a contract for five years at the Porte-Saint-Martin. The first reading took place immediately. After hearing the great "sunrise" scene, the actor got up, walked over to the author, and embraced him. "C'est grand comme l'Himalaya!" he declared. This enthusiasm went some way towards reconciling Edmond to his new interpreter, but by 7th

April, Renard was writing in his diary, "Rostand is already in despair because it is Guitry who will play Chantecler". The poet's fears would prove to be well-founded.

During this brief stay in Paris, Rostand stayed in his hotel and hardly went out. His grief at Coquelin's death, and the difficulties of finding an actor to replace him, had lowered his resistance and he caught another bad dose of flu. This prevented him from paying his respects at another funeral, that of Catulle Mendès. Mendès had fallen under a train, whether by chance or intention was not known. Mendès, a faithful follower and admirer of Rostand, had never known the latter's success, which he had the generosity of spirit to applaud. Lately his life had become even more disordered than before, and he was drinking more. Whenever the Rostands were in Paris, he would visit them, his clothes rumpled, his eyes glassy. Speaking to Renard ("you who are his friend"), just a few days before his death, Mendès had asked him to reproach Edmond for his negligence towards him.[63]

Was Renard still Rostand's friend, however? He had not spoken to Edmond for years, and he did not call on him now. It was not simply that Renard's circle of friends was mainly opposed to the poet and his success: his own envy of Rostand can be seen clearly in his diary. But another reason may have been Renard's own ill-health – he was to die the following year. Contact between the two families was left to Rosemonde, who with Maurice visited the Renards whenever she was in Paris. During a visit on 25th February, she praised her husband: he loves her more than ever, and is "modeste, gentil, bon, généreux" (modest, kind, good, generous). *Chantecler* is the best thing he has written. If it succeeds it could renew the theatre. It's marvellous!

Edmond seems to have preferred not to call on anyone. But the Rostands did give dinner parties in their salon at the Meurice. Among those invited were old friends such as Richepin, who had remarried and left behind his bohemian lifestyle. Henri Bauer was another old friend who called, as did Edmond's publisher Eugène Fasquelle and his wife, along with La Touche, the artist who had worked at Arnaga.

More recent acquaintances were Louis Barthou, Minister of Public Works, and his wife, who were to become good friends.

If his father preferred to keep his own company, Maurice on the other hand was excited by the literary life and salons of Paris. He had made the acquaintance of Jean Cocteau, who had written to him at Cambo, asking for a poem for *Schéhérezade*, a review he was co-founding. Several editions of *Schéhérezade* were published, including, thanks to the efforts of the young enthusiasts, prose by Anatole France, poetry by Guillaume Apollinaire, and drawings by Picasso.

The Rostands left Paris on 10th April 1909 for Cambo, much to Maurice's regret. Now that the question of who was to play *Chantecler* had been settled, there was nothing to keep the poet in Paris any longer, and he was eager to get back to Arnaga. It was too late to mount a production of his play for the current season – rehearsals would begin again in September.

But even in his absence, Rostand's name continued to be brought before the public. Sarah Bernhardt was recording the Nose Tirade from *Cyrano de Bergerac* for Pathé – she had already recited it, wearing a cardboard nose, at one of the salons, as a joke. Another recording would contain part of the First Tableau of *La Samaritaine*, which Sarah had revived again this season, and the Wagram scene from *L'Aiglon*. Rostand's revised version of *La Princesse lointaine* was scheduled for performance in October 1909. It would not, however, be performed in Paris until 1929, long after the death of both writer and intended interpreter.

At Arnaga, Rostand again consecrated himself to his garden and his work. He was writing "Les Douze Travaux" (The Twelve Tasks), a long poem based on the myth of the humiliation of Hercules by Omphale.[64] Hercules has completed his twelve famous exploits and is now resting in luxury at the palace of the queen of Lydia. Unfortunately he has fallen in love with the beautiful but devious queen, Omphale, who tries to humiliate the hero by making him spin for her, offering him in turn twelve different spindles. He evades her intention by using each to illustrate one of his famous exploits. But eventually he runs out of exploits: "You never have enough completed tasks – when you rest on your laurels, you crush them … you're no longer a hero if you stop working". Here Hercules was surely expressing Rostand's sentiments as well as his own.

Sensing her triumph is almost complete, Omphale brings on a dancing dwarf, whose mesmerising twirls, "an insidious trampling on beauty", seem to be saying to him "what's the point?" Hercules feels his strength ebbing away – he takes the next spindle offered to him and begins to spin, breaking out into a sweat as his calloused hands succeed, with intense effort, in spinning a fine thread. Everyone in the court comes to mock his humiliation. He is brought back to himself by a timely cloud spitting lightning and thunderbolts, sent by his father, Jupiter. The terrified courtiers take cover, while the hero calmly uproots a convenient pine tree and, using it as a spindle, gradually spins away all the cloud. Then, spurning the fawning crowd and humbled queen, he strides away to find new deeds of valour to accomplish.

There are many resemblances here with *Chantecler*. Both Omphale and the Pheasant deploy their feminine attractions to tempt the hero away from his duty: the latter will be redeemed by love, the former humiliated for her lack of it. Hercules and Chantecler are both hated for their good deeds, but the weak and foolish still turn to them in time of danger. In both works, too, Rostand stresses the sacred nature of duty, of doing the work allotted to one; he contrasts the purity and beauty of nature with the artificial world of human society, and reiterates that constant vigilance is required to fight the pernicious contemporary attitudes of cynicism, boredom, the sense of purposelessness, and the lack of wonder.

Rehearsals for *Chantecler* began on 27th September, without Rostand. They would be long, slow, and difficult, taking in all one hundred and thirty days.

On 5th October, the Rostands arrived by car in Paris, this time staying at the recently-built Hôtel Majestic, on the avenue Kléber. They had left Arnaga at eleven pm and driven through the night. Even so, a large crowd of well-wishers, journalists and the simply curious was waiting to greet them. There was no hope of avoiding the publicity which Rostand's enemies again claimed was purposely orchestrated by the poet himself. Joachim Gasquet claimed that the Majestic was actually paying Rostand to stay there, on the understanding he would let himself be seen at mealtimes by the rich South Americans who lived in the area.[65] The truth was quite the opposite. Rostand was horrified by all the uproar; he reluctantly agreed to see some journalists but always dined in his room.

Rostand himself was to direct rehearsals. He was determined that everything should go exactly as he wanted, and made both actors and technicians repeat their actions until he was completely satisfied. This particularly annoyed Guitry, who was already resentful of the weight of his costume. As a professional actor of high standing, he was not accustomed to being told what to do. Sometimes Edmond would even take his place to show him exactly what gestures and intonations he wanted him to use.

Rostand's whole family were in the habit of accompanying him to the theatre, including at times Rosemonde's half-brother Henry Lee and his wife, the tutor, Raymond Lerouge and the governess, Miss Day. Simone, playing the Pheasant, found "their friendly chuckles … their whispers, their admiring exclamations and their officious advice" very distracting.[66]

Simone doubted that the realistic approach insisted on by Edmond was the right one. Her doubts would prove well-founded. The actors were much encumbered by the weight of their costumes, and by their lack of freedom for gestures, since their arms were not free. The sheer mechanics of moving the actors round the stage, amongst the more than lifesize props (to make them proportionate to the animals portrayed by the actors), caused difficulties too, while their numbers also raised problems of stage management. Time and again the actual acting of a scene was interrupted by technical difficulties, so that by the end of November, the actors were feeling stale without having perfected their roles.

As the gramophone was still in its infancy, another difficulty was reproducing the sounds of the forest in Act Four. Various bird-song virtuosos were interviewed, but they all specialised in only one song. Not until December was someone found who claimed to be able to imitate all the birds needed, including the all-important nightingale. Everyone stopped work to hear this phenomenon, who worked at the Folies Bergères. To their surprise, he began by announcing: "the Paris-Bordeaux express", complete with train and station noises. Then it was the turn of "the ship in the fog", with lashing waves and a foghorn, followed by "the peasant women at the washplace". At this point, Rostand, in his "gentle voice which hoped to avoid hurting anyone's feelings", reminded the source of these marvellously realised sounds that all they really wanted to hear was the bird songs. The actor replied that it had taken him a year to get his act right, and now he could only reproduce the birdsong if he went through what led up to it![67]

That October, in Rostand's honour, there was a performance of *Les Deux Pierrots* at the Palais d'Orsay for members of the Académie française. On 26th of the same month, Jules Renard's play *La Bigote*, had its successful first performance. Rosemonde and Maurice (but not Edmond) were present, and went backstage afterwards to congratulate the author. Renard was annoyed about a joke played by Tristan Bernard – he had thrown a crumb into the Rostands' box, "for Chantecler"!

Chantecler fever still possessed Paris. It was the perennial topic of salon conversations, the theme of shop window displays, the subject of endless magazine articles. Fashionable dressmakers were overwhelmed by requests for splendid outfits, and those Parisiennes who had long since purchased their dress for the première were praying, "if only *Chantecler* is performed while my dress still looks new!"[68] Rostand himself was besieged by journalists asking for interviews; the hotel apartment, recounts Paul Faure, who had accompanied the poet to Paris, was busy all the time. People asked the poet for assistance, recommendations, jobs; they invited him to preside over banquets and reunions;they asked for his autograph or for money. Rostand responded generously to both the latter requests, but he found all the fuss exhausting. He was upset, too, by so much publicity, much of it dishonest, "he who was so scrupulous and simple himself".[69] The poet was unable even to stroll in the streets without a crowd forming round him. However, he kept his mild demeanor, agreeing courteously to interviews and photographs, and, when absolutely obliged to attend a social function, always dressing with his accustomed elegance.

By the close of 1909, *Chantecler* was still not ready. The première was postponed yet again, until January 1910. Meanwhile Maurice, in contrast to his father, was entering with enthusiasm into the literary life of the capital. He began frequenting salons with Jean Cocteau. Elegantly if flamboyantly dressed, he was delighted to read his poems to a flattering audience.

Rosemonde apparently concealed her son's outings from Edmond, who did not approve of Maurice's behaviour. Rosemonde herself seemed to enjoy being in Paris again. Still youthful and beautiful – "this pretty flower will never decide to fade", sighed Renard in his diary,[70] she often accompanied Maurice to the literary salons, where, because of Edmond's fame and the expectation surrounding *Chantecler*, they were the centre of attention.

Rostand himself had always disliked and avoided such salons because of the flippancy of the conversation and the prevalence of scandalous talk. His caricature of salon behaviour in Act Three of *Chantecler* would cause much offence.

In December Jules Renard and Edmond met again for the first time since 1900. They greeted each other rather coolly. Renard found his friend unrecognisable. "He gives the impression of being a nice old chap ('un gros bonhomme gentil'). The man who is abandoning himself to the torrent and shakes hands on the bank."[71] Rostand still had his headaches and was even more short-sighted, peering at Renard to see if he had aged. He had no appetite – they would lunch on boiled eggs brought from the Astoria. Renard did not find his friend arrogant (was this the fear that had kept him from visiting Rostand?) and they soon seemed to be chatting as before. Rostand was beginning to accept Guitry "[il] vous séduit" (he wins you over), but was convinced *Chantecler* would be a flop. "He's just bluffing", thought Renard. Although he mixed with the rich and famous, his friend seemed to have achieved a kind of indifference towards other people. Edmond said he was bored in Paris and wanted to go back to Cambo. He did not even intend going to the *répétition générale* of his play.

The Renards were invited to dinner five days later. They were served tepid water rather than wine. Looking more carefully at his friend, Renard could now see a few grey hairs, a certain slackness in the cheeks. Rostand was more hesitant in talking, afraid of compromising himself. "You attribute to them the radiant, serene fame that you yourself would like to have", he wrote on his return home. "They don't have it". Perhaps he regretted having kept his distance from his friend all these years.

On January 13th, bookings opened at the Porte-Saint-Martin theatre for the first fifteen performances of *Chantecler*, planned for the end of January. But bad luck continued to dog the play. Rain soon began to fall on Paris in such torrents that the Seine rose to an unprecedented level; by 27th a quarter of Paris was under water and there was no light for rehearsals. The date of the première had to be postponed. Then, just as the floods finally began to recede, Simone's legs were so badly injured in an accident on stage that the première was postponed again. Now it was fixed for 2nd February, but was postponed again at short notice because of a problem with the third act. The public had not heard of the postponement and there was practically a riot when the doors of the theatre were kept closed.

At last, on Monday, 7th February, the all-important *répétition générale* for invited guests took place. (According to Maurice Rostand, there were two *générales*, to avoid offending people.) The crowds outside the theatre were so great that they held up the traffic; the actors themselves were hardly able to get into the theatre. Inside, the rich and famous waited in glittering anticipation. Relays had been set up along the boulevard to the café Weber, where those without a ticket awaited an act-by-act account of the play and its reception.

Some evenings earlier, a preview had been given to friends and sympathisers. They all expected *Chantecler* to be a success. Simone, however, feared that so much prolonged anticipation could only damage the reception given to the play by the public when it was finally performed. She shared her anxiety with the director, Hertz, but he was unconcerned. The theatre was fully booked now for weeks ahead – success or failure, he could not lose.

Rostand also feared the worst. That afternoon of the first *générale*, he wrote to the critic Jules Lemaître from Guitry's dressingroom "Two hours before this battle which I hardly count on winning, so foolish does it seem to me to rely on poetry alone to triumph at the theatre, I want to thank you for the warm words which it appears you spoke with regard to *Chantecler*".[72]

The poet spent the first part of the performance tucked away in the wings, where he could observe the audience closely. His apparent impassivity was belied by his frequent blinking and the way he kept pulling at his moustache. At first, however, all seemed to be well. The audience, avid to see the play so long awaited, were attentive. The Prologue and first act were enthusiastically received. The second act, too, with Chantecler's lyrical evocations to the sun at dawn, seemed to go well to many observers, but Simone remembers feeling that they were beginning to lose the audience. The satire of the Third Act ("The Guinea-fowl's Five O'clock") was not found acceptable, and was received almost in silence. The toad scene in the final act caused open disapproval, drowning the song of the nightingale, and proving, as several present remarked later, that envious toads were present in the auditorium as well as on stage.

Sitting with his father in Simone's box, Jean could sense his unhappiness. But Edmond bore his disappointment with a dignity which impressed Julien Benda, Simone's cousin. "He bore his defeat with a dignity which commanded respect".[73] There were only six curtain calls. Rostand, though called for by the audience, refused to come on stage.

"Have I ever in my whole life seen a living person as pale as Edmond Rostand when the evening was over…I think I can reply I never have", recalled Simone.[74]

Rostand did not attend the première. Instead he awaited news by telephone. But the news was no better. Jules Renard's friend Athis told him there had been wild enthusiasm for the first two acts. But silence had greeted most of the Third Act and there had even been boos in the toad scene of the Fourth Act. Guitry had even refused to give the name of the author; it was Jean Coquelin who announced it.[75]

It was not that *Chantecler* was a flop. But it was not a triumph. By any objective standard, *Chantecler* was a success. It played to full houses in Paris for over three hundred consecutive performances. In late February, three troupes set off in different directions to perform the play in the provinces and even abroad, giving over seven hundred performances in four months. Though Guitry handed over the role in June, after one hundred and fifty performances, Chantecler, in the shape of Pierre Magnier, Romuald Joubé, Dorival and others, continued to crow at the Porte-Saint-Martin until 1st November 1910.

The financial rewards were considerable. Hertz was well able to recoup his lavish expenditure on costumes, decor and publicity. Rostand himself received more than 200,000 francs just in performance rights.

One hundred and thirty thousand copies of the play, with a frontispiece designed by Rostand himself, were published by Fasquelle on 15th February. *Chantecler* also appeared act by act in four consecutive editions of the magazine *L'Illustration*, which also sold well. The publishers Lafitte approached Rostand with a suggestion for a complete illustrated edition of his work.[76]

Posters proclaiming this new edition as the publishing event of the century appeared all over the capital. The shop windows, too, were full of articles inspired by *Chantecler*, including an alarm clock modelled on Guitry's cockerel. Papier-mâché heads of Rostand himself, to top gentlemen's canes, were also popular. In the cafes, jokes still circulated, including the suggested alternative title: "Les Animeaux malades de la veste" (the animals sick of their costume).[77] Magazines such as *Le Théâtre* brought out special illustrated editions. *Paris-Journal* ran a competition for the best epigrams on the play. Parodies of *Chantecler* abounded, with many provincial cities providing their own. One of the first animated cartoon films, by the pioneer Émile Cohl, was based on *Chantecler.*

The press, apart from the nationalist papers, generally reviewed the play sympathetically, both in France and abroad. "The most beautiful work M. Rostand has yet given us", declared Léon Blum,[78] who had approved of the poet's earlier "idealist" plays, but disliked *Cyrano de Bergerac.* Blum's praise was echoed by Adolphe Brisson of *Le Temps* and Duquesnel of *Le Gaulois.* Indeed, most of the critics in the quality papers praised *Chantecler,* albeit with some reservations. Many, like Léon Blum, welcomed Rostand's return to a more poetic treatment of his ideas, and recognized the difficulties of such a play succeeding with a boulevard audience. "An honourable defeat" was Firmin Roz's view in the *Revue bleue.*

Rostand's former teacher, René Doumic, wrote perceptively of the ground-breaking nature of the play and concluded that in *Chantecler* "[Rostand] has burst open the narrow boundaries of the theatre. The poet has challenged the playwright. The latter is not diminished by this test, the poet has grown by it".[79] Robert de Montesquieu wrote a favourable first review in *Gil Blas,* followed, however by a more critical one in *Le Théâtre* on March 1st, claiming Rostand had borrowed ideas from a play by Victor Hugo, "La Forêt mouillé".[80] Later Montesquieu, wrongly convinced he was being caricatured in the character of the peacock, turned completely against Rostand.

The nationalist papers, who could not forgive Rostand for having been a dreyfusard, were however uniformly hostile to *Chantecler. L'Action française* was said to have recruited students to go and boo the play by offering them five francs each.[81] Disproportionately scathing criticisms were levelled at the play in *Les Nouvelles, Paris-Journal,* the *Gazette du Palais* and *L'Humanité.* It seems ironic that such a patriotic play, rooted in the soil of France and starring "le coq gaulois", should have aroused such hostility from the nationalist papers. Many of these writers seem to have genuinely believed that the writer himself was responsible for the huge amount of publicity, publicity which he in fact deplored.

Another major factor in the criticism of Rostand and his work was simply envy of his success, as Jules Romains later admitted. He was one of the new generation of writers interviewed by *L'Opinion* who were dismissive of the play (without having seen it) and of Rostand's abilities generally. It was an article of faith to the avant-garde, whose views were represented by the new periodical, *La Nouvelle Revue Française*, that Rostand was a mediocre poet who relied on a huge publicity machine to make money out of the general public. Jacques Copeau, not yet a ground-breaking theatre director, welcomed the "failure" of *Chantecler*: it was good that Rostand should be publicly discredited for letting his work become a "a valuable stock on the Stock Exchange".[82]

But the most virulent attack on *Chantecler* and on Rostand came from *L'Éclair* in the form of nine successive articles entitled "Le krach Rostand" (The Rostand Crash) written by Joachim Gasquet.[83] Rostand's biographer Apesteguy suggests that *L'Éclair*'s motive for publishing these articles was revenge. In January *L'Éclair* had published, copied from an Italian paper, *Le Secolo*, what purported to be a scenario of the play, along with the "Hymn to the Night". Not only did the paper have no right to reprint the article, the scenario was totally misleading and the verses invented or truncated. The directors of the Porte-Saint-Martin theatre had taken *L'Éclair* to court, demanding one hundred thousand francs in damages. But in view of the financial success of the play, the claim for damages had been reduced to a notional one franc.[84]

Gasquet's articles merely generated extra publicity of the kind he claimed to deplore; his criticisms were so exaggerated that even the *Nouvelle Revue Française*, in an article by Henri Ghéon, felt bound to protest.[85]

"It's a flop that will be performed a hundred times", the playwright Alfred Capus had joked after the first night.[86] Certainly *Chantecler* continued to play to full houses in Paris, drawing visitors from all over Europe as well as France. The touring companies were also doing extremely well in the provinces. And yet, although the booing of the toad scene stopped after twenty or so performances, evidence that it had indeed been orchestrated, there was no doubt that *Chantecler* had not achieved the unmixed enthusiastic reception given to Rostand's earlier successes. Various reasons were put forward for this disappointing result.

The most obvious factor working against the success of the play, quite apart from the play's merits or demerits, was the tantalisingly long wait for the first performance. This had annoyed the public and made the play into rather a joke. By February 7th 1910, as Simone had suspected, the almost hysterical curiosity of the first-night audience would have been almost impossible to satisfy with any play, let alone a symbolic play in verse with animal characters,

The use of birds and animals as characters was a novelty which distanced the audience from the action. Rostand's insistence on realism in the costumes and scenery not only caused his actors much discomfort (and was a major factor in Guitry's resignation in June), but limited their gestures. To Louis N. Parker, Rostand's American translator, they looked like characters in a pantomime, which created quite the wrong ambiance for poetic verse. And as, even with all Rostand's care, the total illusion of reality was impossible, the attempt to achieve it destroyed that other illusion which is part of the charm of the theatre[87] (as the poet himself had so well appreciated in his *Discours de Réception* to the Academy).

The acting, too, left much to be desired. Only Simone, as the pheasant, Jean Coquelin, who played the dog, Patou, Galipaux, the blackbird, and Marthe Mellot, the nightingale, were considered to have acquitted themselves well.[88] The strongest criticisms were levelled at Guitry himself. He was "heavy, muddled, inexact ... he created a gloomy atmosphere, not allowing the whole significance of the work appear". "We ought to call him Sing-Dark [not "Chantecler", Sing-Light]", commented Raoul Aubry.[89]

Constant Coquelin had told his son that this was a role which had to be not only declaimed, but danced.[90] Even Simone, Guitry's acting partner, admitted that "the solemn voice, the restrained acting of Guitry, his concern for truth even when being lyrically expansive" disappointed listeners who were accustomed to Coq's "trumpet".[91] With Coq it would have been different, declared Jean Rostand later. When Rostand recited, at a dramatic critics' matinee, his former sonnet to Coquelin beginning: "Toi, tu poétisais" (You, you used to poeticize), it was warmly applauded, but also taken in some quarters as a direct criticism of Guitry.[92]

There may have been a hidden reason for Guitry's apparent failure to give of his best in the part. Guitry seemed to hate his role, noted Louis N. Parker, and Copeau wrote that the actor seemed to connive with the audience against what he was reciting on stage.[93] Paul Faure felt that Guitry's acting of *Chantecler* was so bad, one wondered whether he was doing it on purpose: "the heavy and uniformly lacklustre way he acted the role of cockerel, which was above all lyrical, smelt of sabotage".[94]

Was this the actor who had exclaimed "C'est grand comme l'Himalaya" on first reading the part? "Guitry will have a prodigious success" wrote Jules Renard in his *Journal* on 22nd January, and Maurice Rostand remembers hearing Guitry declaim some of the great speeches better, he thought, than Coq would have done. Yet on 8th February, Renard was writing in his diary that everyone agreed he [Guitry] was bad.

According to an anecdote told to Mary Marquet by Rostand, Guitry's stolid acting was indeed a deliberate act of sabotage: vengeance for an unfortunate incident which was no fault of Rostand's. At the time, Guitry had a young mistress, Jeanne Desclos. She had already tried to seduce the eighteen-year-old Maurice.[95] At the dress rehearsal, Jeanne was present in Guitry's dressing room when Edmond rushed in after the third Act to congratulate his Chantecler on a splendid performance (he told Mary Marquet he had thought Guitry even superior to Coquelin that evening). As soon as the actor had left, Jeanne threw herself at Edmond and kissed him on the lips. Just then, Guitry returned for something he had forgotten and saw them. He said nothing and went out again. From that moment, Guitry set out to sabotage the play. He recited his lines without expression, "like a first-form schoolboy". He refused to listen to Edmond's explanations and would not accept his offer of a duel, still an accepted way of settling a matter of honour.[96] Nor did Guitry relent. Maïté Dabadié, who attended the ninety-fourth performance, recounts that "Guitry n'a pas joué, il récitait son rôle". He was angry with Rostand, she explains, "the gossip columns would explain why".[97] This seems to corroborate Marquet's account that something happened which upset Guitry and made him Rostand's enemy.

However it may have been, Edmond himself was very disappointed with the acting of his play, as is clear from a letter to Barrès on 10th February. "I hope you haven't seen this play, acted like this", he wrote. And Mary Marquet recalls that, when Rostand saw his fourth Act performed at the *Université des Annales* by Albert Lambert and Marie-Thérèse Pierat, the poet told everyone delightedly "I've seen my play acted for the first time".[98]

But Guitry cannot shoulder all the blame for the "failure" of *Chantecler* in 1910. Other factors were involved, too. One problem was the attempt to marry two distinct styles in one play. The poetic Prologue, evoking the countryside, and the lyricism of the first two acts had been enthusiastically received by the first-night audience. The disparity between this reaction and the incomprehension which greeted the satirical third act, the guinea fowl's "Five o'clock", was very marked. The lyrical speeches of the fourth act, too, were well received.

Simone, writing later with the hindsight of a career in the theatre, felt that it was the choice of subject which made boulevard audiences resistant to the play. "How many of the men and women sitting in the stalls of the Porte-Saint-Martin found themselves capable of sympathising with Rostand's dream ... a veil iridiscent with fable, transparent for an elite, opaque for the majority". *Chantecler* should be performed at the Comédie-Française.[99]

Those who were able to appreciate *Chantecler*, especially those who knew Rostand and knew how personal this work was, felt that it was the poet's greatest play. "Every breath bears the mark of a great heart", felt Simone. "You've written nothing to equal *Chantecler*", wrote Barrès to Rostand in June.[100] Jean Rostand called *Chantecler* "the most moving of my father's works"; for Rosemonde, aware more than anyone of what this play had cost her husband, "*Chantecler* was his very soul".[101] Maurice Rostand agreed: "all of my father is in *Chantecler*".[102]

The use of the word "poem" in many of the assessments of *Chantecler* is significant. As Rostand himself was coming to realise, the ideas he wished to express in the form of a play were less and less suited to the popular stage. In spite of the poet's remarkable gifts for the theatre, what he had written was more of a poem to be read in individual contemplation than a play to engage a boulevard audience. This was probably a major reason for the poet's reluctance to allow *Chantecler* to be performed. The enthusiasm of his wife and the Coquelins, besides the insistence of Hertz, had persuaded him, against his will, to let Coq play the part at the Porte-Saint-Martin; after Coq's death, Rostand felt bound to honour his agreement with Jean Coquelin, whereas the play would almost certainly have had a huge success at the Comédie-Française with Le Bargy in the title role.

Rostand himself was confident of the merit of his play. It had worked really well during rehearsals. He felt that poor acting had come between him and the audience, and that a revival in different circumstances would be a success. In this he was proved correct. The Porte-Saint-Martin revived the play in October 1927. This time, *Chantecler* was an undoubted success, still playing to full houses at the fiftieth performance. Victor Francen, a former Cyrano, played the cockerel; Marthe Mellot, the only member of the original cast, took up once more the role of the nightingale. This production may have been prompted, ironically, by a performance, in Czech, at the National Theatre of Prague the previous March, which was a huge success even in translation.[103] For both productions, the animal costumes were symbolic rather than realistic, and this apparently worked well. There was no booing in the Act Four toad scene: the satire of society in general was not taken personally as in 1910, and the 1927 audience no longer saw themselves pilloried as envious toads. The play could be appreciated as Rostand had intended it to be.

After a long silence when the play went out of print in the sixties, *Chantecler* probably reached its widest audience yet with what Patrick Besnier has called a "brilliant" version for television in 1976.[104]

In 1984, *Chantecler* was revived again, with a flourish of trumpets, at the Avignon Summer Festival, under the direction of Jean-Claude Martin. This was a modern dress production with the actors expressing the human behaviour implicit in the poet's lines. The characters' costumes and behaviour reflected their roles; the woodpecker became the academician imagined by the poet, while the toads were dressed as self-important critics. The audience found the text so modern, they could hardly believe it was genuine. Public and critics alike acclaimed Rostand's play as a masterpiece.[105]

In December 1994, *Chantecler* was successfully revived again by Jérome Savary at the Théâtre National de Chaillot of Paris.

Readers of today will surely agree with the poet's friends and family that *Chantecler* is the most profound, the most lyrical and the most moving of all Rostand's plays. Yet it is hardly known at all outside France, though a few translations exist.[106] In January 1911, Maude Adams, an earlier Aiglon, opened at the Knickerbocker Theatre as Chantecler in an adaptation by Louis N. Parker. This ran for a respectable ninety-six performances. Apart from this production and the one in Prague in 1927, *Chantecler* does not seem to have been performed in translation. This is understandable, as the difficulties are considerable: the poetry, the word play and the topical allusions make the play challenging to translate. A modern translation into English is long overdue.

Inevitably Rostand was distresseded by the mixed reception given to this his most personal play. He told his friend Louis de Robert that he believed now that he would experience no more triumphs like those for *Cyrano de Bergerac* and *L'Aiglon*. He felt his star was setting.[107] Even the elevation to "Commander of the Legion of Honour" could not console him. He would have liked to return immediately to Arnaga, but many obligations kept him in Paris.

There was the reception in his honour, for instance, at the Collège Stanislas. Rostand told the pupils that all his works had cost him enormous effort and suffering. He urged them to remember that "the only true joys result from effort achieved and dificulties overcome", the "leçon d'âme" (lesson for the soul) of *Chantecler*.[108]

Another occasion demanding Rostand's elegant presence was the first performance on stage of his scenario, "Le Bois Sacré", written for Le Bargy in 1908, at Sarah's theatre on 20th April. The action was mimed to the accompaniment of Rostand's verse and Reynaldo Hahn's music. Sarah had also revived *L'Aiglon* again, with great success. There was still talk of her producing *La Princesse lointaine* in the poet's revised version, but nothing came of it. Meanwhile, the Comédie-Française was reviving *Les Romanesques* in the poet's honour. It would reach its hundredth performance at the state theatre in 1911.

Periodicals continued to focus on the author of *Chantecler*. Edmond's poem "La Tristesse de l'éventail", written in 1903, was published in *Touche-à-tout* on 15th February. *La Revue* published the unused scenario Rostand had written long ago for Brada, along with the story of how it was written.[109] In the same issue was a parody of Rostand based on the "Duel Ballad" in Act One of *Cyrano de Bergerac*, one of a series of parodies of the forty "Immortals" [Academicians] by "Un Désillusionné".

Rostand's importance as a writer was also acknowledged in many of the books of literary history and criticism appearing about this time. His name even figured in some of the titles: *De Dumas à Rostand*, by Augustin Filon (Paris,1898), *De Ronsard à Rostand*, by Guido Menasci (Paris, 1901), and Victor Defolie would later publish *De Charles d'Orléans à Rostand*. In 1904, Albert Reggio had contributed a psychological study of Rostand to the series, "Au Seuil de de leur âme". Now, in 1910, Louis Haugmard contributed a slim volume on the poet to the series: "Les Célébrités d'aujourd'hui". The critic J. Ernest-Charles would give Rostand a prominent role in his *Le Théâtre des poètes* (Ollendorff, 1910), and that October, Professor Jules Haraszti would give his perceptive series of lectures on Rostand at the University of Budapest.[110]

In Paris, at the Université des Annales, Adolphe Brisson was also giving lectures on *Chantecler* as part of a series entitled "Le Symbole chez les Poètes".[111] He told the audience that the play was "a flower blossoming in full sun, right at the top of the tree of our race".

Rostand himself went often to the Annales, where he enjoyed reciting his work to the enthusiastic young audience. It was almost the only outing he indulged in, apart from going to the theatre to see dramatists he admired, such as Bataille, Bernstein and Porto-Riche. He would appear in public with a flower in his buttonhole, elegant as always. But he preferred to stay at his hotel, in the company of his friends. One friend who was missing was Jules Renard, who had made his last diary entry on 6th April, and died on 22nd May.

The flamboyant Gabriele d'Annunzio, the Italian poet-dramatist, came to visit Rostand. All Paris was eager to meet d'Annunzio, but he himself was eager to meet the author of *Chantecler*. It was, however, Edmond's son Maurice, a passionate devourer of his work, much of which he knew by heart, who became his friend.

Maurice, now nineteen, was having a marvellous time. Salon life, distasteful to Edmond, offered many pleasures to his son. Rostand himself would have been welcome in the highest circles: he knew Boni de Castellane and the Countess de Greffulhe, the model for Proust's Duchess de Guermantes. But he was only eager to get back to the solitude of Arnaga. One of his last engagements before leaving Paris was attending a charity poetry matinee on 4th June, organised by Sarah at her theatre. The poet recited "La Brouette",[112] the "Hymn to the Sun" and the "Sunrise" speech of Act Two from *Chantecler*. He received a standing ovation. As an encore he delivered his sonnet to Coquelin, which aroused further enthusiasm. It was a heartening note on which to leave for Cambo and home.

Notes – Act IV

[1] Jeanne de Robert, *Le Coeur a ses raisons* (Toulouse, 1987), p. 221

[2] Paris, 1928

[3] Faure, p. 19.

[4] Louis de Robert, *De Loti à Proust* (Paris, 1928), p. 190

[5] Faure, pp. 62-3

[6] L. de Robert, p. 183

[7] "A Krüger", written 26th November, 1901, was published in *Le Figaro* on 9th December 1900, and as a pamphlet by Fasquelle. See *Le Cantique de l'Aile* (Paris, 1922), X.

[8] *Journal*, 11 Dec.1900

[9] "Ce que je fais", *Le Cantique de l'Aile*, XVI

[10] Jules Huret, *Le Figaro*, 8 May 1901

[11] *Le Figaro*, 10 June 1901 (*Interviews*, pp. 219-226)

[12] L. de Robert, p. 198

[13] *Le Cantique de l'Aile*, IX

[14] In *La Ville empoisonnée* (Paris, 1936)

[15] *Journal*, 1st October 1901.

[16] *Archives Arnaga*, quoted Margerie, p. 159

[17] See Chapter Six

[18] "Vichy's Theatrical Venture", *Theatre Survey*, vol 11, no. 2 (Nov.1970), p. 138

[19] *L'Illustration*, 28 Jan. 1939

[20] Jean Rostand to Albert Delaunay, *op.cit*

[21] *Le Temps*, 19 Dec. 1901

[22] *Journal* , 4th Jan. 1902

[23] Faure, p. 65.

[24] Published by Fasquelle the same year; in *Le Cantique de l'Aile*, XXII.

[25] Quoted Premsela, p.144; Margerie, pp.161 and 262.

[26] Simone, *Sous de nouveaux soleils*, p. 63

[27] L. de Robert, p.187

[28] M. Rostand, p. 83

[29] Faure, p. 79

[30] Interview with Georges Bourdon , *Le Figaro*, 10 Jan. 1910

[31] Hobart Ryland, *The Sources of the Play Cyrano de Bergerac* (New York,1936), passim. Margerie has a slightly different version of events (p.162).

[32] 23rd May 1902

[33] Archives Arnaga, quoted in André Triollet's brochure.

[34] Fasquelle, 1903; *Le Cantique de l'Aile*, XIV

[35] 29th May 1903. The incident is recounted by Apesteguy, pp. 216-7

[36] Pen name of Henry Gauthiers-Villars, a well-known wit who had published his wife Colette's early stories as his own.

[37] This sentiment has been shared by many who love the theatre. George Bernard Shaw saw the theatre as the week-day church (*Dramatic Opinions & Essays*, I, p.259

[38] E.-M de Vogüé, *Sous les Lauriers* , pp. 183-216

[39] "Un 'bluff' littéraire: le cas Edmond Rostand" (A literary bluff: the Edmond Rostand case). (Paris: P. Sevin & E. Rey, 1903)

[40] *Journal*, 29th Nov. 1901: "The poor man is reduced to that!" was Renard's comment.

[41] Faure, *L'Illustration*, 28 Jan. 1939, p. 99.

[42] L. de Robert, pp. 187-190

[43] An "interview" at the guineafowl's salon on his method of crowing has totally confused him

[44] Huret, *Interviews*, p. 225

[45] cf. George Bernard Shaw's *Man & Superman*, for example.

[46] There was a fashionable interest in these exotic cockerels, which Rostand would criticize in the play.

[47] *Le Cantique de l'Aile*, XI, i – viii (1911)

[48] Gérard, pp. 135-6

[49] Quoted in Margerie, pp. 178-9

[50] *Nouvelles litteraires, op.cit.*

[51] Jean Rostand, *Le Droit d'être naturaliste* (Paris: Stock, 1963), p. 36

[52] L. de Robert, pp. 191, 199

[53] *Le Temps*, 8 Jan 1905

[54] *Le Cantique de l'aile*, XX

[55] See Barrès, *Mes Cahiers* (Plon, 1931), vol IV, p. 330

[56] It is now open to the public as a Rostand museum.

[57] At Etchegorria, when Rostand was working well, he used to leave his door open. He liked to read aloud as he wrote and his voice could be heard, accompanied by thumps on the table to emphasise the cadences, throughout the house (Faure, p. 133)

[58] Faure, p.166.

[59] *Revue des Deux Mondes*, 56 (1930), pp.539-558; 774-90; *Souvenirs* (Paris, 1930).

[60] *Journal*, 25 Feb. 1908

[61] *Sous de Nouveaux Soleils*, p.165; Apesteguy, pp. 229-230. *Faust* was never completed. See Gérard, pp. 81-93 for extracts.

[62] Margerie, p. 189

[63] *Journal*, 9th Feb. 1909

[64] *L'Illustration*, 25.Dec 1920; *Le Cantique de l'Aile*, XXIV

[65] M. Rostand, p. 128.

[66] *Sous de Nouveaux Soleils*, pp. 170-74

[67] *ibid.*

[68] Renard, *Journal*, 10 Dec.1909

[69] M. Rostand, pp. 128-9

[70] 25th Feb. 1909

[71] *Journal*, 5 Dec. 1909

[72] Apesteguy, p. 248

[73] Benda, "Un Régulier dans le siècle" (Paris, 1938), p. 585

[74] *Sous de Nouveaux Soleils*, p.176

[75] *Journal*, 8 Feb.1910. Jules Renard had been offered two tickets but he was, it seems, not well enough to use them himself.

[76] It would appear in seventy weekly parts at seventy centimes each. Faguet contributed a preface

[77] An allusion to La Fontaine's fable, "Les Animaux malades de la peste". Quoted Ripert, p. 170

[78] *Comoedia*, 8 Feb 1910. Blum became a close friend.

[79] *Revue des Deux Mondes*, 15 Feb 1910

[80] Margerie, p. 264, fn. 31

[81] Marquet, *Ce Que je n'ai pas dit* (Paris, 1975), p. 36; (five francs was the price of a good meal out for two).

[82] *La Grande Revue*, 25th Feb.1910

[83] Feb 13 to 1st March

[84] Apesteguy, pp. 249-250

[85] April 1910, no 16. (Margerie, p. 264)

[86] M. Rostand, p. 130

[87] *Several of my Lives*, p. 228

[88] All were strong supporters of Rostand. Galipaux had refused all major roles for eight years to be sure of a role in *Chantecler* (Apesteguy, p. 248)

[89] Apesteguy, p. 253

[90] Apesteguy, p. 254

[91] *Sous de Nouveaux Soleils*, p. 177

[92] Ripert, p. 172. The sonnet can be found in *Le Cantique de l'aile*, XV

[93] Rostand had criticised this kind of acting behaviour in his *Discours de Réception*.

[94] Faure, p.173

[95] M.Rostand, p. 128

[96] Marquet, 1975, pp. 36-7.

[97] *Lettre à ma nièce sur Edmond Rostand* (Toulouse: Privat, 1970), p. 95

[98] Marquet, 1975, p. 37

[99] *Sous de Nouveaux Soleils*, pp. 177-8

[100] Ripert, pp. 162-3

[101] Gérard, p.126

[102] M.Rostand, p. 130

[103] Apesteguy, p. 257

[104] *Bordas Dictionnaire des oeuvres littéraires de langue française*

[105] The first issue of the French theatre monthly *Theatre Magazine*, (November 1985) was devoted (significantly) to *Chantecler*, including the full text.

[106] See Appendix

[107] L. de Robert, pp. 200-201

[108] Ripert, pp. 171-2

[109] 1 March 1910

[110] Paris: Fontemoing et Cie, 1913

[111] October 1910. The "Université des Annales" had been founded by Adolphe's wife Yvonne Sarcey for the instruction of young people.

[112] (1892), *Les Musardises* (1911 ed.), III,xii

Act Five: The Last Years (1910 – 1918)

La Faisane: *Que vas-tu faire?*
Chantecler: *Mon métier!*
The Pheasant: What are you going to do?
Chantecler: My job!
– (*Chantecler*, Act IV, sc. vii)

IN THE PEACE and privacy of Arnaga, Rostand returned, like his hero
Chantecler, to his work. It was not a dispirited poet who set to work
again, but one who still believed in his destiny. He still had faith in his
play, which he was sure future audiences would appreciate.

Over the next eight years, Rostand would attempt to give form
to some of the other ideas teeming in his brain, some new, some in
his mind for some time. His most ambitious project was the trilogy
already mentioned, in which Faust, Don Juan and Polichinelle would
successively portray the triumph of doubt and cynicism over the will
to create. These negative forces had been combated by Cyrano in
others, and by l'Aiglon, Chantecler and Hercules in themselves; now
the poet, who had until now put so much of himself into his idealistic
heroes, would create protagonists who would embody the attitudes to
life which he deplored.

Polichinelle had been intended for Coquelin; besides, many of
Rostand's ideas for it had been already incorporated into *Chantecler*.
So he now concentrated on his version of Goethe's *Faust*. Faust is a
seeker after truth who becomes tempted away from his path by the
delights of sensuality. In Rostand's version, Faust would save his soul
through returning to his love for Gretchen. Rostand hoped Le Bargy
would incarnate his hero at the Comédie-Française.

As Rostand liked to work on more than one project at a time, he
was also planning a play for Sarah Bernhardt, to be called *Le Théâtre*,
in which she would portray herself, under the name of "Gloriane". Beau
Brummel, the British dandy who had popularised the top hat, also

attracted the poet as a possible subject, as did the robot of Albert le Grand. *L'Automate* would deal with the argument between Albert, who created a human-like robot, and Thomas of Aquinas, who saw this as sacrilege. When Thomas destroys the robot in a fit of rage, it becomes a human being: it is, then, mortality which makes a man human.

This play was intended to be read rather than performed; after the lack of understanding of *Chantecler* in the theatre, Rostand was turning more and more towards writing "unperformable" philosophical plays. If he had lived longer, he would probably, in his son Jean's opinion, have at least completed *L'Automate*.[1] But sadly Rostand was unable to complete any of these projects, and not simply because of his early death. Much of his work ended up in the waste-paper basket, as it failed to reach his own demands of perfection. And his poor health and tendency to depression robbed him of many hours of possible work.

For health reasons and from choice, Rostand preferred to work in bed. He would spend most of the day there, facing the open window into the garden. Here Paul Faure would sometimes come to visit him. Faure remembers the mauve-patterned wallpaper, the sofa loaded with books, the Directoire clock over the mantelpiece. There was little furniture, so that the poet could work undistracted, but there were flowers on the windowsill and pictures on the walls: a portrait of Edmond's mother by Coraboeuf, and Deveria's Victor Hugo. In the corner stood Edmond's ivory-topped cane.[2]

Propped up in bed, Edmond would cover the pages of his notebooks, balanced on his briefcase, with his tiny writing, using a fine pen or a pencil. Notes for future poems would often be adorned with little sketches or doodles. He would also read the Paris papers and the latest books. Often he would be so absorbed that the butler would need to beat the gong more than once for lunch. If he was tired, or wanted to carry on working, his lunch would be brought to him in his room.

Lunch was a lively meal in the Rostand household. Maurice and Jean were now almost grown-up. With their tutor, Raymond Lerouge, the secretary Louis Labat, and the governess, Miss Day, they would hold enthusiastic discussions about a variety of topics, but especially literature and politics, under the indulgent eyes of their mother. If the arguments grew so passionate that the noise reached their absent father, he would send a note to ask what they were discussing, and might then send a contribution of his own, so further inflaming the discussion. But if Edmond was unwell, on the other hand, he might ask them to be a little quieter. This was rarely necessary, as at such times his family were too concerned to make lively conversation.[3]

When Rostand did join his family for lunch, the youthful high spirits of his sons were more restrained. Edmond was often eager to talk about the new book or play he had just been sent by the author. (He kept up-to-date with all the poetry, novels and plays that were published.) He managed to find something to praise in everything, however mediocre the work. Sometimes he would read passages aloud. "It was a delight to hear him", recalled Lerouge. "To the preciseness of his diction, to the warm, pure tone of his voice, he added an awareness of the text which allowed no detail, no nuance of syntax or vocabulary, to escape". When asked how he came to read so well, Edmond would reply that it was a matter of paying careful attention to the thoughts and intentions of the writer. Rostand's appreciation of literature was so sensitive that both Lerouge and Paul Faure thought Edmond could have made an excellent career as a critic, and if the work under discussion had not been successful, especially if it was a play, he enjoyed trying to improve on it himself.

After lunch, served informally in the little studio unless visitors other than intimate friends were present, the family would repair for a while to the salon, often continuing the discussion begun over the meal. In the evenings, the family would sometimes play cards here, but without Edmond, who preferred to relax by reading or sketching, or by talking to a guest in his study.

In the summer, if the weather was fine and he was well, Rostand might work in his garden, either strolling up and down thinking, or writing in the arbour. (His wife remembered that he was always losing pencils outside; one of the gardeners would cycle into Cambo for replacements.) But generally he would work in his room upstairs. Then, towards five o'clock, he would allow himself to go outside, bounding down the steps as if released from prison, and giving a cry of delight at seeing his wonderful garden again.

Rostand's garden at Arnaga was as much an artistic creation as his house and his plays. He had taken great pleasure in designing it, and was forever thinking of new ways to improve it. The formal garden now ran the full length of the plateau, stretching away towards the distant mountains, with its geometrical parterres full of vivid flowers, its lawns and pools with fountains, the whole framed by full-grown trees. Facing the classical orangery across the formal garden was a green arbour, approached through a rose garden, where the busts of Shakespeare, Victor Hugo and Cervantes overlooked the poet as he worked.

On the sides of the hill Rostand had increased the numbers of yellow broom bushes and added many more trees, whose forms were silhouetted against the Pyrenees. Elsewhere, rhododendrons and oleanders shed their colourful petals on the slopes. But at the back of the house, overlooking the valleys of the Arraga and the Nive, the garden was left as natural as possible, so that nothing should detract from the view. Judging by the photographs taken at the time, this quieter side of the house, with its lawn leading down to the stream, was where the family chose to entertain their close friends. Here there were no fountains or flowerbeds, just a few shade trees, the whole enclosed by a hedge of box overrun with small-flowered roses.[4] Edmond no longer needed excursions into the countryside to become close to nature – nature had come to him, in the privacy of Arnaga. Walking in his garden until the stars came out, the poet would find the peace and inspiration he needed. Sometimes, if the evening was fine, dinner would be taken on the terrace.

After Rostand's return from Paris, he added an Italian-style portico to the far end of the formal garden, its colonnades reflected in still pools. Three hundred white doves made wonderful patterns in the sky and against the saffron-coloured awnings over the house windows, specially chosen to set them off. Rostand had taken a fancy to having white animals in his garden – besides the doves there were white cats, white dogs, and white swans to glide beside a small boat on the canal he built soon after, to lead down the length of the formal garden towards the portico.

Inside the house, too, changes were always being made. Even some of the murals were eventually shifted to new homes. The Genlis salon was transformed into a "salon chinois" with the arrival of some fine Chinese lacquer panels, a gift from Edmond's brother-in-law Pierre de Margerie, now serving in the French Embassy in Pekin. Just as when he was a child, Edmond also loved rearranging the furniture, saying it was good exercise if he could not go on his usual walk in the garden because of bad weather.

A life at once simple and luxurious was lived in these splendid surroundings. Edmond's own life consisted mainly of work and walks in his garden. Only a few intimate friends, such as Paul Faure, visited the family. Only when he was going out, or receiving official visitors, did Edmond need to dress elegantly, as he did in Paris. At Arnaga, he wore a brown woollen suit in winter, and a striped white flannel suit in summer, with large tortoise-shell spectacles taking the place of his famous monocle. "No one was more simple, more lacking in arrogance or posing".⁵ His sons, too, though raised in luxury, did not act as if this made them special in any way. True, they had lessons from private tutors, and their own horses to ride. But Rosemonde had always encouraged them to mix with the local boys. Jean would often go up to Cambo to play pelote, and Maurice, when they lived at Etchegorria, had spent many happy hours at the social club there. Rosemonde herself, in the time left to her from running the house, had started to write and publish poetry again.

The sumptuous luxury of Arnaga's interior, and its splendid garden, surprised those who knew Edmond to be a modest man with simple tastes. But Arnaga, to Edmond, was not only his home but also an aesthetic creation, which, like his written works, he wanted to make perfect. He was always conscious of its imperfections, always trying to improve it. But Arnaga's main purpose, which Rostand did succeed in fulfilling, was to provide a beautiful and isolated setting within which he felt relaxed and private enough to write.

Edmond's home at Arnaga, well outside the town, and accessible from the road only by a long drive flanked with hydrangeas, gave the poet the solitude he craved. No casual visitor could come within eyeshot of the house and its gardens. Inevitably, at times, the Rostands would have to welcome important people on *visites d'honneur*, and sometimes their friends from Paris came to stay, but otherwise they led an intentionally isolated life: apart from close friends such as Paul Faure and his wife, only the doctor, the lawyer, and, if Edmond's mother was with them, the curé, would call. This suited Edmond very well: he disliked having to make conversation to people with whom he had nothing in common, and resented any time spent away from his work. And although he enjoyed speculating about what splendid fêtes he could give in the setting of Arnaga, in practice he preferred to keep its beauty and peace for himself and his family.

In any case, Rostand needed quietness to work. His family had long been aware of this. Inspiration was a fickle guest, liable to slip away if disturbed. And inspiration alone was not enough. Contrary to what his critics had assumed, Rostand was not content with what he had written rapidly, when inspired; he continued to revise his work until he was satisfied with it. This was one reason why it took him so long to complete a play or even a poem. In his son Jean's words "he did not accept his facility and wanted to give nothing that was not perfect".[6] Louis de Robert agreed: Rostand would often write something straight off, but he always inspected it minutely afterwards. Rostand himself told Raymond Lerouge that he could not imagine "the gift without the work". This was one reason for his dislike of modern "vers libre" – Rostand preferred to work within the discipline of the traditional verse forms, though, unlike some of his critics, he did not expect other poets to necessarily do the same.[7]

One September evening in 1910, Rostand had an experience which set his inspiration off along a new track. The French aviator, Tabuteau, flew his plane over Arnaga to pay homage to the poet. Rostand immediately invited him to lunch next day, and wrote a sonnet, "Premier Passage sur mon jardin". This was the first of several poems that Rostand would compose over the next ten months to celebrate the amazing achievement of flight.

Rostand hated to leave Arnaga. Several days before a necessary departure, according to Paul Faure, he would become morose, dreading not only leaving his home, but also the whole business of packing, travelling and staying in hotels. But in October he was obliged to make a brief visit to Paris to consult with Fasquelle about the new edition of *Les Musardises*, to be published early in 1911; he also had to visit the publishers Lafitte to discuss their proposed illustrated edition of the poet's *Collected Works*.

While in Paris, Rostand probably attended some of the sessions of the Académie française, though he never travelled up to Paris specially. With his usual modesty, he had told Louis de Robert that he felt he should not attend because he had no "instruction" (education); this was not said to evoke protest – he never did that, says Robert, no, he said it because he felt it was true.[8]

Edmond's friend Charles Le Bargy accompanied him on his return to Arnaga. The actor was planning to retire from the Comédie-Française, and asked his friend for a new two-act play for his farewell performance.

It seemed to Edmond that the short dialogue he'd already written about Don Juan might be made suitable. (And in view of Le Bargy's fondness for amorous adventures, appropriate! Le Bargy had also starred in Molière's *Don Juan* at the Comédie.) Edmond had been thinking of using it as a link between *Faust* and *Polichinelle* in his proposed grand trilogy; sketches of Don Juan can be seen on some of the manuscript pages of *Chantecler*. He promised Le Bargy he would revise the play and write a Prologue for it.

Early in 1911, Edmond was again obliged to travel briefly to Paris for the publication of the new edition of *Les Musardises*. Subtitled "Édition nouvelle 1887 – 1893", it contained many new poems written by Rostand before 1893, mostly written at Luchon in the happy three years following his marriage. These were collected in Part Three, now entitled "La Maison des Pyrenées", replacing the "Le Livre de l'Aimée" of the original edition. Rostand also took the opportunity to remove some other poems to make way for new work in Section Two, which he renamed "Incertitudes".[9]

Twenty thousand copies of this edition of *Les Musardises* were published. Edmond recited some of the new poems at the Université des Annales. He found he had lost none of his popularity – the audience acclaimed him, and women threw flowers on the stage.

On his return to Arnaga, Rostand began to work seriously on what was to become *La Dernière Nuit de Don Juan*. Simultaneously, fired by the achievements of the daring young French aviators, he celebrated them as modern heroes in a long poem, "Le Cantique de l'aile" (The Canticle of Flight).[10] Rostand also wrote five sonnets linked by the theme of flight, which would be published in *Le Figaro* the following year.[11]

In contrast to writing about heroes who inspired people to raise their eyes to the skies, in June 1911 Rostand wrote a sequence of eight sonnets honouring a man who kept his eyes on the ground – Henri Fabre.[12]

As we have seen, Edmond had become interested in Fabre through his son Jean, while he was writing *Chantecler*. Jean later wrote of the similarity between Edmond Rostand and the humble, simple naturalist of Provence. Edmond, too, was a silent, solitary man, who only lived for his work. It was not surprising that Edmond felt an affinity with Fabre. He wrote in a notebook:

> Henri Fabre. A hero. Obsession. Fabre is a modern hero, because of the wall round his garden ... The vocation, the message. To live on and from oneself... unity of life ... not to take on too much ... Nothing should turn us away from our work... Life does not give us time to move around... we must straight away start digging in where we are.[13]

Similar ideas are found in *Chantecler*, and they continued to guide the life of Rostand at Arnaga. He had found the perfect place in which to carry on his work of writing "leçons d'âme" – lessons for the soul.

The apparent ease and happiness of life at Arnaga, however, concealed a growing distance between the poet and his wife.

The joys that Edmond and Rosemonde had shared in the early days of Edmond's fame had been replaced by the burden on the poet of living up to his fame, and producing new works to satisfy the public. Rosemonde had always been his support and encouragement, she had rescued work thrown away in Edmond's moods of despair and helped him to reconstruct it; she had given up her own career to further that of her husband; she had carefully copied out his verse from his tiny, hasty hand-writing, and had learnt his poems and speeches by heart. She had helped to save his life by her careful nursing when he was ill after *L'Aiglon*. She had made a peaceful, happy home for Edmond to work in, and kept importunate visitors from disturbing him. But she could not do her husband's work for him. The strain of creativity, which so often made Edmond ill and subject to nervous crises, was Edmond's alone. The poet's determination to fulfil what he saw as his duty now cut him off, even more than in the past, from his family. Rosemonde, from being the close companion, the sharer in every phase of a new play or poem, was now excluded more and more from the process of creation and so from her husband's life.

Arnaga had been totally Edmond's creation – all Rosemonde had done was offer her usual encouragement of her husband's projects. Rosemonde had been happy at Etchegorria, the villa she had selected for the family to live in. Etchegorria was bright and airy, simple, intimate. Arnaga was less of a home than a prince's palace; it was also isolated, far from the town, and without her beloved mother's presence Rosemonde may have felt lonely. Neither Edmond nor Rosemonde wanted to socialise with the local gentry or the aristocrats of Biarritz. But because of Edmond's desire to work, few friends were invited to visit. Besides, Coq was dead and Sarah away much of the time on her tours of the States and Europe; they scarcely saw Bauer even in Paris; Edmond had fallen out with Hervieu and would soon fall out with Claretie. There were new friends, of course, but they were generally Edmond's. It is not surprising that Rosemonde had enjoyed her recent stay in Paris.

Light-hearted, easy-going, unconventional, simple in her dress and her attitude to life, she had married for love, and still had the passionate heart of a romantic schoolgirl. Speaking of *La Dame aux Camélias* to Jules Renard,[14] she had admitted adoring such sentimental plays. But they bored her husband. Already, in *Les Romanesques*, he was gently making fun of such a romantic attitude to love in real life. "Amusez-vous" was Rosemonde's recommendation to her sons, whereas Edmond extolled the virtues of hard work. Maurice would follow his mother's prescription, Jean his father's.

There had been signs of strain in the relationship for some time. Perhaps one should not read too much into the omission of the love poems to Rosemonde from the new edition of *Les Musardises*, prepared as early as 1903. Something had to be dropped to make way for the poems written between 1890 and 1893, and the love poems were not particularly original. But it is noticeable that Rostand retained several poems expressing his distrust of women.

More significant is the letter Rostand had written to Coq in November 1904, after his long nervous illness, saying he owed it to his wife and family to spend more time with them. "Rosemonde is worth more than Fame, and my children are worth more than my author's rights".[15] This suggests that Rostand was conscious of neglecting his family, and felt he should do something about it. But the family/work conflict could never, in a writer like Rostand who was so conscious of his duty as a writer, be resolved for long in favour of the family. When he was unable to work because of depression, Rosemonde did her best to distract the poet and encourage him to relax by, for instance, putting on a puppet play together, as they had at Etchegorria. But, like his hero Chantecler, Rostand would always, when he was well enough, try to fulfil what he saw as his vocation – that is, to write plays and poetry that would inspire ordinary people with love, joy and courage. In spite of his very real desire to rest from the strain of writing and enjoy the company of his family, and the beauty and peace of the Basque countryside, he had returned, when the nervous crisis was over, to writing *Chantecler*.

The various references to women as distractions to the hero from his duty in *Chantecler* and *Les Douze Travaux* may also reflect the strains within the marriage. Chantecler, in defiance of the Pheasant's instructions to crow only once, to save his voice, crows instead as often as he feels it is his duty to crow, but in secret. This could be a reference to Rosemonde's protectiveness. Both Chantecler and Hercules feel under pressure from the women they love to put their love before their work, and both resist the temptation.

However, from Rosemonde's point of view, she had done all she could to support her husband in his self-imposed task of giving "leçons d'âme" (lessons for the soul). She had given up her own career as a poet to further that of her husband, and cheerfully devoted herself completely to him and her family. Without her encouragement, would Edmond ever have had the courage to share his work with the public? Rosemonde was ambitious for him; she wanted the whole world to know his worth. But now that it did, it seemed that her husband no longer needed her. He had so many other women now to choose from, attracted by his fame. She had turned a blind eye to any philandering in Paris, and had remained faithful herself, in a society in which adultery was common enough. But her simple devotion and still youthful beauty were not enough, it seemed, to satisfy Edmond, who now preferred the company of the spirited, intelligent women of the world who sought him out in Paris, women such as Simone, of whom Rosemonde was distrustful, but in this particular case, without good reason.[16]

Deprived of her husband's company and affection, Rosemonde had turned more and more to her son Maurice, to whom she had always been close, and whose attachment for her had always been unusually strong, ever since, as a very small boy, he had tied a length of cotton to her finger when she was going out for the evening. Jean was silent, self-absorbed, a solitary like his father. Maurice was out-going, lively, imaginative, chatty, a passionate lover of romantic and sentimental literature and he hoped to be a poet and writer like his parents. If Jean had inherited his father's serious, shy, thoughtful side, Maurice represented rather Edmond's "Pierrot qui rit" aspect, which since his fame became a burden was less and less in evidence. To this extent, Maurice may have reminded Rosemonde of past happiness.

When Rosemonde and Maurice had visited Paris alone together in the winter of 1906-7, because Maurice had broken his arm and it needed resetting, the attachment between mother and son was already very close. Renard noted, "Maurice adores his mother. At every moment when he is with her he talks of love".[17] Mother and son wrote a play together in 1908 – a distraction for Maurice when he had had to spend a month in isolation because of scarlet fever. Chiefly the work of Rosemonde, she convinced him it was he who had written "Un Bon Petit Diable", a play based on one of Mme de Ségur's stories.[18]

It was Rosemonde, rather than Edmond, who now encouraged Maurice's writing ambitions – Edmond opposed them, especially when his son began to write for the theatre. In his memoirs, Maurice generously suggests this was because his father wished to spare him the difficulties he himself had had to undergo, which would be multiplied by having such a famous father. Opposition, too, would help Maurice to discover whether he had a true vocation.[19] It had been Sarah Bernhardt who had first recognised and encouraged Maurice's love for the theatre. As for poetry, Jules Renard noted in 1909, having heard him recite, that Maurice had a genuine talent.[20] Like his father, Maurice drew inspiration from Musset and Hugo as well as from the English poets, particularly Shelley. He was a precocious writer. At fifteen, Maurice had translated *La Samaritaine* into English; at nineteen, his first book of poems was published.

Nor did Edmond approve of his elder son's behaviour when the family were staying in Paris in 1909 and 1910: visiting salons, declaiming his poetry, giving interviews to the press and delighting in the attentions of photographers. Edmond did not see in his son's elegant (but too extravagant) attire a desire to copy an admired father; the author of *Cyrano de Bergerac* also deplored Maurice's effeminate, coquettish ways. He cannot fail to have noticed his son's closest friends were all male, while the various fiancées in whom Maurice briefly showed an interest were all sent away disappointed. Homosexuality was against the law at that time, and gay men and women were discreet about their sexual preferences, but Maurice revealed himself boldly in his clothes, his permed hair (dyed to be blond, like his mother's), and in his feminine gestures.

The long period of writing and the eventual, only half-successful performance of *Chantecler* had accentuated the growing rift between Rosemonde and Edmond. The poet had wanted to keep the play from being performed; he thought it more suitable for publication than the theatre, and was afraid the boulevard audience would not understand a play into which he had put so much of his own inner life. In all this he was proved right. It was Rosemonde and Coquelin whose combined flattery and insistence had eventually persuaded him to let the play go forward. But Edmond was becoming suspicious of his wife's unfailing admiration of everything he wrote. After a visit to the Rostands at their hotel on 5th December 1909, Jules Renard noted that Edmond was apprehensive about the reception of his play. "It will be a flop", he had said, " I don't understand anything in the first act any more." Then, turning to his wife, "You always say: 'It's wonderful!' I change it. You still say: 'It's wonderful!'".

Rosemonde's eagerness to get *Chantecler* performed, her extravagant praise of the play in the salons she visited in 1909 with Maurice, their enjoyment of the limelight, were all in contrast to Edmond's own misgivings and his natural desire to be self-effacing. He could hardly help noticing that his wife and elder son delighted in the reflected glory of his fame. Indeed, the behaviour of Rosemonde and Maurice had given useful ammunition to Rostand's enemies. Julien Benda, who occasionally (but reluctantly) attended his cousin Simone's thriving literary and political salon, noted in his diary, "The wife and one of the sons were unbearable … in their conviction that the birth of *Chantecler* was the great event of the century, and in their indignation that the universe might have other concerns." Benda glimpsed Edmond at the first night of *Chantecler*, and thought him "a man capable of an inner life, of thought and even self-criticism". Comparing this impression with the behaviour of Rosemonde and Maurice, Benda wondered whether Rostand was perhaps the type of writer whose entourage had led to their downfall by assuring them that everything that came from them was sublime.[21]

Then again, after Coq's death, Rostand had in fact had little choice but to let Jean Coquelin and Hertz put on the play at the Porte-Saint-Martin theatre, in spite of his misgivings. But it was Rosemonde who encouraged a reluctant Edmond to accept Lucien Guitry for the leading role, Guitry whom Edmond felt was unsuitable for the part, and who in the end all but sabotaged his play.

It was also Rosemonde's overprotectiveness that had allowed his enemies in Paris to misportray her husband's delays in getting *Chantecler* performed as an attempt to increase publicity for the play. By preventing him from seeing the increasingly vicious criticisms of him in the Paris papers, she deprived him of the right to react and defend himself, which he took as soon as he discovered the true situation.

Rostand had always borne with Rosemonde's desire to protect him, even to the extent of taking a groom with him when he went riding. In view of his absentmindedness, he may even have been grateful; at the very least, he could appreciate that this came from her concern for his safety. But he was now becoming aware of how harmful his wife's attitude could be to his own reputation. The exaggerated care with which Rosemonde tried to protect her husband from the slightest contre-temps had in the past annoyed Louis de Robert. Montesquiou would note that Rostand was surrounded by a coterie whom he must find embarrassing. At least four people, besides the family, he claimed, kept up a kind of worship of Edmond, presenting his every act as if it offered some special virtue or grace. These admirers, especially Rosemonde and Maurice, by extension were given publicity for their own actions.[22]

"Edmond loves me more than ever", Rosemonde had told Jules Renard on 25th February 1909. (Why should she make a point of saying this, unless she was unsure of it?) "He has one fault" she had continued, "He won't write". She seems not to have understood her husband's scruples with regard to *Chantecler*. Rosemonde enjoyed the reflected glory that came from her husband's fame, the fame which seemed to give Edmond himself so little pleasure and so much anguish. In encouraging Maurice's ambitions, and by continuing to write herself, she would be able to return to the literary life of Paris, of which her isolation at Arnaga and her husband's dislike of salon society had deprived her for so long.

Even at Arnaga, however, there were occasionally "visites d'honneur" from notables spending the summer season at nearby Biarritz. More enjoyable for the family, though, were the visits from friends: besides Le Bargy, Léon Blum and Louis Barthou, among others, found their way to Arnaga.

Léon Blum, now critic of *Comoedia* (as well as being a lawyer, sociologist, essayist, and many other things), was leading a campaign to keep the theatre at the forefront of modern life. Though his background –the *Revue blanche*, the *Mercure de France* – was hostile to Rostand after *Cyrano de Bergerac*, Blum had understood and admired *Chantecler*, and had written such an appreciative review that the two men put aside previous misunderstandings and became good friends. Blum came often to Arnaga, and his clear thinking, sound judgement and gently persuasive talking impressed Paul Faure, who noted that these qualities, along with Blum's love of the spiritual and his capacity for true friendship, made him very dear to Edmond.

In total contrast to Blum was another new friend, Louis Barthou, who swept through Arnaga like a gust of wind, exuding physical and intellectual vitality. A career politician who was soon to realise his ambition of becoming prime minister, he was also president of numerous societies and was trying to get into the Académie française. Barthou had admired Rostand and cultivated his friendship since *Cyrano de Bergerac*. He knew hundreds of lines of Rostand's poetry and quoted them frequently in his speeches.

In contrast to these friendships with public figures was the relationship which developed between Edmond and the local postman. But Louis Geandreau was no ordinary postman. He had been writing poetry and plays since the age of sixteen. A fervent admirer of Rostand, he took every chance he could to embellish the poet's correspondence, writing affectionate verses or lyrical effusions on the backs of envelopes or the inside of newspaper wrappers. Edmond, amused and intrigued, called the unknown poet "le Sylphe". After Geandreau sent him one particularly beautiful poem under his own name, Rostand invited him to come to Arnaga. As they walked in the garden, talking of poetry, the young man mentioned he was a postman. Light dawned: "You must be 'le Sylphe'", cried Rostand. Geandreau only put his finger to his lips and smiled.[23]

When there were no visitors, the members of the family were all busy with their own concerns. Jean, now sure he wanted to become a naturalist, had been given his own laboratory at Arnaga. Here he spent most of his time outside lessons exploring the wonders of insects and amphibians.

Maurice for his part was revelling in the social and cultural life of Biarritz, where the salon life of the capital continued during the summer months. That summer, Maurice was thrilled to see two of his poems printed prominently in *Le Figaro*, thanks to the kind offices of the editor, Gaston Calmette, a good friend of his parents. These poems were favourably received by many critics, and earned Maurice a letter from a young British student at Oxford by the name of Harold Nicholson. Soon after followed the publication, by Fasquelle, of his first book of poetry, called simply *Poèmes*.

On 27th July, Edmond received official confirmation that he would be made a Commander of the Legion of Honour. He would not receive the insignia until August 1913, and when he did, was shy of displaying his purple cravate in public. Montesquiou noticed that at one social occasion he attended, Rostand kept his coat on to hide the decoration until he saw Hervicu arrive wearing his.[24]

Besides writing his poems on flight and his sonnets to Fabre, Rostand continued to work on other projects. In a light-hearted moment he wrote a poem, "Les Rois Mages", in which the Three Wise Men lose sight of the star they are following.[25] This is a parable-poem like "La Brouette", reflecting Rostand's belief that the simple faith of the humblest brings them closest to God. The star is rediscovered by the least regarded of the three Wise Men, who sees its reflection in the bucket of water he is offering to their animals. This recalls the old hen's sayings in *Chantecler*: "Ce qui voit le mieux le ciel, c'est l'eau du puits" (it is the water in the well which sees the sky best), and "Un rond d'azur suffit pour voir passer les astres" (a circle of sky is enough to see the passage of the stars).

Edmond's work received a brief setback in August when he was involved in a car accident, on his way to visit Simone one morning at Bayonne. (She had rented a villa in the Basque country for the summer with her new husband, Casimir-Périer.) Edmond's chauffeur apparently had a momentary blackout, and the car fell into a ditch. Edmond was trapped underneath the car and lost consciousness. He was lucky enough to escape with severe bruising.

There is a mystery here: the reason for the chauffeur's blackout was apparently that he had been driving all night. Had Edmond been to Paris? Or had the car been returning from delivering a visitor to Paris? What is really strange is that Rostand should have asked the chauffeur to drive on a morning after he had driven all night. His consideration for others was usually very marked. When Edmond had lived in Paris, for instance, Jules Renard had been amused at the poet's unusual sollicitude for his coachman. When he went for supper after the theatre, Edmond could not bear to think of him left outside in the cold and the rain. He would send him a hot toddy, and tell him to return home; he, Rostand, would get a taxi back. But one evening the coachman had come into the café and given notice, because he did not think Rostand was taking him seriously enough.[26]

Disquieting news came from Marseilles. Edmond's father Eugène, now sixty-eight, was suffering from hardening of the arteries, which had gradually prevented him from working and was now threatening to incapacitate him altogether. Eugène and Angèle would be moving to Paris, to live near Eugène's beloved brother Alfred and his wife, who were now living at 22, Avenue de Villiers. Edmond went to Paris that autumn to see them.

On that visit, Edmond was also able to renew contact with Sarah Bernhardt, just back from twelve months in the United States. The indefatigable Sarah was continuing to act in spite of the pain her bad leg still gave her. It had been injured in 1905, on a previous tour, and an operation in 1908 had been unsuccessful. Sarah had spent the summer of 1910 in London, where the second act of *L'Aiglon* had been on her programme. Now she and Edmond together watched a preview of some scenes she had filmed from *La Dame aux Camélias*, renamed *Camille* for the cinema. She had taken enthusiastically to the world of film: Sarah always looked forward rather than back. Now in her seventies, she would continue to act into the Twenties.

That winter, however, Edmond did not travel to Paris for the première of his wife and son's play, *Un Bon Petit Diable*, "being unable to come to Paris for so little", as Maurice puts it in his memoirs. Instead Edmond rented a villa for himself and Jean (who did go to see the play) at Biarritz for part of the winter, and carried on working on his Don Juan play for Le Bargy.

Un Bon Petit Diable was the play Rosemonde had written, with a little help from her son, in 1908. Maurice, turning up to direct rehearsals in his extravagantly elegant costumes, giving interviews and being photographed, just like his famous father, felt he now really was the playwright he had long hoped to become. After all, his play had been accepted by the Gymnase, a leading boulevard theatre, as their Christmas offering for children; actors of the calibre of Galipaux (who had played the blackbird in *Chantecler*), and Marthe Mellot (who had been the nightingale), were taking part.

The première took place on 22nd December 1911. To Maurice's delight and gratification, the play was a success; hardened critics, who had criticized *Chantecler*, had waxed sentimental about this charming little fairy story. Even while appreciating the irony of this, Maurice felt encouraged by the reception of "his" first play, even though there were only thirty performances, and takings were correspondingly small. *Un Bon Petit Diable* was however successful enough to be translated into

English, and performed in New York in 1913. In 1924, it was made into a musical, with music by George Gershwin.

The hectic social life enjoyed during Maurice and Rosemonde's stay at the Astoria more than compensated for the brief run of their play. Maurice visited his favourite salons and was invited to many of the fancy-dress balls of the Christmas season. He dined with actresses and fell in and out of love several times.

Edmond himself returned briefly to Paris in January 1912, to deliver his famous 1896 "Sonnet to Sarah" at the Théâtre Féminin's gala for the actress. While in the capital, Edmond took the opportunity to use his influence with Louis Barthou and others to obtain a posting in Paris for his brother-in-law, Pierre de Margerie, now anxious to leave Pekin. Doubtless Pierre's wife Jeanne wanted, too, to be close to her sick father.

His duties over, Rostand returned to Arnaga and remained there until the autumn. Besides correcting the proofs of his poems on the theme of flight for *Le Figaro*, his main preoccupations were his version of *Faust*, of which he would complete Part One this year, and his play about Don Juan, which had not been ready in time for Le Bargy's farewell performance at the Comédie-Française. The title would be *La Dernière Nuit de Don Juan*. Edmond was also still working on the various other projects already mentioned. But new ideas were continually occurring to him, such as a poem about Penelope, as she waits for the return of Ulysses. Rosemonde quotes some of the only lines remaining in existence, describing a dream Penelope has about the flock of swans she was feeding (doubtless an idea suggested by the swans of Arnaga).[27]

About this time there was a misunderstanding with Sarah about Rostand's new version of *La Princesse lointaine*. The actress had heard a rumour that it was to be offered to the Comédie-Française, instead of, as agreed long ago, to her. She wrote with her customary vigour to Edmond, who sent the following reply: "*La Princesse* is yours. You will play *La Princesse* with your genius which I have always adored, and which remains Unique. I obey my conscience, and to use the word with which you decorate your letter, which I have already burnt, I don't give a damn about the rest".[28]

The summer of 1912 brought the usual visitors to Arnaga. Simone was again spending August in Cambo with her husband. Her tour of America had been so successful that she had been invited to return in October. However, the English version of Rostand's *La Princesse lointaine*, "The Lady of Dreams",[29] had not been well received, having had only twenty-one performances in New York, and even fewer in London.

The summer season, for Maurice, was enlivened by a visit from his friend Jean Cocteau in September. As only close friends of Edmond's were allowed to stay at Arnaga, for fear other visitors would disturb the poet's work, Cocteau stayed at a hotel in Cambo. But the friends met every day, making plans for the future and reading each other their poetry.

Maurice and Jean would also go for rides in Maurice's car, with another friend, the musician Tiarko Richepin, who had been a member of Cocteau's group in Paris, and who was now living with his wife in Cambo. Tiarko was the second son of the Rostands' old friend Jules Richepin; Rosemonde had first known him as a child, in 1906. Now, lonely and neglected, she allowed herself to fall in love with the young man he had become. Tiarko did not let his marriage, which was an unhappy one, stand in the way of reciprocating her feelings. At first, the couple were discreet, and Edmond did not suspect the liaison.

That autumn, the whole family would visit Paris for the preparations for Le Bargy's revival of *Cyrano de Bergerac*, the first production since the death of Coquelin.

Le Bargy had decided to try out his interpretation of Cyrano in the provinces before it was revealed to the Parisian public at the Port-Saint-Martin theatre. This tour proved very successful and augured well for the revival in the capital. Letters went back and forth between author and performer, concerning the new production. Rostand was eager to take advantage of new approaches to staging. "Don't you think we should get a colourist to study all the costumes together? And the colours in the scenes with large groups of people should not be left to chance," he wrote on 21st October. "Very beautiful tableaux could be consciously composed, as is usual now." [10]

Edmond hoped for the kind of magnificent production from Le Bargy that his play would have benefited from at the Comédie-Française. One senses that he would have loved to be allowed to direct and stage the play himself. The casting, too, had to be left to Le Bargy, though here again, Rostand offered advice. Andrée Mégard had been suggested by Hertz for the role of Roxane. But would she be able to express the preciosity and lyricism demanded by the part, and the deep emotion needed in the last two acts? "Let us be wary", wrote Edmond, thinking no doubt of Guitry, "of repeating the mistake we made in *Chantecler* of having verse spoken by actors who are only good in modern plays".

So that Rostand could attend as many rehearsals as his health would allow, the whole family moved to Paris for the winter of 1912-13. Since they intended to stay for longer than usual, they rented a furnished flat in the rue d'Astorg, not far from Edmond's family in the Avenue de Villiers, and, poignantly, near the church of St Augustine, where Edmond and Rosemonde had been married. (Maurice, for his part, was quick to note the proximity of the Countess de Greffulhe's salon.) Here the Rostands would have more privacy than in a hotel, and not have to keep up the fatiguing pretence of being a united family.

While Edmond and Rosemonde, united at least in their desire to see the new production of *Cyrano de Bergerac* fulfil their high expectations, went to attend rehearsals at the Porte-Saint-Martin, Jean had enrolled at several university courses, passing one scientific examination after another with ease. (He obtained his first degree at the age of seventeen.) Maurice naturally returned with delight to the literary and social life of Paris. To his father's chagrin (if he knew), Maurice combined high and low life, taking tea with duchesses and supper with courtesans. He was received again at his favourite salons, such as those of Madame de Pierrebourg and the Duchesse de Rohan, where he was sometimes invited to recite his own verse, leaning in traditional style against the mantelpiece.

The highlight of this Parisian stay, however, for Maurice, was that he finally made the acquaintance of Cocteau's friend Marcel Proust. To literary Paris, Proust was just an amateur and a snob. His friends, however, such as Lucien Daudet, Reynaldo Hahn, and Cocteau, knew him as a man of genius who had written an amazingly original and beautiful novel, *Du côté de chez Swann*, which he was trying to get published by Fasquelle, the publisher of high-class best-sellers like Flaubert, Zola and Rostand.

The meeting took place at a midnight supper at Larue's. When Maurice, having spent the evening at Diaghilev's *Ballets russes*, arrived, Proust was already there, with his friend and admirer Marie Scheikevitch. After an extravagant meal (for which Proust simply signed the bill, then borrowed a large sum of money from the Head Waiter for his own tip and a taxi home), Proust offered to read part of his novel to Maurice. In his memoirs, Maurice describes how he first heard, from the author's own lips, the opening pages of what was to become the first volume of *A la Recherche du temps perdu*.[31]

Maurice's admiration for Proust's genius was shared by his father. Edmond had read and much admired an article by Proust in *Le Figaro* that September, entitled "L'Église du village" (an excerpt from the chapter on Combray). He would have sent a congratulatory telegram to its author, but feared his compliments would be unwelcome to someone he knew was a friend of Montesquiou, Edmond's self-declared enemy after *Chantecler*. But on hearing from Maurice that Proust was trying to get his book published, Rostand very much wanted to help him. He asked Maurice (as he himself was unwell) to send a telegram to Fasquelle, recommending it. "You would give [my father and myself] great personal pleasure by publishing this book in its entirety", Maurice duly wrote. "Literature will be grateful to you." Alas, Fasquelle was unmoved by their pleas, and Proust finally had to pay for the publication of the first volume himself, *chez* Grasset. But Proust never forgot Rostand's kindness.

In the intervals between attending rehearsals and resting, Edmond was renewing acquaintance with the family from whom distance had kept him, apart from brief visits, for so long. His parents had rented accommodation in the rue Jouffroy,[32] which adjoins the Avenue de Villiers where Alexis and his wife lived. Eugène was scarcely recognisable any longer as the highly-respected economist, banker and academician of Marseilles. His condition had deteriorated so much that he had to be looked after by a full-time nurse. In addition to the arteriosclerosis which was gradually killing him, Eugène was also suffering from terrible nervous crises caused by the neurasthenia which also afflicted his children Edmond and Jeanne.

The pain caused to Edmond by seeing his much-loved and respected father in this condition was mitigated somewhat by renewing his relationship with his sister Jeanne. Since her marriage, Jeanne, his younger sister by ten years, had spent most of her time abroad with her husband on his diplomatic postings. Now back in Paris, thanks to Edmond's overtures to his powerful friends, she was continuing to assist her husband Pierre's career by attracting writers and politicians to her salon in the rue de l'Université. Edmond and Jeanne found that, besides the neurasthenia inherited from their father and their Spanish grandmother, they had much else in common. Jeanne's friendship was to give Rostand much-needed support in the future.

Edmond's hopes of protecting himself and his family from the world's attention by staying in an appartment rather than a hotel, were only partly fulfilled. He would have been shocked to read the Abbé Mugnier's entry in his diary for 3rd December 1912, which gives an idea of the malicious gossip current in the salons. The abbé, father confessor to the cream of society, and a great diner-out, had spent the evening with the Félix de Vogüés and others. They had discussed the state of affairs at the Rostands: "it's an impossible household. There's a mad grandfather, ... His son, the great poet who has delusions of grandeur. Maurice, who has waved hair – an impossible character who is on very good terms with Pradier. Mme Rostand on very good terms herself with Richepin's son. And another of his sons who practices vivisection."[33]

The revival of *Cyrano de Bergerac*, was, however, a great success. The new staging, still realistic, with real food this time in the café and battle scenes, but also more modern in style, as Rostand had suggested, was well-received, as was Le Bargy's performance. Rostand, delighted to see his friend at last acting in one of his plays, and looking forward to seeing him as his Don Juan, sent him an enthusiastic telegram, which included the phrase: "I'm particularly glad of a success which comes to me through you, and I hope that this is a sign and a good omen".[34]

It was the first time another actor had played the role in Paris since Coquelin, who had played Cyrano nine hundred and fifty times before his death. Le Bargy brought not only a different temperament to the part, but a different professional background. His more melancholy interpretation of the role did not please everyone, but many, like Maurice Rostand, felt he attained a kind of tragic grandeur in the last act. All in all, he was seen as a worthy successor to the great Coquelin.

Such was the success of the new production of *Cyrano de Bergerac* that the thousandth performance of the play in Paris was attained on 26th April 1913. (It had already had more than two thousand performances on tour.) This was a rare event in those days. Rostand wrote a heartfelt sonnet in honour of Coquelin for the occasion, delivered to a hushed house by Le Bargy/Cyrano, when he presents the Cadets de Gascogne to the Comte de Guiche in Act Two. "I am not the one who should be speaking these lines at the thousandth performance", he proclaimed, and called on the Cadets to join him in saluting:

> *Celui qui de son âme a fait vibrer ces vers*
> *Et de les voir revivre eût pleuré de tendresse.*
> The one who made these verses vibrate with his soul,
> and who would have wept with tenderness to see them revived.

Only two major roles were taken by their original interpreters: Jean Coquelin as Ragueneau, and Desjardins as the Comte de Guiche. The new Christian was Pierre Magnier, who would play Cyrano himself in 1919. From now on, *Cyrano de Bergerac* would be revived almost every year in Paris, with a succession of Cyranos, each with their own special styles and strengths. But for Maurice Rostand: "Only Coquelin was truly wholly Cyrano, because only Coquelin had Cyrano's independence, disdain, courage, both physical and moral, Coquelin who brought to the role the humanity of a Molière and the panache of a Hugo."[15]

Since Le Bargy's revival, there has probably been no day in the year when Rostand's play is not being performed to enthusiastic audiences somewhere in the world. In the United States, Walter Hampden took up the role in the Twenties and made it his own. In Britain, many well-known actors have donned the nose of Cyrano. Of these, Sir Ralph Richardson was long associated with the role: besides his performance on stage in 1946-7, his radio interpretation became a classic. Memorable recent Cyranos on the English stage have included Robert Lindsay, Derek Jacobi and, in the centenary revival of Rostand's play, Anthony Sher. There have also been several television and radio broadcasts in Britain and North America, as well as in France.

Of the many films made of *Cyrano de Bergerac*, José Ferrer's moving portrayal (1951) stands out, along with Steve Martin's witty retelling, *Roxanne* (1987). Jean-Paul Rappeneau's glorious 1990 film starring Gérard Depardieu has brought Rostand's play to modern audiences with a flourish.

Cyrano de Bergerac has been reincarnated in other media as well: as a *kabuki* play in Japan, as a ballet (twice), and in numerous operas and musicals, including one in China in 1997. In the USA, Walter Damrosch's opera was performed in 1913 and 1939. European composers inspired by Rostand's play have included the Italian Franco Alfano, the Belgian Paul Danblon, the Estonian Eino Tamberg, the Pole Goldbach and the Czech J. B. Foerster, while the Dutch composer Johan Wagenaar's overture is well-known.[16]

Rostand's hero has flourished his spotless white plume, his *panache*, all over the world, and will continue to do so as long as human beings have hearts to respond to Cyrano's courage, idealism and integrity.

Reassured as to the success of Le Bargy's revival, and his own continuing popularity, Edmond was able to enjoy the delights of the capital. The hermit of Arnaga became for a while the Parisian man of the world. While *Cyrano de Bergerac* continued to delight the crowds, its author strolled in the Bois de Boulogne, enjoying the spring air. There were of course many official engagements to fulfil, such as attending the sessions of the Académie française; giving a speech at the banquet of the *Association de la Critique,* and inaugurating a bust of Catulle Mendès.

Edmond told the assembled critics that only when opposing views are freely discussed can works of art flourish. He drank a toast to all those who had supported him, but also to those who had opposed him, as they had been no less useful to him: "Roots discover how firmly they have taken hold by the shaking of branches".[37] The bust of Catulle Mendès, Rostand's faithful admirer, was unveiled on 18th May. Edmond expressed his gratitude to Mendès, who had had the generosity of spirit to salute Rostand's success in the field where he himself had failed, that of verse drama.

On one typical day in April, Rostand, along with Edouard de Max and other performers, recited his poems to an elegant audience at a *Fémina* gathering in his honour in the afternoon; the same evening he did the same for an audience of working men and women at the *Université populaire* of the Faubourg St Antoine. Although the poet, accompanied by Maurice, did not arrive until half past eight, the hall had been full since seven o'clock; many present had even arrived at five o'clock, bringing their evening meal with them to be sure of a place. When Rostand left, the workers crowded around him so that he had difficulty in leaving; he shook some of them by the hand. "Did you see that!" one of the lucky ones exclaimed to his friend, "just as if I was a mate!"[38]

In July, Rostand was asked by the theatre manager Gabriel Astruc to suggest composers he would like to put his works to music.[39] Astruc's own suggestions were Puccini for *Cyrano de Bergerac,* Saint-Saëns for *L'Aiglon,* Strauss or Ravel for *Chantecler,* Vincent d'Indy for *La Samaritaine* and Gabriel Fauré for *La Princesse lointaine.* (Massenet, tempted by *Chantecler*, according to Rosemonde, had died the previous year.) None of these ideas was ever implemented, though Rostand's plays would attract other composers.

Besides dining out in society or with his friends, visiting his family, and enjoying the company of beautiful women with Charles Le Bargy, Rostand spent much of his time at the Porte-Saint-Martin, chatting to Le Bargy between scenes. When the new Cyrano was on stage, Edmond talked instead to Andrée Mégard, playing Roxane, whose dressingroom was next door. She has recalled in her memoirs that Edmond, "très jeune de caractère" (rather juvenile in character) was fond of playing tricks on herself and Le Bargy, jumping out from a hiding-place to frighten them when they returned from the stage, before he went off with Le Bargy to supper.[40] This is a side of Edmond that had not been seen for some time, and a sign that he was relaxed and happy again.

One night the joke rebounded on Edmond. He and Andrée had become lovers, and after a quarrel, Edmond wrote "Adieu" in lipstick on her mirror, then hid behind a curtain to see her reaction. However, on her return, Andrée was accompanied by her husband, the actor Gémier. The two were having an argument. Both saw the word on the mirror, but continued arguing. Mégard got ready to leave with Gémier. Edmond, realising that he might be locked in for the night, came out of hiding and said quite naturally to Andrée: "Gémier's right, my dear. Why don't you agree with him?" and Gémier continued the conversation as if nothing had been written on the mirror.

It is clear from this incident, recounted by the actress Mary Marquet, that liaisons and infidelities were an accepted part of theatre life.[41] In Marquet's memoirs she describes several love affairs of her own. When Rostand allowed his sensual side free reign, and took mistresses, he was simply doing what many people in the theatre world took for granted.

But Rostand was about to become the close friend of a woman whose attitude to love was emotional rather than sensual: Anna de Noailles.

Anna was a poet, intense, passionate, lyrical. Edmond and Paul Faure had enthused together about her early novel and later volumes of poetry,[42] but he and she had scarcely met. Anna, then in her early thirties, lived in a social whirl. She knew all the most interesting people in Paris, in politics as well as literature. You would be just as likely to meet Anna at the Élysée Palace as at the Russian ballet. If you were invited to her house at 40 rue Schaffer, she was most likely to receive you in her bedroom, where she spent most of her free time. Her friends included Proust, Cocteau and Simone; she tolerated the admiration of Maurice Rostand, but dropped him after she became friends with his father. Voluble to a fault – she always liked to be the centre of attention at any gathering – she had never paid much attention to Edmond on the rare occasions when their paths had crossed. But she had adored *Chantecler*, seeing it many times and sending tickets to her friends.

Now, in 1913, Anna was determined to make the poet's acquaintance. She took her opportunity at an *Annales* conference that February, where Edmond was reciting his verse. After the recital, she approached him and almost overwhelmed him with her enthusiasm and gushing compliments. This could have been fatal for any friendship between them, for as we know, Edmond could not abide flattery. But the astute Anna, realising her mistake, began to talk instead about Bergson's admiration for his work. Now Edmond was interested, for he revered this philosopher who advocated the primacy of the spirit over the brain.[43] He offered to see Anna home, and their friendship began.[44]

They met again at the Annales in April, where Edmond sat in the front row, with Cocteau and Simone, for a lecture, this time, on Anna herself. Anna was being praised as a great poet; the word "genius" had even been mentioned. And on 4th July the paths of the poets crossed again, at a dinner at the Countess de Greffulhe's.

Perhaps as a result of this further meeting – or other more private ones – Anna invited Edmond to join her at a fourteenth-of-July dinner with some friends at a restaurant, the "Quatre Sergents de La Rochelle", in the Bastille quarter. After the meal, the company went off to finish the evening in bohemian style by drinking beer from the local café. Afterwards Anna asked for a lift home in Edmond's car, and on the way to rue Schaffer, they held hands for the first time. Edmond later wrote to Anna referring to this occasion:"That evening we would have liked to go to the ends of the earth".[45]

Le Bargy's production of *Cyrano de Bergerac* was closing for the summer season. Rostand made preparations for returning home. Even at Arnaga, however, there were official duties for him to fulfil. Mme Poincaré, the wife of the President, invited herself to stay with the Rostands while her husband was on an official visit to Spain. She was treated like a queen at Arnaga: she and Rosemonde were rowed in the gondola on the canal in the formal garden while young Basque women danced the fandango for them.

If Mme Poincaré was welcomed with, literally, a fanfare, and a small child offering flowers, the next visitor had an even warmer welcome. Unfortunately, it was not meant for her, but for someone else.

The Countess de Greffulhe, the toast of society and the main inspiration for Proust's Duchess de Guermantes, was a great admirer and friend of Edmond's. She turned up without notice one day at Arnaga, simply dressed (in her eyes) for the country, with long trailing skirts and a parasol in her black-lace gloved hands; her huge hat was half-hidden by floating veils and she was accompanied by her sister, who had more the appearance of a lady-in-waiting. On learning that the family were about to go to Cambo to watch a match of pelote, she said she would accompany them. As she appeared on Rostand's arm, the whole crowd rose and cried "Vive Sarah Bernhardt!"[46]

Edmond somehow found the energy to be a charming host on these occasions. He also made the effort to write to the young poets he was encouraging, thanking Geandreau, for instance, for giving a talk on him at Bordeaux.[47] But he was again suffering from his nervous illness, which worsened with the departure of the visitors. There were in any case enough reasons to depress Edmond, even if he had not been prone to such illness: the suffering of his beloved father and the failure of his marriage, now confirmed by Rosemonde's love affair with Tiarko Richepin, which she no longer tried to conceal. His eldest son Maurice was a disappointment and even an embarrassment to him. The almost manic activity of Edmond's stay in Paris, and perhaps too, the exhaustion of being so much in the public eye, must also have played their part. Edmond's doctors diagnosed a chill, or perhaps anaemia. But Edmond himself knew that nothing could be done to help him.

In November, Edmond's condition was made far worse by news of two deaths: the first, on the 15th, was that of Ernest de Gorsse, Henry's father. It seems that Edmond made the effort to get to Luchon with his father, who had been a friend of Ernest's. It was a visit which brought back poignant memories, not only of his carefree boyhood, but also of the happy early years of his married life. "Je ne veux plus revenir à Luchon parce que j'y ai été trop heureux", Rostand said to Henry as they stood together by the river Pique (I never want to return to Luchon again because I was too happy there).[48]

Edmond brought his father back with him to Arnaga. He told Le Bargy, in a letter thanking him for the gift of some engravings, that the return to Arnaga was made in an ambulance; since then he had been too busy looking after his father to even open his post. "It's impossible to leave my father. It's the most tiring and the most distressing thing. Especially as we have to be cheerful all the time, and talk to keep him amused. I, who normally say so little, am wearing myself out telling stories and making conversation".[49]

The second death was that of Boris de Tannenberg, his old teacher and friend, who had encouraged him to believe in his vocation throughout those difficult early years.

Rostand was only forty-five, but he had written to Henry in his letter of condolence: "at our age we begin to expect nothing but grief".[50] Now he wrote to his sister Jeanne: "Tannenberg's death has finished me off". He described his sufferings to her, the sister who shared with him the fearful inheritance from their grandmother that was aggravating their father's condition and which from time to time ravaged them, too. "You know what it is like. There's nothing one can do about it. No sleep, debility of the brain, I drag myself around, I'll be like this for at least a year. And I feel as if I'll never be able to put two ideas together again … I've never been so ill".[51]

Jeanne urged him to come to Paris, but Edmond did not want to return to the capital again until he felt better, if he ever did. His next letter was even more pessimistic. "Thank you for your kind efforts to persuade me," he wrote, "but you will not see me in Paris again". Edmond felt that, like his father some years before, he had had a presentiment of his present illness, from which he did not expect to recover. This was why his behaviour had been so manic on his recent visit. "I *knew* I would not come back, hence my feverish gaiety, that I *knew* to be false, and my haste to snatch a few pleasures there, which I *knew* would be the last".

Now he was back in Arnaga, he wrote, he knew this secret presentiment to be correct. He would stay there quietly, on his own, as he had no energy to entertain friends. He did not intend to be a nuisance to anyone: a room, a bed and a few books would be enough for him from now on, unless war broke out, when he would try to offer "some modest final service".

Even in his despair, Edmond remembered to protect his family. "Say nothing to mother", he commanded Jeanne, "and don't come and visit me; if you do, come during one of my "up" periods rather than one of my "downs", but why not rather keep the more sparkling picture you have of me from my stay in Paris?"

To Anna de Noailles, Edmond wrote early in December apologising for not having been in touch with her. He was very ill: he had not even left his room for the past three months. "Think of me as dead. You will not see me again unless by some miracle I become gay and "nice" again, as you used to like me to be. But as long as I'm a wolf and ill, I shall stay in my woods: my friends will not have to look after me or get bitten."[52]

It must have seemed to Rostand during his earlier periods of depression, too, that he would never get better again. But this illness seems to have been tinged with a kind of world-weariness which made even death seem acceptable.

"Don't pity me, mind", he had written to Anna, "for I consider that I have had from life all that it can give, and I desire nothing further,

I think … [sic] I think …). Was this simply a "mid-life crisis"? Or was his pessimism bound up with feelings of impending doom, as the possibility of war with Germany grew ever stronger?

Rostand's friends tried to rally him by appealing to his duty as a writer. Anna wrote back on 23rd December, "Remember you are a famous prisoner who should not stop work for long"; Léon Blum kept telling him he was at the peak of his creativity.[53] In vain. Although he wanted to work, Edmond just could not find the energy to put pen to paper, even if he had been able to get his ideas into some sort of shape.

The fateful year of 1914 dawned and Rostand was still in the grip of his nervous illness at Arnaga. He could not even find the energy to travel to Paris for a fête in Sarah Bernhardt's honour – on 15th January she had finally been awarded the cross of the Legion of Honour. Rostand sent enthusiastic telegrams: "Dear, great friend, I embrace you with all my heart", and later, "every poet and artist has waited impatiently for the time when your huge mass of laurels should at last be bound by this little bit of red ribbon".[54] But although he had been invited to be the one to officially welcome his old friend into the Legion of Honour, Rostand felt unable to travel to Paris. Nor did he go to the Académie française to vote for the philosopher Bergson, in spite of the strong admiration the two men felt for each other.

Raymond Lerouge, the boys' former tutor, returned to Arnaga in January, and would stay until April. He was company for Edmond and Jean while Rosemonde and Maurice were in Paris, where they were spending the whole of the winter season. Parisian life continued as brilliant as ever, a succession of fêtes, dinner parties and literary events. Diaghilev's *Ballets russes* continued to delight audiences; the tango was all the rage, and an American invention, the brassière, was altering the shape of women's fashions.

Maurice and Rosemonde were often in the papers because of the prestige attached to the name Rostand, and both welcomed this attention. Maurice had published another book of poems, *La Page de la vie*, and collaborated with his mother on another retelling of a favourite story, this time from Hans Christian Andersen's "The Little Match Girl". *La Petite Marchande d'Allumettes* opened at the Opéra-Comique on 25th February 1914. Tiarko Richepin had written the music.

The two returned briefly to Arnaga before returning to Paris in April. This time they took a flat for the whole family in the rue d'Artois. The Rostands continued to be in the limelight. Sarah gave a lecture on Edmond at the Annales on 3rd April, and would present *La Samaritaine* at the *Université populaire* of St Denis in May. (This was more likely to have been a reading than a performance; Sarah's leg was now so bad that Dr Pozzi had set it in plaster; she could only walk a few steps at a time.) Relations between the two friends would be briefly soured later this year with a misunderstanding about the performance rights of *L'Aiglon*.

Meanwhile Edmond had been asked by Gabriel Astruc for a poem to celebrate the re-opening of the Théâtre des Champs-Élysées, which Astruc was taking over. As Edmond had not felt able to write anything new, he had sent him "A la Musique", written in 1890 for Chabrier.[55] Astruc had also requested a poem from Edmond in honour of Antoine, who had been ruined by his efforts to promote modern theatre in Paris. This time, Edmond did compose a new poem, for he greatly admired Antoine. He would deliver it later, at Antoine's benefit performance at the Opera. Antoine was going to Istanbul to become director of the Conservatoire there. Edmond's long poem, ending with a rather slangy sonnet, recounted the avant-garde director's achievements, and begged him to stay.[56]

Rostand was beginning to recover his energy and strength. On 16th June, he wrote to Anna de Noailles that he was coming to Paris soon; he did not want to miss the traditional dinner-party on 14th July, "an important date in the history of France and my own".[57] But in fact the visit had planned for some time. In a letter to Le Bargy, undated but written after Edmond's illness, Rosemonde had written "We are coming to Paris in June, [my husband] will read you *Don Juan*".[58]

La Dernière Nuit de Don Juan was the play originally intended for Le Bargy's farewell performance at the Comédie-Française. Le Bargy was now hoping to perform it at the Porte-Saint-Martin theatre. Rostand had been to ill to come to Paris to read him the play. But now Edmond had had second thoughts about it. "It is completely finished, recopied and locked in a drawer", wrote Rosemonde in her letter to Le Bargy. "But ... and it is a big but: Edmond considers that this play, which he wrote without any thought of how it would work as theatre, is perhaps less of a drama than a poem, and unless he changes his mind, he will not let it be performed." (In the published version, the play is called "poème dramatique".) Rosemonde stressed that this was Edmond's attitude, not her own, and that she hoped Le Bargy would be able to change Edmond's mind when he read the actor the play on his return to Paris.[59]

Le Bargy must have succeeded, for plans began for a production of *La Dernière Nuit de Don Juan* at the Porte-Saint-Martin for the following season. But the outbreak of war was to prevent any performance from taking place. Rostand's last play would be performed posthumously, as an act of homage to the poet, in 1922.

La Dernière Nuit de Don Juan was intended to be the link between Rostand's *Faust* and his projected play, *Polichinelle* (Punch). Faust is redeemed, finally, by his love for Gretchen, and so saves his humanity and his soul. But Rostand's Don Juan is incapable of true love, nor is he worthy of hell, though he considers himself a great antihero. He is fit for nothing but to become a puppet, Polichinelle, manipulated by the puppeteer, as he himself had been the slave of his desire. The puppet stage of the last scene of *La Dernière Nuit de Don Juan* would become the actual stage of *Polichinelle*.

Rostand's play about Don Juan is a totally original conception, beginning where other plays leave off. As one of his "lessons for the soul", *La Dernière Nuit de Don Juan*, and Edmond's recently finished translation of Goethe's *Faust, Part One*, are new departures for the poet, in that they present the reverse side of his earlier plays, whose heroes are inspired by the poet's own idealistic attitude to life. Cyrano,

Chantecler and the others cope with disillusion or the defeat of their hopes by holding fast to their ideal, and continuing to live by it, creating good out of misfortune. But Don Juan and Faust react more negatively to their discovery of the world's imperfections.

In speaking of the forbidden fruit of paradise, Faust talks of "rotten apples" while for Don Juan, "every apple has its worm within". Both turn from God to the devil for satisfaction. Faust makes a pact with Mephistopheles. For his part, the Don will work for the devil by debasing human love to the sexual act alone. He will seduce women rather than offer them true love, and make a paradise for himself by forgetting the imperfections of the world in the pleasures of sensuality.

In Rostand's work, as we have seen, pure love is always the ideal and inspiration of the hero and the means of redemption of the heroine. Sensuality is seen as a temptation, distracting human beings from their duty, their work, or from true love. Faust's love for Gretchen proves stronger than his other desires, and so his soul is saved. Don Juan, too, will be given the chance of redemption through love. But after a lifetime of seducing women for his own pleasure, he is unable to devote himself to truly loving just one woman.

Goethe's Mephistopheles incarnates the spirit of negation and cynicism which prevents human beings from doing great deeds or creating beautiful things. It is this defeatist attitude which Rostand always strove to combat. When Don Juan finally realises that in all his life he will have achieved and created nothing, his pride in himself is destroyed, and the devil is finally able to carry him off. He has denied his humanity and is fit neither for heaven nor hell; he is fit only to be a puppet.

Rostand's play begins where Molière's ends, with the statue of the Commander taking Don Juan down the steps of his tomb to Hell. Don Juan shows no sign of fear or remorse; at each step he names one of the women he has seduced. The Commander is so impressed by his courage – or insouciance – that he is prepared to let Don Juan go free, but it is too late: the devil already has a grip on him. However, the seducer persuades the devil to let him return to life for ten more years so that he can do more of what he considers is the devil's own work: "As the corrupter, I am your curate".

This action takes place in the Prologue, which Rostand never completed to his own satisfaction. It was reconstituted for the published version from several much-corrected fragments. Part One begins in Venice, ten years later. A table overlooking the Adriatic is already elegantly laid for supper on the terrace of Don Juan's sumptuous palace; marble steps lead down to the Adriatic. The Don, who arrives reciting the names of his women as he had in the Prologue, tells Sganarelle how much he loves Venice. Every speech of his contains allusions to sensuality and seduction. "Your words always smell a little of the flesh", the devil will tell him.

Sganarelle reminds his master that the ten years are now up, but Don Juan is not perturbed: he thinks the devil has forgotten him, and is intent on continuing his career as seducer by making a new conquest tonight, after the ball. "The future belongs to me", he declares. Just then, a cry is heard from the street, "Burattini!" (Puppets!) Don Juan is reminded of his childhood, and the happy times he spent at the puppet show. He decides to watch Polichinelle perform while eating his supper.

The puppet Punch treats Don Juan very familiarly, calling him him a "confrère…en paillardise" (a fellow libertine). He rings a bell (the hour has already struck once, from the campanile, and from time to time a bell will ring throughout the play, in an increasingly doom-laden way) to mark "the solemn hour in which Don Juan confronts Polichinelle".

The traditional performance begins to unfold. Don Juan constantly interrupts to give Punch advice: "instead of hitting women, make them suffer", but Punch carries on hitting the woman puppet until she is dead. Don Juan then insists on skipping to the scene where the devil comes for Punch's soul; again, Punch rings his bell. The devil-puppet duly appears; Punch tries again and again to beat him, but every stick breaks. "Don't hit the devil, either, make him suffer", again advises

Don Juan. Punch is carried off screaming. "How could you make the devil suffer?" asks the little devil-puppet. "I would not be frightened; I would still have my pride," replies Don Juan. "You will beg me not to take you!" declares the devil-puppet, "I will only carry you off when you are defeated". They shake hands on it and the little devil disappears, leaving the Don wondering what sort of a bargain he has just made with a puppet. But again a bell rings, and out of the puppet box comes the puppeteer: it is the devil himself!

Now Don Juan understands. Quite at ease, he is ready to depart for hell, but first invites the devil, as he had invited the ghost of the Commander, to eat supper with him. Don Juan recalls their first meeting, in the Garden of Eden, when the devil, as the serpent, had invited him to eat the forbidden fruit. In each apple he had bitten into, he had found a maggot, "your horrible miniature". "Every beautiful fruit, you tell us, is nothing but a hidden maggot. That is the great secret that must not be known. Now, knowing it, try to live!" Don Juan decided to renounce the paradise of such a mean-spirited god, and make his own: "For one [paradise] lost, I have regained a thousand". "Mille et trois", corrects the devil, in a reference to the number of women the don claims to have seduced.

"So what is the source of your pride?" asks the devil. "I am the only hero admired by humanity", boasts Don Juan. "I conquered, like Alexander, but unlike him, I conquered alone". When asked what he conquered, or in his word, "possessed", the don calls for his famous list. "To possess is to know" (Posséder, c'est connaître), explains Don Juan. "I clasped to myself their naked souls". He boasts that the list could be torn up, he remembers all the names of the women he has seduced, and everything about them. So the devil tears the list into tiny pieces. Then he suddenly produces a violin and begins to play; the shreds of paper begin to stir, they dance and spin and then fly away over the sea, into which they gently fall.

In the distance, across the sea, a flotilla of gondolas appears.[60] As they draw nearer, the devil explains that each of them bears the Shade of one of the women, alive or dead, that the don has seduced – there are more than a thousand of them. Don Juan takes a candelabra, as night has fallen, and goes to the steps to watch them disembark. Each Shade wears a cloak and mask, and carries a rose and a fan.

Don Juan is not allowed to touch the Shades, or take off their masks, but must discover, since he has boasted that he knows them all, who they are, when they whisper in his ear a brief description of their soul. If he remembers their names, their cloaks and masks will fall. But the don's first attempts to name a Shade are a failure. He continues to move amongst the Shades with his candelabra, trying out name after name as the curtain slowly falls.

As the curtain rises on Part Two, Don Juan is still searching in vain to find a woman he recognises. He is finally forced to admit defeat. "You saw nothing! You knew nothing! You had nothing!" (Tu n'as rien vu! Tu n'as rien su! Tu n'as rien eu!"). The women knew him better than he knew them. But Don Juan tries another defence: "I may not have known them, but I did have power over them – it was I who corrupted them". "No", chorus the Shades, "we were already eager for the crime!" Far from seducing them, Don Juan had been passed like a pawn from one woman to another – it was they who had used him. Don Juan admits he has been duped and humiliated, but finds another cause for pride: he pleased women: "To please is the greatest gift for a man!". But he discovers he pleased them, not for any qualities of his own, but for a variety of petty circumstantial reasons. "So, Prince Charming", taunts the devil, "Are you pleased with this cause for fame?"

Desperately searching for a further source of pride, the Don cries out "My intrepidity! I cared for nothing! I was always the first to leave a relationship. I obeyed only my instinct, leaping over all foolish moral conventions in my progress!" "A progress which was nothing but a flight", counters the devil. "You were afraid of stopping, afraid of loving, afraid you might be made to suffer!" "Lâche!" (Coward!), the Shades taunt him. "Are you still trying to find a destiny where there was only disorder?" asks the devil, ready to lead the don away with him.

Don Juan seems beaten, but then finds new hope for pride in the claim that he was "The Lover", who took women away from other men.

This claim is soon disposed of as the Shades chant "Romeo", "Tristan". They were true lovers, the lovers women dream of. All Don Juan did was profit from hearts already made tender by the thought of them. "But at least I made women suffer", cries Don Juan. The devil gives Don Juan a goblet from the table, and tells him to collect one tear from each of the women, to prove they have suffered for love of him. The goblet is soon full, and as the tears are poured onto the table, the Don is sure he has won his bargain with the devil – he still has a source of pride. But when the devil examines them under his magnifying glass, they all seem to be false.

"Now what is left of your pride? Seek hard!" says the devil. But Don Juan leaps on the word. "Seeking, that's what I was doing", he claims, "I was always looking for a hidden treasure, an ideal." "So your claim to greatness is that you never found your ideal?" asks the devil, but just then he burns his hand on a real tear. It was a tear of pity, not suffering, shed by the White Shade, who comes forward to explain that she gave herself to Don Juan out of pity when she saw that he desired her.

Don Juan does not recognise her, or remember her name, which she tells him – it was not on the list! (The devil has kept a copy in his pocket.) "But at least", he cries, " I only found my ideal once in one thousand and four women!" "Not so", chorus the Shades," "You could have found perfect love with each of us if you had tried. You passed your life in walking by."

The White Shade begs Don Juan to show her tenderness, to try to love her. As long as a flame burns in her tear, he has the chance to save himself by finding he has a heart. Don Juan tries, but finds he cannot promise to be faithful. He realises he would have become bored with just one woman. It was the search itself he sought, he now claims: women were simply a means of transcending himself; he used them to reach a state of exaltation. But when the Shades ask him what he achieved by using them in this way, he is unable to reply.

Now Don Juan realises that he is beaten. He is not a great anti-hero, he is not a great lover; he has nothing to be proud of; he has done nothing, created nothing in his whole life. "Do you then love life to the point of avenging it, Death?" cries Don Juan in his agony. This is the central question of the play: what makes life worthwhile? Rostand's answer is creativity. The only way to overcome the disillusion of finding life is imperfect, the only way to beat death, is to have created, or to have done, something beautiful. "At the moment of death, you must have created [something]".

Even Don Juan's belated memory of having given money to a poor man, "for the love of humanity" cannot save him. The man, summoned by the devil, throws Don Juan's money back into his face. "Libertines have nothing to with Liberty – they break rules only for themselves." Don Juan offers to put his courage and his talents at the disposal of the poor, but when the Shades let fall their cloaks, he knows he is incapable of devoting himself to a cause while beautiful women still exist. "The charms of women stop men doing great deeds", groans Don Juan. "Ah, let me lament the suffering of the male!".

Every claim to pride has now been ripped away. Don Juan has no more illusions about himself. But he will still show no fear, he will go willingly to hell, he demands, indeed, to suffer. But the devil tells him he is not worthy to go to hell, instead he will experience damnation in the hands of others, as a mere puppet. "Grâce! L'éternel feu!" begs Don Juan. "Non! L'éternel théâtre!" is the devil's reply (Mercy! Give me the eternal fires! No! Eternal theatre!). Now Don Juan does struggle, but he is dragged nonetheless to the puppet booth. But the unrepentant Don gains one last satisfaction: he will still amuse the girls, he gloats, right under the eyes of their parents. "You who could fulfil the greatest of destinies", sighs the White Shade as the flame in her tear finally dims. And as Don Juan reappears on the Punch and Judy stage as a puppet, it is she who has the last word: "Quel dommage!" (What a pity!)

La Dernière Nuit de Don Juan contains some wonderfully dramatic moments, lively verse, poetic beauty and much wit. It is also a very personal play. The poet, too, has known "the sufferings of the male"; he has succombed from time to time to the temptations of sensuality. But he has known it was wrong to do so; he has not given up his faith in true love or his belief in the need for a positive, creative attitude to life that is the exact opposite of his protagonist's attitude. Don Juan may have drawn Rostand's attention because of his own susceptibility to female charms. But the archetypal seducer is presented here, almost uniquely in the repertoire, without any admiration for his exploits. Rostand's Don is portrayed as totally contemptible, incapable of true love or any human achievement. Although the women he seduced are shown to have behaved badly too, the Don's cynical view of womenkind is shown as unjustified. It is true that the White Shade alone gave herself to him out of love and pity rather than self-interest, but all the Don's women claimed they were capable of giving him love, if he had been capable of receiving it. Far from being a disillusioned, cynical play, as some have suggested, Rostand's *La Dernière Nuit de Don Juan* is inspired, like his earlier plays, by his idealism.

In March 1922, *La Dernière Nuit de Don Juan* would be produced posthumously at the Porte-Saint-Martin theatre, with *Les Romanesques* as a curtain-raiser. Pierre Magnier played Don Juan. René Doumic wrote that the critics present listened to the play with unanimous emotion and respect –a way of putting right their injustice towards *Chantecler*.[61] But the public was not enthusiastic. Yet again, this was not a play for the boulevard; as Doumic lamented, it should have been put on at the Comédie-Française. Rostand had been right – *La Dernière Nuit de Don Juan* was more suitable to be read than to be performed on stage. It would, however, make a marvellous television play, with all its special effects.[62]

In 1914, plans for Le Bargy's production of *La Dernière Nuit de Don Juan* were going ahead for the autumn season, in ignorance of the war to come. Meanwhile, Edmond was once again part of the social life of Paris. In particular, he renewed his acquaintance with Anna de Noailles.

Anna, like Edmond, had been unwell. She had kept to her bed all winter, claiming to be exhausted. But at a big dinner at Count Primoli's, which Edmond also attended, she was back to her voluble, vehement self, if with an additional edge of bitterness or sarcasm. She flirted mercilessly with the poet, making him blush by quipping, as he tried unsuccessfully to light her cigarette, "so you can't set me alight – what a pity".[63]

It was about this time that Jean Rostand, too, first made the acquaintance of Anna. He was too shy to be anything but overwhelmed by her on this occasion, but in later years he became a valued friend of hers. Maurice found the budding friendship between Edmond and Anna embarrassing, especially as Jean Cocteau, who was a clever mimic, took pleasure in imitating them in conversation together.

The assassination of Arch-Duke Ferdinand at Sarajevo on 28th June shocked those who realised the danger of war if France's ally, Russia, became drawn into a conflict in the Balkans. But diplomacy had averted similar crises before. It would take more than this to disturb the complacency of a society which believed the "Banquet Years" would continue for ever. So social life continued unabated. Maurice had the satisfaction of having his poem, "Septentrion", performed at the *Pré Catalan*, that fashionable place of pleasure in the Bois de Boulogne.

Strenuous diplomatic efforts were being made meanwhile to avoid war. The French president went to Russia on a visit to the Tsar designed to reassure the public. Pierre de Margerie, Edmond's brother-in-law, went with him. In a similar gesture of reassurance, Jeanne de Margerie gave a dinner party, to which Edmond, Anna and such leaders of society as Boni de Castellane and Count Primoli were invited.

By the end of July, however, war began to seem inevitable. On 28th July, Austria sent an ultimatum to Serbia; the same day Russia mobilized in Serbia's defence. Three days later, France, while still hoping for peace through diplomacy, began to mobilise too. Among those called up were the boys' tutor Raymond Lerouge and Simone's friends, the poet Charles Péguy and the novelist Alain-Fournier, whose novel, *Le Grand Meaulnes*, had recently narrowly failed to win the Prix Goncourt.

Rostand knew he would not be called up, in view of his poor health and short-sightedness, but on 31st July, when Germany delivered an ultimatum to Russia, he wrote to President Poincaré offering his services in even the humblest capacity in his secretariat.[64] That same evening, Jean Jaurès, the socialist pacifist leader and a good friend of Rostand's, was assassinated. Jaurès had striven to unite the workers of Europe and so preserve the peace, but patriotism proved stronger than the ideal of universal brotherhood. On 3rd August, Germany declared war on France, and the following day, the day of Jaurès's funeral, the war had begun.

The French troops went off to war full of optimism and patriotic fervour. It was widely expected that they would hold off the Germans, while the Russians would soon reach Berlin. The war should be over by Christmas. But the Germans, guessing correctly that the main French attack would be in Alsace-Lorraine, the provinces lost to Prussia in 1870, advanced on a second front through Belgium and by the 28th August had crossed into France and reached the Somme.

Rostand and his family remained in Paris. As the war moved closer to the capital, Eugène's doctors urged Edmond to take his father to the safety of Cambo, as any excitement was bad for him. But Rostand was reluctant, for patriotic reasons, to abandon the capital, and Eugène would not go without him.

In early September, with the onset of the Battle of the Marne, Paris itself seemed threatened by the German advance. Clemenceau, still the Rostand family's friend, telegraphed Edmond and told him that events were now desperate: he should take his family south to safety; the government, too, was shifting to Bordeaux.

The poet reluctantly agreed. Angèle and Eugène travelled south in the relative comfort of the train. Rostand, with the rest of his household, along with Anna, who suddenly decided to join them with her mother and her son, began the long drive south in three cars.

It proved to be an epic journey. The Rostands and the Noailles were not the only ones travelling south, and accommodation was hard to find. One morning Anna was found having breakfast with the ladies of uncertain virtue who had offered her and her family hospitality on the previous night. On 6th September, the convoy reached Bordeaux, where the government was already installed. Anna planned to stay in Biarritz at first with her sister Helen, so the following day, the Rostands parted with her and her family at Bayonne, and finally safely reached Cambo and home.

Je ne veux que voir la Victoire.
Ne me demandez pas: "Après?"
Après, je veux bien la nuit noire
Et le sommeil sous les cyprès.

Je n'ai plus de joie à poursuivre
Et je n'ai plus rien à souffrir.
Vaincu, je ne pourrais pas vivre,
Et, vainqueur, on pourra mourir.[65]

I only want to see Victory.
Do not ask me: "What then?"
Then I will happily accept black night
and the sleep beneath the cypresses.

There is no more joy for me to seek,
there is no more sorrow for me to endure.
Conquered, I could not live;
as a conqueror, one may die.

These four years when France was at war were to be the last four years of Rostand's life. They would also be the saddest, though he was to experience unexpected joy, too. Rostand was devastated by the war. His imagination could envisage all too clearly the horrors of the battlefield, as in the Wagram scene in *L'Aiglon*; his compassionate heart suffered deeply with the bereaved and wounded. The poet who had put his heart and soul into his hero Cyrano longed to fight for his country, but had to content himself with putting all his energy and passionate love for France into serving and inspiring those who did fight for her.

Had Rostand known he was soon to die, would he have tried to complete some of his unfinished plays, or to create new works still at the stage of being vague ideas? It is unlikely. Rostand's concern for the soldiers at the Front, and for the wounded he would soon be helping to comfort, would always have taken precedence. His creativity in the next four years was devoted almost completely to writing letters to the Front and composing patriotic poems with which he hoped to encourage and inspire his compatriots during the war. These poems were printed in newspapers such as *Le Gaulois* and *Le Figaro*, and some were later collected into a posthumous anthology, *Le Vol de la Marseillaise*.[66]

In the peace of Arnaga, the noise and horror of war were far away, though always present in everyone's mind. A few days after the Rostands arrived home, the news from the Front improved: the French and British allied forces had driven the Germans back beyond the Marne. Both sides now dug themselves into trenches. It became clear that there would be no swift end to the war.

There was no question of returning to Paris: Eugène was very ill, and being nursed by Angèle in the Red Room. In any case, the war itself soon came to the Basque country, in the form of hundreds of soldiers wounded in the Battle of the Marne. Edmond had been excused military service because of his poor health and short sight, and was again rejected when he presented himself to the recruitment office in Bayonne as a volunteer. He then asked to join the 18th section of military nurses. Though this request was accepted, Edmond had meanwhile found worthwhile work to do in the hospitals at Bayonne and Biarritz. Here he comforted the wounded as well as he could, writing and reading their letters, bringing them whatever necessities they needed, and listening with humility to their horrific experiences. The courage and panache of these young soldiers filled him with admiration and hope for the future of France.

Life settled into a routine. A new hospital, Larressore, soon opened close to Cambo. The nurse in charge was Louis Barthou's wife, whose officiousness sorely tried Edmond's patience. He went there every day to work as an administrator, but he also spent a lot of time with the wounded. Rosemonde worked in the same hospital as a nurse. Sometimes Anna would accompany Edmond on his walks round the wards, helping him to distribute money and tobacco, and talking volubly to the wounded.

Anna had soon joined the Rostands at Cambo. She and her son Anne-Jules, and her mother, the Princesse de Brancovan, rented a villa found for them by Rosemonde. Edmond's friend Paul Faure was delighted to meet the woman whose poetry he had so long admired. This "miraculous woman", with her slight figure, looked so fragile, and yet on her rested the immensities of thought and poetry, he thought.[67] Small wonder that Rostand, too, would fall under her spell.

The Villa Brimbirion was close enough to Arnaga for Anna to visit every day. While her fourteen-year-old son rode his bicycle round the gardens, Anna would talk with Edmond, or sit amicably knitting for the soldiers at the Front with Rosemonde, when the latter was not nursing at Larressore. Anna's vibrant presence even made an impression on Eugène, who in a rare lucid moment in October composed a quatraine in her honour.

Anna agonised with the whole of her passionate poet's nature about the fate of the fighting soldiers. She told Paul Faure that she was no longer interested in the beauty of nature – it was human beings who now commanded all her attention. She wrote heartfelt poems about the young Frenchmen at the Front. Her husband Mathieu was among them, having enlisted in the 27th dragoons. But Rosemonde's mind was at rest: her lover Tiarko Richepin had not gone to the Front with the rest of his regiment. She had arranged this with Rostand's friend, Louis Barthou. Barthou had used his prestige as a recent head of government to ensure that Tiarko stayed in Biarritz, where Rosemonde could visit him frequently.

This ideal arrangement, for the lovers, came to an end when Jules Richepin came to Cambo and insisted that his son should go and fight for his country like his compatriots. In spite of Rosemonde's entreaties, Tiarko had to give in. Once he had left for the Front, she departed for Paris, taking Maurice with her.

With Rosemonde away, the friendship between Anna and Edmond soon developed into a deeper intimacy, which gave Rostand immense satisfaction. But, as with Anna's long and passionate relationship with Barrès, this was a meeting of minds rather than a physical relationship.[68]

By December, however, Anna was talking of returning to Paris. She gave many reasons, but perhaps one that remained unspoken was a fear of committing herself too deeply to her fellow poet. By the end of January, she had gone, taking her mother and son with her. Edmond was alone again, with his son, his sick father, and his anxious mother, who was in such despair about Eugène's illness that the family feared she would not survive his death.

Rostand had many friends in the Basque country, but they could not replace Anna. His old friend Simone was no longer in Cambo. She had spent the summer there as usual, with her faithless husband Claude Casimir-Périer and Alain-Fournier, with whom she was in love. When war broke out and the two men were called up, she had stayed on with Alain-Fournier's parents. Simone, too, had been helping in local hospitals. But on hearing of Alain-Fournier's death on 22nd September, she had returned, distraught, to Paris. By then she had already suffered the loss of Charles Péguy, the poet and her dear friend; in 1915, she would also lose her husband.

Sarah Bernhardt had been in Bordeaux, much against her will, since the end of August. She had only left Paris because Clemenceau had told her she was on a list of hostages to be taken if the Germans entered the capital. But by October she had left for Paris again, as she was, as usual, short of money; the theatres were reopening again at the end of the year. With the need to entertain the French and Allied troops enjoying leave in the capital, not only the theatres, but cafés, too, were opening, with waitresses rather than waiters. Although revues and other light-hearted shows were soon revived, the first offerings at the theatres were patriotic plays, among them Rostand's *Cyrano de Bergerac*, starring Jean Daragon. This, like the other productions, opened with a matinee for the wounded. Sarah would be performing in *Les Cathédrales*, a long poem written for her by Eugène Morand, celebrating the cathedrals of France damaged in the war.

The year 1915 would be a year of contrasts for Edmond. It began painfully. Eugène finally died on the 20th January. His body was taken to Marseilles, where it lay in state at the family bank. Here the citizens of Marseilles came to pay their respects before Eugène was buried in the Rostand tomb at St Pierre cemetery. The funeral ceremonies were long and tiring, the formal eulogies endless. Not only were the Rostands one of the major families in Marseilles, but Eugène himself had been highly respected for his achievements and well-loved for his philanthropy. Angèle's Catholic faith gave her the strength to cope, to her family's relief, but Edmond found it all exhausting. To add to his misery, Rosemonde suddenly left Marseilles before the official ceremonies were complete. She had heard that Tiarko Richepin, in the front line, had been wounded. Rosemonde left to visit him immediately, taking Maurice with her.

This behaviour made his bereavement even harder for Edmond to bear. His sisters were already angry with Rosemonde for her open affair with Tiarko. Now they were also deeply offended and urged Edmond to make a complete break with his wife. But he was reluctant to do so. He did not want to upset his son Jean, and Rosemonde herself later begged for a second chance. The couple would finally agree to live apart for the time being, but Edmond's sisters continued to press him for a definitive separation.

Rostand wrote in despair to Anna on 30th January that he wished he could have died fighting for his country rather than go through such misery.[69] These were not empty words. He wrote in similar terms to Pierre Clarac, a soldier correspondent who became a close friend.[70]

On 2nd February Edmond learnt that his poet friend, Louis Geandreau, had been killed on 13th January while leading his men into battle near Soissons. Rostand was broken-hearted at the loss of this young man of so much promise. At least two other writers known to Edmond, Ernest Psichari and Guy de Cassagnac, both the sons of family friends, had also died recently at the Front. "Les rossignols tombent de toutes les branches" (the nightingales are falling from every branch), Rostand would write later, referring to the forest scene in *Chantecler* (Act IV, sc. 6).[71]

The same month Rostand learnt that Sarah was returning to Bordeaux to have her right leg amputated. It had been giving her increasing pain, which no treatment seemed to alleviate, so with characteristic aplomb, she decided to get rid of it. Rostand travelled to Bordeaux to offer moral support, but it was Sarah who called out to him "Courage, mon ami" as she was wheeled into the operating room. The operation was completely successful, but Sarah hated the wooden leg she was given. She had another made for her out of rubber, but found it most convenient to do without that, too, being instead carried around in style in a kind of palanquin whenever possible.

Anna and Edmond were still writing to each other, but Edmond felt that, though Anna's letters were, if anything, more affectionate, she was quite glad of the distance between them. Anna was, it seems, too conscious of her position to want to be compromised by being seen in public with Rostand. He had booked a room for her in Bordeaux at the Hotel Terminus where he was staying with Jean and Miss Day for Sarah's operation, but she had not come.

As the war dragged on, Rostand considered whether he should use his popularity and skills as a public speaker to travel to neutral countries such as Italy and the United States, to urge them to join the Allies. As he hated travelling, this would have been a noble sacrifice for his country. But in the event, he was too ill that spring to fulfil this plan. He was unable to even go to the Larressore hospital. So, resting in bed at Arnaga, he used his time and energy instead to correspond with troops at the Front.

Edmond adopted a section of the 34th Infantry Division, and soon had a huge correspondence with soldiers of all ranks. Many became good friends, such as Pierre Clarac, who declared later that it was the generosity, nobility and depth of soul revealed in the poet's letters that sustained him over the next four years of fighting.[72] Edmond, for his part, was reassured to think he had contributed at least something to the war effort. He wrote to Clarac that his latest letter was "very consoling for the poet who feels useless, whom they hadn't wanted in the army, who suffers, and needs people to repeat to him sometimes that he hasn't been useless".[73]

"The good he did remains indisputable", wrote Jean Suberville, another of Rostand's correspondents, who later wrote a book about him.[74] "The ardent appeal of one soul to another" of these personal letters moved their recipients deeply. But through his plays, the poet had already inspired a much greater number of combatants.

Rostand's appeal was to the heart and soul, not the intellect. The heroism which refused to take itself too seriously; courage that faced danger with a smile or a joke, which he had summed up in the word "panache", was felt to incarnate the French spirit. Some army divisions adopted Chantecler as their emblem; others called themselves after Cyrano. *Cyrano de Bergerac* was a favourite to be performed at the theatres at the Front, along with the numerous parodies inspired by it, such as *Cyronac de Bergerot, Les Cadets de France*, and Suberville's own *Cyrano de Bergerac aux tranchées*. Men about to risk their lives on the battlefield drew courage and inspiration from Rostand's plays. His friend Geandreau was just one of many officers who read aloud to his troops from *L'Aiglon* and the other major plays. So did two NCOs from the 12th Cavalry Division, who wrote to tell the poet of the pride they felt in defending him, and their gratitude for giving them "la force consciente de bien mourir" (the conscious strength to die well).[75] The wounded, too, found consolation in Rostand's work – many were the copies of *Cyrano, Chantecler* and *L'Aiglon* sent to the poet, found under the pillows of those that had died.[76]

"There are words which, spoken before people gathered together, have the strength of a prayer. There are thrills which, experienced in common, are equal to a victory", Rostand had claimed in his "Discours de Réception" at the French Academy. (Il y a des paroles qui, prononcés devant des hommes réunies, ont la vertu d'une prière. Il y a des frissons éprouvés en commun qui équivalent à une victoire.) He had wished to give his audiences "leçons d'âme". Now the generation inspired by Cyrano was putting Rostand's "lessons for the soul" into action.

That summer, Maurice visited his father and brother at Arnaga. He was spending the season in Biarritz – some society life continued in spite of the war. Amongst other activities, Maurice was acting scenes from *L'Aiglon*. He was still writing for the theatre, but now in prose. It may have been Maurice who persuaded Edmond to take on Émile Agostinelli as his chauffeur in May. Proust had been looking for a post for the destitute Émile, brother of his great love, Alfred Agostinelli, for many months. It was acts of kindness like this that made Edmond remembered with so much affection after his death.[77]

In October, with no sign of an end to the war, Rostand decided to return to Paris. He was concerned about his Uncle Alexis's health and would also be able to see more of his mother, who was now living with Alexis and his wife at their home in the avenue de Villiers. His sister Juliette, too, was also in Paris; her flat was just across the street from Anna's house in rue Scheffer. Rostand himself took a comfortably-furnished flat south of the river at 4, avenue de la Bourdonnais.[78] The huge bulk of the Eiffel Tower, which Edmond considered ugly until a circlet of lights was added to it, loomed up nearby. "Now the skeleton has a soul", he told a visiting friend, Guillaume de Saix.[79] The flat was on the ground floor, and from the salon-cum-study, French windows opened onto a small garden with the trees and greenery of the Champ de Mars beyond. This was, perhaps, the closest Rostand could get in Paris to a rural outlook.

Here Edmond was looked after for the rest of the war (except when visiting Arnaga) by his sons' former governess, Miss Daÿ, who put into his pockets before he went out whatever he might need: money, pen, wound–up watch, spare monocle – the poet was still absent-minded.[80] Jean soon moved in with him. He and Maurice had both decided to join the war effort. They had been aware that their father was suffering from their earlier non-participation in the war, but both deplored violence. Edmond, too, was a socialist and pacifist, and counted Joseph Reinach and Léon Blum among his close friends. But he believed that in fighting Germany, France was not only protecting herself, but was also preserving civilisation. The idea that his country was the sole guardian of truth and freedom found expression in many of his war poems, but this sentiment was not shared by his sons, who believed France had no monopoly of these qualities.

Jean found work that suited him in the laboratory of the Val de Grâce, preparing anti-typhus vaccine for the men in the trenches. Maurice became a nurse, work he found very tiring. He was assigned to an annexe run by the *Dames de France* in the Duchesse de Rohan's house, a house where in happier times he had read his poetry in the salon. At first, Maurice had stayed with friends, but later he moved to a small flat in the Quai d'Orsay, near enough to his father's flat to eat there if he wished. But Maurice preferred to keep his distance and lead his own life. Edmond's sons were not the only young people spared the call-up who were now getting involved in the war. Maurice's friend Jean Cocteau had joined an amateur ambulance unit, wearing an elegant uniform designed by Paul Poiret.

At the Front, both sides remained dug into the trenches. Rostand visited the front lines in Champagne and Alsace at the end of October as part of a group of writers and politicians including Maurice Barrès, the playwright Edmond Haraucourt, Fernand Laudet (editor of the *Revue Hebdomaire),* and Joseph Reinach. But it was Rostand who received the warmest welcome from the soldiers. He was devastated to learn later of the death of the general and some of the officers he had met in Alsace.

October also saw the death in Paris of Paul Hervieu, who had worked so hard to get Rostand elected to the Académie française.

On his return from the Front in November, Edmond went with Anna to see the première of a film by Sacha Guitry (Lucien's son), *Ceux de chez nous,* at the Théâtre des Variétés. Guitry had approached the leading proponents of the arts in France: Rodin, Monet, Antoine, Saint-Saëns, Anatole France and Sarah Bernhardt and others, asking if he could film them at their work. The film was sponsored by the government as part of an effort to improve national morale. Rostand was filmed in Guitry's garden, drawing Reims cathedral, which had been partly destroyed by the enemy, then writing his sonnet about it.

Guitry introduced the poet as: "the most famous, the most dazzling and the most curious dramatic author of our time".[81]

The year 1915 had begun badly for Edmond, but it was ending on a more hopeful note. Not only was he reassured as to his position as France's most popular national poet, but he was about to make the acquaintance of a tall blonde actress who would give him a new zest for living. She was just twenty years old, and her name was Mary Marquet.[82]

Mary Marquet, known to her friends as Maniouche, came from a theatrical family. Her father and mother, Marcel and Louise Marquet, both acted at the Odéon. Mary herself had won the second prize for tragedy at the Conservatoire in 1914. She was now under the wing of Sarah Bernhardt, acting at the actress's own theatre, the Théâtre Sarah Bernhardt. Sarah had watched over Mary's career since she was twelve, when she had convinced Mary's parents that though their daughter was unusually tall, this need not prevent her from becoming a successful actress.

That winter of 1915, Mary was taking part with Sarah in the poetic recitation *Les Cathédrales*, already mentioned. Rostand arrived for the *répétition générale*, which he spent sitting drowsily in the wings. But when Marquet began to declaim her contribution, Rostand suddenly took notice. "Whose voice is that?" he asked. A few days later, he suggested to Sarah that Mary should take the part of l'Aiglon in the planned Christmas production.

Sarah, who until very recently had played the part in its many revivals, in spite of her bad leg, schooled the young actress in the part for two solid weeks. But just before the première, she became unwell. Rostand had expressed a wish to see his new duc de Reichstadt, so Sarah sent Mary to rehearse with him instead. On 15th December, Marquet arrived as requested at 4, ave de la Bourdonnais. She had to wait for a while, impressed by the elegant furniture and décor, the engravings and portraits on the walls, the huge table loaded with magazines and newspapers in the tiled vestibule, the thick carpet leading down the hall. Edmond's visitor turned out to be the philosopher, Bergson. Once he had left, Marquet recited her lines to the poet for two hours. Edmond was impressed with her acting ability, and even more with the young woman herself. Marquet, for her part, was overwhelmed by her meeting with the poet. Still a virgin, she vowed to herself that Rostand and no other man should become her first lover.[83]

Marquet's interpretation of *L'Aiglon* was a success. The play continued for three weeks over Christmas.[84] Rostand sent congratulations and an invitation to supper. Before she left, they exchanged their first kiss. But, although very much attracted by the young actress, Rostand was also aware of the difference in their ages. That did not deter Marquet, but, as she wrote to Rostand afterwards, her own self-respect required that she would not give herself to a man who did not love her in return.

Rostand reassured her that his feelings were genuine. The next time they had supper together, they made love. Only one thing spoilt the evening for Marquet: Edmond refused to believe that Marquet was a virgin. After all, this attractive young woman had been connected with the theatre for six years. Marquet was mortified. This could have been the end of the relationship even before it began. But Marquet was in love; she forgave Rostand's scepticism, but was still not sure whether he reciprocated her own feelings. In June, she left for Trouville for a holiday with some girlfriends.

Rostand wrote Mary an affectionate, teasing letter from Paris, thanking her for her cards and letters and excusing himself for not replying before.[85] But within eight days of her departure, he had sent a witty telegram, asking that "the parcel despatched in error" should return to Paris by the next train. His warm welcome as she stepped off the train left no doubt in Mary's mind about the future of their relationship.

However, Edmond swore Marquet to secrecy. His marriage to Rosemonde was over, he told her, but Anna de Noailles still had a claim on him. She even expected him to marry her if her husband died in the war.[86] As Marquet knew, Anna telephoned him every day and he went to her house twice a week for dinner. Here he would meet army generals and leading politicians, so apart from the pleasure of her company, he would also hear the latest news.

Rostand spent the whole of 1916 in Paris. But in spite of his new friendship with Marquet, this year was to be for Rostand, as he would write later, "l'année douloureuse".[87] He was concerned for his widowed mother and for the health of his uncle Alexis. He continued to correspond with soldiers at the Front and to welcome to his flat any *poilus*[88] on leave in Paris, even though he found such visits tiring. The news from the Front was discouraging. The Germans were trying to force their way to Verdun and in trying to hold them back, the French were sustaining heavy losses. It would not be until July that Germany finally gave up its offensive. The same month the Allies began their counter-attack at the Somme.

In June, while Mary had been away in Trouville, Rostand had been with Anna to see the Cecil B. de Mille film, *Forfaiture*.[89] This was considered the first 'psychological' film, and it made a great impression on Edmond. In a letter to Marquet, he commented: "we should be making films like this in France … it proves that the cinema has a great future".[90] The Americans were already realising the potential of the cinema, while the French were still making 'theatrical' films, sticking to the old conventions of the stage. According to Guillaume de Saix, Rostand was himself thinking of writing a film scenario, like his *Le Bois Sacré*, about La Fontaine, a favourite writer of his. He had already chosen the title: *Une Journée du bonhomme*.[91]

Rostand was again writing poems inspired by the events of the war. The journalist Ajalbert had asked for suggestions as to how best to commemorate the fallen. Rostand replied with the verses entitled "Le Nom sur la Maison". Here he proposed that the names of the dead heroes should be inscribed above the doorway of their homes, or in some other suitable place in their village. [92] This suggestion received a warm response. That autumn, Edmond was invited to Lyons by the mayor, his friend Édouard Herriot, to talk to the public about his idea. He also recited this poem and another, "Disparus", on a similar theme.[93] Subsequently many villages took up his suggestion. After the war, a committee, "L'Oeuvre Edmond Rostand", was formed to promote it.

Sarah visited the Front this year as a volunteer in the Théâtre des Armées. Rostand's poetry was included in her programme. Sarah was now seventy-two, and had only the one leg, yet she impressed Béatrice Dussane, a young actress who accompanied her, by her vitality and the response she was able to evoke in the troops. "At first sight, she seemed like a little heap of cinders", remembered Dussane, " but as soon as she started to act, the heap of cinders came alive and started throwing out sparks". In all the difficulties of that four-day tour, Sarah remained brave and cheerful, arousing admiration rather than pity from her fellow actors and actresses.[94]

That autumn, the indefatigable Sarah was off to the United States again, where she planned to spend the whole of 1917. *La Samaritaine* was included in her programme. Though one aim of Sarah's visit to America was undoubtedly to raise money – her generosity meant that she was always short of it – she also intended do all she could to encourage the States to enter the war on the side of the Allies.

Personal grief was added to Rostand's concern for his country with the death of his mother on 12th September. It was some consolation that he and the rest of the family were at his mother's side when she died at Alexis's home. In October, Edmond again had the wretched experience of accompanying the body of one of his parents to Marseilles, where his mother was buried next to Eugène. "What courage you have to have after reaching middle age", wrote Rostand to Henry de Gorsse. "This is the greatest pain it is possible to know".[95] Rostand's grief was expressed in a poem: "So, my country is in danger...". But although the heart is weak, the soul is strong. These deaths strengthen the poet's love for his country and his will to survive.[96]

The winter of 1916-7 was unusually harsh. To make things worse, there was a shortage of coal and even food. After the slaughter at Verdun and the Somme, with over 190,000 Frenchmen killed, morale was low amongst troops and populace. Some politicians, especially the former premier Caillaux, were openly talking of trying to arrange an armistice. Rostand deplored Clemenceau's attacks on Caillaux in January. But he felt that this war was a just war: France was defending civilisation itself.

According to Simone, Rostand told her that spring: "I'm not at all happy, caught between a tall blonde who bores me and a small brunette who tires me out".[97] This may simply have been a disparaging remark to a woman whose affection the poet wished to keep. But even if there was truth in the remark, the tall blonde was gradually replacing Anna in Rostand's affections. Rostand must have decided that, for his own peace of mind at least, he must choose between the two women who loved him. He chose Mary.

In the spring of 1917 there were many patriotic efforts to raise morale and generate funds for various war charities. Rostand was much in demand to compose and recite new poems, and the applause with which his contributions were received left no doubt about his continuing popularity with his countrymen and women. Rostand was also writing prefaces, in particular an affectionate personal one for Louis Geandreau's posthumous collection of poems, *Le Ciel dans l'eau*.[98] To preface *Les Livres de guerre*, he composed a dramatic poem, using some of his translation of Faust.[99]

A more light-hearted task was to contribute a letter-preface to the parody, *Cyronac de Bergerot*, by André Hallu and Gabriel Manetche, sergeants in the 36th infantry regiment.[100] In the Prologue, the authors explain that they have given the heart of Cyrano to the *poilu* of today. The action and verses keep ingeniously close to the original. This is yet further proof of the influence of Rostand's works, especially *Cyrano de Bergerac*, on his compatriots at the Front.

On the thousandth day of the war that April, Rostand recited to great applause a specially written poem[101] at a benefit performance for the Red Cross, held at the Palais de la Légion d'Honneur. The capacity audience gave generously as Rostand himself carried round a collecting plate afterwards. Mary Marquet stood at the back, rather self-conscious, as her liaison with Rostand was now becoming known, but proud to see the popularity of her lover.

At the beginning of April, the United States had finally agreed to join the Allies fighting in France. On the 15th, La Fraternelle du Spectacle held a gala at the Sorbonne to celebrate this momentous decision. With the Americans on their side, the French felt, the war could soon be won. Edmond's poem to mark the occasion, which he recited himself, was warmly applauded by an audience excited and relieved by the good news. At the end of the tenth ovation, Rostand told the audience, "Don't shout, 'Vive Rostand', shout 'Vive Wilson'".

Rostand paid another visit to the Front in May, to the Noyon sector near Compiègne. He was shocked to see how close to Paris the Germans were dug in. But the reforms of Pétain were improving morale in the French trenches, and there had been no widespread fighting on the scale of the previous year. With the imminent entry of the United States into the war, Edmond felt he could allow himself to return at last to Arnaga. After reciting his poetry at the Théâtre Sarah Bernhardt in June, he left Paris for Cambo. Mary Marquet joined him soon after.

Even neglected as it had been while the gardeners were at the Front, Arnaga was still a place of beauty and peace. Mary stayed in a hotel in Cambo until the red guest room was ready for her. In her biography, she makes no mention of how long she stayed, but she may have left before Paul Faure came to stay with Rostand at Arnaga in July. One of their visitors was Léon Blum.

Paul Faure does not mention Marquet. He describes a quiet summer with his friend. They dined nightly on the terrace, listening to Fritz Kreisler and Reynaldo Hahn on an old gramophone that Coquelin had given Rostand long ago. Rostand generally spent the day in his bedroom as usual: working, reading, and writing letters to the Front. Several poems in the *Vol de la Marseillaise,* such as "Le Faucheur basque" and "Grognards pyrénéens", were probably inspired by this stay.

Rostand and Faure also paid a visit to Georges Courteline, the humorous novelist, who was staying with his wife at nearby Hendaye.

Because of the proximity of the Basque country to the frontier, national guards stopped them at each village to examine their papers. They paid Rostand flattering attention, and one roused the villagers, who came out to applaud their famous neighbour.[102]

Raymond Lerouge called at Arnaga on leave in the early autumn and found Rostand in good spirits. The poet felt that the end of the war was in sight, and was optimistic that the French people would emerge from it morally stronger.

Another Rostand was in the Basque country that summer. Maurice was again spending the season in Biarritz, socializing and acting. His play, *La Messe de cinq heures*, was performed in July at the Théâtre Réjane on behalf of a war charity. Maurice was no longer a nurse: he had been demobbed because of an infected arm. Although he now also lived, when in Paris, at the avenue de la Bourdonnais (but at number 52), he had been seeing less of his father recently. In his autobiography he mentions "misunderstandings" without elaborating, but it seems likely that Edmond disapproved of his openly effeminate behaviour and his liaisons with young men. Maurice did call at Arnaga that autumn – his first visit there since October 1915 – but he found it deserted. Edmond had returned to the capital.

"I'm returning to Paris in early September", Rostand had written in a long, encouraging letter to the wife of André Lamande, only recently married and now posted as missing. "Don't tell anyone, but for you I'll be there." It was this kind of thoughtfulness that caused Guillaume de Saix, who quotes this letter, to write "to know him was to love him".[103]

The flat at 4, avenue de la Bourdonnais was the first port of call in Paris for many soldiers on leave, especially those from Provence with whom Rostand had made friends through his letters. Soldiers such as Pierre Clarac and Guillaume de Saix, who remembered vividly the small salon-study with its walls lined with books, and the huge vase of hydrangeas brought from Arnaga. Émile Ripert, a provençal poet who greatly admired Rostand, and who would write his biography,[104] was another caller, as was Jean Suberville, mentioned earlier. Edmond would write a letter-preface for the latter's one-act plays.[105]

Suberville was just one of the many young writers who turned to Rostand for help and were not turned away. The previous March, for instance, the poet had urged the Comédie-Française to put on Paul Géraldy's first play, *Noces d'Argent*.[106] Rostand always did all he could to support young writers, whether they were in or out of uniform. "He was so ready to help the young", wrote Sacha Bernard, a young Genevois writer who had sent Edmond a copy of his book, *La Vie de L'Aiglon* in 1911, and corresponded with him ever since.[107]

The writer Pierre Benoît, too, always remembered Rostand's kindness to him when, young and unknown, he and Jean Giraudoux once dined with Anna de Noailles. Edmond was the only other guest. Not only did the poet do all he could to help them feel at ease, but he afterwards walked part of the way back to the station with them. " No later journey surpasses this one in emotion", recalled Benoît later.[108] This kindness was typical of the poet. "Rostand's kindness was only equalled by his unpretentiousness", claimed Sacha Bernard. This was also the view of the poet Fernand Gregh: "[he was] at one and the same time infinitely distinguished in his soul, his manners and his words, and so unaffected, so kind, so agreeable, in spite of his crushing fame for which he seemed almost to apologise...he truly was The Poet and The Frenchman".[109]

In November 1917 the Bolsheviks, now in power in Russia, signed a peace agreement with Germany. France had lost a major ally; the Americans, meanwhile, were still mobilising. The Germans decided to make one last all-out attempt to win the war. Two separate attacks foundered after initial advances. However, from April on their mighty "Big Bertha" gun intermittently bombarded Paris, just 75 miles away.

The Parisians continued their daily lives with panache, in spite of the shells. Strips of paper were put across the windows of the shops, sometimes in attractive patterns, to preserve them from shattering in the blasts. The poet admired the tenacity of the French spirit, making even such practical measures defiant works of art. The resulting poem,

"Mignonne, allons voir si la vitre", was, Edmond told Mary Marquet, addressed to her.[110]

Certainly, if he had become a soldier, Rostand would have distinguished himself by his sang-froid and courage. Marquet recounts how he was once entertaining some Italian soldiers when the siren sounded. She would have run to the shelter, but Edmond asked her instead to sing at the piano for their visitors. Then the shells began to fall, but it was not until they were really close that Edmond reluctantly agreed that they should seek cover.[111]

Edmond had taken two rooms above his own at the ave de la Bourdonnais for Maniouche, as he did not consider it safe for her to travel back and forth to her parents at rue de Tournon. When there were no *poilus* visiting, he was continuing to write verse. He was working on a major poem, to be entitled "Le Vol de la Marseillaise", in which he would evoke the French national song, and its continuing inspiration. At the end of the afternoon, Edmond and Mary would usually take a taxi to visit Alexis, whose health was still giving concern. (Alexis's wife later took him to Marseilles, to stay at Valmante, the home of Edmond's sister Juliette.)

Although the Germans were still threatening Paris, the arrival of American troops brought fresh hopes of an end to the war. Rostand and Marquet were among the Fourth-of-July crowds cheering members of the expeditionary force as they marched down the Champs-Elysées. The couple had bought armfuls of flowers, which they and those around them showered on the soldiers.

The Germans, for their part, felt sure of victory if they could only take Paris. They launched another offensive on the capital. Clemenceau was even warned by his chief of command that the government should consider leaving. But a successful counter-attack by Mangin three days later saved Paris; the Allied fortunes began to change. The Germans had thrown everything they had into this last effort and their resources were now exhausted, while fresh American troops were arriving all the time. At last, victory for the Allies seemed to be within reach.

Reassured about the progress of the war, Rostand wrote to Paul Faure on 27th July that he was thinking of returning to Arnaga, depending on his uncle's health; he hoped to bring back Reynaldo Hahn with him and invited Faure to come and stay. Rostand was feeling more cheerful than for some time, and not only because of the good news from the Front. He and Rosemonde were at last near to an agreement about a separation. Maurice, too, had paid a friendly call on him.

Mary and Edmond returned to Arnaga in August. The garden was already looking better cared for, since some of the gardeners had been demobbed. The couple enjoyed its peace and beauty, in the company of Paul Faure and Edmond's secretary and friend, Louis Labat. Jean Rostand would join them at the end of the month on his release from his laboratory. Among the many acquaintances who visited was the music critic Samazeuilh, asking on behalf of a colleague permission from the poet to set La Princesse lointaine to music. Rostand was able to tell him that a foreign music editor had already made enquiries about the setting of all his works to music.[112] Again, the friends dined every evening on the terrace. As Hahn could not join them after all, they played the gramophone instead, or Mary performed at the piano. Faure has evoked the delight of those evenings, as the sun went down behind the mountains and the warm south wind brought them the scent of flowers from the garden and the slow, grave sound of the church bell at Espelette.[113]

Rostand had found with Mary Marquet a new joy in living. He envisaged a happy future for them together at Arnaga. Although he still had bad times, when he would withdraw into himself rather than burden his friends with his neurasthenia, he soon became himself again. Even his boyish high spirits and love of practical jokes were reasserting themselves: one September evening he dressed up in a cardinal's robe, turned out the lights and gave his friends and dinner guests a fright.[114] During the meal which followed, Dr Jacquemin, the chief doctor at the Larressore hospital, could not stop talking about the terrible Spanish Flu epidemic. He gave it as his opinion that the best way to be safe from it was to stay away from the large towns.

This Rostand was fully intending to do. He wanted to divorce Rosemonde and marry Mary, and live quietly at Arnaga in future with Mary and his son Jean. He had already persuaded his friend Paul Faure to build a house for himself and his wife nearby. In future, Rostand wished to visit Paris as little as possible, and this was made easier by the fact that Rostand was distancing himself from the theatre, a process which had begun even before *Chantecler*. The plays he now wanted to write were more suitable for reading than for being performed. Convinced, too, that the future lay with the cinema rather than the stage, he also planned to write film scenarios. As for Mary's career as an actress, he had persuaded her to give up the stage in order to live with him in the Basque country. Rostand's dream for some time had been to live a peaceful country life, far from the demands of fame.[115]

As the war entered its final stages, Rostand stayed on at Arnaga, working on his long poem, *Le Vol de la Marseillaise*. The final part, entitled "Elle se pose" (she alights), would celebrate the triumphant return of the Marseillaise, personified as a winged figure, to Strasbourg, where it had originated. Rostand intended to write it as soon as the armistice had been signed. He had already obtained clearance to go with friends to Strasbourg, for inspiration. But "Elle se pose" would never be written.

When the news came that the Armistice was about to be signed, Rostand felt he had to be in Paris. He took the evening train on 10th November, with Mary and Miss Day. He had wanted Mary to remain behind with Jean, because of the Spanish flu epidemic, but she insisted on coming with him.

Edmond found it hard to leave his beloved Arnaga, bursting into tears as he left.[116] He seemed to have a premonition that he would never return. That morning, though not normally superstitious, he had been shaken by a couple of bad omens. Mary had been light-heartedly telling his fortune with the cards, but several had come up in spades, including the ace. Later, as they sat by the fire, one of Edmond's white pigeons blundered into the room and collapsed dead in front of the chimney.[117]

However, in the excitement of reaching his flat in Paris just before the armistice cannon boomed out from the Eiffel Tower close by, such omens were forgotten. Edmond walked the streets with Mary until evening, mingling with the exultant crowds and chatting to acquaintances they happened to meet. On his return he began to compose *La Belle au bois s'éveillant*, a symbolic celebration of France's reawakening after the war.[118]

Rostand had another reason for returning to Paris for a while. He was expected at rehearsals for the traditional end-of-year revival of *L'Aiglon* at the Théâtre Sarah Bernhardt, and was already in touch almost daily with Sarah about the production. As Mary had given up the stage for him, the leading role had been given instead to his old friend Simone.

Rehearsals were going well under the direction of Sarah's son Maurice. Simone, more mobile than Sarah, with her bad leg, had asked him for several changes and though these had been agreed, she was eager for Rostand to arrive and give the author's approval.

Simone was not only Edmond's friend, but also his devoted admirer. Of his appearance at this time, she has left us this description:

"He was a man of short stature with a delightful face. His black eyes shone with the gentleness acquired by those who have the taste for dreaming and often give themselves up to it. His strong and well-modelled aquiline nose ensured the perfection of his profile; his mouth was rather large, and the points of his chestnut-coloured moustache, often twisted by a small white hand, scarcely extended beyond it ... A delicate pale and silky skin covered his cheeks and forehead, which, being mostly hairless, reflected the light."

Simone had noticed two contrary habits to which Rostand was prone: sometimes he was reflective; then he would suddenly take an interest again in the person he was talking to, looking sometimes into their eyes and then away again, showing with the curve of his mouth his incredulity at the difference between their words and their behaviour. But no one took offence at this apparent light mockery, because his voice was warm and his words kind. He was a man who loved, understood and pitied his fellow human beings.[119]

From 13th November, Edmond was directing rehearsals for *L'Aiglon* at the Théâtre Sarah Bernhardt. Mary went with him. Also present at rehearsals was Simone's new husband, François Porché. He was an old and close friend of Simone's whom she had nursed him back to health after the war. "Le doux Porché" (gentle Porché), a symbolist poet who wrote plays in verse, had much in common with Edmond and they quickly became friends.

With Rostand's usual enthusiasm, he leapt on stage one day to show an actor how he wanted him to deliver speech, throwing off the heavy coat needed to keep out the freezing draughts. Both Mary and Simone were concerned, remembering the almost fatal illness he had contracted in 1900, also at rehearsals for *L'Aiglon*. Rostand's health was always fragile, and he had been suffering slightly from bronchitis when he returned to Paris.

Rehearsals were going well. But Rostand, with his habitual interest in clothes, had decided the double-collared royal-blue coat Sarah had worn in the First Act was now unsuitable. He wanted to change it to one of fine black cloth, pinched at the waist like that of an 1830 dandy. This was agreed and the coat ordered. The day before it would be ready, Simone had to stop a stagehand from sweeping the stage and filling with clouds of dust the auditorium where she sat with Rostand and her husband, whose health was also uncertain. When, the next evening, they visited the tailor's after rehearsals, Simone was horrified to hear Rostand give a dry cough as he waited outside while she tried on the coat. On the way home Rostand continued to cough in the cab as he talked animatedly to François.

The next day Rostand woke with a high temperature and the beginnings of influenza. He was nursed by Miss Day and Mary Marquet. When Simone, alerted by a phone call from Miss Day, called after rehearsals, she found he had been in bed with a high temperature since morning. With his typical thoughtfulness for others, Rostand was mainly concerned that François would not have caught the flu from him.

The feverish flu continued for the rest of the week. At this stage, the illness did not appear life-threatening. There seemed no need to summon Jean from Arnaga, but he came anyway on the Sunday as he himself was too anxious for his father to remain at Arnaga. Meanwhile both François Porché and Mary Marquet had succumbed to influenza themselves. Mary had gone home to her parents in rue Tournon, and François was being cared for by Simone. It transpired that they both had the mild form of Spanish flu.

But that weekend it became clear that Rostand's flu was of the virulent variety. His temperature soared. Jean and Miss Day looked after him, with advice from the doctor, Dr Renaud, who prescribed only hot drinks and aspirin, and some cuppings.[120] On Monday 25th November, Rostand dictated a letter to his sister Juliette, asking her to look after Jean if he should die. But the same day his temperature dropped a little. Maurice, who telephoned for news as soon as he heard from a colleague that his father was ill, was told there was no cause for alarm. Jean was able to send reassuring telephone messages morning and evening to Mary Marquet.

On the Wednesday, Simone was finally able to leave François, now reckoned to be out of danger, to call on Rostand. The following day she called again after rehearsals, and met Professor Faisans who had been called in after another deterioration in Rostand's condition. But he was not able to offer any better suggestions for treatment. Simone was not impressed. But there was a slight drop in Rostand's temperature on the Friday.

This improvement was short-lived. Rostand was now suffering from double pneumonia, as a result of the Spanish Flu. When he saw an oxygen cylinder being brought in to help him breathe, the poet realised he was going to die. "C'est un peu tôt" (it's a little soon), he apparently said. He was only in his fiftieth year; he had so many ideas for works that he wanted to write, and a new life with Marquet seemed to promise him happiness for the future. But he kept calm until the end, following the course of his illness with painful lucidity.[121]

Saix was just one of the many friends and colleagues who called to see or enquire after the poet during his illness. He was looked after by his sisters Juliette Mante and Jeanne de Margerie, his son Jean, Miss Day, Louis Labat, his old friend Valentine Feydeau and others. By the first of December, all the family, apart from Alexis, had arrived. Mary Marquet, still weak from flu, had joined them. But Anna de Noailles, fearful of contracting the dreadful disease herself, kept in touch by telephone.

There was a certain tension amongst those who waited at the flat in the avenue de la Bourdonnais while Rostand was dying. Neither Rosemonde nor Mary Marquet wished to share their grief with the other. Simone has described the scene as she sat in the dining room with the wife and the mistress, each avoiding the other's eyes. Maurice, with his friend, stood to one side, while Edmond's sisters were in the adjoining salon, which led to Edmond's bedroom. Maurice had greeted Simone with an affectionate kiss. His brother Jean was with their father.

Rosemonde, her face set, drew closer to Simone. Perhaps sensing the latter's sympathy, she began pouring into her ear an account of all the occasions when her husband had been unfaithful. Simone, listening incredulously, remembered her own suspicions.[122]

Anna de Noailles had sent the abbé Mugnier to give absolution to the dying man. She had told him Rostand was asking for him. This is unlikely, but the abbé's intervention did not seem out of place. Although Rostand had not been an orthodox Christian, his whole attitude to life was a spiritual one. The abbé, too, was a compassionate and broadminded man, a true Frère Trophime.[123]

The abbé called again in the evening. He noted in his diary that the women caring for the poet were agitated because Rostand was refusing to see Rosemonde. Jeanne de Margerie told him how much Edmond loved his son Jean, and said that his private life had been very unhappy.

At 4 am on the morning of Monday 2nd December, Rostand awoke from his stupour and murmured "Agonie! Agonie!" (I am dying!). He was having great difficulty in breathing when the abbé Mugnier administered the sacraments just after 9 am. Rostand's sisters Jeanne and Juliette, along with Mary Marquet, stood by in tears.

Later Mary was called in again to receive a last kiss from the man she had hoped to marry. Marquet believed that the abbé had made the sign of the cross over both of them, as if consecrating their relationship. But according to the abbé's own account, he did not even know who she was at that time.

At 11.30 am, Edmond Rostand lapsed into a coma. He died at 1.20 pm. Those who were with Rostand for his final moments saw his eyes open and look upwards as if at some wondrous vision. Juliette told Guillaume de Saix later: "his beautiful eyes grew larger and his eyes looked up and up, as if he was following his soul. He certainly had a vision in his last moments." She continued, " I have watched many dear ones die, but I have never seen such a look; anyone who was not a believer would have been gripped, troubled and perhaps even converted by it."[124]

Rostand's body was laid out on his divan in his small study, the room where he had been accustomed to entertain his friends. Only the poet's head and hands were visible above the sheets, his hands holding a rosary, perhaps put there by his sisters. On the table, the inkstand was veiled in black. The scent of Rostand's favourite tobacco still pervaded the air of the candle-lit room.

Notes – Act V

[1] Interview with Albert Delaunay, *op.cit.*

[2] Faure, pp 181-2

[3] Lerouge, *op.cit.*

[4] See Faure, pp182-190 for a vivid decription of the gardens of Arnaga in Rostand's time, now restored

[5] Lerouge, *op.cit.*

[6] Albert Delaunay, *op. cit.*

[7] Rostand satirised this attitude in *Chantecler*: *Le coq-qui-se-mêle-de-tout*: "Le Cocorico libre! Il est obligatoire!" (Act III, sc. v)

[8] L. de Robert, p. 194

[9] See Chapter Two.

[10] *L'Illustration*, 29 July 1911, and in the posthumous anthology, *Le Cantique de l'aile* (Fasquelle, 1922), I

[11] *Le Cantique de l'aile, II – V*

[12] *Le Cantique de l'aile, XI*

[13] *Le Droit d'être naturaliste* , pp. 27-8

[14] 23rd Jan 1907

[15] See Act Four

[16] Simone, who writes candidly in her memoirs about her marriages, a love affair, and her platonic friendships with literary men such as Péguy, mentions Rostand only as a dear and respected friend.

[17] *Journal*, 23 January 1907

[18] It would be performed in December 1911

[19] M. Rostand, p. 125

[20] *Journal,* 25 Feb 1909

[21] Benda, *Un Régulier dans le siècle*, vol 49, II, p. 585

[22] Montesquiou, Count Robert de, *Les Pas effacés* (Paris, 1923), vol. I, pp. 32-40

[23] Geandreau, *Le Ciel dans l'Eau*, Préface (Paris, 1917).

[24] *Les Pas effacés*, vol. I, p. 32

[25] In *Le Cantique de l'aile*, p.28

[26] *Journal*, 16 Jan.1905

[27] Gérard, pp. 98-9

[28] Margerie, pp. 211-2; p.265

[29] By Louis N. Parker

[30] Hepp-Le Bargy, "L'Amitié d'Edmond Rostand et Charles Le Bargy", *Revue des Deux Mondes* (June 1986),p. 613

[31] M. Rostand, pp. 171-2

[32] An appropriate address, as the philosopher Jouffroy had been Rosemonde's mother's uncle.

[33] *Journal* (Paris, 1985), p. 247

[34] Hepp-Le Bargy, p. 613

[35] M. Rostand, p. 75

[36] See my M.Phil. thesis, *Edmond Rostand's Success: Cyrano de Bergerac* (University of East Anglia, 1977) for more details.

[37] Gérard, pp. 79-80

[38] "Comme à un copain!" *Annales*, 15th December 1918 , quoted Ripert, pp. 179-80

[39] Letter of 18th July 1913, Archives nationales, quoted by Margerie, pp. 218; 265

[40] *Et l'on revient toujours*, quoted Hepp-Le Bargy, p .613-4

[41] *Marquet*, 1975, pp. 40-41

[42] *Le Coeur innombrable* (1901), *L'Ombre des jours* (1902), *Les Éblouissements* (1907)

[43] Henri Bergson (1859-1941) His *L'Évolution créatrice*, published in 1907, had made his ideas widely known. He proposed that life was constantly evolving, and suggested that intelligence, intuition etc. sprang from some kind of Life Force, which he called "L'Élan vital". Such an idealistic approach, a counter to the scientific materialism of the time, naturally attracted Edmond.

[44] François Broche, *Anna de Noailles, un mystère en pleine lumière* (Paris, 1989), p. 301

[45] Margerie, pp. 219; 265, fn. 15

[46] M. Rostand, *Confession*, pp. 176-7

[47] 16th September. Letters between Geandreau and Rostand were printed in *L'Européen* , 4 Dec. 1929 (Premsela, p.216)

[48] Reported by Henry de Gorsse at the unveiling of a bust of Rostand at that very spot (P. de Gorsse (ed.), *A la Mémoire d'Edmond Rostand*, Paris: Fasquelle, 1922)

[49] Undated letter, quoted Hepp-Le Bargy, p. 620

[50] Undated, Archives Gorsse, quoted Margerie, pp. 220; 265

[51] Undated letters sent to Jeanne in December 1913, quoted Ripert, pp. 181 -3

[52] Margerie, p. 219

[53] Margerie, p. 220

[54] Quoted and translated by Joanna Richardson, *Sarah Bernhardt* (London, 1959), p. 169

[55] See Act One

[56] 20th June 1914; published by Champion the same year.

[57] Margerie, p. 221

[58] Hepp-Le Bargy, pp. 616-7

[59] *ibid.*

[60] According to Rosemonde, the little red gondola on the canal of Arnaga was the inspiration for the whole play (Gérard, p. 197)

[61] *Revue des Deux Mondes*, 7th period, vol. 8, pp. 703-8

[62] *La Dernière Nuit de Don Juan* was first published in *L'Illustration*, 27th January 1921, and by Fasquelle the same year. See the Appendix for translations.

[63] Ferdinand Bac, quoted Broche, pp. 316-7

[64] Margerie, p. 222; p. 265

[65] Poem found in a notebook after Rostand's death; see *Le Vol de la Marseillaise* , p. 354

[66] Fasquelle, 1919

[67] Faure, pp. 213-4

[68] Anna told the abbé Mugnier that she and Barrès had never been lovers (Broche, p. 292)

[69] "Quel atroce malheur que je n'ai pas pu aller bien finir à la guerre!", quoted Margerie, p. 228

[70] Quoted by Migeo, pp. 127-8

[71] In his preface to Geandreau's book of poems, *Le Ciel dans l'Eau* (Paris, 1917)

[72] In his preface to Dabadié, *Lettre à ma nièce*

[73] Migeo, pp. 127-8

[74] *Edmond Rostand, son théâtre, son oeuvre posthume* (Paris: Chiron éditeurs, 1921), pp. 121-3.

[75] *Ibid.* p.120

[76] Jean Rostand to Albert Delauney, *op.cit*

[77] G.D.Painter, *Proust*, (London, 1959), 1977 ed., vol.1, p. 223.

[78] It now bears a commemoratory plaque.

[79] *Comoedia*, 2nd Dec 1926.

[80] "Miss est une providence", Rostand told Guillaume de Saix (*Comoedia*, 2nd Dec. 1926)

[81] Andry, *Edmond Rostand: le panache et la gloire* (Paris: Plon, 1986), pp. 182-3

[82] There is no mention of Mary Marquet or Edmond's separation from Rosemonde in the early biographies of the poet. It was not until Migeo's *Les Rostands* (1973) that any hint of the failure of the Rostands' marriage was given by Rostand's biographers.

[83] Mary Marquet's experiences are recounted in her two autobiographies: volume I: *Ce que j'ose dire* (Paris: Jean Dullis, 1974), and volume II: *Ce que je n'ai pas dit* (Jean Dullis, 1975)

[84] *Les Romanesques* would also be revived that February, at the Comédie Française

[85] Quoted in full in *Ce que j'ose dire*, pp. 48-9

[86] Marquet, 1975, p. 57

[87] "The Year of Pain" (*Le Vol de la Marseillaise*, XL)

[88] "Poilu", the popular name for the French soldiers of the 1914-18 war. Copious body hair ('poils') was thought to be a sign of courage.

[89] *The Squaw Man*, 1914

[90] Marquet, 1975, p. 49

[91] *Comoedia*, 2nd Dec. 1926

[92] See *L'Eveil*, 1st June 1916.

[93] Both poems are in *Le Vol de la Marseillaise* (XXII, XXI); Rostand's speech was published in *Lectures pour tous*, 15th Dec. 1916

[94] *Reines de théâtre, 1633 – 1941* (Lyons, 1944), pp. 198-9

[95] Ripert, pp. 184-7

[96] "L'Année douleureuse", *Le Vol de la Marseillaise*, XL

[97] *Ce qui restait à dire*, p.153

[98] The title refers to shell-holes full of water, but Geandreau may also have had in mind one of the old hen's aphorisms in *Chantecler*: "Ce qui connait le mieux le ciel, c'est l'eau du puits" (Act I, sc. vi).

[99] (Paris, 1917). This was probably "Les Deux Propagandes" (*Le Vol de la Marseillaise*, XLI)

[100] This witty parody is in the British Library (11735 c54) (Gironde, 1918)

[101] "Mille fois que le jour est né…" is not in *Le Vol de la Marseillaise*, but "Complainte de celui qui va quêter " (XLII), may also have been written for this occasion.

[102] Faure, pp. 222-4.

[103] *Comoedia*, 2nd Dec. 1926. Lamande was later found to be alive, but a prisoner.

[104] *Edmond Rostand* (Hachette, 1968). Ripert would become a professor at the University of Aix.

[105] *Cyrano de Bergerac aux tranchées*, and *La Grogne et les Étoiles*.

[106] Géraldy would become a successful playwright.

[107] *A L'Ombre de Marcel Proust* (Paris, 1980), pp. 50-51.

[108] When representing the Académie française at the ceremony in 1952 to dedicate a monument to Rostand at Cambo (*Revue des Deux Mondes*, Sept 1952 no. 18, pp. 253-4).

[109] Quoted by Ripert, p. 191.

[110] Parodying Ronsard's famous poem. ("Les Belles Fenêtres", *Le Vol de la Marseillaise*, LII); Marquet 1974, pp. 74-5

[111] Marquet 1974, pp. 77-79

[112] "Le Théâtre d'Edmond Rostand et la musique", *Mercure de France*, 1st June 1937.

[113] Faure, p. 288

[114] Faure, p. 235

[115] Rostand once told Guillaume de Saix that if he could live life over again, he would have nothing to do with literature, but would be a gentleman farmer, living in a humble house with flowers round the window. (*Comoedia*, 1926)

[116] Saix, *Comoedia*,1926

[117] Marquet, 1974, pp. 88-89

[118] "The Sleeping Beauty awakes" (Apesteguy, p. 282).

[119] *Ce qui restait à dire*, pp. 136-7.

[120] A procedure involving placing a heated glass on the skin, to draw out blood or fever.

[121] Saix, *Comoedia*, 1926

[122] *Ce qui restait à dire*, pp. 149-151.

[123] The gentle priest of *La Princesse lointaine*

[124] Saix, *Comoedia*, 2 Dec. 1926

Epilogue

Oui, tout passe! Le rêve et ses visions blanches,
La gloire et le bonheur, l'amour d'un être cher
...
Tout passe, mes amis...
Yes, everything passes away! The dream and its pure visions,
fame, happiness, the love of a dear one
...
everything passes away, my friends.[1]

THE FUNERAL SERVICE in Paris on 4th December was kept simple in accordance with Rostand's wishes. Early in 1919, his body was taken to Marseilles, where it lay in state for three days in the public library. Then, after a farewell service at the church of Gros Caillou, the poet was buried beside his father and mother at the Cimetière de Saint Pierre. The son of Marseilles had finally returned to his Provençal roots.

The obituary writers were united in praise for Rostand's achievement in restoring to the French public a sense of pride in their own heritage, while those writers who had known Edmond personally took the opportunity to counter the false picture painted of him by some newspapers at the time of *Chantecler.* "He was uncomplicated, sensitive, noble-hearted and modest", wrote François Chantavoine in the *Journal des Débats.*[2] "He inspired friendship and profound esteem in those who knew him well."

One writer who regretted Rostand's untimely death was Marcel Proust. In a letter of condolence to Edmond's friend Louis de Robert, Proust wrote that Edmond's kind letters over the last few years had made him feel very close to the poet. How he now wished he had accepted Edmond's recent invitation to visit him. "It seems he possessed qualities completely the opposite of the faults attributed to him [by sections of the press]", he added. [3]

The production of *L'Aiglon* at the Théâtre Sarah Bernhardt that December went ahead, as Rostand would have wished. It was, as usual, a great success. At the Porte-Saint-Martin theatre, Pierre Magnier took on the role of Cyrano, and continued to play it for several years.

In February 1919, Rostand's war poems were collected and published as *Le Vol de la Marseillaise* to coincide with his funeral. This is an uneven collection which does little to enhance Rostand's reputation as a poet. Although it includes some moving patriotic verse, and poignant tributes to the dead, there are also several poems, written merely in response to events, which the poet himself would probably not have chosen to include.

Rostand's death was officially commemorated all over the country that February, especially in Provence. At Toulon, a bust was unveiled to Rostand; in Marseilles, a one-act play in verse, "Au Balcon de Roxane", was performed. There were also revivals of Rostand's plays in translation abroad. In London, Robert Loraine's *Cyrano de Bergerac* filled theatres from March to October. Louis N. Parker's version of *L'Aiglon*, starring Marie Lohr, ran for thirty days at the Globe.

There was much speculation about what unpublished works the poet had left for posterity. *La Dernière Nuit de Don Juan,* of which the Prologue was still in draft, was known to be intended by Rostand for the Porte-Saint-Martin theatre, with Le Bargy and Edouard de Max in the main roles. But the decision to go ahead lay in the hands of Edmond's executors, his son Jean and his secretary Louis Labat. There was also the long awaited revised version of *La Princesse lointaine*, in which Sarah Bernhardt was to play Rudel, the dying poet.

Other plays Rostand was known to have been writing for Sarah included *Faust, Jeanne d'Arc, La Maison sans miroirs* and *L'Étoile* (perhaps another title for the long-planned *Le Théâtre*). Other unfinished works were the play about Albert le Grand's robot, *L'Automate*, and a scenario for cinema, "La Belle au bois dormant".[4] The reason for so many unfinished works was Rostand's well-documented conscientiousness. As Saix commented, "Il remettait cent fois ses ouvrages" (he used to go over his work a hundred times), until satisfied he could do no better.[5]

Of all these works, only *La Dernière Nuit de Don Juan* and the revised version of *La Princesse lointaine* would eventually be performed. Meanwhile in a flurry of publishing activity, many previously unpublished works appeared. *Les Douze Travaux*, written in 1910, was printed in the *L'Illustration* Christmas issue of 1920. The following February, Fasquelle published *La Dernière Nuit de Don Juan*. Also in 1921 Rostand's early essay, *Deux Romanciers de Provence*, was published by Champion, with a preface by the poet and admirer of Rostand, Émile Ripert. The almost equally youthful "Un Rêve" appeared in *Les Oeuvres libres* the same year.[6] Fasquelle began publishing Rostand's *Théâtre Complet* in 10 volumes, while Lafitte would complete their Illustrated edition with two new volumes in 1924. Fasquelle also collected Rostand's major later poems into *Le Cantique de l'Aile* in 1922, while *Choix de Poésies*, which included extracts from his plays as well as poems, would follow in 1925. Reminiscences of the poet by his friends, and admiring studies of his work, appeared in article and book form throughout the Twenties.

In March 1922, *La Dernière Nuit de Don Juan* was finally performed at the Porte-Saint-Martin, with Pierre Magnier as Don Juan. The critics listened unanimously "with emotion and respect" to the posthumous work of Edmond Rostand, according to René Doumic, who felt this put right a little of their injustice in 1910 towards *Chantecler*.[7] And *Chantecler* itself was finally vindicated in 1927, when it was revived with great success at the Porte-Saint-Martin Theatre. Even the 50th performance was sold out.

The revised version of *La Princesse lointaine* was performed in 1929, too late for Sarah Bernhardt, who had died in 1923. It, too, was a success.[8]

Cyrano de Bergerac continued to thrill audiences regularly at the Porte-Saint-Martin and later moved to the Théâtre Sarah Bernhardt. However it would not be until 1939 that it was finally staged at the Comédie-Française, signalling Rostand's belated acceptance by the establishment. *Cyrano de Bergerac* continues to be Rostand's best-known work, performed all round the world – there can never be a day when it is not being performed somewhere, in some form or language. The brilliant film by Jean-Paul Rappeneau starring Gérard Depardieu introduced Rostand's play to a whole new generation.

L'Aiglon, too, has been revived on stage and on air many times, and always to public acclaim. Even Rostand's less well-known plays are appreciated by afficianados and reappear from time to time in translation. It is sad that only *Cyrano de Bergerac* and *L'Aiglon* have been consistently kept in print in France, though *Chantecler*, perhaps Rostand's greatest play, is now in print again after two successful modern revivals.[9]

Meanwhile, life continued for those who survived Rostand. Mary Marquet withdrew from the theatre for a while, but went on to a successful career as an actress at the Comédie-Française and later on the boulevards. She was to play the role of l'Aiglon over two hundred times. During the Second World War, Marquet gave poetry recitals, including Rostand's work in her repertoire.

Rosemonde never remarried. She returned to writing poetry, and she and Maurice became familiar figures in the salons, an inseparable pair. She wrote a self-effacing and lyrical account of her husband's career in 1935 and lived until 1953.

Maurice's career, as poet, critic, novelist and especially playright, never reached the heights of his father's, but produced some successful plays such as *La Gloire* (1921), which starred Sarah in her last appearance on the stage. Perhaps his best-known work is *L'Homme que j'ai tué*, a pacifist novel which became a well-known film in the Thirties. After his father's death, Maurice's writing took on a new depth, which he attributed in his memoirs to direct inspiration from his father's spirit. He died in 1968, his father's centenary year.

In 1919, Jean returned for a while to Arnaga, and married his cousin Andrée Mante soon after. Their son, François, was born in 1922. Jean and Andrée settled in Ville d'Avray, near Paris, where Jean's world-wide reputation as a biologist and philosopher began to grow. He died in 1977.

Rostand's beloved Arnaga was sold in 1923. After several owners, it was bought by the Cambo Town Council and made into a museum in the poet's memory. Paul Faure was its first custodian. The house and grounds have now been restored to something of their earlier glory: a worthy memorial, and well worth visiting for its atmosphere, its beauty and its collection of personal letters and photographs.

In the domain of literature, Rostand had no lasting inheritors apart from his son Maurice. Many of the young poets inspired by him, such as Louis Geandreau, died in the war. After Émile Ripert's first collection of poems, *Le Chemin blanc*[10] and tributes such as the "Rostanderaie" in François Moutran's *Soleil sur les Palmiers*,[11] Rostand's influence on poetry seems to have vanished.

Likewise there was no renaissance of the poetic drama in France. The plays in verse by Geandreau and Suberville that were published were not, it seems, performed. François Porché, Simone's husband, did have some verse plays performed, as did Maurice Rostand and one or two others. But they made no real impact on the general public. Rostand's contemporaries preferred to write in prose. The success of *Cyrano de Bergerac* and *L'Aiglon* did not, as Faguet had hoped, lead to a new flowering of the French Romantic drama or the drama in verse. But they did continue to be popular, in France and abroad, themselves.

There have been major new productions of *Cyrano de Bergerac* in Paris every decade, beside the numerous other productions elsewhere. *L'Aiglon* was being performed in France at least every five years up to the Sixties; *Chantecler* has been revived in France twice in the last two decades.

Rostand's centenary in 1968 attracted little interest. But the centenary of *Cyrano de Bergerac* in 1997 was celebrated world-wide.

There are plaques, busts and other memorials to Edmond Rostand all over France, but his most worthy memorial, one that will live for ever, is his work. Cyrano, Chantecler and l'Aiglon in particular are heroes who will continue to inspire our own and future generations. *Vive Cyrano! et vive Rostand!*

Notes – Epilogue

[1] Excerpt from a free translation made by Rostand in his youth from a sonnet by the Spanish poet, Manuel del Palacio (quoted in *Journal des Débats*, 27 Dec. 1918, p. 1054)

[2] 6th Dec. 1918, p. 969

[3] Quoted in Jeanne de Robert, *Le Coeur a ses raisons* , p. 131

[4] Gérard, pp. 98-100.

[5] *Comoedia*, 1919

[6] In volume one of a new series featuring unpublished work by well-known writers (Paris: Fayard)

[7] *Revue des Deux Mondes*, March-April 1922

[8] Published in *Petite Illustration*, 9 Nov. 1929. For a detailed discussion of the changes Rostand had made to the text, see Premsela, pp.43-45

[9] See the Appendix for details of translations and editions of Rostand's plays. My M.Phil. thesis has further information on later performances of the plays, and their reincarnation in musical and other media.

[10] Fasquelle, 1904

[11] Champion, 1921

Appendix

English Translations and

Critical Editions of Rostand's Plays

Cyrano de Bergerac: major translations into English

Gertrude Hall, *Cyrano de Bergerac*, verse (New York: Doubleday & McClure, 1898; London, 1900) and in numerous anthologies in 1930s and 40s. Also on internet at www.encyclopediaindex.com.

Howard T. Kingsbury, *Cyrano de Bergerac*, blank verse (Boston & London, 1898) The version used by Richard Mansfield; in anthologies as late as 1970.

Gladys Thomas & Mary F. Guillemard, *Cyrano de Bergerac*, blank verse (New York: G.Munro, 1898; London: Heinemann,1898) Many re-editions.

Mrs Henderson Dangerfield Norman, *Cyrano de Bergerac*, rhymed verse, in *Collected Plays of Edmond Rostand*, vol. 1 (New York & London: Macmillan, 1921)

Brian Hooker, *Cyrano de Bergerac*, verse (New York: Holt, Rinehart & Winston, inc., 1923; London: Allen & Unwin, 1924) Replaced Howard Kingsbury's version for Walter Hampden and later actors, until 1960s. Numerous re-editions; still in print.

Humbert Wolfe, *Cyrano de Bergerac* (London: Hutchinson, 1937; New York: Peter Pauper Press, 1941) Written for projected film by Orson Welles, with Charles Laughton as Cyrano. Exuberant rhyming verse, faithful to original but now rather dated.

James Forsyth, *Cyrano de Bergerac* (Chicago: Dramatic Publishing Co., 1968). Much praised stage version.

Anthony Burgess, *Cyrano de Bergerac*. (1) Adapted version for Tyrone Guthrie Theatre, Minneapolis; also used for 1973 musical in New York (New York: Knopf,1971). (2) Closer but still free and vivacious version in rhythmic verse for 1983 RSC performance in London (London: Hutchinson, 1985). Drawn on for subtitles in J-P Rappeneau's 1990 film. Still in print, various editions (e.g. Vin Books, 1990; Bantam Books, 1981).

Lowell Bair, *Cyrano de Bergerac* (New York: Signet Classics, 1972; London: Penguin, 1991). Prose version, but close to original, with notes. Still in print.

Christopher Fry, *Cyrano de Bergerac*, (London: OUP, 1975). In "chiming" couplets, and true to Rostand's idealism. Reissued in 1998 in paperback in Oxford World's Classics Series.

Edwin Morgan, Edmond Rostand's *"Cyrano de Bergerac"* (Manchester: Carcanet Press, 1992). "Racy new translation into Glaswegian", for the Communicado production, Glasgow. Still in print.

Amongst many other translators of *Cyrano de Bergerac* are Patrick Garland, Charles Renauld, Helen B. Dole, C.H. Bissell & W. Van Wyck, Edna Kruckmeyer and H.Whitehall.[1]

Cyrano de Bergerac: introductions in English

E. and L. Dubose, *Rostand's "Cyrano de Bergerac"*, Cliffs Notes Series (Lincoln, Nebraska, 1971) Still in print.

Edward Freeman, *Cyrano de Bergerac*, Glasgow Introductory Guides to French Literature, 34 (University of Glasgow, 1995) Recommended and still in print.

Cyrano de Bergerac: critical editions in English

Oscar Kuhns, *Cyrano de Bergerac* (New York, 1899). Reissued in revised edition by H.W.Church, up until 1970.

A.G.H.Spears, *Cyrano de Bergerac* (New York, 1921, 1962)

N.Scarlyn Wilson, *Cyrano de Bergerac* (London & Paris, 1933)

H. Ashton, *Cyrano de Bergerac* (Oxford, 1942, 1962)

E.A. Bird, *Edmond Rostand: "Cyrano de Bergerac"* (Toronto and London: Methuen Educational Ltd., 1968, 1970)

Geoff Woollen, *Cyrano de Bergerac* (London:Duckworth, for Bristol Classical Press, 1994) excellent up-to-date study, with introduction, notes and bibliography. Still in print.

Cyrano de Bergerac: critical editions in French

Jacques Truchet, *Cyrano de Bergerac, édition critique*, with illustrations (Paris: "Lettres Françaises", Imprimerie Nationale, 1983) Scholarly and authoritative.

Numerous annotated editions available in paperback, eg in Gallimard's Folio series, Petits Classiques Larousse, Classiques Hatier, Flammarion, Presses Pocket, Livre de Poche, Classiques Hachette, etc.etc.

L'Aiglon: translations into English

No recent translations. Earlier versions include:

Louis Napoleon Parker, *The Eaglet*, in verse (New York: R.H.Russell, 1900)

Mrs Henderson Dangerfield Norman, *The Eaglet*, rhymed verse, in *Collected Plays of Edmond Rostand*, vol. 2 (New York & London: Macmillan, 1921)

Basil Davenport, *The Eaglet* (New Haven: Yale University Press, and London: Oxford University Press, 1927)

Clemence Dane, *The Eaglet*, free adaptation with music by Richard Addinsell (New York: Doubleday, Doran & Co., 1934)

L'Aiglon: critical edition in French

Patrick Besnier, *L'Aiglon* (Paris: Collection Folio, Éditions Gallimard, 1986)

Chantecler: translations into English

No recent published translation. Earlier versions include:

Gertude Hall, *Chantecler* (New York, 1910)

John Strong Newberry, *Chantecler*, in verse (New York, 1911)

Mrs Henderson Dangerfield Norman, *Chanticleer*, in rhymed verse, in *Collected Plays of Edmond Rostand*, vol. 2 (New York & London: Macmillan, 1921)

C.H.Bissell & W.Van Wyck, *Chantecler* (with *Cyrano de Bergerac*) (Los Angeles,1947)

Chantecler: editions in French

Chantecler (Paris: "Les Introuvables", Éditions l'Harmattan, 1996)

Chantecler, *Théâtre Magazine*, Nov.1985

Chantecler, *L'Avant-Scène théàtre*, 959 (Dec.1994, reprinted 1999)

The other plays: translations into English

1) La Princesse lointaine

No translations still in print. Mrs Norman's rhymed version, *The Princess Far Away*, is in *Collected Plays of Edmond Rostand*, vol. 1 (New York & London: Macmillan, 1921). Other versions include: Anna Emilia Bagstad, *The Princess Far-Away*, verse (Boston: R.G.Badger, 1921); John Heard, junior, *The Far Princess* (New York: Holt, 1925).

2) La Samaritaine

No translations still in print. Only published version is by Mrs Henderson Dangerfield Norman, *The Woman of Samaria*, rhymed verse, in *Collected Plays of Edmond Rostand*, vol. 1 (New York & London: Macmillan, 1921)

3) La Dernière Nuit de Don Juan

No translations still in print. Dolores Bagley, *The Last Night of Don Juan*, in O.Mandel (ed.),*The Theatre of Don Juan* (Lincoln, USA, 1963) is recommended.

4) Les Romanesques

Very popular with amateurs at one time. Variously entitled *The Romantics* (Mrs Henderson Dangerfield Norman, in *Collected Plays of Edmond Rostand*, vol. 1 (New York & London: Macmillan, 1921); *The Romancers* , by Mary Hendee (New York, 1899), Anna Emilia Bagstad, in *Poet Lore*, 32, no. 4 (1921), and Barrett H. Clark, a prose version (New York: Samuel French, 1915) The latter has been the main choice for actors and anthologies.

George Fleming (Julia Constance Fletcher), *The Fantasticks*, in free rhyming verse (New York and London, 1900), was reprinted in 1925, 1929.

5) Les Deux Pierrots

Also popular with amateurs. Most recent version is V. & F. Vernon's: *The Two Pierrots, or The White Supper*, in *Modern One-Act Plays from the French* (New York: Samuel French, 1933; London: Allen & Unwin, 1935)

Amy Lowell's *Weeping Pierrot and Laughing Pierrot* (New York & Boston, 1914), has music by Jean Hubert, i.e., Alexis Rostand.

The other plays: annotated editions in English

La Princesse lointaine, French text, English notes. ed. J.L.Borgerhoff (Boston, 1909)

The Fantasticks, English notes by W.A.Darlington, for a radio performance (London: BBC, 1929)

More information about Rostand's plays and their reincarnations in various media may be found in my Master of Philosophy thesis.

NOTES – APPENDIX

[1] A detailed comparison of six translations will be found in my Master of Philosophy thesis, *Edmond Rostand: Cyrano's Success* (University of East Anglia, England, 1977).

Bibliography

(All works published in Paris unless stated otherwise)

Biographies and Studies of Edmond Rostand

AMOIA, Alba, *Edmond Rostand* (Boston: Twayne Pub's, 1978). In English. Literary study of Edmond Rostand's work.

ANDRY, Marc, *Edmond Rostand: le panache et la gloire* (Plon, 1986). Lighthearted, anecdotal biography.

APESTEGUY, P., *La Vie profonde d'Edmond Rostand* (Fasquelle, 1929). Reverent study of the poet and his inner life.

DABADIE, Maïté, *Lettre à ma nièce sur Edmond Rostand* (Toulouse: Éditions Privat, 1970). Personal and idealistic.

ESPIL, Pierre, *Edmond Rostand, une vie* (Bayonne: Éditions de Mondarrain, 1998). Modern biography based on memories of Paul Faure, Rostand's friend at Cambo.

FAGUET, Émile, "La Vie et l'oeuvre d'Edmond Rostand", avant-propos to *Oeuvres complètes Illustrées* (Lafitte, 1921).

FAURE, Paul, *Vingt Ans d'intimité avec Edmond Rostand* (Plon, 1928). Rostand's life after moving to the Basque country.

GÉRARD, Rosemonde, *Edmond Rostand* (Charpentier-Fasquelle, 1935). Mme Edmond Rostand's account of the poet's life and successes.

GRIEVE, J.W., *L'Oeuvre dramatique d'Edmond Rostand* (Les Oeuvres représentatives, 1931). Derivative study of the plays.

HARASZTI, Prof. Jules, *Edmond Rostand* (Fontemoing et cie, 1913). Perceptive study of the poet's work (lectures originally given at Budapest University).

HAUGMARD, L., *Edmond Rostand: Biographie-critique etc.* (Sansot et cie, 1910). Slim volume written for the *Célébrités d'aujourd'hui* series.

LAUTIER, A., KELLER, F., *Edmond Rostand, son oeuvre* (Paris, 1924). Brief study with good bibliography.

LLOYD, Susan M., *Edmond Rostand's Success: Cyrano de Bergerac* (M. Phil. thesis for University of East Anglia, 1977).

LUTGEN, Odette, *De Père en fils (Psychobiographie, 1679 – 1964)* (Plon; Geneva: La Palatine, 1965). Psychological study of Edmond Rostand and his family.

LYET, Dr, *Le Style et la psychose maniaco-dépressive, Edmond Rostand* (Thesis for Faculty of Medicine, Paris, 1949).

MAGNE, Émile, *Les Erreurs de documentation de "Cyrano de Bergerac"*, with autograph letter by Edmond Rostand (Éditions de la Revue de France, 1898; *Revue de Paris*, June, July, Aug., 1898).

MARGERIE, Caroline de, *Edmond Rostand ou le baiser de la gloire* (Grasset, 1997). Excellent modern biography drawing on family archives.

MIGEO, Marcel, *Les Rostands* (Stock, 1973) Biographical study of Edmond Rostand, his wife Rosemonde Gérard, and his two sons, Maurice and Jean.

MILLER, E.V.W., *The Dramatic works of Edmond Rostand* (B.Litt. Thesis, Oxford, 1966-7).

PAGE, Dorothy, *Edmond Rostand et la légende napoléonienne dans "L'Aiglon"* (Champion, 1928)

PREMSELA, Martin J., *Edmond Rostand* (Amsterdam: J. M. Meulenhoff, 1933) In French. The most scholarly and thorough account of Rostand's work in any language.

RICTUS, Jehan, *Un Bluff littéraire, le cas Edmond Rostand* (P. Sevin et E. Rey, 1903). Bitter and misguided attack on Edmond Rostand.

RIPERT, Émile, *Edmond Rostand, sa vie et son oeuvre* (Hachette, 1968). Enthusiastic and readable biography, published to celebrate the centenary of Rostand's birth by the Provençal poet Ripert, former professor at the University of Aix.

SUBERVILLE, Jean, *Edmond Rostand, son théâtre, son oeuvre posthume*, 2nd ed. (Chiron, 1921). Updated edition of Suberville's 1919 study, "Le Théâtre d'Edmond Rostand" (Éditions et Libraires).

Select Bibliography of Other Works

(with date of first publication)

Memoirs and Biographies

Antoine, *Mes souvenirs sur l'Odéon (Paris, 1928)*

Baring, Maurice, *Sarah Bernhardt* (London, 1933)

Barrès, Maurice, *Mes Cahiers*, vol. IV (Paris, 1931)

Benda, Julien, *Un Régulier dans le siècle* (Paris, 1938)

Bernard, Sacha, *A l'Ombre de Marcel Proust* (Paris, 1980)

Billy, André, *L'Époque 1900* (Paris, 1951)

Broche, F., *Anna de Noailles, un mystère en pleine lumière* (Paris, 1989)

Brisson, Adolphe, *Portraits intimes*, vol. II (Paris, 1896)

Brisson, Pierre, *Autre Temps* (Paris, 1949)

Castelot, André, *L'Aiglon: Napoléon Deux* (Paris, 1959; London, 1960 (English edition))

Christophe-Charles, *La Crise littéraire à l'époque du naturalisme* (Paris, 1979)

Claretie, Jules, *La Vie à Paris*, vol. VII (Paris, 1904)

Emboden, W., *Sarah Bernhardt* (London, 1974)

Gourmont, Rémy de, *Promenades littéraires* (Paris, 1922)

Guitry, Sacha, *If I remember aright* (Methuen, 1935); *Si j'ai bonne mémoire* (Paris, 1934)

Hahn, Reynaldo, *La Grande Sarah: souvenirs* (Paris, 1930)

Huret, Jules, *Interviews de littérature et d'art* (Paris, 1984)

Huret, Jules, *Loges et coulisses* (Paris, 1901)

Huret, Jules, *Sarah Bernhardt* (Paris, 1899), with preface by Edmond Rostand

Joannis, Claudette, *Sarah Bernhardt "Reine de l'attitude..."* (Paris, 2000)

Marquet, Mary, *Ce que je n'ai pas dit* (Paris, 1975)

Marquet, Mary, *Ce que j'ose dire* (Paris, 1974)

Montesquiou-Fezensac, Count Robert de, *Têtes couronnées* (Paris, 1916)

Montesquiou-Fezensac, Count Robert de, *Les Pas effacés* (Paris, 1923)

Morand, Paul, *1900* (Paris, 1941)

Moreau, Dr Laurent, *Hommage à Edmond Rostand* (Avignon, 1931)

Pac, Henri, *Luchon et son passé, nouvelle edition* (Toulouse, 1991)

Parker, Louis Napoleon, *Several of my lives* (New York, 1928)

Reggio, A., *Au seuil de leur âme: études de psychologie critique* (Paris, 1904)

Renard, Jules, *Journal* (Paris, 1925-7)

Renard, Jules, *Lettres inédites* (Paris, 1957)

Richardson, Joanna, *Sarah Bernhardt* (London, 1959)

Robert, Louis de, *De Loti à Proust* (Paris, 1928)

Robert, Jeanne de, *Le Coeur a ses raisons* (Toulouse, 1987)

Rostand, Jean, *Le Droit d'être naturaliste* (Paris, 1963)

Rostand, Maurice, *Confession d'un demi-siècle* (Paris, 1948)

Rostand, Maurice, *Sarah Bernhardt* (Paris, 1950)

Simone, Mme, (Pauline Benda), *Ce qui restait à dire* (Paris, 1967)

Simone, Mme, *Sous de nouveaux soleils* (Paris, 1957)

Works on Literature and the Theatre

Antoine, *Le Théâtre (Paris, 1932)*

Chesterton, G.K, *Twelve Types: a book of essays* (London 1906)

Doumic, René, *Essais sur le théâtre contemporain* (Paris, 1905)

Doumic, René, *Le Théâtre nouveau* (Paris, 1908)

Dussane, B., *Reines de théâtre 1633-1941* (Lyons/Montreal, 1944)

George-Michel, Michel, *Gens de théâtre que j'ai connus 1900-1940* (New York, n.d.)

Howarth, W.D., *Sublime and Grotesque: A Study of French Romantic Drama* (London, 1975)

James, *The Scenic Art: notes on acting and the drama, 1872-1901* (London, 1949)

Lemaître, Jules, *Impressions de théâtre*, vols. IX,X (Paris, 1896, 1898)

Sarcey, F., *Quarante ans au theatre*, vols.. VII, VIII (Paris, 1902)

Shaw, G.B., *Our Theatres in the Nineties* (London, 1932)

Shaw, G.B., *Collected Letters, 1898-1910* (London, 1972)

Shaw, G.B., *Dramatic Essays and Opinions*, I (London, 1907)

Articles and Speeches

Bauer, Gérard, "Le Panache de Cyrano", *Annales Conferencia,* 37th year, no.12 (15 Dec. 1948), 508

Benoît, Pierre, "Le Souvenir de Rostand", *Revue des Deux Mondes*, 18 (Sept. 1952), 253-8

Besnier, Patrick, preface to *L'Aiglon* (Gallimard Folio, 1986)

Brulat, Paul, "Rostand Écolier", *Annales politiques et littéraires*, 15 Dec. 1918

Clarac, P., "Lettres d'Edmond Rostand pendant la guerre", *Revue des Deux Mondes*, 1 Dec. 1928

Delauney, Albert, "Edmond Rostand par Jean Rostand. Un entretien", *Nouvelles littéraires*, 2119 (1968), 1,2

Favalleli, Max, "La Triumphale Première de *Cyrano de Bergerac*", *Paris-Presse -l'Intransigeant* (8 Feb. 1956), 2

Fletcher, J.C. ("George Fleming"), "M. Edmond Rostand and the literary prospects of the Drama", *Edinburgh Review,* CICII (Jul-Oct.1900), 307-321

Gérard, R. and others, *"Cyrano de Bergerac"*, *L'Illustration*, 28 Jan. 1939

Gorsse, Henry de, "L'Enfance pyrénéenne d'Edmond Rostand", *Revue de France*, V (1921), 75-102 (Fasquelle, 1922)

Gorsse, Pierre de, ed., "A la Mémoire d'Edmond Rostand" (Fasquelle, 1922)

Gorsse, Pierre de, "Edmond Rostand, Poète français d'inspiration commingeoise" (*Revue de Comminges*, 1950-1) (Toulouse, 1951)

Hepp-Le Bargy, M., & Hepp, J., "L'Amitié d'Edmond Rostand et de Charles Le Bargy", *Revue des Deux Mondes* (June 1986), 608-621

Lecrique, C., "Hommage à Edmond Rostand & Rosemonde Gérard", *La Grive* (Oct 1952, Oct. 1953)

Margerie, Roland de, in *Marseille III*, 70 (Jan-Feb. 1968), 25-32

Marie, André, "Un Hommage à Edmond Rostand", *Revue des Deux Mondes*, 18 (Sept. 1952), 177-184

Payoud, Jean, in *Le Petit Marseillais* (11th April 1930)

Poizat, A., "Edmond Rostand", *Le Correspondent*, 273 (1918), 789-97

Pons, Maurice, "L'Année Cyrano", *Revue de Paris*, 63rd year (March 1956), 115-20

Rat, M., "Quand l'enfant Rostand découvrait Cyrano", *Les Nouvelles littéraires*, 42nd year, no. 1901 (6th Feb. 1964), 3

Saix, Guillaume de, *Comoedia*, 2 Dec. 1926, 1; *Comoedia*, 24 Oct. 1919, 1

Samazeuilh, G., "Le Théâtre d'Edmond Rostand et la musique", *Mercure de France*, 1 June 1937

Véber, Pierre, in *Le Gaulois* (11 May 1922), 1

Vogüé, Vicomte E. Melchior de, "Réponse au discours de réception de Edmond Rostand, 4th June 1903" (Paris, 1903, and in *Sous les Lauriers*, Paris, 1911)

Weber, Jean, "Rostand, 'sans qui les choses ne seraient que ce qu'elles sont'", *Les Annales* (Conferencia), 228 (Oct.1969), 3-33

The Collection Auguste Rondel, at the Bibliothèque de l'Arsenal, Paris, contains contemporary reviews etc. relating to Rostand's works.

Works of Edmond Rostand

Oeuvres complètes illustrées, 5 vols. ed. Pierre Lafitte, with preface by
Émile Faguet (Paris: Hachette, 1911) Two further vols. added in
1924.
Oeuvres complètes, 10 vols. (Paris: Fasquelle, 1921-26).

Plays, Listed Chronologically with Date of First Publication

1888: Le Gant rouge (Archives nationales, Liasse F18-1036)
1891: Les Deux Pierrots ou le Souper blanc, lever de rideau en vers;
published as Pierrot qui pleure et Pierrot qui rit, with music by Alexis
Rostand (Heugel, 1899); revised version in Je Sais tout , Dec.1909;
bound with Les Romanesques (Fasquelle, 1923)
1894: Les Romanesques, comédie en trois actes en vers (Fasquelle,
1894)
1895: La Princesse lointaine, pièce en quatre actes en vers (Fasquelle,
1895); revised version (Fasquelle, 1929)
1897: La Samaritaine, évangile en trois tableaux en vers (Fasquelle,
1897)
1897: Cyrano de Bergerac, comédie héroique en cinq actes en vers
(Fasquelle, 1898)
1900: L'Aiglon, drame en six actes en vers (Fasquelle, 1900)
1908: Le Bois sacré, pantomime en vers, L'Illustration, Christmas 1908
(extracts only); L'Illustration, 23 April 1910
1910: Chantecler, pièce en quatre actes en vers (Fasquelle, 1910)
1912: La Dernière Nuit de Don Juan, poème dramatique en deux parties
et un prologue (Fasquelle, 1921)

Prose Works, Listed Chronologically

1887: Deux Romanciers de Provence: Honoré d'Urfé et Émile Zola
(Champion, 1921)
1887: "Le Costume du petit Jacques", Le Gaulois, 2 May, 1-2
1903: Discours de réception à l'Académie française, le quatre juin, 1903
(Fasquelle, 1903)

plus numerous prefaces and "lettres-préfaces".

Verse Anthologies

Les Musardises (Lemerre, 1890)

Les Musardises, édition nouvelle, 1887-1893 (Fasquelle, 1911)

Le Cantique de l'aile (Fasquelle, 1922). Contains all the major poems written 1893 –1914.

Le Vol de la Marseillaise (Fasquelle, 1919). Poems written during the 1914-18 War.

Choix de poésies (Fasquelle, 1925). Poems and extracts from Rostand's plays.

Major Poems Published Separately, Listed in Order of Composition

"A la Musique", with musical score by Emmanuel Chabrier (Paris, 1914)

"Un Rêve", in *Les Oeuvres libres*, vol.1, (Fayard, 1921)

"Pour la Grèce", 11 March 1897 (Fasquelle, 1897); in *Le Cantique de l'aile*, XXIX

"La Journee d'une Précieuse" (written 1899), *Lectures pour tous*, Jan. 1900; in *Les Élégantes* (Hachette, 1913) and *Le Cantique de l'aile*, CXXIX – CLXXI

"A Kruger" (written 26 Nov. 1900), *Le Figaro*, 9 Dec. 1900 (Fasquelle, 1900); *Le Cantique de l'aile*, LXVII

"A Sa Majesté l'Impératrice de Russie", *Le Gaulois*, 20 Sept. 1901; in *Le Cantique de l'aile*, XLI – LV

"Un Soir à Hernani", *Le Gaulois*, 4 March 1902 (Fasquelle, 1902); in *Le Cantique de l'aile*, CVXXII – CC

"Le Verger", *Le Figaro*, 22 April 1903 (Fasquelle, 1903); *Le Cantique de l'aile*, LXXXVI

"Les Douze Travaux" (written in 1909), *L'Illustration*, Christmas, 1920

"A Antoine", in *A Antoine* (Champion, 1914)

See also *Poésie castillane contemporaine* (Paris:Perrin et Cie, 1889), which includes several French versions written by Rostand.

See also *Six Mélodies*, with musical score by Emmanuel Chabrier (Enoch, 1890), which includes three poems by Rostand.

Index

Printed in the United Kingdom
by Lightning Source UK Ltd.
9595100001B